Praise for Pakistan: Between Mosque and Military

"A very valuable addition to the existing literature."
—*International Affairs*

"Taking years of first-hand experience of Pakistani politics, Haqqani's narrative weaves disparate strands into an informative and authoritative tale."
—*Far Eastern Economic Review*

"For gaining a grasp of the situation and its implications for the United States, there may be no better place to begin than *Pakistan: Between Mosque and Military*."
—*Commentary*

"In Pakistan, a nation that the United States has been happy to use without ever bothering to understand, the global war on terror will be won or lost. In this cogent, well-informed and extraordinarily informative book, Husain Haqqani describes in detail the unholy alliance between Islamists and military officers that has shaped Pakistan's past and may well determine its future. An important and disturbing tale, deftly told." ·
—**Andrew J. Bacevich,**
Author of *The New American Militarism: How Americans Are Seduced by War*

D0931833

Pakistan

Between Mosque and Military

Husain Haqqani

CARNEGIE ENDOWMENT FOR INTERNATIONAL PEACE
Washington, D.C.

Carnegie Endowment for International Peace
1779 Massachusetts Avenue, N.W., Washington, D.C. 20036
202-483-7600, Fax 202-483-1840
www.CarnegieEndowment.org

To order, contact Carnegie's distributor:
The Brookings Institution Press
Department 029, Washington, D.C. 20042-0029, USA
1-800-275-1447 or 1-202-797-6258
Fax 202-797-2960, E-mail bibooks@brook.edu

Composition by Stephen McDougal
Printed by United Book Press

Library of Congress Cataloging-in-Publication data

Haqqani, Husain, 1956-
Pakistan : between mosque and military / Husain Haqqani.
    p. cm.
    Summary: "This book analyzes the origins of the relationships between Islamist groups and Pakistan's military, and explores Pakistan's quest for identity and security. Tracing how the Pakistani military has sought U.S. support by making itself useful for concerns of the moment, author Husain Haqqani offers an alternative view of political developments in Pakistan since the country's independence in 1947"—Provided by publisher.
    Includes bibliographical references and index.
    ISBN-13: 978-0-87003-223-3 (cloth)
    ISBN 10: 0-87003-223-2 (cloth)
    ISBN-13: 978-0-87003-214-1 (pbk.)
    ISBN-10: 0-87003-214-3 (pbk.)
    1. Civil-military relations—Pakistan. 2. Islam and politics—Pakistan. 3. Pakistan—Armed Forces—Political activity. 4. United States—Military relations—Pakistan. 5. Pakistan—Military relations—United States. I. Carnegie Endowment for International Peace. II. Title.

JQ629.A38C585 2005
322'.5'09549—dc22   2005012396

---

15 14 13 12 11 10   10 9 8 7   1st Printing 2005

Contents

Foreword

Of all the United States' partners in the global war on terrorism, Pakistan is the most vexing and arguably the most important. For years it has been accused of encouraging terror, through support of the former Taliban government in Afghanistan and by promoting armed opposition to Indian control of Kashmir. Following the events of September 11, 2001, however, Pakistan cast its lot with the United States, providing assistance to U.S. military operations in Afghanistan and sharing valuable intelligence. Today, Pakistan is simultaneously a breeding ground for radical Islam and a key ally in the U.S. effort to eliminate terror in South Asia and worldwide.

This ambiguous relationship is rooted in the historic alliance between Islamists and the Pakistani military—the subject of Husain Haqqani's fascinating political history of this young, troubled state. Haqqani, a visiting scholar at the Carnegie Endowment, political commentator, and former Pakistani diplomat, examines the entire period of Pakistan's statehood, from which he masterfully extracts the key factors that have shaped the contours of the country's evolution.

Haqqani shows how perceptions of Pakistan's external and domestic threats have produced a debilitating partnership of expediency between Islamists and the military. Government officials have not only used Islam to unify the multiethnic and multilingual Pakistani state, they have also used it to reinforce Pakistani identity in opposition to India's predominantly Hindu population. Conflict with neighboring India has mainly benefited the Pakistani military, which has used its exalted status to play a decisive role in government policy, even during periods of civilian rule. Haqqani contends that while Pakistan's leaders have repeatedly courted religious nationalism to advance their personal agendas, they have rarely been able to control its less desirable effects. "The historic alliance between Islamists and Pakistan's military has the potential to frustrate antiterrorist operations, radicalize key segments of the Islamic world, and bring India and Pakistan to the brink of war yet again," he warns.

Pakistan: Between Mosque and Military is an articulate and convincing plea for a return to civilian-led government and an end to the Islamist-military alliance. As Haqqani amply demonstrates, reliance on this partnership has stoked the flames of conflict, impeded efforts to control terrorist operations, and diverted precious resources from the country's considerable development challenges. In doing so, Haqqani firmly rejects the view that greater democratic participation will empower Islamic extremists.

Now more than ever, the fates of the United States and Pakistan are tightly intertwined. From counterterrorism to nuclear nonproliferation, effective cooperation with Pakistan is a *sine qua non* for the success of critical U.S. foreign policy goals. The harrowing discovery of the A. Q. Khan network in 2003—a Pakistan-based operation that had for years been selling nuclear bomb designs and equipment to North Korea, Iran, Libya and elsewhere—is only the most recent example of this troubled interdependence. Given the central role Pakistan plays in whether or not the U.S. reaches so many of its foreign policy objectives, partnership with this South Asian power is sure to be a high priority well into the future.

Between Mosque and Military is a timely and original contribution to our understanding of one of the U.S.'s most enigmatic allies. At this particularly critical juncture in the U.S.-Pakistani relationship, Haqqani's trenchant analysis and practical recommendations deserve our closest attention.

Jessica T. Mathews
President, Carnegie Endowment for International Peace

Acknowledgments

This book is the result of my lifelong passion for understanding the history and politics of my homeland and for creating a democratic Pakistan. In a sense everyone in Pakistan who has contributed to my learning and the evolution of my ideas has contributed to this book. That includes my neighbors, teachers, and friends from my days as a student activist with Islamic sympathies; my many colleagues as a journalist; and the several Pakistani officials who I worked with, or for, during my days in government.

My father, Muhammad Saleem Haqqani, taught me at an early age to question the officially distorted version of events in Pakistan. My mother, Saeeda Saleem Haqqani, continues to support me, as she has done at every stage of my life. She believed in me through the many controversies in which I have been embroiled.

I learned about the ethos of Pakistan's civil bureaucracy from Roedad Khan, Saeed Mehdi, Anwar Zahid, and Ijlal Zaidi. Zaidi was, in addition, also helpful in figuring out several mysteries of Pakistan's political development.

Pakistan's military and intelligence services try very hard to remain inscrutable. My understanding of these institutions was made possible by my acquaintance with Generals Aslam Beg, Asad Durrani, Hamid Gul, Jehangir Karamat, Zulfikar Khan, Asif Nawaz, Abdul Qayyum, and Syed Refaqat. Generals Durrani and Refaqat have remained friends, notwithstanding our occasional differences of opinion and outlook. I also value my friendship with several colonels and junior officers in the Pakistani military establishment but they would probably not like to be named in a book of this nature.

ix

Among Pakistani political figures, I am grateful to Benazir Bhutto for a free exchange of ideas during our decade-long association. My analysis has also benefited from exchanges with Qazi Hussain Ahmed, Professor Khurshid Ahmed, Kamal Azfar, Hamid Nasir Chattha, Syed Munawwar Hasan, former president Ghulam Ishaq Khan, Ghulam Mustafa Jatoi, Shafqat Mahmood, Sardar Abdul Qayyum, Anwar Saifullah, Nawaz Sharif, and Manzoor Wattoo.

The friendship of several American diplomats and scholars has been invaluable. Among them I would like to mention Jerry Brennig, Stephen Cohen, William Milam, Robert Oakley, Robin Raphel, Teresita and Howard Schaffer, Michele Sison, and Marvin Weinbaum.

Nuscie Jamil, Maleeha Lodhi, Najam Sethi, and Nasim Zehra provided friendship, guidance, and help even when we disagreed vehemently. With Nuscie and Najam, our agreements have become greater than our disagreements over time. The advice of Ardeshir Cowasjee, Amina Jilani, Arif Nizami, Sherry Rahman, Muhammad Salahuddin, Mahmood Sham, Mujibur Rahman Shami, and Sajjad Mir was always helpful as was the friendship of Khawaja Ashraf, Sophia Aslam, Yahya Al-Husseini, Zia Khokhar, Mian Saleemullah, and Aniq Zafar. The fear of criticism by my mother-in-law, Akhtar Ispahani, helped me fine tune my argument in several places.

The Carnegie Endowment for International Peace provided me the opportunity and the environment for actually thinking through and writing this book. My special thanks are due to the endowment's president, Jessica Mathews, and vice presidents Paul Balaran and George Perkovich. Carnegie librarians Kathleen Higgs and Chris Henley helped me find even the most obscure reference material without complaint. The publications team, notably Carmen MacDougall, Phyllis Jask, and Sukhi Sahni, put up with missed deadlines and offered much needed encouragement in the final stages of the book's writing, production, and marketing.

My research was greatly assisted by Carnegie junior fellows Faith Hillis, Alexander Kuo, and Revati Prasad, as well as interns Fariha Haque and Anirudh Suri. My students Shilpa Moorthy, Aparna Pande, and Humza Tarar were helpful in locating some of the material used in the notes.

My children Huda Haqqani and Hammad Haqqani sacrificed much of their summer vacation and endured broken promises of their father's company as I conducted my research. By the time the book was completed, their question "How far are you with your book?" had become a major reason for my wanting to finish the project. Although Maha and

Mira were away from their father during this period, I am sure their reactions would not have been different from those of their siblings.

The most significant source of inspiration and support in my life is my wife, Farahnaz Ispahani. Farah, as she is known to her American friends, provides the emotional and intellectual anchor that is needed for any major endeavor. I am grateful to Farah for her support and encouragement, as well as her many helpful specific comments that made this book possible. I look forward to the benefit of her partnership for the rest of my life.

I would like to add that the views expressed in this book are solely mine, as are any mistakes and errors.

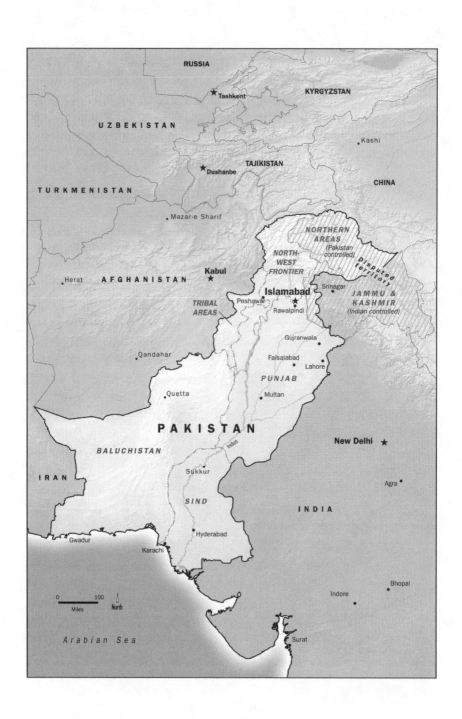

1

Introduction:
Identity and Ideology

Pakistan for more than a decade has been accused of supporting terrorism, mainly because of its support for militants opposing Indian rule in the disputed Himalayan territory of Jammu and Kashmir and also its backing of the Taliban government in Afghanistan. After September 11, 2001, when terrorists attacked the World Trade Center and the Pentagon, Pakistan heeded U.S. pressure to reverse course and take a stand against terrorism. Pakistan became a key U.S. ally, facilitating U.S. military operations in Afghanistan and sharing intelligence about Al Qaeda operatives. Nevertheless, terrorists continue to operate in, and from, Pakistan. The country is now a target and a staging ground for terrorism while it is simultaneously seen by U.S. policy makers as the key to ending terrorism in South Asia.

Pakistan's future direction is crucial to the U.S.-led war against terror, not least because of Pakistan's declared nuclear-weapons capability. The historic alliance between Islamists and Pakistan's military, which is the subject of this book, has the potential of frustrating antiterrorist operations, radicalizing key segments of the Islamic world, and bringing India and Pakistan yet again to the brink of war.

Pakistan's Islamists made their strongest showing in a general election during parliamentary polls held in October 2002, when they secured 11.1 percent of the popular vote and 20 percent of the seats in the lower house of Parliament. Since then, they have pressed for Taliban-style Islamization in the North-West Frontier Province (NWFP) bordering

1

Afghanistan, where they control the provincial administration. Pakistan's military ruler, General Pervez Musharraf, has made repeated pronouncements to reassure the world of his intention to radically alter Pakistan's policy direction away from its recent Islamist and jihadi past. In a major policy speech on January 12, 2002, Musharraf announced measures to limit the influence of Islamic militants at home, including those previously described by him as "Kashmiri freedom fighters." "No organizations will be able to carry out terrorism on the pretext of Kashmir," he declared. "Whoever is involved with such acts in the future will be dealt with strongly whether they come from inside or outside the country."[1]

Musharraf's supporters described his speech as revolutionary.[2] He received international applause and support as well. Pakistanis tired of years of religious and sectarian violence agreed with Musharraf's statement that "Violence and terrorism have been going on for years and we are weary and sick of this Kalashnikov culture . . . The day of reckoning has come." But soon it became apparent that Musharraf's government continues to make a distinction between "terrorists" (a term applied to Al Qaeda members who are mainly of foreign origin as well as members of Pakistan's sectarian militant groups) and "freedom fighters" (the officially preferred label in Pakistan for Kashmiri militants). The Musharraf government also remains tolerant of remnants of Afghanistan's Taliban regime, hoping to use them in resuscitating Pakistan's influence in Afghanistan in case the U.S.-installed regime of President Hamid Karzai falters.

This duality in Pakistani policy is a structural problem, rooted in history and a consistent policy of the state. It is not just the inadvertent outcome of decisions by some governments (beginning with that of General Muhammad Zia ul-Haq in 1977), as is widely believed.

Since the country's inception, Pakistan's leaders have played upon religious sentiment as an instrument of strengthening Pakistan's identity. Under ostensibly pro-Western rulers, Islam has been the rallying cry against perceived Indian threats. Such rulers have attempted to "manage" militant Islamism, trying to calibrate it so that it serves its nation-building function without destabilizing internal politics or relations with Western countries. General Zia ul-Haq went farther than others in "Islamizing" Pakistan's legal and educational system, but his policy of Islamization was the extension of a consistent state ideology, not an aberration.

Islamist groups have been sponsored and supported by the state machinery at different times to influence domestic politics and support the military's political dominance. In the South Asian region, the Islamists have been allies in the Pakistan military's efforts to seek strategic depth in Afghanistan and to put pressure on India for negotiations over the future of Kashmir. Relations between ideologically motivated clients and their state patrons are not always smooth, which partly explains the inability of Pakistan's generals to completely control the Islamists in the post-9/11 phase. The alliance between the mosque and the military in Pakistan was forged over time, and its character has changed with the twists and turns of Pakistani history.

Pakistan's state institutions, especially its national security institutions such as the military and the intelligence services, have played a leading role in building Pakistani national identity on the basis of religion since Pakistan's emergence as an independent country in August 1947. This political commitment to an ideological state gradually evolved into a strategic commitment to jihadi ideology—ideology of holy war—especially during and after the Bangladesh war of 1971, when the Pakistani military used Islamist idiom and the help of Islamist groups to keep secular leaders who were supported by and elected by the majority Bengali-speaking population out of power. Rebellion by the Bengalis and their brutal suppression by Pakistan's military followed. In the 1971 war, Pakistan was split apart with the birth of an independent Bangladesh.

After the 1971 war, in the original country's western wing, the effort to create national cohesion between Pakistan's disparate ethnic and linguistic groups through religion took on greater significance, and its manifestations became more militant. Religious groups, both armed and unarmed, have become gradually more powerful as a result of this alliance between the mosque and the military. Radical and violent manifestations of Islamist ideology, which sometimes appear to threaten Pakistan's stability, are in some ways a state project gone wrong.

The emergence of Pakistan as an independent state in 1947 was the culmination of decades of debate and divisions among Muslims in

British India about their collective future. After the consolidation of British rule in the nineteenth century, Muslims found themselves deprived of the privileged status they enjoyed under Mughal rule. Some of their leaders embraced territorial nationalism and did not define their collective personality through religion. They opposed British rule and called for full participation in the Indian nationalist movement led by the Indian National Congress of Mohandas Gandhi and Jawaharlal Nehru. Others felt that Muslims had a special identity that would be erased over time by ethnic and territorial nationalism centered primarily on the Hindu majority in India.

Coalescing in the All-India Muslim League and led by Muhammad Ali Jinnah, these Muslim nationalists asserted that India's Muslims constituted a nation separate from non-Muslim Indians and subsequently demanded a separate homeland in areas with a Muslim majority. British India's Muslim-majority provinces lay in its northwest and northeast, leading to Pakistan comprising two wings separated by India until the eastern wing became the new state of Bangladesh in December 1971. Pakistan's creation represented the acceptance of the two-nation theory, which had been periodically articulated long before the formal demand for recognition of a Muslim nation in 1940 but had never been fully explained in terms of how it would be applied. Although Pakistan was intended to save South Asia's Muslims from being a permanent minority, it never became the homeland of all South Asia's Muslims. One-third of the Indian subcontinent's Muslims remained behind as a minority in Hindu-dominated India even after partition in 1947. The other two-thirds now lives in two separate countries, Pakistan and Bangladesh, confirming the doubts expressed before independence about the practicality of the two-nation theory.

Pakistan's freedom struggle had been relatively short, beginning with the demand by the All-India Muslim League for separate Muslim and non-Muslim states in 1940 and ending with the announcement of the partition plan in June 1947. Although the Muslim League claimed to speak for the majority of Indian Muslims, its strongest support and most of its national leadership came from regions where Muslims were in a minority.[3] Even after the Muslim League won over local notables in the provinces that were to constitute Pakistan, it did not have a consensus among its leaders over the future direction of the new country. Issues such as the new nation's constitutional scheme, the status of various ethno-linguistic groups within Pakistan, and the role of religion and theologians in matters of state were still unresolved at independence.

Leaders of the Muslim League had given little thought to, and had made no preparations for, how to run a new country. One possible explanation for this lack is that the demand for Pakistan was "devised for bargaining purposes to gain political leverage for Muslims."[4] Several Muslim leaders, notably poet-philosopher Muhammad Iqbal in 1930, proposed schemes for power sharing between the religious majority and minorities in independent India. They claimed that India's Muslims constituted a separate nation by virtue of their unique history and cultural differences with the Hindu majority. This claim to nationhood, however, was not necessarily a claim to separate statehood. A separate Muslim nation could have remained part of a federal or confederal India under special power sharing arrangements and that may have been the original intention of the Muslim League leadership.[5] According to this argument, the refusal of the Indian National Congress to contemplate such power-sharing and to accept the notion of a multination state led inadvertently to partition and the creation of a sovereign Pakistan.

While seeking recognition of a separate Muslim nation, Jinnah had managed to pull together various elements of Muslim leadership in India, creating communal unity through ambiguity about the final goal. He was "using the demand for Pakistan to negotiate a new constitutional arrangement in which Muslims would have an equal share of power"[6] once the British left the subcontinent. Historian Ayesha Jalal has elaborated on the impact that Indian Muslim politics of the time made on the demand for Pakistan as well as the nature and contradictions of that demand:

Once the principle of Muslim provinces being grouped to form a separate state was conceded, Jinnah was prepared to negotiate whether that state would seek a confederation with the non-Muslim provinces, namely Hindustan, on the basis of equality at the all-India level, or whether, as a sovereign state, it would make treaty arrangements with the rest of India . . . If they were to play their role in the making of India's constitutional future, Jinnah and the Muslim League had to prove their support in the Muslim-majority provinces. Such support could not have been won by too precise a political programme since the interests of Muslims in one part of India did not suit Muslims in others . . . Jinnah could not afford to wreck the existing structure of Muslim politics, especially since he had nothing plausible to replace it with. This is where religion came to the rescue . . . Yet Jinnah's resort to religion was not an ideology to which he was ever committed or even a device to use against rival communities; it was simply a way of giving a semblance of unity and solidity to his divided Muslim constituents. Jinnah needed a demand that was specifically ambiguous and imprecise to command general support, something specifically Muslim though unspecific in every other respect. The intentionally obscure cry for a "Pakistan" was contrived to meet this requirement . . . Jinnah could not afford to state precisely what the demand for "Pakistan" was intended to accomplish. If the demand was to enjoy support from Muslims in the minority provinces it had to be couched in uncompromisingly communal terms. But the communal slant to the demand cut against the grain of politics in the Muslim provinces, particularly the Punjab and Bengal, where Muslim domination over undivided territories depended upon keeping fences mended with members of other communities.[7]

One result of Jinnah's elaborate strategy was that India's Muslims demanded Pakistan without really knowing the results of that demand. Once Jinnah's demand for recognition of Muslim nationhood had been characterized as a demand for India's division, Jinnah's critics pointed out that any division of India along communal lines would inevitably have to include a division of the two major provinces, Punjab and Bengal, along similar lines.[8] A few months before independence, Khwaja Nazimuddin, who later became Pakistan's second governor general as well as its second prime minister, candidly told a British governor that he did not know "what Pakistan means and that nobody in the Muslim League knew."[9] What may have been an effort to seek recognition for

Muslims as a nation in minority moved millions of Indian Muslims into expecting a separate country, the running of which Muslim leaders had made no preparations for. By May 1947, Jinnah was telling a foreign visitor that "even if 'driven into the Sind desert,' he would insist on a sovereign state."[10]

Jinnah and his colleagues in the Muslim League had not contemplated a Pakistan that did not include all of Punjab and Bengal. If the entire scheme was designed to increase the Muslims' bargaining power in post-British India, the division of India had to be between Muslim-majority provinces and Hindu-majority provinces. "Without the non-Muslim-majority districts of these two provinces [Bengal and Punjab], the [Muslim] League could not expect to bargain for parity between 'Pakistan' and 'Hindustan.'"[11]

The British agreement to concede the demand for Pakistan was based partly on the outcome of the 1945–1946 elections for a Constituent Assembly and various provincial assemblies. The elections were organized on the basis of limited franchise and separate electorates for various religious communities, a practice in vogue in India since 1909. The Muslim League won 75 percent of the Muslim vote and all the Muslim seats in the constituent assembly. Only 15 percent of the population had the right to vote on the basis of literacy, property, income, and combatant status.[12] It can be said with some certainty that literate, salaried, and propertied Muslims as well as those who had served in the British army supported the Muslim League. The views of the Muslim peasantry and illiterate masses were less clear.

To shore up Muslim support, the Muslim League appealed to religious and communal sentiment. Although Jinnah—by then known as Quaid-i-Azam (the great leader)—and most of his principal deputies in the campaign for Pakistan were secular individuals, the Muslim League's 1945–1946 election campaign was based almost entirely on Islamic rhetoric. The Indian National Congress secured the assistance of "nationalist" Muslim clerics organized in the Jamiat Ulema Hind (Society of Indian Scholars) to attack the Islamic credentials of Jinnah and other Muslim League leaders. The Muslim League responded by rolling out its own theologians. The result was the almost total identification of Pakistan with Islam in the course of the campaign. The rural Muslim masses were encouraged to develop "a vague feeling that they would all become better Muslims once a Muslim state was established."[13]

Before extending their support to the Muslim League, some religious leaders demanded assurances from Jinnah that Pakistan would follow Islamic laws. Jinnah offered these assurances, as professor Khalid bin Sayeed notes:

> In a letter to the Pir of Manki Sharif, the [Muslim] League leader clearly stated in November 1945: "It is needless to emphasize that the constituent Assembly which would be predominantly Muslim in its composition would be able to enact laws for Muslims, not inconsistent with the Shariat laws and the Muslims will no longer be obliged to abide by the Un-Islamic laws. . . ." In the League meetings that the Quaid-i-Azam addressed, particularly in the Muslim majority areas, Islam with its symbols and slogans figured very prominently in all his speeches. Addressing the Pathans, he said, "Do you want Pakistan or not?" (shouts of Allah-o-Akbar) (God is great). Well, if you want Pakistan, vote for the League candidates. If we fail to realize our duty today you will be reduced to the status of Sudras (low castes) and Islam will be vanquished from India. I shall never allow Muslims to be slaves of Hindus. (Allah-o-Akbar.)[14]

In Punjab, where the Muslim elite had been reluctant followers of Jinnah, the tide was turned with the help of conservative religious elements. A Pakistani scholar and former diplomat explains:

> The spectacular victory of the Muslim League in the Punjab elections in 1946 (79 of the 86 Muslim seats as against only 2 out of 86 Muslim seats in 1937) cannot be understood only in terms of Quaid-i-Azam's charisma. One cannot ignore the use that was made of the religious emotions by the ulema [Islamic scholars], the *sajjada nashins* [hereditary heads of Sufi shrines] and their supporters. The thrust of their message was simple; those who vote for the Muslim League are Muslims, they will go to Heaven for this good act. Those who vote against the Muslim League are kafirs [non-believers],

they will go to hell after their death. They were to be refused burial in a Muslim cemetery . . . The Quaid-i-Azam was not unaware of the use of religion in this manner by the Muslim League, although on principle he was opposed to mixing religion with politics . . . And yet it is a fact that the people of Pakistan talked in the only idiom they knew. Pakistan was to be the laboratory of Islam, the citadel of Islam.[15]

In what was an early, but by no means the last, effort at attributing religious status to Pakistan's political leadership, several Muslim League leaders from Punjab added religious titles, such as Maulana, Pir, or Sajjada Nashin to their names in "dubious pretensions to piety."[16] In the end, the clerics and hereditary religious leaders reduced the argument in favor of creating Pakistan to a simple question of survival of Islam on the South Asian subcontinent.

The sort of logic these religious leaders used was best summarized in one of the speeches of Maulana Abdus Sattar Khan Niazi. He said, "We have got two alternatives before us, whether to join or rather accept the slavery of Bania Brahman Raj in Hindustan or join the Muslim fraternity, the federation of Muslim provinces. Every Pathan takes it as an insult for him to prostrate before Hindu Raj and will gladly sit with his brethren in Islam in the Pakistan Constituent Assembly. A Pathan is a Muslim first and a Muslim last."[17]

The 1945–1946 election enabled the Muslim League to claim that it was the sole representative of the Muslims. Jinnah interpreted the vote as a mandate for him to negotiate on behalf of Muslims, a position the British had no choice but to accept. The election campaign generated religious fervor, and its result seemed to indicate that the Muslims were unhappy at the prospect of being dominated by Hindus; but the election results did not settle the question of what India's Muslims really wanted. Jalal points out that even the limited Muslim vote "had not ratified a specific programme because no programme had actually been specified. No one was clear about the real meaning of 'Pakistan' let alone its precise geographical boundaries."[18] The Muslim League still did not form the government in most of the Muslim-majority provinces, making it impossible to divide India neatly into Muslim-majority and -minority provinces and then allowing two parties, the Muslim League and the Congress, to negotiate a future constitutional arrangement as equals.

Having decided to end colonial rule over India, the British conceded the demand for Pakistan by agreeing to divide India as well as the provinces of Punjab and Bengal. The Pakistan that was created was communally more homogenous but economically and administratively a backwater. Communal riots involving Muslims, Hindus, and Sikhs resulted in massive migrations from Pakistan to India and vice versa, although no such shifts of population had been envisaged by Pakistan's founders. The communal basis of partition, coupled with the religious frenzy generated by it, made religion more central to the new state of Pakistan than Jinnah may have originally envisaged.

The circumstances of the Muslim League's apparent success in the 1946 elections foreshadowed the difficulties confronting Pakistan's leaders once the new country was created. The campaign for Pakistan had, in its final stages, become a religious movement even though its leaders initiated it as a formula for resolving post-independence constitutional problems. This created confusion about Pakistan's raison d'être, which Pakistan's leadership has attempted to resolve through a state ideology. The Muslim League did not retain mass support in the areas that became Pakistan within a few years of independence, especially after universal adult franchise was recognized. The abstract notion of a Pakistan that would be Muslim but not necessarily Islamic in a strict religious sense was confronted with alternative visions. The elite that demanded an independent Pakistan was now challenged by groups that appealed to the wider electorate, most of whom did not have a say in the 1946 election that led to partition. Religious leaders who had been brought belatedly in to campaign for the Muslim League were joined by theologians who had not supported the demand for Pakistan, and they started calling for the new country's Islamization. Others sought to build Pakistan as a loose federation of Muslim majority provinces, with an emphasis on ethnic and regional cultures.

To complicate matters further, when Pakistan was finally born, it faced an environment of insecurity and hostility, with many Indian leaders predicting the early demise of the new country. A former Pakistani foreign minister explained half a century later that the new country found itself beset with problems:

> The partition plan of 3 June 1947 gave only seventy-two days for transition to independence. Within this brief period, three provinces had to be divided, referendums organized, civil and armed services bifurcated, and assets apportioned. The telescoped timetable created seemingly impossible problems for Pakistan, which, unlike India, inherited neither a capital nor government nor the financial resources to establish and equip the administrative, economic and military institutions of the new state. Even more daunting problems arose in the wake of the partition. Communal rioting led to the killing of hundreds of thousands of innocent people. A tidal wave of millions of refugees entered Pakistan, confronting the new state with an awesome burden of rehabilitation.[19]

Getting the new state on its feet economically presented one of the major challenges. Pakistan had virtually no industry, and the major markets for its agricultural products were in India. Pakistan produced 75 percent of the world's jute supply but did not have a single jute-processing mill. All the mills were in India. Although one-third of undivided India's cotton was grown in Pakistan, it had "only one-thirtieth of the cotton mills."[20] The non-Muslim entrepreneurial class, which had dominated commerce in the areas now constituting Pakistan, either fled or transferred its capital across the new border. The flight of capital was attributed to "uncertainties about Pakistan's capacity to survive and the communal disturbances."[21] The U.S. consul in Karachi estimated in July 1947 that, in early June, Rs. 3 billion were sent out of the Punjab alone. Capital transferred from the province of Sindh stood at between Rs. 200 and Rs. 300 million.[22] This amounted to shrinking the revenue base of the new country even before it was formally created. The monetary assets of the Pakistan government were held by the Reserve Bank of India and, given the atmosphere of hostility between partisans of the Indian National Congress and the Muslim League, the division and transfer of assets was by no means a smooth process. Pakistan's earliest government officials feared the "economic strangulation" of their new country and saw a Hindu design to force Pakistan to its knees.[23]

Pakistan's evolution as a state and nation was deeply influenced by these economic and political challenges and the early responses of Pakistan's leaders to these challenges. The ambiguity that had united the supporters of Pakistani independence could no longer be maintained now that the country had come into being. Jinnah could not now break completely from the communal rhetoric preceding independence even though he was concerned about aggravating the communal violence already stoked during partition.

Three days before Pakistan's independence was formalized and Jinnah became the new dominion's governor general, he addressed Pakistan's Constituent Assembly on August 11, 1947. This speech suggests that Pakistan's founder and Quaid-i-Azam expected the new country to be a homeland of Muslims but that he did not expect a role for religion in its governance:

> You are free, free to go to your temples; you are free to go to your mosques or to any other places of worship in this state of Pakistan. You may belong to any religion or caste or creed that has nothing to do with the business of the state. As you know, history shows that in England conditions some time ago were much worse than those prevailing in India today. The Roman Catholics and the Protestants persecuted each other. Even now there are some states in existence where there are discriminations made and bars imposed against a particular class. Thank God, we are not starting in those days. We are starting in the days when there is no discrimination, no distinction between one caste or creed and another. We are starting with this fundamental principle that we are all citizens and equal citizens of one state. The people of England in course of time had to face the realities of the situation and had to discharge the responsibilities and burdens placed upon them by the government of their country, and they went through that fire step by step. Today, you might say with justice that Roman Catholics and Protestants do not exist, what exists now is that every man is a citizen, an equal citizen of Great Britain, and they are all members of the

nation. Now I think we should keep that in front of us as our ideal and you will find that in course of time Hindus would cease to be Hindus and Muslims would cease to be Muslims, not in the religious sense, because that is the personal faith of each individual, but in the political sense as citizens of the State.[24]

Pakistan's secularists have interpreted Jinnah's August 11 speech as a clear statement of intent to build a secular state.[25] Although the speech was widely publicized at the time in an attempt to quell the communal riots that accompanied partition, subsequent official accounts of Jinnah's life included only an edited version of the speech. References to religion having no role in the business of state had been taken out.[26] In any case, Jinnah died within a year of independence, leaving his successors divided, or confused, about whether to take their cue from his independence eve call to keep religion out of politics or to build on the religious sentiment generated during the political bargaining for Pakistan. On-the-ground political realities determined their direction.

The greatest support for Pakistan had come from Muslims living in regions that did not become part of the new state. These Muslim minority regions, now in India, also provided a disproportionate number of the Muslim League's leadership, senior military officers, and civil servants for Pakistan's early administration. Interprovincial rivalries, ethnic and language differences, and divergent political interests of various elite groups had remained dormant while Pakistan was only a demand. Now that it was a state, these became obstacles to constitution writing and political consensus building. India, which became independent along with Pakistan in 1947, agreed on a constitution in 1949 and held its first general election in 1951. Pakistan's first constitution was not promulgated until 1956, and within two years it was abrogated through a military coup d'état.

Pakistan, unlike India, did not go through a general election after independence. Instead, indirect elections through provincial assemblies substituted for an appeal to the general electorate. Provincial elections, held in the Punjab and the NWFP in 1951, were tainted by allegations of administrative interference, whereas the center was often at loggerheads with the elected leadership in Sindh. The Muslim League, which had led the country to independence, was swept out of power in the country's eastern wing in 1954 amid a rising tide of Bengali awakening.

Jinnah's successors chose to patch over domestic differences in the independent country the same way that Muslim unity had been forged during the pre-independence phase. They defined Pakistani national identity through religious symbolism and carried forward the hostilities between the Indian National Congress and the All-India Muslim League by building India-Pakistan rivalry. The dispute over the princely state of Jammu and Kashmir and continued criticism of the idea of Pakistan by Indian politicians and scholars helped fuel the view that "India did not accept the partition of India in good faith and that, by taking piecemeal, she could undo the division."[27] The fears of dilution of Muslim identity that had defined the demand for carving Pakistan out of India became the new nation-state's identity, reinforced over time through the educational system and constant propaganda.

The focus on rivalry with India as an instrument of securing legitimacy and authority for the new Pakistani state defined the locus of political power within Pakistan and influenced the relationship between the state and its citizens. Pakistanis were being conditioned to believe that their nationhood was under constant threat and that the threat came from India. Within weeks of independence, editorials in the Muslim League newspaper, *Dawn*, "called for 'guns rather than butter,' urging a bigger and better-equipped army to defend 'the sacred soil' of Pakistan."[28] This meant that protecting Pakistan's nationhood by military means took priority over all else, conferring a special status upon the national security apparatus. It also meant that political ideas and actions that could be interpreted as diluting Pakistani nationhood were subversive. Demanding ethnic rights or provincial autonomy, seeking friendly ties with India, and advocating a secular constitution fell under that category of subversion. Ayesha Jalal points out:

> If defense against India provided added impetus for the consolidation of state authority in Pakistan, paradoxically enough, it also served to distort the balance of relations between the newly formed center and the provinces. Nothing stood in the way of the reincorporation of the Pakistan areas into the Indian union except

the notion of a central government whose structures of authority lacked both muscle and the necessary bottom. So in Pakistan's case defense against India was in part a defense against internal threats to central authority. This is why a preoccupation with affording the defense establishment—not unusual for a newly created state— assumed obsessive dimensions in the first few years of Pakistan's existence. An insecure central leadership of a state carved out of a continuing sovereign entity found it convenient to perceive all internal political opposition as a threat to the security of the state. In the process the very important distinction between internal and external security threats was all but blurred.[29]

Although before partition Jinnah had never spoken of Pakistan as an ideological state, a Pakistani ideology was delineated by his successors soon after independence. Islam, hostility to India, and the Urdu language were identified as the cornerstones of this new national ideology. Emphasis on Islamic unity was seen as a barrier against the potential tide of ethnic nationalism, which could undermine Pakistan's integrity. It was also argued that India would use ethnic differences among Pakistanis to divide and devour the new country.[30] Very soon after independence, "Islamic Pakistan" was defining itself through the prism of resistance to "Hindu India." It was also seeking great-power allies to help pay for the economic and military development of the new country.

The emphasis on Islam as an element of national policy empowered the new country's religious leaders. It also created a nexus between the "custodians of Islam" and the country's military establishment, civilian bureaucracy, and intelligence apparatus, which saw itself as the guardian of the new state. Inflexibility in relations with India, and the belief that India represented an existential threat to Pakistan, led to maintaining a large military, which in turn helped the military assert its dominance in the life of the country.[31] The search for foreign allies who could pay for the country's defense and economic growth resulted in Pakistan's alliance with the West, especially the United States.

Each element of this policy tripod—religious nationalism, confrontation with India, and alliance with the West—influenced the other, sometimes in imperceptible ways. Sometimes one factor required distortions and convoluted explanations to manage the other. Thus, India had to be painted by Pakistan as an enemy of Islam in order to bolster Pakistan's self-image as a bastion of Islam. The United States had to be persuaded of the value of Pakistan's strategic location and its anticommunist credentials to be able to secure weapons, which were needed to confront the Indians. During its history, the greatest threats to Pakistan's central authority came from groups seeking regional autonomy, ethnic rights, or political inclusion; however, successive Pakistani governments linked these threats to either an Indian-inspired plan to weaken Pakistan or "communists," even though communist influence in Pakistan was minuscule.

The first formal step toward transforming Pakistan into an Islamic ideological state was taken in March 1949 when the country's first prime minister, Liaquat Ali Khan, presented the Objectives Resolution in the constituent assembly. The resolution laid out the main principles of a future Pakistani constitution. It provided for democracy, freedom, equality, and social justice "as enunciated by Islam," opening the door for future controversies about what Islam required of a state. The Objectives Resolution was a curious mix of theology and political science. It read:

Whereas sovereignty over the entire universe belongs to Allah Almighty alone and the authority which He has delegated to the State of Pakistan, through its people for being exercised within the limits prescribed by Him is a sacred trust;

This Constituent Assembly representing the people of Pakistan resolves to frame a Constitution for the sovereign independent State of Pakistan;

Wherein the State shall exercise its powers and authority through the chosen representatives of the people;

Wherein the principles of democracy, freedom, equality, tolerance and social justice as enunciated by Islam shall be fully observed;

Wherein the Muslims shall be enabled to order their lives in the individual and collective spheres in accordance with the teachings and requirements of Islam as set out in the Holy Quran and the Sunnah;

Wherein adequate provision shall be made for the minorities to freely profess and practice their religions and develop their cultures;

Wherein the territories now included in or in accession with Pakistan and such other territories as may hereafter be included in or accede to Pakistan shall form a Federation wherein the units will be autonomous with such boundaries and limitations on their powers and authority as may be prescribed;

Wherein shall be guaranteed fundamental rights including equality of status, of opportunity and before law, social, economic and political justice, and freedom of thought, expression, belief, faith, worship and association, subject to law and public morality;

Wherein adequate provisions shall be made to safeguard the legitimate interests of minorities and backward and depressed classes;

Wherein the independence of the Judiciary shall be fully secured;

Wherein the integrity of the territories of the Federation, its independence and all its rights including its sovereign rights on land, sea and air shall be safeguarded;

So that the people of Pakistan may prosper and attain their rightful and honored place amongst the nations of the World and make their full contribution toward international peace and progress and happiness of humanity.[32]

Non-Muslim opposition members and a solitary Muslim parliamentarian expressed serious qualms about committing the new state to "ordering their lives in accordance with the teachings and requirements of Islam." But Liaquat Ali Khan described it as "the most important occasion in the life of this country, next in importance only to the achievement of independence."[33] In one way, it was. After the Objectives Resolution there was no turning back from Pakistan's status as an Islamic ideological state.

Soon, prominent individuals within the government mooted proposals for adopting Arabic as the national language and for changing the script of the Bengali language from its Sanskrit base to an Arabic-Persian one.[34] The president of the Muslim League, Chaudhry Khaliquz-zaman announced that Pakistan would bring all Muslim countries together into Islamistan—a pan-Islamic entity.[35] The Pakistani government also convened a world Muslim conference in Karachi in 1949, to promote pan-Islamism.[36] This conference led to the formation of the Motamar al-Alam àl-Islami (Muslim World Congress), which has since played a crucial role in building up the feeling of Muslim victimization that subsequently fed the global Islamist movement. Toward the end of 1949, the Pakistani government reached out to the governments of other Muslim countries to try to form an Islamic conference. Only Egypt and Saudi Arabia showed any interest.[37]

Delegates from eighteen Muslim countries attended an international Islamic economic conference, organized at Karachi, in November 1949. Finance Minister Ghulam Muhammad, who subsequently became governor general and was an important architect of Pakistan's alliance with the United States, called for "a system of collective bargaining and collective security" for Muslim nations.

Pakistan's pan-Islamic aspirations, however, were neither shared nor supported by the Muslim governments of the time. Nationalism in other parts of the Muslim world was based on ethnicity, language, or territory. Most Arab governments, as well as secular states such as Turkey, were wary of a religious revival. One of the earliest Western scholars of Pakistani politics, Keith Callard, observed that Pakistanis seemed to believe in the essential unity of purpose and outlook in the Muslim world:

Pakistan was founded to advance the cause of Muslims. Other Muslims might have been expected to be sympathetic, even enthusiastic. But this assumed that other Muslim states would take the same view of the relation between religion and nationality. In fact, the political upsurge elsewhere was based largely on territorial and racial nationalism, anti-Western, anti-white. Religion played a part in this, but it was a lesser part than color, language, and a political theory of violent opposition to colonialism and exploitation. If a choice had to be made [by other Muslim states between friendship with India or Pakistan], India, as the more powerful, more stable and more influential, was likely to have the advantage.[38]

Although Muslim governments were initially u
Pakistan's pan-Islamic aspirations, Islamists from the
drawn to Pakistan. Controversial figures such as the ,
grand mufti of Palestine, Al-Haj Amin al-Husseini, and leaders of Islamist political movements like the Arab Muslim Brotherhood became
frequent visitors to the country. Pakistan's desire for an international
organization of Islamic countries was fulfilled in the 1970s, with the creation of the Organization of Islamic Conference (OIC). During Pakistan's
formative years, however, pan-Islamism was more important for
Pakistan's efforts to consolidate its national identity than as the main-
stay of its foreign policy.

The strongest objections to the Islamic ideological paradigm being
imposed on the new state came from Pakistan's eastern wing. Bengali-
speaking Muslims from what is now Bangladesh, hoping their more
numerous population would guarantee them at least an equal say in
running a new country's affairs, had supported the idea of Pakistan, but
West Pakistani soldiers, politicians, and civil servants dominated
Pakistan's government. Within a year of independence, Bengalis in East
Pakistan were rioting in the streets, demanding recognition of their language, Bengali, as a national language. Soon thereafter, in the western
wing of the country, ethnic Sindhis, Pashtuns (also known as Pathans),
and Balochis also complained about the domination of the civil services
and the military's officer corps by ethnic Punjabis and Urdu-speaking
migrants from northern India.

Liaquat Ali Khan was not a religious man himself and most members
of the first constituent assembly were members of the country's secular
elite. They had clearly been influenced in their decision to declare Pakistan an Islamic state by the realization that Pakistanis had multiple identities. The experience of language riots by Bengalis in East Pakistan had
pointed out the difficulty of subsuming ethnic identities into a new Pakistani identity. Religion was an easier tool of mobilization. Making being Pakistani synonymous with being a good Muslim was considered
the more attainable goal. Given the reality that Islam meant different
things to different people, however, the development of an ideological
state could not be left to the will of the people. Institutions of state had to

control the process of building the new nation. Ensuring the supremacy of these state institutions required greater centralization of authority.

The secular elite assumed that they would continue to lead the country while they rallied the people on the basis of Islamic ideology. They thought they could make use of Muslim theologians and activists, organized in religious parties such as the Majlis-e-Ahrar (Committee of Liberators) and Jamiat-e-Ulema Islam (Society of Muslim Scholars). Pakistan had inherited the "religious sections" of the British intelligence service in India, which had been created to influence different religious communities during colonial rule. The religious sections had often manipulated these groups to ward off pressures for Indian independence. With classic divide-and-rule thinking, leaders of the British Raj assumed that they would have better administrative control if groups within the various religious communities, especially Hindus and Muslims, could be persuaded to pursue sectarian issues.[39] After independence, the Pakistani intelligence organizations hoped to use the same tactic against perceived and real threats to the state. The religious organizations were small in number and stigmatized by their pre-independence opposition to the idea of Pakistan, but they could make statements that secular officials could not. Particularly appealing was the prospect of using theologians to create an impression of pressure from below for policies that did not otherwise capture the imagination of the people.[40]

The Pakistani government could also take advantage of the religious groups, as was the case during the anti-Ahmadi riots in Lahore in 1953. The Ahmadis (also known as Qadianis or Ahmadiyyas) assert that they are Muslims, follow the teachings of a nineteenth century messiah, Mirza Ghulam Ahmad (whom they consider a prophet), and do not recognize the obligation of jihad. Orthodox Muslims had always considered Ahmadis a non-Islamic cult because of their refusal to acknowledge that Muhammad was the final prophet of God. After the 1951 Punjab elections, Punjab's chief minister, a member of the Muslim League, used the links his provincial secret service had with Islamist groups to foment popular agitation calling for legislation that would declare the Ahmadis non-Muslims for legal purposes.

The plan was that violent street protesters would call for the resignation of Pakistan's first foreign minister, Sir Zafarulla Khan, who was an

Ahmadi, and bring down the federal government. The Punjab chief minister, Mumtaz Daulatana, hoped to benefit from the fall of the central government and expected to become prime minister. The riots could not be calibrated, however, and law and order collapsed and the army was called in to control the situation through a declaration of martial law in Lahore, the capital of Punjab.

The events of that year highlighted three interlinked problems that have dogged Pakistan's internal politics over the past fifty years: part of the state apparatus used religion and religious groups for a political purpose. The extent of the religious groups' influence and the sentiment unleashed by them could not be controlled. And the military stepped in to deal with the symptoms of the chaos generated by religious-political agitation, without any effort to deal with its causes.[41]

The anti-Ahmadi riots brought into the limelight Maulana Sayyid Abul Ala Maududi and his Jamaat-e-Islami (Islamic Society or Islamic Party). Founded in 1941, the Jamaat-e-Islami was different from other religious groups. It was neither sectarian nor an association of theologians of a particular Islamic school. The Jamaat-e-Islami was an Islamist party similar to the Arab Muslim Brotherhood. Maulana Maududi, its founder, aimed his calls for Islamic revival at middle-class professionals and state employees rather than traditional mullahs. He had not been part of the campaign for Pakistan and had been critical before partition of the Muslim League's "un-Islamic" leadership, but his writings had supported the theory that Muslims were a nation distinct from non-Muslims. Vali Nasr points out that "communal rights for Muslims" was the common theme of both organizations: "The Jamaat and Muslim League each legitimated the political function of the other in furthering their common communalist cause . . . The Jamaat legitimated communalism in Islamic terms and helped the League find a base of support by appealing to religious symbols. The Muslim League, in turn, increasingly Islamized the political discourse on Pakistan to the Jamaat's advantage, creating a suitable gateway for the party's entry into the political fray."[42]

Maulana Maududi's emphasis before Pakistan's creation was on religious and spiritual revival, and he had commented on politics without taking part. He had hoped to create a large cadre of pious Muslims who would not aspire to power and would lead by example. The process of independence seems to have changed his mind. If Jinnah—a Western-educated and, by all accounts, nonpracticing Muslim—could inspire India's Muslims to create a state by appealing to their religious sentiment, Maulana Maududi reasoned there was scope for a body of practicing Islamists to take over that state.

Maulana Maududi (1903–1979) was a prolific writer. He argued that Islam was as much an ideology as a religion.[43] The Islamic ideology, according to Maulana Maududi, carried forward the mission of the prophets, which he described as follows:

1. To revolutionize the intellectual and mental outlook of humanity and to instill the Islamic attitude toward life and morality to such an extent that their way of thinking, ideal in life, and standards of values and behaviour become Islamic.
2. To regiment all such people who have accepted Islamic ideals and moulded their lives after the Islamic pattern with a view to struggling for power and seizing it by the use of all available means and equipment.
3. To establish Islamic rule and organize the various aspects of social life on Islamic bases, to adopt such means as will widen the sphere of Islamic influence in the world, and to arrange for the moral and intellectual training, by contact and example, of all those people who enter the fold of Islam from time to time.[44]

The Jamaat-e-Islami adopted a cadre-based structure similar to that of communist parties. It built alliances with Islamist parties in other countries, recruited members through a network of schools, and hoped to be the vanguard of a gradual Islamic revolution. The party's call for Islamic revolution did not have mass appeal, however, even though its social service helped create a well-knit, nationwide organization within a few years of partition. The Jamaat saw its opportunity in working with the new state's elite, gradually expanding the Islamic agenda while providing the theological rationale for the elite's plans for nation building on the basis of religion. Jamaat-e-Islami's cadres among students, trade unions, and professional organizations, as well as its focus on building its own media, made it a natural ally for those within the government who thought that Pakistan's survival as a state required a religious anchor.[45]

The Pakistani establishment immediately after partition was wary of Maulana Maududi. Some saw rudiments of totalitarianism in his concept of pious leadership while others considered Jamaat-e-Islami's revolutionary rhetoric dangerous. Muslim League leaders saw Maulana Maududi as a rival claimant for popular support. Some were concerned about the claim to leadership by someone who had not participated in the campaign for Pakistan's creation. Liaquat Ali Khan advised civil servants and military officers against joining the Jamaat-e-Islami and even clamped down on the organization in 1948, banning its newspapers and arresting its leaders.[46]

Liaquat Ali Khan's admonition did not prevent the state apparatus from adapting or adopting some of Maulana Maududi's ideas in their own nation-building enterprise. The Jamaat-e-Islami benefited from close ties with Muslim League leaders, such as Punjab chief minister Nawab Iftikhar Mamdot, who were "eager to enlist the support of Islamic groups such as the Jamaat"[47] in battles against political rivals. Maulana Maududi continued to be disliked by the pro-Western interior minister, Major General Iskander Mirza, and the army chief, General Ayub Khan, both of whom later rose to the office of Pakistan's president. These members of the permanent state establishment encouraged the creation of other religious groups more amenable to official control, which in turn influenced the politics of Jamaat-e-Islami.

Maulana Maududi's idea of regimenting Muslims and instilling a belief system in their thinking was not very different from the objectives of Pakistan's top-down nation builders, who considered regimentation necessary to iron out the creases in the design of a nation-state united primarily by the religion of its citizens. Pakistan's early elite embraced Maulana Maududi's message even as it opposed the messenger. To them the concept of a religious state was desirable as long as it did not entail ceding power to a group of theologians. Maulana Maududi, on the other hand, sought power for the *saleheen* (the pious ones). The Jamaat-e-Islami summed up its philosophy in the slogan, "The country is God's; rule must be by God's law; the government should be that of God's pious men."

In December 1947, a group of students inspired by Maulana Maududi's writings formed the Islami Jamiat-e-Talaba (Islamic Students Society, also known as Jamiat or by its initials, IJT). Although essentially the student wing of the Jamaat-e-Islami, the IJT was greatly influenced by the methods of the Egyptian Muslim Brotherhood, which were more radical than the constitutional gradualism advocated by Jamaat-e-Islami.[48] The IJT became involved in student politics, which enabled it to act as a big tent for center-right students opposed to Marxist student groups on Pakistan's college campuses. IJT members clashed violently with rival, mostly left-wing, student groups and engaged in agitation on issues affecting students. In addition to providing a large cadre for recruitment for the Jamaat-e-Islami, the IJT also created a wide circle of "fellow travelers" in Pakistan's educational system, civil services, and the military's officer corps. As IJT members graduated to membership in the parent organization, Jamaat-e-Islami became more overtly political; it no longer stuck to a single modus operandi and was now willing to explore all possible avenues toward expanding its influence and ideology.

Maulana Maududi outlined a nine-point agenda for Islamic revival. Some of the points, such as the need to "break the power of un-Islam and enable Islam to take hold of life as a whole" were not particularly appealing to the ruling elite. Others points, such as his ideas for intellectual revolution and defense of Islam, could be useful in building an Islamic national identity for Pakistan. Maulana Maududi defined intellectual revolution as an effort to "shape the ideas, beliefs and moral viewpoints of the people into the Islamic mould, reform the system of education and revive the Islamic sciences and attitudes in general."[49] This plan for shaping and molding ideas provided the basis later in Pakistan's life for creating a national culture and history that traced Pakistan's origins to the arrival of Islam in South Asia.

The Pakistani state, in its various campaigns against ethnic nationalists and leftists who did not agree with a centralized state, similarly adopted Maulana Maududi's notion of defense of Islam against "political forces seeking to suppress and finish Islam and [to] break their power in order to make Islam a living force."[50] Pakistan was now the bastion of Islam and an Islamic state, even if the pious elite did not yet rule it. Critics and enemies of the state could now be called enemies of

Islam and their ideas described as threats to Islam's emergence as a living force.

One of Maulana Maududi's earliest contacts with the Pakistani establishment was Maulana Zafar Ahmed Ansari, who had served as office secretary of the All-India Muslim League and who shared Maulana Maududi's vision of a greater role for religion in Pakistan. Both Maulana Ansari and Maulana Maududi were consulted by the first head of the country's civil service, Chaudhry Muhammad Ali, who subsequently became Pakistan's prime minister. Maulana Maududi was also invited to speak on Pakistan's state radio to elaborate his vision of an Islamic state. The Jamaat-e-Islami played a key role in mobilizing theologians to favor an Islamic constitution. It maintained a hard-line posture against India and helped the state by describing leftists, secularists, and ethnic nationalists as "anti-Islam unbelievers." When Muhammad Ali, as prime minister, finally thrashed out a Pakistani constitution in 1956, it included the Objectives Resolution in its preamble, transformed the Constituent Assembly into the National Assembly, and declared Pakistan's official name to be "the Islamic Republic of Pakistan." Pakistan became the first Muslim country to use the religious appellation in its constitutional name. Maulana Maududi's followers credited their leader's influence for this achievement. Since then, the Jamaat-e-Islami has emerged as Pakistan's most well-organized and internationally visible religious party although the number of its followers as a proportion of the total population has remained small.

Maulana Maududi was initially also critical of Pakistan's alliance with the United States, but he gradually tempered his criticism and focused more on combating communism. However, Jamaat-e-Islami's critique of Western civilization and values helped shape the Pakistani state's later worldview of suspicion toward the United States. Pakistani Islamists did not seriously challenge the plans of Pakistan's leaders to build their economy and military with U.S. assistance, but they periodically questioned U.S. intentions, which enabled Pakistan's rulers to cite opposition from both right and left in fulfilling their end of the bargain when Pakistan became a U.S. ally.

A parallel development during Pakistan's formative years was the rise to power of the military and civil bureaucracy. The politicians of the

Muslim League had little or no administrative experience and relied heavily on civil servants inherited from the Raj. The Kashmir dispute as well as the ideological project fueled rivalry with India, which in turn increased the new country's need for a strong military. The military and the bureaucracy, therefore, became even more crucial players in Pakistan's life than they would have been had the circumstances of the country's birth been different. There were fewer Muslim than Hindu officers in the highest echelons of the British Indian army and civil service. For the first few years, British generals commanded Pakistan's military, and British officers also filled many important civil service positions. Midrank Muslim officers, eager for promotions, accused the British of favoring India and played the religious card to move British officers out.[51]

At partition Pakistan had received 30 percent of British India's army, 40 percent of its navy, and 20 percent of its air force.[52] Its share of revenue, however, was a meager 17 percent, leading to concerns about the new state's ability to pay for all its forces. Within days of independence, Pakistan was concerned about its share of India's assets, both financial and military. India's decision to delay transferring Pakistan's share of assets increased the bitterness of partition. Mohandas Gandhi, the father of modern India, recognized the importance of containing that bitterness in India-Pakistan relations; in fact, he went on a fast in January 1948 and demanded that Pakistan's share of the monetary assets be paid.[53] But Pakistanis were not fully satisfied by the terms of the partition. They felt strongly that the Indians as well as the British had created additional problems for the new country while dividing the assets and, especially, in demarcating the border.

If Indian leaders were openly hostile to the idea of Pakistan, global public opinion had also been lukewarm to partition. *Time* magazine, while reporting on the independence of India and Pakistan, wrote that "Pakistan was the creation of one clever man, Jinnah"[54] and compared it unfavorably to the "mass movement" leading to India's independence. The dominant Indian narrative of independence demonized Jinnah and spoke of Pakistan's creation as a tragedy. Indian intellectuals and officials routinely predicted that India and Pakistan would become one nation again. Vijay Lakshmi Pandit, the sister of India's Prime Minister Nehru who

served as Indian ambassador to the United States told an A
paper in 1951, "We agreed to partition because failure to do so wou󠁪u
have perpetuated foreign rule."[55]

Persistent questioning of the wisdom of their nationhood bred insecurity among Pakistanis about the viability of their new state. Pakistanis
responded with a parallel narrative justifying the creation of Pakistan
that blamed the Hindu leadership of Congress for threatening Muslim
identity and culture and thereby making separation inevitable. Pakistanis
also defended their founder, Jinnah, whom they considered the *Quaid-e-
Azam* (great leader). Although much thought might not have gone into
creating the separate state of Pakistan, considerable effort was now ex-
pended on defining, justifying, and protecting it. Pakistani insecurity
was reinforced whenever Indians or other foreigners alluded to the futility of Pakistan's creation. Pakistanis were concerned about the prospect of India "undoing" the partition and the attitude of India's post-
independence elite, which continued to speak in terms of the inevitability
of "reunification," did not help in allaying Pakistani fears.

Among the contentious issues born out of the partition was that of
the princely state of Jammu and Kashmir. During the Raj, 562 princely
states had retained varying degrees of administrative independence
through treaties with Britain concluded during the process of colonial
penetration. Jammu and Kashmir was one of them. The treaty relation-
ships conferred "paramountcy" on the British and, in most cases, control over defense, external affairs, and communications. The end of the
Raj also marked the end of paramountcy. At the time of partition, the
British asked the rulers of these states to choose between India and Pakistan, taking into consideration geographical contiguity and the wishes
of their subjects.[56]

Kashmir's contiguity with Pakistan and its Muslim majority created
the expectation of its inclusion in the new Muslim country. The state's
ruler at the time of partition, Maharajah Hari Singh, sought to retain
independence even though a segment of his Muslim subjects wanted
Kashmir to become part of Pakistan.[57] It has been argued that Indian
Prime Minister Jawaharlal Nehru had thought through a grand strategy
for the princely states, including a design to ensure the inclusion of Jammu
and Kashmir in the independent Indian state.[58]

Most Pakistani leaders and scholars, as well as some Western authors, have also implicated the last British viceroy, Lord Mountbatten, and members of his staff in the "conspiracy" to draw the boundary in a manner that Kashmir would abut both India and Pakistan. Under the partition plan, the province of Punjab was to be divided between India and Pakistan on grounds of contiguity and majority of religious affiliation. Two Muslim-majority *tehsils* (subdivisions) in Gurdaspur district were awarded to India by the Boundary Commission led by British judge Sir Cyril Radcliffe. This provided overland access to Kashmir from India.[59] Had the map of the Punjab been drawn differently, Kashmir could have ended up with road access only to Pakistan and a natural mountainous frontier with India. This would have precluded any effective Indian claim on the princely state.

The chaotic condition of government in the newly born state of Pakistan left little room for planning grand strategy. Pakistanis felt cheated over the Boundary Commission award. Concern about the future of Kashmir was addressed by support for the pro-Pakistan All-Jammu and Kashmir Muslim Conference that led an agitation against the Maharajah.[60] Pashtun tribesmen were hastily trained to enter Kashmir; they were supported by Pakistani military officers. The fact that a British general headed the new Pakistani army limited the scope for a declaration of war against the ill-equipped forces of a British-allied maharajah.

Pakistan's first move in Kashmir was an unconventional war, begun with the assumption that the Kashmiri people would support the invading tribal *lashkar* (unstructured army) and that the maharajah's forces would be easily subdued. Little, if any, thought had been given to the prospect of failure or to what might happen if the Indian army got involved in forestalling a Pakistani fait accompli against the Kashmiri maharajah.

Maharajah Hari Singh sought Indian military help and signed the instrument of accession with India to secure military assistance.[61] India's prime minister, Jawaharlal Nehru, sent in Indian troops to fend off the Azad (Free) Kashmir forces. Pakistan continues to dispute Hari Singh's accession, arguing that it was not the result of a voluntary decision and that he was not competent to accede to India because he had signed a standstill agreement with Pakistan earlier.[62]

The Indian army secured the capital, Srinagar, and established control over the Kashmir valley and most parts of Jammu and Ladakh before a cease-fire was declared and United Nations (UN) peacekeeping troops arrived. The critical consequence of the 1947–1948 war and the subsequent cease-fire was that it conferred upon India the position of a status quo power, holding most of the population and significant territory of Jammu and Kashmir, including its capital, Srinagar. Kashmir continues to bedevil India-Pakistan relations. The role of the conflict, beginning soon after partition, in the ideological evolution of Pakistan is most relevant to the subject of this study.

Muslim officers of Pakistan's army involved in the Kashmir military operation of 1947–1948 used the Islamic notion of jihad to mobilize the tribesmen they had recruited as raiders for the seizure of Kashmir. Akbar Khan, who rose to the rank of major general before being implicated in a 1951 conspiracy to overthrow the government, commanded the Kashmir liberation forces.[63] He adopted the nom de guerre of Tariq, after the Muslim conqueror of Spain, Tariq bin Ziyad.[64] Religious scholars were invited by the government to issue fatwas (Islamic religious opinions issued by a mufti or jurisconsult) declaring the tribesmen's foray into Kashmir as a jihad, and both the tribesmen and the military officers assisting them were described as mujahideen. Notwithstanding the fact that the Pakistani army had been created out of the British Indian army and had inherited all the professional qualifications of its colonial predecessor, within the first few months of independence it was also moving in the direction of adopting an Islamic ideological coloring.

With an ongoing war in Kashmir and the need to maintain the military that had come as Pakistan's share, Pakistan's central government was forced to allocate 70 percent of its projected expenditure in its first year's budget for defense.[65] The prospect of conflict with a much larger neighbor bent upon denying Pakistan's right to exist also led to the strengthening of the country's intelligence services. Pakistan's intelligence services were particularly attentive to the prospect of domestic political forces cooperating with the country's external enemies. As in many insecure states, in Pakistan the line between preventing the nation's enemies from causing it harm and declaring everyone who disagrees with the government an enemy of the nation was blurred. In addition to the civilian Intelligence Bureau (IB), each of Pakistan's provinces had a special branch in its police force that dealt primarily with local intelligence. Each arm of the military (the army, navy, and air force) had its own intelligence service. In 1948, the Inter-Services Intelligence (ISI) directorate was created, primarily to coordinate strategic intelligence gathering. The IB and the provincial special branches had been involved in politics since the British Raj, spying on dissidents and playing one group of natives against another. The military intelligence services became politicized in their effort to find a great-power patron for an economically and militarily weak Pakistan.

If concerns about national identity led to an emphasis on religious ideology, the need for keeping the military well supplied resulted in Pakistan's alliance with the United States. Even before partition, Jinnah had indicated that Pakistan's foreign policy would be oriented toward the Muslim world but that there would be an expectation of U.S. support. "Muslim countries would stand together against possible Russian aggression and would look to the U.S. for assistance," he told a visiting U.S. diplomat.[66] After independence, Jinnah's emphasis on alliance with the United States increased, and he believed that Pakistan could extract a good price from the United States for such an alliance in view of Pakistan's strategic location. Margaret Bourke-White, a *Life* magazine reporter-photographer, reported that Jinnah told her that "America needs Pakistan more than Pakistan needs America . . . Pakistan is the pivot of the world, as we are placed . . . [on] the frontier on which the future position of the world revolves."[67]

Bourke-White had interviewed Jinnah soon after partition and referred to that interview in her book, which was published within two years of the founding of Pakistan. That 1947 interview and Bourke-White's observations, based on conversations with Pakistani officials in 1947–1948, reveal the underlying assumptions of Pakistan's relations with the United States for the next five decades:

"Russia," confided Mr. Jinnah, "is not very far away." This had a familiar ring. In Jinnah's mind, this brave new nation had no other claim on American friendship than this—that across a wild tumble of roadless mountain ranges lay the land of the Bolsheviks. I wondered whether the Quaid-i-Azam considered his new state only as an armored buffer between opposing major powers. He was stressing America's military interest in other parts of the world. "America is now awakened," he said with a satisfied smile. Since the United States was now bolstering up Greece and Turkey, she should be much more interested in pouring money and arms into Pakistan. "If Russia walks in here," he concluded, "the whole world is menaced . . ." In the weeks to come I was to hear the Quaid-i-Azam's thesis echoed by government officials throughout Pakistan. "Surely America will give us loans to keep Russia from walking in." But when I asked whether there were any signs of Russian infiltration, they would reply almost sadly, as though sorry not to be able to make more of the argument. "No, Russia has shown no signs of being interested in Pakistan . . ." This hope of tapping the U.S. Treasury was voiced so persistently that one wondered whether the purpose was to bolster the world against Bolshevism or to bolster Pakistan's own uncertain position as a new political entity."[68]

Bourke-White attributed the interest of Pakistan's founders in foreign affairs to the "bankruptcy of ideas in the new Muslim State."[69] Pakistan, she observed, had a policy of "profiting from the disputes of others," and she cited Pakistan's desire to benefit from tension between the great powers and Pakistan's early focus on the Palestine dispute as examples of this tendency. "Pakistan was occupied with her own grave internal problem, but she still found time to talk fervently of sending 'a liberation army to Palestine to help the Arabs free the Holy Land from the Jews,'" she wrote. "Muslim divines began advocating that trained ex-servicemen be dispatched in this holy cause. *Dawn*, the official government newspaper, condemned the 'Jewish State' and urged a united front of Muslim countries in the military as well as the spiritual sense. 'That way lies the salvation of Islam,' said one editorial."[70]

Liaquat Ali Khan, Jinnah's anointed successor and Pakistan's first prime minister, explained the three fundamental interests that would define Pakistan's external relations: "integrity of Pakistan, Islamic culture and the need for economic development."[71] Maintaining Pakistan's integrity was a euphemism for ensuring adequate defense and military preparedness; it implied Pakistan's need of a great-power patron to help pay for its defense. When Liaquat Ali Khan addressed a Western audience, as when he stated the three fundamental interests, his Islamic rhetoric was diluted by couching it in cultural terms. In the domestic arena, however, he continued to use the term, "Islamic ideology," making it possible for Islamist ideologues to assert their role as interpreters of that ideology.

The United States was Pakistan's great-power patron of choice, crucial as a source of weapons and economic aid. Alliance with the United States became as important a part of the plans for consolidating the Pakistani nation and state as Islam and opposition to Hindu India. At one stage, Liaquat Ali Khan even suggested that Pakistan would have "no further need to maintain an army," let along a large one, if the United States was ready to "guarantee Pakistan's frontiers."[72] In one of its first overtly political initiatives, Pakistan's intelligence community fabricated evidence of a communist threat to Pakistan to get U.S. attention:

> Since the cease-fire in Kashmir, the joint services intelligence had been fabricating increasingly bizarre reports about the fledgling local Communist party and its purported plans to destabilize the state. An early attempt to get attention from London and Washington was "a most hair-raising leaflet . . . which talked . . . of subterranean armies of shock troops, planned attacks on 'nerve centers,' shadow governments" and so on. By the summer of 1949, the director of military intelligence, Brigadier Shahid Hamid, had started dreaming up phantoms and spent the better part of his waking hours "seeking funds and authority to establish a large secret civilian intelligence agency." The brigadier had touched [a] sensitive nerve among senior bureaucrats. The finance minister himself showed a keen interest in the matter and began exploring the possibility of receiving help from American intelligence to build an "Islamic barrier against the Soviets."[73]

In May 1950, Liaquat Ali Khan visited Washington at the invitation of President Harry Truman and was warmly received. During the visit he declared Pakistan's alignment with the United States.[74] Although India remained Pakistan's main military concern, the first Pakistani prime minister went along with the theme of fighting the communist menace. He supported U.S. actions in Korea, which he described as being aimed at "saving Asia from the dangers of world communism."[75] U.S. economic aid started flowing to Pakistan soon after Liaquat's trip to Washington. Liaquat balanced his generally pro-West policy with a refusal to align Pakistan completely with the United States "unless Washington guaranteed Pakistan's security against India."[76]

The push for formalizing a treaty relationship with the United States even without specific guarantees regarding India came from the army, which was concerned about keeping itself well supplied. In 1951, General Ayub Khan became the first Pakistani commander in chief of Pakistan's army, marking the indigenization of the military and ending the transition role of British officers. In the same year, Liaquat Ali Khan was assassinated. Before the assassination, Liaquat, his foreign minister, Sir Zafarulla Khan, and General Ayub Khan initiated talks about military cooperation with the United States. In September–October 1953, General Ayub Khan visited Washington "at his own volition," ahead of a visit by Pakistan's civilian head of state and foreign minister.[77] He sought a "deal whereby Pakistan could—for the right price—serve as the West's eastern anchor in an Asian alliance structure."[78]

The new U.S. administration, led by President Dwight D. Eisenhower, sought to reduce U.S. involvement in military operations of the type undertaken in Korea by building the military capability of frontline states such as Pakistan, Iran, Turkey, and Iraq. This plan of building a "northern tier of defense" against Soviet expansion required Pakistan's participation. Pakistan's leaders of the time saw in it an opportunity to secure the resources and material for the country's military. During his independent visit to Washington, General Ayub Khan "made a favorable impression on both [Secretary of State John Foster] Dulles and [his chief military adviser, Admiral Arthur W.] Radford. Indeed, by this time the mystique of the martial Pashtuns with their splendid warrior traditions was beginning to take firm hold in Washington. Ayub, himself a Pathan and in person an impressive man, was readily seen as epitomizing the best of these traditions. Better still, he was in a position to deliver the goods and seemed willing to do so."[79]

Pakistan concluded a joint defense treaty with the United States in 1954 and became part of the Southeast Asia Treaty Organization (SEATO). From Pakistan's point of view, the relationship was one of quid pro quo. Pakistan would get U.S. arms as well as substantial aid to cover the costs of economic development. The United States would secure Pakistan's membership in alliances it considered necessary. Pakistan subsequently also became part of the Baghdad Pact and the Central Treaty Organization (CENTO). The deal ensured the resources needed to protect the integrity of Pakistan and the need for economic development—two of the three fundamental national interests identified by Liaquat Ali Khan.

The third element—Islamic ideology—remained in the picture, but its priority was lowered for the moment. Appeals to Islamic sentiment against godless communism fit in well with Pakistan's alliance with the United States; however, as Liaquat had himself realized, while dealing with Americans it was not expedient to go beyond mild references to Islamic culture and the importance of religious roots. The United States, in a policy statement, had made it clear that "[a]part from Communism, the other main threat to American interests in Pakistan was from 'reactionary groups of landholders and uneducated religious leaders' who were opposed to the 'present Western-minded government' and 'favor[ed] a return to primitive Islamic principles.'"[80]

At home, however, the domestic audience continued to be given the full dose of Islamic ideology. This created a dichotomy for the Pakistani state. On the one hand, it had to take into account U.S. expectations on a range of issues, from attitudes toward India to attitudes toward developments in the rest of the Islamic world. On the other hand, it had to contend with opposition from more eager Islamists, who saw a close relationship with the United States as impeding Pakistan's ideological growth. At home, Pakistan's leaders dealt with the problem partly by portraying the alliance with the United States in terms of ensuring Pakistani security vis-à-vis India and acquiring Kashmir although, in fact, Washington had given no clear guarantee about Kashmir. In their eagerness to seek alliance with the United States, Pakistani officials had exaggerated their commitment to fighting communism and had even pledged that U.S. military aid would not be used against India.[81]

The United States, after getting Pakistan's participation in SEATO and CENTO, fulfilled Pakistan's demand for military equipment and economic aid. In the quest for U.S. support, Ayub Khan had gone so far as telling a U.S. official, "Our army can be your army if you want."[82] However, Washington's expectation of a centrally positioned landing site for possible operations against the Soviet Union and China was not met. Shirin Tahir-Kheli points this out in her study of U.S.-Pakistan relations:

> Despite the overwhelming disparity in the power equation, Washington was not able to convince Ayub—who as commander in chief of the army was the key relevant figure—to grant full access rights. Ayub tantalized Washington with possible offers of such facilities and manpower only if the price was "right." There were three main reasons for his demanding the maximum price.
>
> First, Ayub fully recognized the enormous costs of Pakistan's military expansion program, which could not be borne indigenously. Second, he was aware of the resentment the cost of military expansion would engender in the civilian sector if the funds were abstracted from the civilian budget and allocated for defense. Washington represented a possible way out of the dilemma because it could become the source not only for military assistance but for other economic aid. Ayub could thus become a national hero for bringing home both guns and butter, so to speak. Third, Ayub was keenly aware that Pakistan needed its military for defense against India and could not deplete its ranks in pursuit of U.S. options. The only way Pakistan could play that proxy role, in his view, was if Washington guaranteed Pakistan's security against India.[83]

While Pakistan did not provide the military facilities the United States sought as part of the strategy for the containment of communism, it permitted U-2 reconnaissance flights and listening posts that were aimed at the Soviet Union. The United States had to be content with looking upon its investment in Pakistan as one that would bear fruit only over time.[84] Ayub Khan's bargaining for greater military and economic assistance became the norm for his successors. General Zia ul-Haq drove a similarly hard bargain when the United States sought to expand an anticommunist insurgency in Afghanistan after the 1979 Soviet invasion of that country. General Musharraf, too, followed Ayub Khan in seeking the right price for cooperation in the war against terrorism after September 11, 2001. While the Pakistanis bargained well for military and economic assistance, the United States has generally had to be modest in its ambitions about what it could hope to achieve. Pakistan's real or projected limitations and compulsions have repeatedly been cited during the execution stage of deals based on a quid pro quo, limiting the fulfillment of U.S. expectations.

The most significant result of the U.S. treaty relationship was to enhance General Ayub Khan's standing within the Pakistani ruling elite and, more important, provide an increased role for the military in Pakistan's subsequent development. The military was already a significant institution, one that existed well before the country came into being. It had fought India in 1947–1948, helped resettle the refugees, and provided crucial assistance during national disasters such as floods. Now it had emerged as the major reason for U.S. interest in Pakistan. The political leadership, on the other hand, was mired in infighting that—at least in the eyes of the military and the civil bureaucracy—could jeopardize Pakistan's survival. The same year he secured Pakistan's relationship with the United States, Ayub Khan wrote a memo entitled "A short appreciation of present and future problems of Pakistan."[85] He was preparing for a military takeover of Pakistan; this was his blueprint for governance.

Between 1954 and 1958, members of Pakistan's permanent state structure—the civil services and the military—enhanced their share of power although they did not completely dispense with trappings of a parliamentary democracy. Soon after Liaquat's assassination in 1951, the civil servant finance minister, Ghulam Muhammad, became governor general. Major General Iskander Mirza, graduate of the Royal Military Academy Sandhurst and one-time member of the British Indian political service, succeeded him.

General Ayub Khan remained a constant power broker throughout this period, playing a behind-the-scenes political role. In 1953 he was named defense minister. This marked a break from the tradition of parliamentary government, which requires cabinet ministers to be members of Parliament. Ayub Khan remained a constant factor in Pakistan's circle of power between 1951 and 1958, even though the country went through seven prime ministers and several cabinets during this prolonged period of political uncertainty.

The rise to power of the civil-military complex ended the process of political bargaining in defining the direction of Pakistan. These primarily British-trained men "deferred to the experts, minimized the role of the politicians and tried to isolate the clerics."[86] But that did not mean they had abandoned the notion of building a nation through administrative fiat and with the help of an ideology. The bureaucrats, backed by the military, attempted to reduce the domestic role of religion by ignoring, for example, calls for Sharia rule. But religious sentiment continued to be exploited in responding to what came to be described as the Indian threat. The civil-military complex adapted the ideology of Pakistan to mean demonization of India's Brahmin Hinduism and a zealous hostility toward India. Domestic political groups demanding provincial autonomy or ethnic rights were invariably accused of advancing an Indian agenda to dismember or weaken Pakistan.

Iskander Mirza had impressed Western statesmen and diplomats as a secular man, but, when it came to India, his reaction was visceral and not very different from the more religiously inclined politicians or bureaucrats. Before Iskander Mirza abrogated the 1956 constitution and imposed martial law in 1958, he confided his intention to Sir Alexander Symon, the British high commissioner.[87] Immediately after what amounted to a coup d'état, when Sir Alexander advised him to make an early statement about peaceful intentions toward India, Mirza ignored that advice.[88]

General Mirza imposed martial law on October 7, 1958, ostensibly to save the country from its political drift. Although General Mirza's coup d'état had been planned for some time, the immediate provocation for such a drastic move came when a confrontation between various political factions in the East Pakistan legislative assembly turned into a brawl and resulted in the death of that assembly's deputy speaker. In August 1958, almost two months before what was to be Pakistan's first direct military coup d'état, the British high commissioner at Karachi reported the possibility of the military's direct assumption of power;[89] General Iskander Mirza had shared with the high commissioner the view that democracy was unsuited to a country like Pakistan, even as plans were publicly laid out for general elections. The high commissioner reported that the president had told him of his intention to intervene "if the election returns showed that a post-electoral government was likely to be dominated by undesirable elements."[90] Sir Alexander noted parenthetically that the term "undesirable" was not defined and "no doubt the term may include any persons who are unlikely to vote for Iskander Mirza as president."[91]

By September 23, 1958, the British high commissioner was reporting the suspicion that "the President himself may take a hand in the provocation of violence in order to clear the way for the intervention of the army and the postponement of elections."[92] Later, on September 27, General Mirza confided to Sir Alexander his conviction that democracy would not work in Pakistan and that "the time had come for him to act."

"What he had in mind," wrote Sir Alexander in a letter to the Commonwealth Relations Office in London, "was (after the army's intervention had cleared the ground) to appoint 20 to 30 good men, if he could find them, to reshape the constitution and govern the country."[93] But martial law shifted the power balance completely in favor of the military, making it untenable for Mirza to remain in charge. Twenty days later, on October 27, 1958, General Ayub Khan, the army chief, assumed the presidency.

Ayub Khan announced a comprehensive program of reforms and styled himself as a revolutionary leader. Most of these reforms were in the temporal domain, but the question of ideology did not escape attention. In a 1960 *Foreign Affairs* article, Ayub Khan reinforced Liaquat Ali Khan's definition of Pakistan's crucial interests and spoke of "the peculiar strains which confronted Pakistan immediately on its emergence as a free state."[94] The first of these strains was described as ideological and Ayub Khan declared his intention of "liberating the basic concept of our ideology from the dust of vagueness." Ayub Khan explained the importance of his plan to build a Pakistani nation from the top. "Till the advent of Pakistan, none of us was in fact a Pakistani," he wrote, "for the simple reason that there was no territorial entity bearing that name." Before 1947, "our nationalism was based more on an idea than on any territorial definition. Till then, ideologically we were Muslims; territorially we happened to be Indians; and parochially we were a conglomeration of at least eleven smaller provincial loyalties."[95] Ayub Khan expected his military coup, which he described as a revolution, to resolve these contradictions.

In the same article, Ayub Khan also argued that Pakistan could be "submerged under the tidal wave of Communism" and that Pakistan was entitled to "claim still more" aid from western nations, especially the United States for "reasons of history." As Pakistan had "openly and unequivocally cast its lot with the West," the western nations had "a special responsibility to assist Pakistan in attaining a reasonable posture of advancement."[96]

Ayub Khan's prescription for national consolidation was to combine ideology and economic development aided by the west. An alternative strategy had been argued by Pakistan's most popular post-independence politician, Huseyn Shaheed Suhrawardy, who served as prime minister in 1956–1957 only to be ousted by the civil-military combine. Suhrawardy, who was barred from politics by Ayub Khan, challenged the concept of Pakistan as an ideological state. Emphasis on ideology, he argued, "would keep alive within Pakistan the divisive communal emotions by which the subcontinent was riven before the achievement of independence."[97] Suhrawardy argued in favor of seeing "Pakistan in terms of a nation state" wherein a "durable identity between government and people derived from the operation of consent."[98] Suhrawardy supported a pro-western foreign policy and saw little gain for Pakistan in impractical visions of pan-Islamism.[99] He felt, however, that the government should explain the rationale of Pakistan's external relations to the people and secure their support for its alliances abroad instead of operating secretly.

It was Ayub Khan's vision, however, that prevailed and Pakistan's military put its weight behind the notion of an ideological state. The success of Ayub Khan's policy of close ties with the United States and Pakistan's economic development under his rule impressed many observers at the time. Ayub Khan, who promoted himself to field marshal, was praised as a reformer and a visionary, a genuinely enlightened dictator. Among Ayub Khan's reforms were the consolidation of state control over education and the media.

At this time, the study of Islam or "Islamiyat" began receiving considerable emphasis.[100] The study of history, geography, and civics at primary and secondary school levels was collapsed into a single subject called social studies. Curricula and textbooks were standardized, presenting a version of history that linked Pakistan's emergence to Islam's arrival in the subcontinent instead of it being the outcome of a dispute over the constitution of postcolonial India. The history of Islam was presented, not as the history of a religion or a civilization, but as a prelude to Pakistan's creation. Muslim conquerors were glorified, Hindu-Muslim relations were painted as intrinsically hostile, and the ability of Pakistanis to manage democratic rule was questioned. Ayub Khan's revolution was characterized as an important step toward the consolidation of Pakistan. The field marshal's successors required the study of the same themes at undergraduate level as Pakistan studies and diluted the exaggerated praise of Ayub Khan, but they retained the contrived historical narrative and expanded the emphasis on Islam. The Ministry of Information and the Bureau of National Reconstruction ensured that a message similar to that taught in schools was available to adults through radio, television, films, magazines, books, and newspapers.

Ayub Khan's close companion and his secretary for information, Altaf Gauhar, revealed several years after Ayub Khan's death that "In 1959 Ayub had written a paper on the 'Islamic Ideology in Pakistan,' which was circulated to army officers among others."[101] Ayub Khan also explained his views on the subject of ideology in his autobiography:

Man as an animal is moved by basic instincts for preservation of life and continuance of race but as a being conscious of his power of thinking he has the power to control and modify his instincts. His greatest yearning is for an ideology for which he should be able to lay down his life. What it amounts to is that the more noble and eternal an ideology, the better the individual and the people professing it. Their lives will be much richer, more creative and they will have a tremendous power of cohesion and resistance. Such a society can conceivably be bent but never broken . . . Such an ideology with us is obviously that of Islam. It was on that basis that we fought for and got Pakistan, but having got it, we failed to define that ideology in a simple and understandable form. Also in our ignorance we began to regard Islamic ideology as synonymous with bigotry and theocracy and subconsciously began to feel shy of it. The time has now come when we must get over this shyness, face the problem squarely and define this ideology in simple but modern terms and put it to the people, so that they can use it as a code of guidance.[102]

Ayub Khan then proceeded to define and outline the issues of a simplified Islamic ideology: "True that in [Islamic] society national territorialism has no place, yet those living in an area are responsible for its defense and security and development. Attachment to the country we live in and get our sustenance from is therefore paramount."[103] "Moreover, considering that the people of Pakistan are a collection of so many races with different backgrounds, how can they be welded into a unified whole whilst keeping intact their local pride, culture, and traditions."[104]

Contrary to widespread perception, Ayub Khan was not a secularist; neither was he averse to the notion of Pakistan having a state ideology. Being a straightforward soldier, he did not have time for an elaborate theory of the Islamic state such as the one proposed by Maududi. He simply wanted to do what he perceived was good for the state and declare it as Islamic.

Ayub Khan did not think highly of the ulema and spoke of their conflict with "the educated classes." He also did not like the complicated and mutually contradictory versions of religion offered by theologians and clearly opposed their role in governance. Ayub Khan wanted the state to exercise the function of religious interpretation and wanted an Islamic ideology that would help him in the "defense and security and development" and the "welding" of Pakistan's different races into a unified whole. He envisioned Islam as a nation-building tool, controlled by an enlightened military leader rather than by clerics. His vision was shared by most of his fellow military officers even though some had started reading Maududi and other theoreticians of the Islamic state. Some had even started developing close relations with religious scholars.

One element of Ayub Khan's thinking that overlapped with the ideas of religious-political leaders related to the characterization of India as a

Hindu state and of Hindus as irreconcilable enemies of Islam and Muslims. "It was Brahmin chauvinism and arrogance that had forced us to seek a homeland of our own where we could order our life according to our own thinking and faith," he wrote in his autobiography.[105] In Ayub Khan's view:

> The Indian theoreticians were claiming boundaries from the Oxus to Mekong . . . India was not content with her present sphere of influence and she knew that Pakistan had the will and the capacity to frustrate her expansionist designs. She wanted to browbeat us into subservience. All we wanted was to live as equal and honorable neighbors, but to that India would never agree . . . There was the fundamental opposition between the ideologies of India and Pakistan. The whole Indian society was based on class distinction in which even the shadow of a low-caste man was enough to pollute a member of the high caste.[106]

Without wanting to emphasize piety or get involved in the fine points of theology, Ayub Khan wanted Pakistani nationalism to reflect pan-Islamic aspirations and a fear of Hindu and Indian domination:

> The countries in [the Muslim] region from Casablanca to Djakarta are also suspect in the eyes of the major powers because most of them profess the faith of Islam. Whatever may be the internal differences among these countries about Islam, and regardless of the approach to Islam, which each one of these countries has adopted, it is a fact of life that the Communist world, the Christian World, and Hindu India treat them as Muslim countries.
> India particularly has a deep pathological hatred for Muslims and her hostility to Pakistan stems from her refusal to see a Muslim power developing next door. By the same token, India will never tolerate a Muslim grouping near or far from her borders.[107]

In a sense, Ayub Khan was the first Pakistani leader with international stature who convinced the world of his modernizing bona fides without giving up religious prejudices. His lack of outward religious observance, his distance from the ulema, and his careful choice of words abroad helped create his image as a latter day Atatürk or a Muslim de Gaulle; however, Ayub Khan moved Pakistan further along the road of a state-sponsored ideology. The military leadership, assuming that the military would remain in control, saw no threat to the state from the Islamists. Acceptance of an Islamic ideological state, however, led to the inevitable claim by Islamists of their right to define the contours of that state.

Ayub Khan was a firm believer in the policy tripod developed within the first few years of Pakistan's creation: he identified India as Pakistan's eternal enemy, Islam as the national unifier, and the United States as the country's provider of arms and finances. In his particular mixture of the three key elements of state policy, however, hostility toward India and friendship with the United States took precedence over Islam as unifier.

During Ayub Khan's first few years in power, the religious parties were generally kept out of the orbit of power, partly because Ayub Khan sought to cultivate the image of an enlightened Muslim leader in the West. This led to the Jamaat-e-Islami joining up with secular parties opposed to military rule. At one point, Ayub Khan banned the Jamaat-e-Islami under a law regulating political parties, but the Supreme Court forced him to withdraw the ban.[108] The Jamaat and some officials in Ayub Khan's regime cooperated with each other, however, so that the Jamaat would use its Islamist contacts in Arab countries over the Kashmir issue.[109]

When Ayub Khan introduced the 1962 constitution that provided for a presidential system with indirect elections for president, its initial version deleted "Islamic" from Pakistan's official name and used the term "Republic of Pakistan." Under the protest of religious parties, the indirectly elected National Assembly restored the original designation, "Islamic Republic of Pakistan." With the new constitution in force, martial law ended although the constitution was widely unpopular and seen as an instrument of one-man rule in the country. Ayub Khan saw the country "behaving like a wild horse that had been captured but not yet tamed."[110]

To tame the wild horse, Ayub Khan mobilized the machinery of state to suppress dissent. The brunt of the repression had to be borne by ethnic nationalist groups and mainstream political parties, although the Jamaat-e-Islami was also not spared for aligning with them against the new constitution. When Ayub Khan held the first indirect presidential election under this constitution in January 1965, the opposition parties nominated Fatima Jinnah, the sister of Pakistan's founder, as their joint candidate. The main issue in the elections was parliamentary democracy versus Ayub Khan's system of controlled governance. Ayub Khan pointed to his achievements in international relations and in the economic sphere but felt overwhelmed by the vociferous opposition to his domestic policies by politicians he thought he had already discredited. As a general who saw his role as keeping the nation together, Ayub Khan could not adjust to competitive politics. He asked his administrative and intelligence machinery to deal with the opposition's attacks.

Among the various political strategies used by Ayub Khan's Interior Ministry (which controlled the domestic intelligence service) in that campaign was a fatwa declaring that Islam did not allow a woman to be head of state.[111] Maududi, committed to Fatima Jinnah's candidacy, said a woman could be head of an Islamic state but it was not desirable. In the ensuing controversy, the government persuaded or bribed many clerics. One pro-Ayub holy man, Pir Sahib Dewal Sharif, "claimed that in the course of meditation, the Almighty had favored him with a communication which indicated divine displeasure with the Combined Opposition Parties."[112] The episode undermined Ayub Khan's original plan of keeping clerics at a distance.

Ayub Khan's foreign policy also started running into some difficulty after the election of John F. Kennedy, in 1960, which sought to strengthen U.S. relations with India. President Dwight D. Eisenhower and Secretary of State Dulles had been impressed by Ayub Khan and the potential for Pakistan's participation in their "northern tier of defense" strategy. Dulles had told the U.S. Congress of his belief that the Pakistanis "are going to fight any communist invasion with their bare fists if they have to."[113] India's unwillingness to join U.S.-sponsored treaties had given Pakistan an advantage in the eyes of Dulles, who looked upon Indian nonalignment as immoral, but Pakistan had not provided the kind of support for the U.S.-led alliances that the United States had hoped for. Pakistan, on the other hand, felt that it needed greater U.S. support, especially in the resolution of the Kashmir dispute. By the time President Kennedy took office, both sides felt they were no longer getting what they wanted from the relationship.

Ayub Khan started warming up to China just as the Kennedy-Johnson administration sought to build closer ties with India. In his July 1960 *Foreign Affairs* article, Ayub Khan had pointed to the need for cooperation between India and Pakistan: "As a student of war and strategy, I can see quite clearly the inexorable push of the north in the direction of the warm waters of the Indian Ocean. This push is bound to increase if India and Pakistan go on squabbling with each other." But four years later, Ayub Khan was willing to forgo containment of China to secure advantage against India. In a new *Foreign Affairs* piece, "Pakistan-American Alliance—Stresses and Strains," published in January 1964, the Pakistani leader explained that the priority for Pakistan was to ensure its security against India, and he voiced the Pakistani grievance that the United States was not helping on that front.[114]

The problem of Pakistanis and Americans having different priorities in their alliance came to a head at the time of the Sino-Indian border war of 1962. During that war, the United States provided military assistance to India. Pakistan's view was that supply of U.S. arms to India should be linked to a Kashmir settlement; otherwise India would use U.S. weapons against Pakistan, a U.S. ally. Pakistan also turned down U.S. suggestions that Pakistan mend fences with India and back away from an entente with the People's Republic of China. Pakistan reached an agreement on demarcating its border with the Chinese, including territory that was formally part of the disputed state of Jammu and Kashmir. It also became the first noncommunist country to begin commercial flights to the People's Republic.

Pakistan's leaders had been clear from the beginning that they were allying with the United States only to offset the disadvantages in resources Pakistan had inherited at the time of partition and that they did not completely share the U.S. worldview. Well before he became president, in July 1958, General Ayub Khan wrote a paper for *Asian Review* on Pakistan's defense requirements: "We have proven and trusted manpower that can do the fighting; but that manpower by itself, unless married up with the necessary modern equipment, is really not much use;

and the only country that equipment can come from is America."[115] Now that he had secured some equipment, Ayub Khan wanted to raise the ante and sought U.S. pressure on India for resolution of the Kashmir dispute. He also asked his brain trust to work out a plan for breaking the stalemate in Kashmir.

The Bureau of National Reconstruction, Ayub Khan's intelligence and research outfit, had published a study of Pakistan's security requirements and recommended that the country look beyond the alliance with the United States in ensuring its defense. The study claimed that in addition to the threat from India, Pakistan had also inherited all the problems of defense of British India owing to Afghanistan's claim on Pashtun tribal areas in the country's northwest and the possibility of a Russian push for warm waters through Afghanistan and Pakistan. The study argued:

Pakistan must be prepared for the day when [the relationship with the United States] is dissolved or loosened . . . Then our "proven and trusted manpower" should be able to hold its own ground. To meet this situation, Pakistan should turn to its own ideology and inherent strength. The duty of self-defense (Jehad) which Islam has ordained makes it incumbent upon everyone to contribute toward the national defense. It also underlines the importance of individual effort and initiative which have become extremely important under conditions of modern warfare.[116]

The Bureau of National Reconstruction's proposed solution to Pakistan's security problems was irregular warfare:

In its manpower, Pakistan is very fortunate. In some of the regions, people have long traditions of irregular fighting. Now that they have got a homeland and a state based on their own ideology they are bound to show great courage and determination to defend them. Then why not train irregular fighters whom even the existing industries of Pakistan can well equip? Of course, they will have to be politically conscious. They will have to be aware of the stakes involved in such a struggle, which is bound to be protracted. Their training in warfare will have to be strenuous and wide in scope. The irregular fighter will have to be shrewd, familiar with local environment factors, aware of the psychology of his own people and of the enemy and of the political consequences of the struggle.

Irregular warfare can help in reducing the crucial nature of the initial battles of Pakistan. It can help in spreading out prolonging action. The essence of this irregular warfare is to deny the enemy any target and keep attacking him again at unexpected places . . .

Lack of military formalities in the eyes of military experts seems to detract from the respectability of irregular warfare. But actually, it is this lack of formal logic and system which is making it increasingly important in this age of missiles and nuclear weapons."[117]

The 1964 death of India's long-serving prime minister, Jawaharlal Nehru, at a time of Muslim unrest in the Indian-controlled parts of Kashmir, encouraged anti-India hard-liners in Pakistan to test this doctrine of irregular warfare, albeit in an offensive posture. Infiltrators were sent into Kashmir in August 1965, hoping to ignite a wider uprising. On September 6, India retaliated by widening the war along Pakistan's international border. The United States suspended supplies of arms to both India and Pakistan, causing disappointment in Pakistan because of the country's greater dependence on U.S. weapons. The war ended in a stalemate, denying Pakistan the military advantage it had hoped to seek.

The 1965 war with India had several consequences, each important for Pakistan's future. First, it bred anti-Americanism among Pakistanis on the basis of the notion that the United States had not come to Pakistan's aid despite being its ally. Second, it linked the Pakistani military closer to an Islamist ideology. Religious symbolism and calls to jihad were used to build the morale of soldiers and the people. Third, it widened the gulf between East and West Pakistan as Bengalis felt that the military strategy of Ayub Khan had left them completely unprotected. Fourth, it weakened Ayub Khan, who lost the confidence of the United States by going to war with India and of his own people by his being unable to score a definitive victory against India.

On the first day of India's offensive against the Pakistan border, Ayub Khan addressed the nation and set the tone for the India-Pakistani relationship for years to come:

Indian aggression in Kashmir was only a preparation for an attack on Pakistan. Today [the Indians] have given final proof of this and of the evil intentions, which India has always harbored against Pakistan since its inception. The Indian rulers were never reconciled to the establishment of an independent Pakistan where the Muslims could build a homeland of their own. All their military preparations during the last 18 years have been directed against us.

They exploited the Chinese bogey to secure massive arms assistance from some of our friends in the West who never understood the mind of the Indian rulers and permitted themselves to be taken in by India's profession that once they were fully armed they will fight the Chinese. We always knew that these arms will be raised against us. Time has proved this is so.

Now that the Indian rulers, with their customary cowardice and hypocrisy, have ordered their armies to march into the sacred territory of Pakistan, without a formal declaration of war, the time has come for us to give them a crushing reply which will put an end to India's adventure in imperialism . . . The 100 million people of Pakistan whose hearts beat with the sound of 'La ilaha illallah, Muhammad Ur Rasool Ullah' [There is no God but God and Muhammad is His messenger] will not rest till India's guns are silenced.[118]

Pakistan's state-controlled media generated a frenzy of jihad, extolling the virtues of Pakistan's "soldiers of Islam." An officer of Pakistan's Inter-Services Public Relations wrote years later:

There was a spurt of gallantry stories, of divine help, of superhuman resistance and of unrivalled professional excellence in the face of overwhelming odds . . . The story of the suicide squad—a band of dedicated soldiers who acted as live mines to blow up the advancing Indian tanks in the Sialkot sector—became one of the most popular war legends. There was no end of stories about divine help. People, both soldiers and civilians, had actually "seen with their eyes" green-robed angels deflecting bombs from their targets—

bridges, culverts, mosques—with a wave of the hand. Soldiers were reported shooting enemy aircraft with their .303s [rifles].[119]

Several junior officers who saw action in that war, including some who rose to become generals, came back to describe it as a struggle of Islam and un-Islam—terminology previously used only by religious ideologues such as Maududi.[120]

The Pakistani people were told by the state that they had been victims of aggression and that the aggression had been repelled with the help of God. The propagation of this view needed the help of religious leaders and groups. The traditional ulema and Islamists used the environment of jihad to advance their own agenda, and one agenda item was that they should be accepted as custodians of Pakistan's ideology and identity. After the war, several state-sponsored publications were devoted to building the case that one Muslim soldier had the fighting prowess to subdue five Hindus.

In discussions with U.S. diplomats, however, Ayub Khan acknowledged that the war had begun as a result of Pakistan's forays in Kashmir.[121] That did not stop Ayub Khan from seeking U.S. intervention on behalf of Pakistan and the Pakistanis from feeling aggrieved when the United States did not help. The official Pakistani attitude was summarized in a conversation between the Canadian high commissioner and Ayub Khan. During the war the Canadian diplomat asked the Pakistani president what he wanted. Ayub Khan replied, "We want Kashmir but we know we can't win it by military action. If only you people would show some guts, we would have it."[122]

The war ended within seventeen days with a UN-sponsored cease-fire, but was far from decisive. Official propaganda convinced the people of Pakistan that their military had won the war. Pakistan had occupied 1,600 square miles of Indian territory, 1,300 of it in the desert, while India secured 350 square miles of Pakistani real estate. The Pakistani land occupied by the Indians was of greater strategic value, as it was located near the West Pakistani capital, Lahore, and the industrial city of Sialkot as well as in Kashmir. Moreover, although Pakistan had held its own against a larger army, it came out of the war a weakened nation. The U.S.-Pakistan relationship had lost its initial strength, Kashmir was still unsettled, and inattention from the central government was upsetting the Bengalis in East Pakistan more than ever. Domestic factors were also causing unrest in Sindh and Balochistan.

The situation immediately after the 1965 war presented an opportunity for the civil-military combine to see the limitations of its nation- and state-building enterprise. Basing Pakistani nationalism on hostility toward India had led the country into a war that had attained none of Pakistan's war aims. It diverted precious resources away from economic development and weakened the links between the country's two wings. Neither Ayub Khan nor his deputies realized that it was time to move away from the ideological tripod. The belief persisted that Pakistan's success depended on an Islamic nationalism, confrontation with India, and external alliances to help the country acquire weapons and pay for development. Evidence to the contrary was either brushed aside or hidden from the Pakistani people.

When Field Marshal Ayub Khan met Prime Minister Lal Bahadur Shastri of India in Tashkent in January 1966, he agreed to swap the territory seized by both sides during the recent war. Brought to believe that the war had ended in a Pakistani victory, the public found it difficult to understand why "objective reality on the ground" had forced an "unfavorable" settlement on Pakistan. The Tashkent agreement also made no mention of Pakistan's demand for a plebiscite in Kashmir, which made the people wonder why Pakistan's "military victory" did not bring it any gain in territory or at least the promise of a future favorable settlement. Ayub Khan's foreign minister, Zulfikar Ali Bhutto, resigned from the cabinet and led critics in suggesting that "political surrender" at Tashkent had converted a military victory into defeat.

Ayub Khan resigned as president in March 1969 after several months of violent demonstrations against his government. Instead of transferring power to the speaker of the National Assembly, a Bengali, as required by his own constitution of 1962, Ayub Khan returned the country to martial law. The army chief, General Agha Muhammad Yahya Khan, became Pakistan's president and chief martial law administrator and ruled by decree, without a constitution.

2

Defending Ideological Frontiers

Pakistan's second military regime, led by General Yahya Khan, was relatively short-lived (1969–1971), but its impact on the country was long lasting. The preoccupation of Pakistan's ruling elite now was to fend off challenges to its dominance from populist political parties. In East Pakistan, the Awami League (AL, founded by Huseyn Shaheed Suhrawardy, who had earlier articulated the vision of Pakistan as a secular nation-state) was questioning the cultural and economic neglect of the Bengali majority by the central government and demanding greater autonomy. The Awami League's leader, Sheikh Mujibur Rahman, campaigned for a six-point program that envisaged a loose confederation between Pakistan's two wings rather than a centralized state controlled by the Punjabi-dominated military. Bengalis also sought an easing of tensions with India and a reduction in military spending. Instead of waking up to Bengali concerns, the Pakistani establishment accused the Awami League of being India's Trojan horse, seeking the country's dismemberment. In West Pakistan, the Pakistan Peoples Party (PPP), led by Zulfikar Ali Bhutto, demanded economic reform and a closer alignment with China against India. Both parties ignored the ideological concept of Pakistan and were seen as a threat to the strategy for national survival nurtured since independence.

Soon after assuming power, Yahya Khan extended the military's role as the guardian of Pakistan's "ideological frontier," a notion that has prevailed ever since. He held Pakistan's first general election on the basis of universal adult franchise but tried to undercut the influence of left-wing and ethnic political parties by covertly promoting religious ones. The law under which the elections were held prescribed a fundamental role for Islamic ideology in Pakistan's future constitution. In foreign affairs, Yahya Khan benefited from the election of Richard Nixon as president of the United States. Nixon remembered Pakistan as an ally from the Eisenhower-Dulles era and wanted Yahya Khan to act as an intermediary in his opening to the People's Republic of China. The revival of Pakistan's alliance with the United States led Pakistan's rulers to believe that their scheme of building Pakistani statehood on the basis of Islam, anti-India sentiment, and external (primarily U.S.) economic and military assistance was still valid, and that the United States would not challenge it.

The transition from Ayub Khan to Yahya Khan had demonstrated the Pakistani military's unwillingness to trust civilian institutions even when the institutions had been carefully built under military supervision during Ayub Khan's decade in power. The last months of Ayub Khan's regime had witnessed massive and violent demonstrations in both parts of Pakistan—East and West. The demonstrators included left-wing groups protesting inequalities in distribution of wealth, Bengalis demanding a fair share in the country's power structure, and Islamists seeking a greater role for religion in public life. This great variety of groups all agreed on the need for greater democracy.

Ayub Khan could have resigned and allowed a constitutional transfer of power, paving the way for fresh elections for president and a national assembly. A free election would probably have resulted in a legislature committed to reversing the scheme of indirect elections Ayub Khan had introduced. Politicians clearly preferred the parliamentary form of government to the presidential system. It was the rise of regional parties seeking greater provincial autonomy that most concerned Ayub Khan and the military. The generals saw anyone calling for regional autonomy or ethnic identity as pro-India. They were concerned that an emphasis on the regions would weaken central authority and undermine the concept of an Islamic Pakistan.

After a decade of arguing that a system suiting Pakistan's genius had been created, the generals now felt the need for another direct military intervention. On March 24, 1969, Ayub Khan wrote a letter to the army chief, Yahya Khan, formally seeking martial law. Ayub spoke of the military's "legal and constitutional responsibility to defend the country not only against external aggression but also to save it from internal disorder and chaos."[1] The transfer of power from one general to another defined the military's role as final arbiter in political matters and recognized the military's supraconstitutional authority. Herbert Feldman wrote that the transfer led to the belief among civilians that "whenever it was felt in General Headquarters that things were not going according to the taste and opinion of senior officers, the armed forces (in effect the army alone) would move in or contrive to do so."[2] The *Economist* described Ayub Khan's ouster and replacement by Yahya Khan in an editorial titled "Tweedle Khan Takes Over."[3]

Yahya Khan did not follow Ayub Khan in presenting himself as a political reformer or the writer of a new Pakistani constitution. Instead he announced his intention to hold elections for a constituent assembly, open to all political parties. Publicly Yahya Khan expressed the hope that politicians would maintain "the integrity of Pakistan and the glory of Islam"[4] and said he would seek to retire after transferring power to civilians. In private conversations, however, senior commanders admitted that they were "attempting to insure that the Constituent Assembly (CA) is so fragmented as to render impossible the drafting of a constitution."[5] The military wanted the populace "to realize that the politicians cannot act unitedly," providing justification for continued military rule.[6]

Yahya Khan allowed relative freedom to the media and the political parties, but his scheme for elections did not reflect a desire to disengage the military. Instead, it reflected thinking within the top brass that they could not ignore the popular sentiment that had manifested itself during several months of rioting in the streets against Ayub Khan. The author of the scheme for military dominance by other means was Major General Sher Ali Khan, scion of the princes of Pataudi in India, who had served as Pakistan's ambassador in Malaysia after retiring from the army. Yahya Khan brought back Sher Ali Khan as minister for information and national affairs in his martial law regime. According to Roedad Khan, a senior civil servant, who served as secretary for information at the time:

The central concept in Sher Ali's thought was that the reason the military was able to snatch the initiative from politicians after the fall of Ayub was not because of its fire power. He wrote [to Yahya Khan] (in effect): "If we had to shoot our way through Nawabpur Road [the main road in Dhaka] we would have had a conflagration on our hands that no amount of fire power in our control could have handled."

The strength of the army which enabled it to seize the initiative from incompetent politicians in March 1969, he argued, lay in its charisma. This was a precious political resource that once lost would not be easily retrieved. It existed because the mass of the people had not actually encountered the army directly. For them it was a mythical entity, a magical force, that would succor them in times of need when all else failed. In the minds of the people, unlike the bureaucracy and the politicians with whom they had daily contact and whom they knew to be corrupt and oppressive, the army was the final guarantor of Pakistan and its well-being.

This charisma, Sher Ali argued with much force, was based on false premises and was, therefore, extremely fragile. It existed only because the common people had no actual contact with the army and did not realize that army personnel were fashioned by the Almighty from the same clay as other Pakistanis. Direct contact with the army would disillusion the people and destroy the charisma—a resource that had to be cherished and conserved for it was invaluable in times of crisis.

The logic of Sher Ali's strategy was not that the army should give up power. On the contrary, it was meant to be a prescription for the perpetuation and safeguarding of the power of the army in the state and national affairs. A necessary condition for the Sher Ali formula to work in the interest of the oligarchy was to have a badly divided parliament and warring political parties, so that the army could assume the role of a referee. A great deal of effort was devoted to supporting weak parties to ensure that they make a good showing.[7]

The Sher Ali formula required behind-the-scenes manipulation of the political process, to increase the number of political contenders, as well as identification of "patriotic" factions against "unpatriotic" ones. The regime's political operation was divided into three parts. First, the National Security Council headed by Major General Ghulam Umer periodically assessed the political prospects of the major parties, diverted resources to various factions of the Muslim League and the religious parties, and recommended regime policies that might favor the parties committed to the ideology of Pakistan. Second, the intelligence services—the military ISI and the civilian IB—monitored and infiltrated left-wing and regional parties, spread disinformation against them, and mobilized attacks by religious groups against their un-Islamic and foreign-inspired beliefs. Third, the Information Ministry mobilized a propaganda drive to create the specter of Islam and Pakistan being in danger, polarizing the country between Islam Pasand (Islam loving) on the one hand and communists, socialists, and secularists on the other.

Although aimed at the civilian population, the ideological indoctrination undertaken during Yahya Khan's rule—which lasted less than three years—deeply influenced the Pakistani military. As explained by Brigadier A. R. Siddiqi, who was then serving as head of the military's public relations arm, Inter-Services Public Relations, the professional military image was replaced by a "politico-ideological image":

Expressions like the "ideology of Pakistan" and the "glory of Islam" used by the military high command were becoming stock phrases. Messages issued by the service chiefs and the President on the occasion of Defense Day reflected the ideological overtones. They sounded more like high priests than soldiers when they urged the men to rededicate themselves to the sacred cause of ensuring the "security, solidarity, integrity of the country and its ideology." They praised the people for their "determination, courage and high ideals in the best tradition of Islam . . ." [General] Sher Ali took the regime to the point of no return on the road to ideological involvement. He went from place to place preaching and pontificating about the Islamic ideology. He even talked of his personal relationship with God with whom, he playfully quipped, he had been "on a direct line" five times a day without anybody's help or assistance. Sher Ali called himself an "ideological man . . ." To be sure,

Yahya himself liked and encouraged Sher Ali's ideological P[ublic] R[elations]."[8]

At the time, most senior military officers, like Yahya Khan and Sher Ali, had been trained by the British and were not observant in religious matters. Some of them noticed the ideological slant and, unaware of the regime's covert political strategy, considered it against the regime's promise of political neutrality. Some of them thought that the information minister was getting carried away with his personal beliefs. When their views were brought to Yahya Khan's notice, Siddiqi says, the president explained that it was regime policy:

The president was of the view that if Sher Ali had been merely trying to propagate and promote the Islamic ideology, he was perfectly justified in doing so. After all, it was no crime to preach Islam. Wasn't it the duty of every Muslim—particularly one in authority—to do so? Yahya admitted that his regime was neutral and interim but that did not deter him or one of his senior ministers from talking and preaching Islam. He was certainly "not neutral where the integrity of Pakistan and the glory of Islam" were concerned.[9]

Yahya Khan had successfully clarified that belief in a national ideology based on Islam had nothing to do with personal piety or lack of it. It was a strategy for national integrity, and the military—as an institution—had adopted it. The military's adoption of Islamic ideology conferred legitimacy on its right to rule Pakistan and was seen by Yahya Khan and his colleagues as the key to continued military preeminence in the country's political life. This emphasis on religious ideology had more than symbolic significance:

Within a short time after the re-imposition of Martial Law [under Yahya Khan] a distinctly obscurantist tendency had begun to develop. This had much to do with an unconstructive harping on Islam, and during the ensuing months it seemed as if no one could talk about anything else. In July [1969] Martial Law Regulation

No. 51 appeared which included the specification of a maximum penalty of seven years' rigorous imprisonment for any person who published, or was in possession of, any book, pamphlet, etc., which was offensive to the religion of Islam. How anyone was to decide what was, or was not, offensive to Islam does not seem to have been considered. For example, are views held by Shias offensive or tolerable? And what of the views of the Qadian [*sic*] community? Moreover, there already existed abundant legislation on blasphemy, on offending the susceptibilities of classes of persons, etc. . . . The import of all books, newspapers, etc., originating in India was prohibited throughout the country and on about 12 July Dr. Fazlur Rahman's book on Islam [advocating modern interpretation of religious texts] was banned . . . In West Pakistan a symposium to discuss academic freedom reached the consensus that such freedom must be allowed but only to the extent that it did not conflict with the ideology of Pakistan. It is not necessary to comment upon the hopeless lack of realism in such pronouncements nor on the dangers inherent in them.[10]

The military authorities had acquired for the government the right to censorship in the name of preventing religiously offensive material. Freedom of academic thought was severely curtailed and eventually led to the emergence of ideological vigilantes on campuses and the media. More significant, the regime opened a Pandora's box on the question of what was and was not Islamic—a problem that became more pronounced during the subsequent military regime of General Zia ul-Haq.

Yahya Khan's regime also persisted with its plan for "diversification of political forces" and scheduled elections for October 1970 but later postponed them until December. The election campaign that began in January thus lasted a whole year. The official plan called for an honest casting of ballots and an honest count. Official influence on the outcome of the polls was to be managed not through the rigging of the ballot but by manipulation of the process leading to the elections.

A major part of this plan depended on handing out money to various contestants. Under a martial law order, the regime took over the plentiful funds of Ayub Khan's faction of the Muslim League. The IB also raised funds from industrialists and businesspeople to finance the election-related activities of Islam Pasand parties and candidates.[11] By the end of 1969, the Jamaat-e-Islami was spearheading a major "campaign for the protection of ideology of Pakistan," claiming that Pakistan was under threat from atheistic socialists and secularists. Several ulema of different schools of thought had been persuaded by the IB to sign a joint fatwa declaring socialism and secularism as *kufr* (disbelief), leading to a struggle between orthodoxy and modernism. The major targets of this campaign were the Awami League, which described itself as secular, and the PPP, which advocated Islamic socialism.

By the time the election campaign officially opened on January 1, 1970, a battle was raging between Islam and socialism.[12] Islamist vigilantes violently confronted their secular rivals on university campuses and in trade unions. A strike by journalists in April–May was used by General Sher Ali Khan as an excuse to purge state and privately owned media of leftists and secularists. The purged journalists were replaced by Jamaat-e-Islami cadres, amplifying the Islamists' propaganda.

Religious leaders who disagreed with the Jamaat-e-Islami's interpretation of Islam were encouraged to form their own parties, resulting in the emergence of Markazi Jamiat Ulema Islam (Central Society of Islamic Scholars) and Jamiat Ulema Pakistan (Society of Pakistani Religious Scholars) as political actors a few months before elections. One reason for encouraging these alternative religious parties was also to ensure control over the direction of religious politics. The Jamaat-e-Islami was too well organized and ideological to be trusted on its own, and other Islamic groups could act as a check on its ambitions.

The well-funded Islamists confronted the PPP in West Pakistan and the Awami League in the eastern wing and, judging by their visibility in the media, were quite powerful. Their attacks on the PPP focused on the "un-Islamic lifestyle" of the party's popular leader, Zulfikar Ali Bhutto, and they stooped so low as to allege that his mother had been a Hindu. The Awami League was accused of close ties with Bengali Hindus, and it was alleged that the party was funded by India. The ideological debates engaged the attention only of the military-bureaucratic complex and conservative urban intellectuals, however; for the rural masses bread-and-butter issues were more important, and here the Awami League's promise of greater power for impoverished Bengalis and the PPP's calls for income redistribution had a tremendous advantage.

The intelligence services were facilitating the Islamists' organizations, and the information ministry was projecting them as potential winners. The downside to this preelection fix was twofold: involvement with one set of parties blinded the intelligence services to the strength of others and the prospect of victory made the Islam Pasand parties vulnerable to greater factional rivalry. On May 31, 1970, several Islamic parties observed Shaukat-e-Islam (glory of Islam) Day. It was not a coincidence that the day was named after the term that General Yahya Khan publicly used for one of the two conditions that political parties had to fulfill to deserve a share in governance of Pakistan. (The other term, "integrity of Pakistan," was explained by the Islamists as the natural consequence of adherence to true Islam). Massive rallies around the country on Shaukat-e-Islam Day convinced the regime that ideological polarization between Islam and un-Islam would contain the influence of the secular and regional parties while it would allow them adequate representation in a truncated Parliament to keep a facade of democracy. On the day of the rallies, the ISI detachment in East Pakistan headlined its situation report to headquarters: "Massive show on Shaukat-e-Islam Day by Muslims indicate their unflinching faith in Islamic cum Pakistan ideology."[13]

The military's estimate of the various political parties' strength underwent some changes during the course of the election campaign, but at no stage did it expect a single party to emerge as the clear winner. Major General Umer, head of the National Security Council under Yahya Khan, joined the Muslim League after retiring from the army. He explained that the military's attempt to bring about the unification of the various Muslim League factions and its support for the Islam-loving parties were based on its assessment of electoral prospects:

The conclusion was that no single party would be able to get an absolute majority. As the election campaign progressed it became clear that the Awami League would be confined to East Pakistan and Peoples Party to West. Jamaat-e-Islami might be able to get stray seats in both the wings but the number would be small. In the circumstances Muslim League was considered as the only national party which might win a sizeable number of seats in both the wings provided its three factions combined. It may still not be the largest party but its presence will be conducive to a positive atmosphere.[14]

The intelligence services had "estimated that although the Awami League would get the greatest number of seats and would perhaps be the single largest political party at the center, it would need the support of other parties to form a government."[15] Major General Muhammad Akbar, who headed the ISI at the time, predicted a season of bargaining after the election. He used the term *bandar bat* (monkeys dividing the spoils)[16] for the future political process. Ironically, the Pakistani military and intelligence services had a poorer understanding of the country's mood than some foreign observers. The U.S. consul general reported that the British deputy high commissioner in Dhaka, Roy Fox, predicted on June 6, 1969, that Sheikh Mujibur Rahman and the Awami League would "emerge as overwhelming victor" in any election.[17]

The U.S. ambassador to Pakistan, Joseph Farland, had also read the wind successfully with the help of his political officers in the field. In a July 3, 1970, cable to the State Department, he summarized his assessment of the election campaign:

As of now, the road to election seems clear of serious obstruction. Beyond October 5 [the scheduled date for the election], the picture is exceedingly murky. If the Awami League and the CML [Council Muslim League], perhaps with the NAP(R) [National Awami Party led by Abdul Wali Khan], can form an effective coalition on a constitutional basis tolerable to Yahya and the military, there is hope for the future of this heterogeneous Islamic state. This is a very big "if." But it seems to us that any other presently conceivable alternative would likely render exceedingly bleak the prospect for the continuation of a united Pakistan."[18]

But the military saw itself as remaining in charge after the election and considered its meddling both sufficient and necessary to protect the unity of Pakistan under a unitary and ideological constitution. In the several memoirs written by Pakistani generals on the period, they express considerable regret at the military's failure to predict the election results correctly. The generals remain reluctant to this day to admit that the military regime was wrong in trying to influence the outcome of an election it claimed would freely elect the country's future constituent assembly. In view of the subsequent secession of East Pakistan, some have even suggested that allowing a free and fair election with universal adult franchise may have been the real mistake of Yahya Khan and his military colleagues.[19]

Pakistan's military leadership had always believed that the country's situation could never go out of its control; this may have been part of the reason for their confidence that the election results would be as they desired. Most of Pakistan's generals belonged to the West Pakistani provinces of Punjab and the NWFP. Some were from the Urdu-speaking minority that moved to Pakistan from northern India after partition. They were all products of the British concept of martial races, which had led the British in India to recruit soldiers only from certain ethnic groups. The Bengalis had not been deemed a martial race by the British, which meant very little representation of East Pakistan in Pakistan's army. In 1947, Bengalis constituted only 1 percent of Pakistan's army; by the 1960s, theirs numbers were up to only 7 percent.[20] In the officer corps, the difference was even sharper.

Pakistan's bureaucracy similarly had far fewer Bengalis than West Pakistanis. In 1966, only 27,648 government officials out of a total of 114,302 belonged to East Pakistan.[21] Although East Pakistan was the country's major foreign-exchange earner, it received a smaller share of federal investment. In 1969–1970, West Pakistan's per capita income was 61 percent higher than Bengali per capita income.[22] East Pakistan was seething with anger, but West Pakistani officers—suffering from what can best be described as colonial hubris—were unable to feel the depth of this sentiment. There was clearly no willingness to let the Bengali majority play a leading role in the country's governance. A U.S. diplomat sensed this when he reported to Washington in November 1969: "Re East Pakistan, one also senses a growing undercurrent that beyond some intangible point the West Pak landlord-civil service-military elite might prefer to see the country split rather than submit to Bengali ascendancy."[23]

Beginning with Ayub Khan, there was also a tendency to look down upon Bengalis as inferior to West Pakistanis. This primarily racist attitude was tied in with a contrived ideological notion as well. The military and its intelligence services started to believe that Pakistan's majority Bengali population was closer to Hindus and therefore somehow less loyal to the Pakistani ideology they had crafted. In his autobiography, Ayub Khan wrote:

East Bengalis, who constitute the bulk of the population [of Pakistan], probably belong to the very original Indian races. It would be no exaggeration to say that up to the creation of Pakistan, they had not known any real freedom or sovereignty. They have been in turn ruled by the caste Hindus, Moghuls, Pathans or the British. In addition, they have been and still are under considerable Hindu cultural and linguistic influence. As such they have all the inhibitions of down-trodden races and have not yet found it possible to adjust psychologically to the requirements of the new-born freedom.[24]

Efforts by Pakistan's rulers to forge a more or less homogenous Islamic nation did not sit well with the Bengali masses, who resented the West Pakistani tendency to see the East's cultural affinity with Bengali Hindus as somehow un-Islamic. Some religious leaders from West Pakistan spoke of the need for "purifying" the Bengali Muslims. The state machinery encouraged the imposition of cultural uniformity based on Islam. Pakistan's nation builders refused to recognize the cultural diversity among Muslims of different regions. The Bengalis felt that their rights and cultural identity were being eroded under the cloak of Islamic ideological nationalism. Moreover, Pakistan's confrontation with India and the massive defense spending were hurting East Bengal's economy. The Bengali Muslim intelligentsia, which in 1947 had actively sought the creation of Pakistan, had started feeling a greater cultural affinity with Hindus in West Bengal than with the Muslims in West Pakistan.

For Bengalis, their exclusion from the military-bureaucratic power structure left politics as the only avenue for seeking socioeconomic justice. Since partition, popular Bengali politicians tended to be secular in outlook and often courted the support of East Bengali Hindus who constituted 20 percent of their province's population. In the context of democratic politics, this made sense; if the pre-partition principle of separate electorates based on religion had been maintained after independence, East Bengal would have lost its majority within the new country.

The need to dilute East Pakistan's majority led West Pakistan's politicians in the early years of the new country to argue for retaining separate electorates. In their pursuit of a fairer share in Pakistan's power structure, the East Bengalis within a few years of Pakistan's independence were moving in a direction opposite to the ideological paradigm created by the predominantly West Pakistani civil-military complex. Robert Jackson explains that the trajectory of Bengali thinking was quite different from the thinking of Pakistan's rulers:

Alongside their commitment to Islam they possessed a deep loyalty to their Bengali culture, and they were schooled in parliamentary traditions and the practice of the rule of law. In every way except their common faith, the attitudes of the East Bengalis differed from those of their fellow-Pakistanis in the western provinces.[25]

The West Pakistani elite, and particularly the military, responded to Bengali political activism with charges of collusion with India. Almost every leading Bengali political figure after partition was at one time or another accused of working in conjunction with India's intelligence services. A. K. M. Fazlul Haq, the mover of the 1940 resolution effectively demanding the nation of Pakistan, was impugned. The Awami League's founder, Huseyn Shaheed Suhrawardy, was barred from politics by Ayub Khan. Sheikh Mujibur Rahman had also been accused by Ayub Khan's government of conspiring "to separate East Pakistan through a revolt, which was to have been armed and financed by India."[26] The so-called Agartala conspiracy case, which accused Mujibur Rahman of planning an insurgency with the help of India and Bengali officers in the Pakistani army, was dropped on the demand of opposition demonstrators during the last days of Ayub Khan. The decision by Yahya Khan to allow Sheikh Mujibur Rahman and the Awami League to participate freely in the 1970 general election was predicated on the assumption that the League's popularity (and, by extension, the demand for Bengali rights) would be contained through coalition politics controlled by the military.

As it turned out, the regime's expectation of a truncated Parliament was not fulfilled. When the votes were counted on December 7, 1970, the Awami League had won more than 72 percent of the popular vote in East Pakistan and ended up with 160 seats out of 300 contested seats. Its uncontested winning of 7 seats reserved for women gave it a total of 167 seats in the 313-member National Assembly. Only two National Assembly seats from East Pakistan went to representatives who were not members of the Awami League.[27] In the provincial assembly election on December 17, the Awami League secured 89 percent of votes cast and won 288 out of 300 seats in East Pakistan. The Jamaat-e-Islami secured only two seats, with 3 percent of the popular vote.[28]

In West Pakistan, the PPP won 81 out of 138 seats for the National Assembly, mainly from Sindh and Punjab. The addition of four seats reserved for women would take its tally up to eighty-five. Its share of the popular vote, however, was 38.89 percent.[29] Balochistan and the NWFP gave a plurality to the Pashtun nationalist National Awami Party (NAP) and the orthodox Jamiat Ulema Islam (JUI), which had aligned itself with the left-wing parties instead of other Islamists. The Islam-loving parties fared poorly. The three factions of the Muslim League combined won eighteen seats. The Jamiat Ulema Pakistan (JUP) ended up with seven seats, while the Jamaat-e-Islami managed only four seats. The Islamic parties' share of the popular vote was around 10 percent nationwide.

In its efforts to ensure a strong showing by the Muslim League factions and the religious parties, the regime had inadvertently caused these parties to become overconfident. They had failed to forge alliances that might have increased their share of seats even with their limited share of votes. The architect of the election scheme, Major General Sher Ali Khan, was disappointed at the poor performance of the Islam Pasand parties. He predicted that the election results would lead to Pakistan's breakup and proposed they should be scrapped.[30] While the regime's behind-the-scenes maneuverings were kept secret from the public, Yahya Khan was receiving praise for holding the first free and fair election in Pakistan's history. As far as national and international opinion was concerned, Yahya Khan was fulfilling the promise he had made upon assuming power:

I have no ambitions other than the creation of conditions conducive to the establishment of constitutional government. It is my firm belief that a sound, clean and honest administration is a prerequisite for sane and constructive political life and for the smooth transfer of power to the representatives of the people elected freely and impartially on the basis of adult franchise. It will be the task of these elected representatives to give the country a workable constitution and final solution to all other political, economic and social problems that have been agitating the minds of the people.[31]

It was difficult to cancel the election results at this stage. Yahya Khan and the military could have withdrawn from the scene gracefully and allowed politics to take its course, but they decided to continue to manipulate the situation. In their minds they could not accept a constitutional arrangement that would have weakened central authority and diluted their ideological predisposition.

At the time, the mandate of the majority of Pakistanis—the Bengalis—was clear. They wanted a radically decentralized Pakistan and a drastic revision of the existing economic arrangements. Neither was acceptable to the West Pakistani establishment. Anticipating "positive" election results, Yahya Khan already had a draft constitution in mind, which would have increased provincial autonomy somewhat but nowhere near what was sought by the Awami League, which was now backed by an overwhelming majority of Bengali people. As for a fairer allocation of national resources, West Pakistani economists argued it would be disastrous for West Pakistan's economic growth. The Punjabi deputy chairman of Pakistan's Planning Commission said, "The West Pakistan growth could not be arrested to increase allocations for East Pakistan."[32] Instead of incurring the cost of removing disparities at a faster rate, West Pakistan's establishment preferred using force and risking the country's division. Soon after the elections, a general visiting Dhaka told his military colleagues, "Don't worry . . . we will not allow these black bastards to rule over us."[33] Six days after the election, the *New York Times* published an article titled "Vote Jolts Punjabis." It contained a remark by a man on the street in Lahore that summarized Punjab's sentiment: "The Punjab is finished . . . We will be ruled by Sindh and Bengal."[34] The Awami League leader Sheikh Mujibur Rahman was Bengali and the PPP leader Zulfikar Ali Bhutto was from Sindh.

In the military's view, Sheikh Mujibur Rahman was an Indian-backed secessionist, although calling for a new constitutional arrangement during the course of elections for a constituent assembly could hardly be called secessionism. Sheikh Mujibur Rahman declared immediately after the elections that he would take into account West Pakistani views while writing the new constitution, but that the fundamentals of the constitution would have to be secular and confederal, in accordance with the Awami League's manifesto, which also called for changing the name of East Pakistan to Bangladesh. By participating in the national elections, and winning them, the League had acquired for itself the right to alter the terms of East Bengal's inclusion in Pakistan.

Secession is usually the demand of a minority against a majority, whereas the Bengalis constituted the majority within a united Pakistan. Parallels have sometimes been drawn by Pakistani generals with the use of force in the U.S. Civil War and in other countries to prevent secession. The case of East Pakistan–Bangladesh is unique because a majority arrived at through a free election was being denied the right to include its preferences in the country's constitution. The military's plans for a democratic facade for military rule had gone awry, and war resulted from the desire of the military and its intelligence services to remain preeminent.

Yahya Khan's senior Bengali adviser at the time, Dr. G. W. Choudhury, asserts that before the election Sheikh Mujibur Rahman had assured Yahya Khan of his willingness to modify his demands and that this had created an expectation on the military's part of some give-and-take.[35] When the process of negotiation started, the military did not find the Awami League as flexible as it had desired. In February 1971, Yahya Khan belatedly scheduled the session of the constituent assembly for March 3 but later postponed it indefinitely, ostensibly at the demand of Zulfikar Ali Bhutto, the major elected leader from West Pakistan. Bhutto demanded an agreement with the Awami League on the basic principles of the constitution before he would agree to attend an assembly meeting.

In view of the subsequent civil war and Pakistan's breakup, the circumstances of the postponement of the elected assembly's first session have been the subject of considerable debate in Pakistan. The military's apologists as well as Bhutto's opponents blame Bhutto for adopting an undemocratic attitude when he refused to acknowledge the rights of the Bengali majority party.[36] Bhutto's associates and some impartial observers, however, blame the military leadership. The overwhelming sentiment among the West Pakistani elite against letting the Bengalis dominate Pakistan made it more likely that Bhutto and the military acted in concert, in the interest of West Pakistan as they perceived it.[37]

Later, when the country broke up amid humiliating circumstances, each side had to point the finger at the other for playing the main role in that humiliation. The role of India in supporting the Bengalis is also highlighted in Pakistan's accounts of the events. Although there is no doubt that India encouraged Bengali nationalism and supported the creation of an independent Bangladesh with arms once civil war started, the slide into civil war in erstwhile East Pakistan was primarily the result of a Pakistani internal power play.

The military liked neither Bhutto nor Mujib, the two leaders with the most votes and the highest number of seats in the newly elected National Assembly. The postelection environment required an accommodation on the part of the generals with someone other than the "Islam-loving parties" that had badly lost in the elections. Unlike Mujib, who had vowed to make Pakistan secular, Bhutto's PPP declared its creed to be "Islam, socialism, and democracy." Bhutto had served as foreign minister under Ayub Khan, had promised a "thousand-year war" with India, and maintained social ties with several generals. Some generals had even favored him privately out of fear of religious conservatism.[38] The PPP's founding documents contained a reference to jihad against India.[39] The party's public anti-Americanism disturbed the pro-U.S. generals, but that was not enough to disqualify Bhutto in the generals' eyes as a countervailing force against East Bengali populism. Yahya Khan and his closest colleagues decided to pit Bhutto against Mujib and retain power for themselves.

The generals also employed the Islamic parties against both Bhutto and Mujib in an effort to impose their own constitution and deny elected representatives the free hand Yahya Khan had originally promised. The process of inflaming religious sentiment started soon after the election. In January, the official media played up the publication of the *Turkish Art of Love,* a book apparently written by a Jewish author of Indian nationality, which was alleged to desecrate the prophet of Islam. Violent demonstrations against the book's publication were orchestrated by religious groups,[40] giving them an opportunity to mobilize cadres that might have been demoralized by the election result. The author's ethnicity projected a link between India and an attack on Islam. Because Pakistan's intelligence services have been known to orchestrate religious demonstrations unrelated to the political issues of the day—to help religious groups flex their muscles as well as to keep religious sentiment within the country on the boil—it has been suggested that during the campaign polarizing Islamists against secularists and socialists, agents provocateurs resorted to shouting slogans against Islam to fire up popular emotion.[41] The riots against the book allegedly desecrating Prophet Muhammad laid the foundation for the return of the Islamists to center stage at a time when political bargaining involving the military regime, the PPP, and the Awami League occupied the nation's attention.

Yahya Khan on March 1 announced the indefinite postponement of the National Assembly session. The Awami League responded by calling for civil disobedience. For the next several days, the military virtually lost control of East Pakistan to Awami League mobs. Bangladesh flags replaced the Pakistani standard in the province. These developments are described by Bangladeshi scholar Talukder Maniruzzaman:

> Sheikh Mujib called for a "non-violent, non-cooperation movement" against the central government of Pakistan for an indefinite period. In an impressive display of unity all government employees (including the judges of the High Court) absented themselves from their offices and promised to continue to do so for as long a period as Mujib chose. At this point Mujib's residence became the new Secretariat of Bangladesh.

After the first two days of boycott, during which the army's attempt to restore normal administrative functioning met with total non-cooperation from all officers of the government and stiff resistance by the rebellious people, the army on orders of the General-in-charge of the eastern command withdrew to its barracks. From March 4, 1971 policy directives designed to restore normalcy began to be issued from 'the Bangladesh Secretariat' at Sheikh Mujib's house. These directives, issued in the name of Bangladesh on March 4, March 7, March 9, March 11 and March 15 helped to keep the Bangladesh economy moving and to maintain law and order.

From this point too Radio Pakistan Dacca was renamed Dacca Betar Kendra (Dacca Radio Center) by Bengali broadcasters. It began issuing news bulletins about revolutionary happenings in Bangladesh and to broadcast regularly the song *Amar Sonar Bangla* (My Golden Bengal), already declared the national anthem of Bangladesh by the Central Students Action Committee. It also played patriotic and revolutionary Bengali songs . . . When at a mammoth public meeting in Dacca on March 7, 1971, Sheik Mujib demanded a) withdrawal of Martial Law; b) transfer of power to elected representatives; and c) withdrawal of troops to the barracks, he actually called for the "juridical recognition of the de-facto situation in Bangladesh.". . . Whilst the establishment of a de facto government by Sheikh Mujib was one dimension of the first phase of the revolution in Bangladesh, the other unique aspect of this phase was the militant mood of the common people. Every day from March 1 to March 25, 1971 innumerable processions chanting slogans like "Joi Bangla" (Glory to Bengal) or "Swadhin Bangladesh Zindabad" (Long Live Independent Bangladesh) paraded the streets of Dacca. These usually ended at Road 32 Dhanmandi (Mujib's home), where the crowds received assurances from Sheikh Mujib that Mukti (emancipation) of Bangladesh would be achieved. Similar demonstrations took place in all other cities and towns of Bangladesh.[42]

Sheikh Mujibur Rahman was mounting pressure on the central government through these street protests but refrained from making a unilateral declaration of independence for Bangladesh. The military re-gime organized three-way negotiations, among the Awami League, the PPP, and the government, with no settlement. In the course of the nego-tiations, military strength in East Pakistan was bolstered and plans drawn up to deal with the secessionist threat:

> The civil as well as the military officers who had gathered around Yahya Khan goaded him to take action. In their opinion the Awami League did not enjoy the support of the majority of the population of East Pakistan and the people did not have the stamina for pro-longed opposition. Therefore, the upsurge of Bengali nationalism and their demands would cool down in a few days after military action. He was assured that short and harsh action taken would bring the situation under control and the politicians would be cowed down. The killing of a few thousand would not be a high price for keeping the country together. Handing over of power to Mujibur Rahman, a proved traitor would be a blunder and history would never forgive Yahya Khan for this. This advice, unfortunately, co-incided with Yahya Khan's own ideas. He believed, "show them the teeth and they will be all right."[43]

The decision to use force against the Bengali people was not supported by those West Pakistani military officers who had served in the eastern wing for any length of time and therefore knew the local mood. The military governor of East Pakistan, Admiral S. M. Ahsan, and the mili-tary commander of East Pakistan, Lieutenant General Sahibzada Yaqub Khan, both argued that the political situation would not change with military measures. Yaqub Khan explained later that Yahya Khan:

> . . . thought a "whiff of the grapeshot" would do the trick and the reimposition of the rigors of martial law would create no problems . . . He remained adamant regarding postponement [of the Na-tional Assembly session] unless Mujib could be persuaded to make concessions on the Six Points to enable Bhutto and other West Pa-kistan leaders to attend the assembly session.[44]

Ahsan and Yaqub Khan both resigned and a new military commander, Lieutenant General Tikka Khan, was brought in to enforce national unity. The attitude of the army was summed up by the general officer commanding, Major General Khadim Hussain Raja, who told an Awami League sympathizer within the hearing of fellow officers: "I will muster all I can—tanks, artillery and machine guns—to kill all the traitors and, if necessary, raze Dacca to the ground. There will be no one to rule; there will be nothing to rule."[45]

The military crackdown, codenamed Operation Searchlight, began on the night of March 25, 1971. The operation's basis for planning clearly stated:

A. L. [Awami League] action and reactions to be treated as rebellion and those who support [the League] or defy M. L. [Martial Law] action be dealt with as hostile elements . . . As A. L. has widespread support even amongst E. P. [East Pakistani] elements in the Army the operation has to be launched with great cunningness, surprise, deception and speed combined with shock action."[46]

Troops moved with full force against Awami League supporters, students at Dhaka University, and Bengali Hindus. Sheikh Mujibur Rahman was arrested and transferred to West Pakistan. Foreign journalists were rounded up and expelled from the province to prevent them from seeing the slaughter. Eyewitness accounts spoke of soldiers blowing up newspaper offices and several rooms in the university hostel shouting "Allah Akbar" (God is great)—the Muslim battle cry in the face of enemies of Islam. There is no evidence of the Awami League at this point having any military capability. Siddiq Salik, who worked as an officer in the Pakistan army's public relations directorate and was present in Dacca cantonment throughout the military operation, offers the following account of the night of March 25, 1971:

The first column from the cantonment met resistance at Farm Gate, about one kilometer from the cantonment. The column was halted by a huge tree trunk felled across the road. The side gaps were covered with the hulks of old cars and a disabled steam-roller. On

the city side of the barricade stood several hundred Awami Leagu-
ers shouting *Joi Bangla* slogans. I heard their spirited shouts while
standing on the verandah of General Tikka's headquarters. Soon
some rifle shots mingled with the Joi Bangla slogans. A little later a
burst of fire from an automatic weapon shrilled through the air.
Thereafter it was a mixed affair of firing and fiery slogans, punctu-
ated with the occasional chatter of a light machine gun. Fifteen
minutes later the noise began to subside and the slogans started
dying down. Apparently, the weapons had triumphed.[47]

The one-sided contest between slogans and guns, however, did not
remain so for long. Many Bengali officers and soldiers of the Pakistan
army deserted their units before they were disarmed. They, along with a
large number of Awami League activists and East Bengali Hindus, went
across to India and with Indian assistance formed the Mukti Bahini
(emancipation army). India described the Pakistani military action as
genocide of the Bengali people and used the presence of large numbers
of Bengali refugees in India as the basis for involvement in internal developments in East Pakistan. Pakistan's military had succeeded in transforming the political debate about Pakistan's future constitution into a
civil war as well as another contest between Islamic Pakistan and Hindu
India. Admiral Ahsan (the military governor who conducted the elections and resigned on the eve of military action) admitted to U.S. officials later that "[p]rior to March at least, separation was not Mujib's intention" and "India's position has despite public outcry been relatively
moderate and its hands before the events in March were relatively
clean."[48]

The Pakistani military aimed its operation against Awami League
supporters, which meant an overwhelming majority of East Pakistan's
population in view of the League's massive support base. Every account
of that period speaks of the Pakistan army's brutality in dealing with
people it labeled secessionists, traitors, and Hindu agents. In its editorial on March 31, almost a week after the beginning of the military crackdown, the *New York Times* pointed out that the brutality in dealing with
the Bengali majority seeking a different basis for remaining part of Pakistan was likely to strengthen the secessionist argument:

Acting "in the name of God and a united Pakistan," forces of the West Pakistan–dominated military government have dishonored both by their ruthless crackdown on the Bengali majority . . . Any appearance of "unity" achieved by vicious military attacks on unarmed civilians . . . cannot . . . have real meaning or enduring effect. The brutality of the Western troops toward their "Moslem brothers" in the east tends only to confirm the argument of the outright secessionists.[49]

Soon the divide was less between Awami League supporters and the government and more between East and West Pakistan.

Controversy continues over the number of civilian casualties resulting from the Pakistan military action. Sheikh Mujibur Rahman subsequently put the number at three million and General Tikka Khan admitted to thirty-four thousand Bengalis killed.[50] In an interview more than two decades later, Major General Farman Ali Khan, who was head of civil affairs in the martial law administration of East Pakistan, acknowledged that the Pakistan army might have killed as many as fifty thousand Bengalis.[51] Major General Farman Ali Khan also admitted to a U.S. official, off-the-record, that as many as six million refugees may have gone to India and that the army wanted to clear East Bengal of all Hindus.[52]

The Mukti Bahini engaged in its own carnage, targeting non-Bengali civilians, although this appears to have been in retaliation for actions by the Pakistan military. In August, when the Yahya Khan regime published its *White Paper on the Crisis in East Pakistan,* it effectively acknowledged that the Bengali atrocities followed rather than instigated the violence by the Pakistani military. The white paper gave a chronological account of major events before and after the military crackdown. The Bengali attacks against non-Bengalis apparently took place after the Pakistani military operation began on March 25.[53] A Pakistani general commented that "elements of the Pakistan army went berserk and took their revenge by spraying bullets at random, setting whole villages on fire and committing wanton acts of murder."[54] A large number of Bengalis were also killed as they tried to cross into India as refugees.

The commander of Pakistan's forces in East Pakistan, General Tikka Khan, was soon nicknamed "Butcher of Bengal" in the international media although he was acting neither alone nor without orders. Most of the leading figures in the Pakistan military during that period have written memoirs blaming each other for cowardice, lack of strategic thinking, or excessive use of force. Lieutenant General A. A. K. Niazi, who took over command from Tikka Khan in April 1971, described the initial military operation:

> On the night between 25/26 March 1971, General Tikka struck. Peaceful night was turned into a time of wailing, crying, and burning. General Tikka let loose everything at his disposal as if raiding an enemy, not dealing with his own misguided and misled people. The military action was a display of stark cruelty more merciless than the massacres at Bukhara and Baghdad by Chengiz Khan and Halaku Khan ... General Tikka ... resorted to the killing of civilians and a scorched earth policy. His orders to his troops were: "I want the land and not the people ..." Major General Farman had written in his table diary, "Green land of East Pakistan will be painted red." It was painted red by Bengali blood.[55]

To this day most Pakistani generals remain unconvinced that their attitudes toward the Bengali population of their country were wrong, and they offer various explanations for the military's excessive violence against the Bengalis. Lieutenant General Gul Hassan Khan, who was chief of general staff at the time and later became commander in chief, tried to explain General Tikka Khan's actions in terms of the army's reaction to insults by the Awami League while it effectively controlled East Pakistan during the phase of civil disobedience:

> Prior to the take-over by General Tikka Khan, our troops had been confined to cantonments. Their movement was limited, owing to the insults and abuse heaped upon them and at times they were subjected to attacks by the Awami League followers. To make matters worse, their ration of fresh supplies was discontinued by Bengali contractors and their electricity and water supplies were cut off. This was a totally dismal picture. It was natural that when

Army action was ordered the troops could not possibly forget the indignities they were subjected to by the Awami League minions.[56]

That the army may have wanted to teach the Bengalis a lesson for not treating it well is confirmed by the conversation between General Yahya Khan and Sheikh Mujibur Rahman during one of their last meetings. According to Dr. Kamal Hosain, then a close associate of Sheikh Mujibur Rahman and later foreign minister of Bangladesh, Yahya Khan received the Awami League leaders with a large glass of whisky in hand and said, "Sheikh Mujib, tell your boys they cannot treat the army with disrespect. We must all work for the glory of Islam and the integrity of Pakistan together." Dr. Hosain was struck by the irony of the invoking of Islam with whisky in hand, given Islam's prohibition of alcohol.[57] But Yahya Khan was simply identifying the military leadership's priorities centered on a Pakistani nation, held together in the name of Islam by a military that civilians were not allowed to question even when the civilians had received an overwhelming mandate in a general election. General Tikka Khan was in no way solely responsible for the savagery, and it did not stop after he relinquished command.

Yahya Khan addressed the nation the day after the beginning of the military operation. He accused Sheikh Mujibur Rahman of treason, announced the banning of the Awami League, and imposed press censorship. Most West Pakistanis, especially the Islam-loving parties, supported his decision. Junior officers of the army expressed satisfaction that "the Bengalis have been sorted out well and proper—at least for a generation."[58] During meetings with military officers in cantonments, Yahya Khan was consistently told by his fellow officers that he "should not concede too much to the politicians."[59] Those officers posted in the cantonments in East Pakistan showed no sign of remorse over the murder and mayhem, and their lives were characterized by "evening and late-night parties."[60] Only a handful of soldiers suffered from the strain of fighting fellow Muslims and erstwhile Pakistanis. The behavior of individual officers reflected the corporate thinking of the army at the time, which was the final solution of Bengali nationalism.[61] Just as Islamic sentiment had characterized Pakistan's past military confrontations, the war against the Bengali people was also characterized as a war for Pakistan's Islamic identity.

The Pakistani military projected the conflict in East Pakistan as a counterinsurgency drive, and at home the troops were presented as mujahideen fighting the enemies of Islam. Propaganda emanating from West Pakistan also focused on the Hindu influence and the actions of anti-Muslim forces as responsible for the crisis in the eastern wing. Every statement by India in favor of the Bengalis was cited as evidence of how the Awami League had been an instrument of Indian influence to begin with. India's intervention had certainly aggravated the situation, but it was hardly the principal cause of the goings-on in East Pakistan. West Pakistani opinion, however, was being shaped almost exclusively by the government and the Islamist elements that dominated the media.

The impact of the massive propaganda campaign against secularism as *kufr* and anti-Islam was fresh in the minds of most people. Although they had ignored that campaign at the time of elections, some of its messages resonated with them during the course of a distant war. Moreover, the popular political force in West Pakistan, the PPP, was unwilling to stand up to the military over atrocities in East Pakistan. Bhutto wanted to retain good relations with the ruling generals so that his chances of coming to power in the western wing were not jeopardized. He could not ignore the possibility that after eliminating political opposition in the eastern wing, the military could easily use force against West Pakistan's elected leadership. For that reason alone, he thought it prudent not to go beyond asking for only a share in political power regardless of his election victory.

When he took over from Tikka Khan, General Niazi cast himself in the mold of a religious zealot:

> During his talks to the troops [Niazi] quoted copiously from the Quran, the Sunnah [traditions of Prophet Muhammad] and the history of Islam. [He would say] "The way of life offered by the Quran is known as Islam—another word for peace. Essentially Islam preaches peace under normal circumstances. But being a realistic way of life it realizes that constant maintenance of peace depends on the ability to repel force." ... [He also said,] "As Muslims

we have always fought against an enemy who is numerically and materially superior. The enemy never deterred us. It was the spirit of jihad and dedication to Islam that the strongest adversaries were mauled and defeated by a handful of Muslims. The battles of Uhad, Badar, Khyber and Damascus are the proof of what the Muslims could do" . . . Niazi's lectures gave a religious tinge to the military operations in East Pakistan . . . [He also said,] "We have an enemy whose goal and ambition is the disintegration of Pakistan."[62]

In addition to motivating the troops with religious frenzy, the regime gave the Jamaat-e-Islami, the various factions of the Muslim League, the Nizam-e-Islam Party, and the Jamiat Ulema Pakistan—the parties that had lost the election to the Awami League—a semiofficial role. Members of these parties formed peace committees throughout Pakistan's eastern wing, at district and even village levels. These parties functioned as the intelligence network of the Pakistan army,[63] especially after the Mukti Bahini launched its guerrilla war against Pakistani forces.

Once a semblance of order had been restored in Dhaka and other major cities, the military regime focused on developing a new political strategy. It decided to disqualify a large number of Awami League members of the national and provincial assemblies on grounds that they had collaborated with the enemy or challenged the integrity of Pakistan. Lists for disqualification were prepared by the IB and ISI. Of 160 Awami League members of the National Assembly, 72 were disqualified, leaving the party with only 86 seats in the 313-seat assembly.[64] In the East Pakistan provincial assembly, 191 out of 288 Awami League representatives were disqualified from membership, leaving the party with a minority of 95 seats out of 300.

The vacant seats were to be filled theoretically by special elections, but the military arranged for six Islamist and Islam-loving parties to form an alliance called the United Coalition Party. A special cell headed by Major General Farman Ali Khan then proceeded to allot the vacant seats to different parties, ensuring that the Islamist candidates would be elected unopposed. This apportionment of seats would have given six Islam-loving parties (the three factions of the Muslim League, the Pakistan Democratic Party, Nizam-e-Islam Party, and the Jamaat-e-Islami)

121 seats in the National Assembly, making their inclusion in a future coalition government necessary. The PPP was offered five seats, primarily to prevent it from objecting to this distribution of spoils, although it had not fielded a single candidate from East Pakistan in the general election. The largest share of unopposed seats—fifty—was allocated for the Jamaat-e-Islami, which became a major force in Parliament with fifty-four seats notwithstanding its poor electoral performance and small share of votes barely a few months earlier.[65]

After fragmenting the elected structure, Yahya Khan proceeded to finalize a constitution for the country with the help of a committee of experts. Constitution writing was no longer to be entrusted to the elected National Assembly. In addition to retaining the offices of president, supreme commander, and commander in chief of the army, Yahya Khan proposed to retain martial law powers. The future constitution gave the military president "special responsibilities for the preservation of the integrity and ideology of Pakistan and for the protection of fundamental rights."[66] Yahya Khan reportedly believed that "the country needs a 'Turkish-type' constitution under which [the] commander in chief of the armed forces would be president and effective leader of the country."[67] The generals had decided to write into the constitution their role as defenders of Pakistan's ideology.

In addition to altering the makeup of the national and provincial assemblies through an arbitrary reallocation of seats won by the Awami League, the military regime also recruited the Islamists to aid in its counterinsurgency effort. India had closed its airspace to Pakistani planes even before the military crackdown against the Bengalis, making it difficult to airlift large numbers of troops from West Pakistan to East Pakistan. At the beginning of the military operation, there were only twelve thousand West Pakistani soldiers in the eastern wing.[68] Eighteen thousand Bengali troops of the Pakistan army either had been disarmed or had deserted. Additional troops had to be flown in, via Sri Lanka, raising troop strength to thirty-four thousand.[69] The Pakistan army needed the bulk of its forces in West Pakistan, however, because Pakistan's strategic doctrine at the time maintained that "the defense of East Pakistan lay in the West," meaning that any Indian threat against the eastern wing would have required a Pakistani counterattack from West Pakistan.

Logistic difficulties combined with strategic doctrine resulted in a massively outnumbered Pakistan army facing a restive population of some sixty million, thousands of whom had by now taken up arms with Indian training and assistance.

The army decided to raise a *razakaar* (volunteer) force of one hundred thousand from the civilian non-Bengalis settled in East Pakistan and the pro-Pakistan Islamist groups. The Jamaat-e-Islami and especially its student wing, the Islami Jamiat-e-Talaba (IJT), joined the military's effort in May 1971 to launch two paramilitary counterinsurgency units. The IJT provided a large number of recruits.[70] By September, a force of fifty thousand *razakaars* had been raised. Secular West Pakistani politicians complained about "an army of Jamaat-e-Islami nominees."[71] The two special brigades of Islamist cadres were named *Al-Shams* (the sun, in Arabic) and *Al-Badr* (the moon). The names were significant for their symbolic value. Islam's first battle, under Prophet Muhammad, had been the Battle of Badr, and these paramilitary brigades saw themselves as the sun and the crescent of Islamic revival in South Asia. General Niazi, commander of Pakistan's eastern command, later explained the role of the *razakaars:*

> A separate *Razakaars* Directorate was established . . . Two separate wings called *Al-Badr* and *Al-Shams* were organized. Well educated and properly motivated students from the schools and madrasas were put in *Al-Badr* wing, where they were trained to undertake "Specialized Operations," while the remainder were grouped together under *Al-Shams*, which was responsible for the protection of bridges, vital points and other areas.
>
> The *Razakaars* were mostly employed in areas where army elements were around to control and utilize them . . . This force was useful where available, particularly in the areas where the rightist parties were in strength and had sufficient local influence.[72]

Bangladeshi scholars accused the Al-Badr and Al-Shams militias of being fanatical. They allegedly acted as the Pakistan army's death squads and "exterminate[ed] leading left wing professors, journalists, littérateurs, and even doctors."[73] *Al-Badr* reportedly killed "10 professors of Dacca University, five leading journalists (including the BBC correspondent), two littérateurs and 26 doctors in Dacca alone."[74] Numerous supporters of the Jamaat-e-Islami and Islami Jamiat-e-Talaba lost their lives during clashes with Mukti Bahini. These numbers increased significantly when Bengali nationalists settled scores after the creation of Bangladesh.[75]

The regime was not helped by the political maneuvers, and the military situation on the ground remained precarious for Pakistani forces. India had become fully involved in supporting the Bengali resistance,[76] and international sympathy for the Bengali people was widespread. One of India's concerns was the radicalization of its own West Bengal state and its northeastern region, which had recently witnessed communist militancy. If Bengali refugees from Pakistan were unable to return to their homes, they might end up as recruits in the communist Naxalite insurgency. Within East Pakistan there was stalemate. The Pakistan army was unable to eliminate the guerrillas, and the Mukti Bahini on its own lacked the firepower to force a Pakistani withdrawal. The pressure of international opinion could have convinced Pakistan to end repression, release Sheikh Mujibur Rahman, and negotiate an end to the civil war with the elected leadership of the Bengali people, but the United States decided to tilt in Pakistan's favor, making it easier for Yahya Khan to ignore international pressure.

U.S. support of Yahya Khan's military regime had little to do with the merits of the issue relating to East Pakistan and Bengali nationalist aspirations. It was, as had been the case in the past, a function of Pakistan's military leadership making itself useful to the United States in its global grand design.

Yahya Khan took the helm in Pakistan in March 1969, two months after the inauguration of Richard Nixon as the thirty-seventh president of the United States. Nixon had visited Pakistan four times in official as well as private capacities and had "recognized U.S. interests in Pakistan early."[77] Nixon saw the replacement of Ayub Khan by Yahya Khan as an opportunity to rebuild U.S. relations with Pakistan. Ayub Khan had moved Pakistan closer to China and had allowed the Soviet Union to play the role of peacemaker after the 1965 war with India. Although Nixon was a personal friend of Ayub Khan, he understood that his time had passed and that a new military ruler in Pakistan would probably be keen to get into the good graces of the United States. When Nixon and his assistant for national security affairs, Henry Kissinger, were planning their initiative for normalizing relations with China, they decided to invite Yahya Khan to act as the intermediary in this major diplomatic coup:

> Nixon's fifth visit to Pakistan in July 1969 came amidst a temporary diplomatic lull [in U.S.-Pakistan relations], as the country prepared for election. It was a brief visit, but momentous. Nixon asked General Yahya Khan to act as a conduit between Washington and Peking and explore the possibility of normalization of relations between the two countries. Yahya agreed and promised to carry out the task in utmost secrecy. In return, Nixon assured Yahya of his goodwill and a place for Pakistan in his emerging strategy.[78]

Yahya Khan facilitated Henry Kissinger's secret trip to China via Rawalpindi, an act that earned him President Nixon's gratitude and sympathy. Throughout the ensuing crisis in East Pakistan, the U.S. president insisted on toughness toward India and a tilt toward Pakistan. Soon after the beginning of the military crackdown in March 1971, the U.S. consulate general reported in classified cables that "the Pakistani military forces were on a reign of terror. They were systematically seeking out and killing Awami League leaders and members, including student leaders and university faculty."[79] Consul General Archer Blood asked that the U.S. government express shock at the Pakistani military's behavior. The embassy in Islamabad modified the request and recommended that "deep concern" be expressed, but Washington decided to "hold off taking a position."[80] When U.S. citizens were evacuated from East Pakistan, the Pakistani government insisted that they first fly from Dhaka to Karachi on Pakistan International Airlines aircraft before they left the country. The United States could have evacuated its citizens to Bangkok, which was geographically closer, but the Pakistanis wanted to earn revenue on the return flight of planes that were ferrying troops to the eastern wing.

The U.S. government described the army repression in East Pakistan as "an internal Pakistani matter." U.S. public opinion, however, was very critical of Pakistan's conduct. On April 7, 1971, an editorial in the *New York Times* declared, "Washington's persistent silence on recent events in Pakistan is increasingly incomprehensible in light of eyewitness evidence that the Pakistani Army has engaged in indiscriminate slaughter."[81] Members of the U.S. Congress criticized President Nixon's Pakistan policy. Members of the staff remaining at the U.S. consulate in Dhaka sent a collective "dissent channel" telegram calling for condemnation of the Pakistan military's repression. President Nixon was not swayed by criticism in Congress and the media. Instead of heeding the call of his man on the ground, Nixon at one stage ordered the transfer of Consul General Archer Blood. Secretary of State William P. Rogers expressed displeasure that the staff at Dhaka was "writing petitions rather than reports."[82]

As the crisis dragged on, the White House ignored proposals for pressuring Pakistan to arrive at a political solution involving the elected Bengali leadership.[83] Pakistan's generals interpreted the U.S. tilt as a guarantee of U.S. intervention on behalf of Pakistan. Yahya Khan, confident in his role as secret intermediary between China and the United States, ignored the international clamor over Pakistani atrocities against the Bengalis and adopted a harder line. In an address to the nation in June 1971, for example, he asked the nation to express "gratitude to Almighty Allah" for the army's intervention in East Pakistan. A British journalist, unaware of the source of Yahya Khan's excessive confidence, expressed surprise at his arrogance and his insistence on the military's preeminence as well as the unifying power of religious symbols:

The [Pakistani] President to be sure extended his "fullest sympathy" to those who had been "terrorized and uprooted." The cause of the suffering of these people, however, was not the Army but "secessionists, anti-social elements, miscreants, rebels, infiltrators, mischief mongers, and saboteurs," a litany of villains familiar to all students of authoritarian regimes . . . Nothing in his address was more eloquent of the bankruptcy of the President's policies than the constantly reiterated appeal to the faith of the Prophet [Muhammad] . . . Bengalis heard the President invoke the threat of external enemies who were doing "their level best to undo our dear country . . . a people whose life is pulsating with the love of the Holy Prophet, whose hearts are illuminated with the light of *Iman* [purity of Islamic faith] and who have an unshakeable reliance on the help of almighty Allah . . . The constitution, the President said, must be "based on Islamic ideology" and must be "the constitution of the Islamic Republic of Pakistan in the true sense.". . . The militant ring of Islam in this context is unmistakable. "Every one of us," the President declared, "is a Mujahid (holy warrior)."[84]

Around the same time, after a visit to Dhaka, the U.S. ambassador, Joseph Farland, reported, "Army officials and soldiers give every sign of believing they are now embarked on a jihad against Hindu-corrupted Bengalis."[85] He did not suggest a U.S. role in dissuading the Pakistan army from pursuing this jihad, arguing instead that "none of the post–World War II insurgencies have been ended with a negotiated peace."[86] In the U.S. ambassador's view, the "civil differences" in Pakistan, too, would be resolved only by "the logic of war."

In July, after the announcement of Nixon's trip to China and the revelation of the critical role of Pakistan in arranging it, there was euphoria in West Pakistan. Hassan Zaheer, a senior civil servant at the time, wrote later:

Although no one was very clear how the new development was going to help Pakistan extricate itself from the mess, the army's faith in the omnipotence of U.S. support was reinforced. The [Pakistani] Foreign Office expected to be rewarded for services rendered, and started dreaming of a Washington-Islamabad-Beijing axis against the evil designs of its neighbor."[87]

The unrealistic faith in the United States and the Chinese led Pakistan's rulers to reject political options, and they persisted with a military approach in dealing with the Bengalis. Until fairly late in the year, Pakistani generals continued to believe that they would not have to fight a war with India, which left them free to focus on pacifying East Pakistan.[88] India, meanwhile, signed a friendship treaty with the Soviet Union. By November, an India-Pakistan war seemed imminent.

Indian military incursions into Pakistan's eastern wing started on November 21, but they fell short of all-out war. On December 3, 1971, Pakistan attacked India from the west in the hope of forestalling the fall of East Pakistan. This gave India an opportunity to directly march into East Pakistan and help the Bengalis create Bangladesh. On December 14, as Indian forces surrounded Dhaka, the Pakistani high command told the besieged garrison that "Yellow and White help expected from North and South shortly"[89]—a reference to imaginary Chinese and U.S. military help that simply postponed cease-fire and surrender negotiations by the eastern command.[90] Of course, neither China nor the United States intended to enter the war on Pakistan's behalf even though they continued to support it diplomatically. General Yahya Khan was simply trying to persuade the eastern command to halt the Indian advance long enough for a UN resolution that would forestall a humiliating surrender of Pakistani troops and the permanent split of the country. Saving face for the West Pakistani military leadership was more important than facing the on-the-ground realities of the military situation in East Pakistan.

President Nixon's pro-Pakistan tilt failed to save Pakistan's unity. Critics of Nixon's policy have made the argument that it encouraged Pakistan's military leaders in their repression against the Bengalis and their persistence with their imposed model of Islamic ideological nationalism:

> Kissinger had informed Zhou Enlai that while the US "would strongly oppose any Indian military action" its disapproval could not "take the form of military aid or military measures on behalf of Pakistan." A statement of this kind to Yahya Khan would have had a salutary effect in two ways. Firstly, Yahya would have been compelled to review his options of either carrying on the barren policy of repression or of initiating some realistic political measures to resume the constitutional process. Secondly, the moderates in the army, though small in number, would have gained greater influence in the inner counsels of the regime for a more practical approach. True, a blunt statement of the US stand on a political settlement would have jeopardized Yahya's position because he had

closed his options by calling Mujib a traitor whom it might have been difficult for him to deal with. But the junta would have found some way to fall in line with U.S. wishes. In the isolated situation from July onwards, Yahya and his generals were depending entirely on the US to see them through the crisis. It was not correct in the circumstances to assume, as Kissinger did, that the generals would have spurned political pressures of the friendly power which they regarded as their main strength . . . Paradoxically, the view of the "anti-Pakistan" State Department that Yahya should be made to face political realities would have served Pakistan's interests better than the friendly drift of the White House.[91]

Christopher Van Hollen, who was deputy assistant secretary for Near Eastern and South Asian Affairs at the State Department from 1969 to 1972 and saw firsthand the U.S. decision making during the Bangladesh crisis, wrote later with the benefit of hindsight:

American interests would have been better advanced in 1971 if Nixon and Kissinger had curbed their penchant to cast the Indo-Pakistan conflict in superpower global terms and, instead, had adopted the more realistic goal of trying to resolve the dispute in the South Asian regional context. The United States should have issued an early public statement deploring the military repression in East Pakistan and followed with cessation of all U.S. military supply, quickly closing any loopholes that later developed. If these actions had been explained to President Yahya in advance through diplomatic channels—as reflecting the strong humanitarian and human rights concerns of the U.S. public and Congress—they would not have jeopardized the China initiative, which was intrinsically very much in Pakistan's and China's interest. U.S. influence was limited both in India and Pakistan but such an initial public position would have increased the bona fides of the Nixon administration in urging restraint upon India; because there were few external options open to Yahya, such a stance should not have reduced U.S. leverage over the Pakistani president in encouraging him to reach a political settlement in East Pakistan.[92]

The United States, however, only pressured India and even ordered the U.S. Seventh Fleet to move to the Bay of Bengal, ostensibly to prevent India from dismembering Pakistan altogether. The Indian prime minister, Indira Gandhi, ignored these pressures, and the Indian military broke through Pakistani ranks in the eastern wing all the way to Dhaka. Pakistani forces in the eastern wing surrendered to the Indian military on December 16, 1971. Approximately ninety thousand West Pakistani soldiers and civilians were transported to India as prisoners of war. The erstwhile province of East Pakistan had finally become Bangladesh.

Four days after the surrender, on December 20, 1971, Yahya Khan was removed from power in disgrace by his senior commanders. During the thirty-three months he held power as chief martial law administrator, Yahya Khan had qualitatively enhanced the alliance between Pakistan's security establishment and the Islamists. The civil war between Bengali Muslims and an army dominated by Muslims from Punjab did not lead to adequate questioning of whether Islam's role was sufficient cement to hold Pakistan together. Instead, the secession of East Bengal with Indian military assistance strengthened the political role of Islam in Pakistan. The institutional hatred of the Pakistan military for Hindu India increased phenomenally because the military now sought to avenge its humiliation in Bangladesh.

The Pakistani establishment also remained convinced of the need for U.S. economic and military support in maintaining its vision of Pakistan. The failure of the United States to help militarily to save Pakistan's unity was interpreted as a betrayal, and it led to the view that, although Pakistan should continue to seek U.S. assistance, it should neither depend on the United States nor trust it.

3

Old and New Pakistan

The breakaway of East Pakistan to become Bangladesh was the most traumatic event in Pakistan's short life as an independent nation. The country's population was reduced by more than half. Pakistan lost a significant portion of its territory, its geopolitical role in Southeast Asia, and an important segment of its economy. More important was the psychological setback that came from defeat at the hands of India. Islamic ideology had obviously proved insufficient to keep Bengalis part of Pakistan. The prestige of the Pakistan army—called by General Sher Ali Khan the invisible charisma that enabled the rule of the country—had also been shattered.

Over the years, Pakistani generals had popularized the view that one Muslim had the fighting prowess of five Hindus. They had operated on the assumption that the "Indians are too cowardly and ill-organized to offer any effective military response, which could pose a threat to Pakistan. Ayub Khan genuinely believed that 'as a general rule Hindu morale would not stand more than a couple of hard blows at the right time and place.'"[1] Now 79,700 of Pakistan's regular soldiers and paramilitary troops were prisoners of war in Indian hands, along with 12,500 civilian internees.[2] Moreover, the army had failed to fulfill its promises of fighting until the last man. The eastern command had laid down arms after losing only thirteen hundred men in battle. In West Pakistan, too, twelve hundred military deaths had accompanied lackluster military performance.[3]

Pakistan's alliance with the United States, which had helped train and equip its massive military, had failed to guarantee the country's integrity. Pakistan's ruling elite had expected religious nationalism, confrontation with India, and alliance with the West to ensure the country's survival and success under the stewardship of a civil-military complex. The civil-military elite's policy tripod, which was meant to ensure Pakistan's security, had failed to prevent the country's breakup. The mood in what remained of Pakistan was summed up by a U.S. academic who was in Pakistan at the time:

Even the idea of Pakistan as the homeland for Muslims in South Asia no longer appeared valid . . . Many Pakistanis, especially those moving into positions of responsibility in government and business, are not as sure of the idea of Pakistan and its future as their fathers and older brothers. Disillusionment, uncertainty, cynicism, and pessimism are all adjectives which might appropriately describe the intellectual climate in the country . . . Bifurcation may have removed more than a geographical area from Pakistan; an intangible loss of confidence has occurred and many doubt that it can be restored.[4]

The people of West Pakistan were not mentally prepared for the bad news when Dhaka fell to Indian forces. State-controlled media in West Pakistan had been projecting imaginary victories of the Pakistan army. The religious parties had plastered the walls in major cities with posters and stickers bearing the slogan "Crush India." Even after Indian troops, accompanied by Western war correspondents, entered the city of Jessore and were welcomed by the local population, the government-owned *Pakistan Times* described Jessore as "the Stalingrad of Pakistan." The newspaper's editor, Z. A. Suleri, wrote: "Our solider is a wholly different species from others, especially from his Indian counterpart. He is armed in the weapons; but he is also armed in *Iman* [purity of Islamic faith]."[5] Official Pakistani briefings used false assertions that local people demonstrated against Indian aggression to counter Indian claims, which were verified by the international media, about the fall of East Pakistani towns.[6] Only four days before the surrender in Dhaka, Radio Pakistan announced, "The question of any surrender is ruled out because our troops are determined to lay down their lives."[7]

Although the military high command knew better, until the very end it did not prepare the people of West Pakistan for defeat. Finally sketchy reports of a grim military situation and fighting against all odds were released. Only during the afternoon of December 16, 1971, around the time of the formal surrender ceremony at the Race Course grounds in Dhaka, did the Pakistan government put out a twenty-seven-word statement: "Latest reports indicate that following an arrangement between the local commanders of India and Pakistan, fighting has ceased in East Pakistan and Indian troops have entered Dhaka."[8] For West Pakistanis, fed on rhetoric of imminent victory in jihad, this was an anticlimax. The war had been lost, and the tables could not be turned.

A segment of the military leadership remained more concerned about its ability to continue to rule the remaining portion of the country, which explains its desire for a soft sell. In the general headquarters (GHQ) in Rawalpindi, the chief of general staff told the head of the military's public relations department, "Go and prepare the nation mentally for the shock . . . Tell them any damned thing. It's your bloody job. No country should expect more from its armed forces. What could any army do, faced with such overwhelming odds?"[9]

The magnitude of military defeat and all that it meant for Pakistan was not easy for the Pakistani people to swallow. Spontaneous demonstrations erupted on the streets of major cities. Individuals on government-run television and radio stations departed from their scripts and started criticizing the ruling junta. There were also "tremors in the army."[10] Air Marshal Asghar Khan describes the machinations and chaos within top military ranks:

A couple of days after the surrender, Gul Hassan Khan, the chief of the General Staff, went round the key army formations to gauge the mood and came back convinced that there was great resentment against Yahya Khan who must be persuaded to leave. He and Rahim Khan, Chief of the Air Staff, spoke with Yahya Khan who agreed reluctantly to step down from the office of President but insisted that he should retain the post of Commander in Chief

of the Army. It was decided that . . . General Hamid Khan, the
Chief of Staff of the Army, should address the officers of the General Headquarters and all the GHQ officers above the rank of major were assembled for a talk. The meeting ended in confusion because the officers were not prepared to listen to General Hamid
Khan, who appeared to be lobbying for his own take-over from
Yahya Khan.[11]

During the heckling of the army's chief of staff, officers demanded
that the army initiate prohibition in its messes because the coterie of
generals at the apex of power, including Yahya Khan, had a reputation
for being hard drinkers. Some units revolted and insisted that power be
transferred to the elected representatives of the people.[12] There was general momentum for transfer of power, as a senior civil servant put it,
"from a deflated, humiliated Yahya to Bhutto, the man of the hour who
possessed all the qualities of leadership—courage, drive, energy, elo-
quence, and a sense of history."[13] When a general close to Yahya Khan
tried to depute an elite commando unit, possibly to arrest Zulfikar Ali
Bhutto, the leader of the majority party in the western wing, as he returned from abroad, junior officers simply ignored his request.[14]

These developments made it impossible for Yahya Khan to continue
in power.[15] For his part, Yahya Khan had planned to address the nation
on radio and television on December 17, 1971, the day after the surrender of Pakistani forces in Dhaka, and announce the outlines of a new
constitution that, in his view, would "preserve and promote the ideology of Pakistan."[16] But the total collapse of loyalty to him by junior military officers and civil servants made it impossible for him to do so. Bhutto
arrived from Rome, where he had stopped on his way back from the
United States, to accept power that was handed over by General Yahya
Khan.

In the absence of a constitution, Bhutto took over as president and
chief martial law administrator, the positions that Yahya Khan had held.
Bhutto retired Yahya Khan with full benefits and honors. The same mag-
nanimity was shown to other generals who had tried even at the last
stage to prevent the induction of a civilian head of state. Bhutto's nomination of Lieutenant General Gul Hassan Khan as the new army chief

led to the common belief that Lieutenant General Gul Hassan Khan had been the leading figure in the military officers' revolt against Yahya Khan.[17] Lieutenant General Gul Hassan Khan claimed in his memoirs that he found out about Bhutto having become president only after the fact and that he accepted the command of the army after receiving Bhutto's assurance of no political interference in the armed forces.[18] Officers involved in the revolt against Yahya Khan also deny any knowledge of the actual dynamic of the transfer of power; one of them suggested that the heckling of General Hamid Khan at GHQ was "contrived."[19]

The question of who persuaded Yahya Khan to transfer power peacefully to Bhutto is important because it bears significantly on some of Bhutto's controversial decisions as well as on the circumstances of his ouster from power. If the coterie of generals close to Yahya was bent upon denying power to Bhutto and Lieutenant General Gul Hassan Khan was not actively involved in securing it for the PPP leader, the only element of the military that could have forced the transfer of power was the senior generals in military intelligence. It is interesting that Bhutto did not retire Major General Akbar Khan, who headed the ISI during the 1970 elections; neither did he retire his successor, Major General (later Lieutenant General) Ghulam Jilani Khan, the head of the ISI at the time of transfer of power. In fact, General Jilani continued to head the ISI throughout Bhutto's years in office. According to Bhutto, General Jilani influenced his choice of army chief when Bhutto chose General Zia ul-Haq, who later overthrew Bhutto and executed him. Except for a handful of Yahya's colleagues, most military officers involved in implementing Yahya Khan's failed strategy of political diversification with the help of religious parties kept their jobs, and, in fact, they gained from vacancies at the top. Bhutto's left-wing lieutenants argue, with some justification, that Pakistan's intelligence services helped the return of civilian rule at this stage primarily to maintain their, and the military's, institutional primacy.[20]

The military, as an institution, needed a popular civilian leader to pick up the pieces after Pakistan's breakup. By allowing Bhutto to come to power, the generals also expected to deflect criticism from their own conduct in East Pakistan. They could now focus political debate on

Bhutto's role in breaking up the country by failing to reach accommodation with Sheikh Mujibur Rahman. Bhutto's many political opponents were happy to pick up that theme from the day he came to power, which helped restore the military's standing within a short time. The military leadership did not feel the need to change its basic assumptions about centralization of authority, rivalry with India, and dependence on external assistance to fuel that rivalry. Even out of power, the military could depend on its Islamist allies to pressure Pakistan's new ruler against shaping a new Pakistan that was radically different from the old.

Zulfikar Ali Bhutto was the first civilian politician to rule Pakistan in almost two decades. From the time Ghulam Muhammad, a civil servant, had become Governor-General in 1951, real power had been wielded by the civil-military complex. Bhutto's Pakistan Peoples Party had been formed only four years earlier, in 1967. It was not a well-structured political party, and its popular support as well as its organization revolved primarily around Bhutto's charisma. To most Pakistanis, however, Bhutto and the PPP represented radical change. An analysis of the PPP's vote in the 1970 election explained the party's appeal to the people:

> The key [Bhutto] slogan was *"roti, kapra, makkan"* [bread, clothing, shelter] . . . a secular demand for a better life for the less privileged . . . Islam could not be eliminated—that would be unthinkable in Pakistan—but emphasis could be placed elsewhere and was. Such a program was hardly designed to appeal to the traditional rural elite and mullahs and thus that avenue of campaigning was very largely closed to the PPP.
>
> [There was also] . . . a stronger relationship between the level of development and modernization and the vote for the PPP . . . [T]he PPP polled more votes in the rapidly modernizing areas . . . [It] represented radicalism in Pakistani politics. It came out against the established order and the groups represented in it. A vote for the PPP was therefore a vote against the system by people who had been alienated from it.[21]

Soon after his assumption of power, a Pakistani writer noted "the secularization of politics brought about by President Zulfikar Ali Bhutto and his party's ascendancy" and explained:

In the nineteenth century, the great Muslim reformer, Sir Syed Ahmad Khan, successfully wrested the leadership of the Muslims from the hold of the orthodox divines and sent them on the road to modernism . . . [T]his trend continued to predominate in politics until 1947. But soon after the death of Muhammad Ali Jinnah in 1948, there was a resurgence of the rightist [Islamist] parties. Lacking economic and social programs, politicians adopted obscurantist tactics and religious sentiments for the furtherance of their respective political aims. It is to Bhutto's abiding credit that he launched a political party with a socialist manifesto, thereby bringing to the fore urgent economic and social issues that are directly relevant to the teeming millions, and successfully detaching religion from politics. Despite the obfuscation and pettifogging of the rightist parties, the Pakistan Peoples Party (PPP) swept the polls and consummated the process of political secularization initiated by Sir Syed Ahmad Khan. From now on economic issues will determine the dynamics of politics.[22]

To accomplish the goal of secularization Bhutto would have had to dismantle the ideological paradigm that had been created by the civil-military complex and at least some of the first generation of Pakistan's politicians. Bhutto espoused a vision for Pakistan with "social standards . . . comparable to those in parts of Europe."[23] He spoke of "fighting prejudice and obscurantism," promoting "equality of men and women, . . . restoration to . . . the citizen of Pakistan the dignity which is his due," and "easy access to education and medical care throughout the country."[24] But he also believed in continued confrontation with India. It was his policy toward India, combined with his authoritarian tendencies, that impeded the prospect of meeting his declared goals in other respects.

Pakistan could not significantly expand social-sector spending without reducing its military budget. Continued confrontation with India, based on an ideological imperative, provided the justification for higher defense budgets. It also moved Bhutto away from his goal of secularizing the Pakistani state. Bhutto also failed to curtail the role of Pakistan's intelligence services and, in some cases, even extended that role to maintain his own supremacy in domestic politics. The security services influenced the civilian Bhutto administration to make decisions that eventually allowed the military to regain the prestige and control it enjoyed under Ayub Khan and Yahya Khan. Once again, Islamic groups acted as allies of the civil-military complex in ensuring its viceregal domination.

Bhutto's mass popularity had been the result of both his secular-socialist rhetoric and his anti-India stance. Until the decisive defeat of the Pakistan army by India in 1971, most Pakistanis did not see the contradiction between their socioeconomic ambitions and their aspirations to compete with India militarily. Since partition, the military, aided by its control of most of Pakistan's resources, had cultivated an image of invincibility. It had managed to cover up its strategic failures until the fall of Dhaka. Now, with the military's standing at an all-time low, an opportunity for change existed. Bhutto's convictions relating to India dictated a different course:

Bhutto projected India as an enemy of Islam and Muslims and, therefore, an inveterate foe of Pakistan, determined to dismember it. He presented himself as a fearless and capable thwarter of India's designs and described his adversaries as its appeasers or agents. He would continue a policy of confrontation with India until it conceded self-determination to the people of Kashmir and stopped its persecution of Indian Muslims. If and when these conditions were met, he would offer Pakistan's cooperation but under no circumstances would he accept India's domination.[25]

This stance caused Bhutto to follow a national security policy that did not differ dramatically from the one pursued by the preceding military regimes. To avoid embarrassing the army, Bhutto kept secret the report of an inquiry commission examining the loss of East Pakistan. Extracts of the Hamoodur Rehman Commission Report (named after the inquiry commission head, the Supreme Court chief justice at that time) have been released some thirty-three years later and still raise questions about the "strategic delusions" and "character" of Pakistan's generals. The release of the report soon after Pakistan's split would have been devastating for Pakistan's army. By withholding the report, Bhutto did the military a favor. He followed that decision with a media campaign emphasizing the military's contributions during disaster relief and as defenders against a hostile neighbor. These measures helped the military to recover from the loss of prestige resulting from the 1971 debacle and to overthrow Bhutto in 1977 as a result of a situation created primarily by his Islamist political opponents.

Bhutto forged a diverse electoral coalition that included middle-class socialists, landlords from Punjab and Sindh, industrial workers, students, and even some industrialists. While forging this coalition, Bhutto promised different things to different people. Like Pakistan's founder, Muhammad Ali Jinnah, Bhutto was somewhat ambiguous about his actual design for Pakistan. Jinnah had mobilized South Asian Muslims for a homeland of their own without getting into the details of how that homeland would be run. Bhutto built a constituency against the concentration of wealth and power but left insufficiently defined the details of how he hoped to effect fundamental change in Pakistan:

Zulfikar Ali Bhutto's success at the polls in 1970 was due in large measure to a constituency that sought a complete overhaul of the country's political, economic and social institutions. Deeply troubled by the re-acquisition of political power by the traditional leaders during the latter [part] of the Ayub era, the most articulate component of the Bhutto constituency demanded "modernization"—and *Mawashrati Taraqi*, its Urdu equivalent—was used freely by Bhutto and his supporters [but] it was not defined very clearly ... In coming to power, therefore, Bhutto brought with him a party that wanted to totally restructure the country's institutions but had not achieved a consensus on the shape the new structure was to take. The designs that were offered ranged from a Westminster-type of parliamentary democracy to a Soviet style "dictatorship of the proletariat." Bhutto did not let his own preferences be known to his various constituencies. The impression that he sought to convey was that of "keeping my options open," a strategy that reassured his followers as well as his opponents.[26]

Bhutto was in a unique position to shift the emphasis on ideology of the old Pakistani establishment and strengthen those aspiring to redefine the basis of Pakistan's nationhood. The circumstances in which he came to power, however, required that he should establish his authority before attempting to redefine Pakistan. He did so by identifying potential sources of threat to his authority and using martial law powers within the first few months to consolidate his power. Bhutto's critics attribute his authoritarian actions to his "intolerance" and "resolve . . . to wrest all power into his own hand."[27] His admirers, however, argue that his conduct was partly the result of his view of himself as a revolutionary leader trying to build a new order.[28] There is no doubt, however, that Bhutto's failure to build and strengthen civil society contributed to both his ouster from power and the further descent of Pakistan into a military-dominated semitheocracy.

Pakistan's religious parties, notably the Jamaat-e-Islami, opposed Bhutto from the day he took office. Because during the 1970 election campaign they described him and his socialist ideology as a threat to Islam, it was not possible for religious leaders to accept that Bhutto or his party had a role to play in rebuilding Pakistan after the debacle of division.[29] As soon as Bhutto assumed power on December 20, 1971, the student wing of the Jamaat-e-Islami burned effigies of him in Lahore and declared the day a "black day."[30]

The Islamists used the influence they had built in the media under Yahya Khan to attack Bhutto for continuing martial law. They also questioned the notion of a civilian martial law administrator. When Pakistan television showed the film of the surrender ceremony in Dhaka in a news bulletin, the Jamaat-e-Islami led public protests against what it described as an attempt to humiliate the army. The military, too, saw this as part of Bhutto's efforts to malign the army, a fact revealed by the army's commander, Lieutenant General Gul Hassan Khan, in his memoirs.[31]

The private views of the military and the public posture of the Islamists showed an unusual degree of commonality. In early 1973, the amir, or head, of the Jamaat-e-Islami even went as far as appealing to the army to overthrow Bhutto's government because of "its inherent moral corruption."[32] Bhutto banned some Islamist publications and detained Jamaat-e-Islami leaders and activists under emergency powers he retained. In the case of the army, he was content to establish his ascendancy over it by changing its command. The new army chief, now designated chief of army staff instead of commander in chief, was General Tikka Khan, who took over from Lieutenant General Gul Hassan Khan in March 1972. Tikka Khan was reputed to be a professional soldier, and his reputation for being the "Butcher of Bengal" militated against his being able to garner sufficient civilian support for a military coup d'état. Bhutto felt he had the situation under control. At the end of 1972, a U.S. observer of the Pakistani scene wrote:

> Bhutto [has] things pretty well in hand; real, potential and imaginary opponents in the military and civil service were either dismissed or replaced by individuals more to Bhutto's liking; others were sufficiently cowed and would not overtly challenge presidential authority . . . Bhutto has accomplished a considerable amount in a short time. The United States has reinstituted economic assistance, there are indications that the Chinese are providing both economic and military assistance, and the international trade and commercial position of Pakistan appears improved.[33]

Within two days of becoming Pakistan's president and, ostensibly, its absolute ruler, Bhutto visited the U.S. ambassador at his residence, primarily to seek U.S. economic and military assistance. The ambassador reported to Washington that Bhutto believed India had "never truly recognized partition nor in fact had been reconciled to it."[34] Instead of curtailing defense expenditures to reflect the reduced boundaries and population of Pakistan, Bhutto maintained military spending and, by extension, the potential for military dominance. In February 1972, barely two months after Pakistan's massive military defeat, Pakistan offered the United States naval bases along the Balochistan coast in return for rearming the Pakistani forces.[35] The proposal was communicated not only at the diplomatic level. The foreign liaison officer of ISI sought a meeting, sanctioned by superior officers, with an officer in the U.S. military mission to ask whether the United States would be interested in establishing bases in Pakistan.[36] The Pakistan military had started quietly to rebuild itself and, as in the past, sought U.S. assistance in doing so. This time Pakistan's offer of bases showed it was willing to go farther than before.

The United States decided, at least for the time being, not to encourage Pakistan in building itself as a military equal of India with U.S. support. The offer for bases was politely declined. Secretary of State William P. Rogers summarized the new situation in South Asia and perceived U.S. priorities in a memorandum to President Nixon:

It is clear, given the major change in the South Asian equation after the December war that we could not and should not seek to build up Pakistan as any kind of strategic counter-weight to India. As we see it our basic policy objective in South Asia should now be to encourage movement toward a broad political settlement which would replace the sharp political-military confrontation that has plagued the Subcontinent for more than 20 years. In Pakistan this would require in addition to our continued support for its territorial integrity and economic growth that we encourage Bhutto in every way open to us to move in the direction of a basic settlement with India and that we avoid any action in the military field that would encourage Pakistan again to postpone the difficult decisions it must make if it is to reach basic accommodation with its stronger neighbor. We would encourage India to recognize that a magnanimous policy toward Pakistan will serve India's longer term interest by contributing to stability in the region.[37]

The opportunity for creating a new South Asian equation came when the president of residual Pakistan, Zulfikar Ali Bhutto, met the Indian prime minister, Indira Gandhi, at Simla for peace talks in June 1972. It was hardly a meeting of equals. Bhutto had to secure the return of 5,139 square miles of Pakistani territory occupied by India and obtain the release of Pakistani prisoners of war from an Indian leader who had humiliated and broken his country. He pleaded with Gandhi not to insist on including a final resolution of the Jammu and Kashmir dispute in any bilateral agreement although, from India's point of view, this would have been the ideal opportunity to impose a solution. The dispute over Kashmir had been poisoning India-Pakistan relations, and settling it could pave the way for normalization of relations between the two countries, gradually overcoming Pakistan's psychosis that India sought its destruction. Gandhi was persuaded by Bhutto's argument that his fragile civilian government would probably be toppled by the Pakistani military, which would accuse him of losing Kashmir in addition to the loss of East Pakistan.

The compromise reached by Bhutto and Gandhi was to declare that "the two countries are resolved to settle their differences by peaceful means through bilateral negotiations."[38] The cease-fire line in Jammu and Kashmir was declared the Line of Control, interpreted by the Indian signatories to suggest that actual control was now synonymous with legal possession. For India, this meant that the phase of international pressure to hold a plebiscite was over. Bhutto claimed later that he had saved Pakistan from the ultimate humiliation of completely giving up its claim to Kashmir,[39] but Pakistan's religious parties described the Simla Agreement as a sellout to India and organized street demonstrations against normal relations with Pakistan's enemy.

The Simla accord facilitated the exchange of thirty-six thousand Bengalis remaining in Pakistan with ninety thousand Pakistani prisoners of war. A majority of the repatriated military personnel returned to the army. Some of them, like Major General Farman Ali Khan, had been part of the effort by the Yahya Khan regime to alter the results of the 1970 election through the scheme of unopposed special elections. Others had participated in maligning the Bengalis as being under Hindu and Indian influence. Almost all had been affected by the cooperative effort between Islamist groups and the army in the civil war. Some officers maintained personal contacts with the Islamists and shared their ideas.

Bhutto made no effort to sever the Islamist-military linkages forged in the last days of East Pakistan. Immediately after the 1971 war, Bhutto spoke to U.S. officials of how Mrs. Gandhi had laid the basis for "Bangladeshes all over [the] subcontinent,"[40] meaning that the breakup of one state emerging from the 1947 partition could lead to other separatist movements encouraged by neighboring states. Bhutto obviously had in mind the prospect of revenge against India by encouraging movements similar to the one that had resulted in the creation of Bangladesh. He was also concerned about the "bug of secession" spreading in West Pakistan in the absence of the balance that had existed between Pakistan's two wings.[41] Bhutto's fears and plans for "new Pakistan" were not very different from the fears and plans of the rulers of "old Pakistan."

Bhutto was not averse to maintaining an ideologically oriented army and may even have thought of the Islamists as a useful pressure group in his own grand design, shared by Pakistan's military, for reviving Pakistan's regional stature as a counterweight to India. Bhutto was confident of his popularity within Pakistan. He did not consider the Islamic parties, which he had defeated so decisively in an election not long before, as a serious domestic challenge. For their part, the Islamists were not content with a limited role in confronting ethnic nationalism and rallying the nation against Pakistan's external enemy, India. They joined with Bhutto's secular opponents to carve out a role for themselves as serious contenders for political power.

From the point of view of Pakistan's national security establishment, the Islamist designs were not a bad thing. The military had been forced to concede power to Bhutto because of its failure to keep the country together, and it could not intervene in politics again without a decent interval. The military would now wait for Bhutto to make mistakes and let the Islamists take him on politically, keeping their ideological agenda alive.

After the Simla accord and repatriation of prisoners of war, it was inevitable that Pakistan would have to recognize a sovereign Bangladesh. The world's major powers had recognized the new state, and Pakistan had no hope of returning its former eastern wing into its fold. Sheikh Mujibur Rahman, who had become president of Bangladesh after his release from a West Pakistan prison by Bhutto, had threatened to put Pakistani military officers on trial for war crimes—a prospect unacceptable to the Pakistani military. The more suspicious minds in the military worried that Bhutto would give a wink and a nod to such trials as a means of discrediting the generals who had plotted to keep him out of power, but Bhutto apparently had no such intention. He sought to use Pakistan's recognition of Bangladesh as a bargaining ploy for setting aside war crimes trials.

Bhutto's suggestion that Pakistan recognize Bangladesh as an independent country did not go uncontested at home. The Jamaat-e-Islami led a campaign against the recognition and started a campaign called

"Bangladesh na-manzoor" (Bangladesh is unacceptable). During the course of this campaign, Islamist student activists addressed gatherings on campuses and in mosques, publicizing the view that the separation of East Pakistan was the result of a conspiracy led by Bhutto. They contended that soon after the 1970 election Bhutto had said, *"Udhar tum, Idhar hum"* (You over there, we over here), which was interpreted to mean that he wanted absolute power in West Pakistan and therefore approved of East Pakistan breaking away. The phrase became widely attributed to Bhutto though he had never used those words. Khalid Hasan explained that *"Udhar tum, Idhar hum"* was the headline in a pro-PPP newspaper on March 15, 1971, and reflected a headline writer's summary of Bhutto's formula for sharing power after the December 1970 election.[42] The "Bangladesh na-manzoor" campaign had no other apparent purpose than to absolve the Pakistani military of blame for the loss of East Pakistan. Islamists were making the case that the civil war in East Pakistan did not negate the essential elements of Pakistan's ideology because the war had been instigated by internal conspirators (Bhutto) and foreign aggressors (India).

Although Bhutto had moved swiftly to restore Pakistan's morale and international standing, Pakistan was in no position to immediately revive its competition with India. Pakistan's national security establishment identified Afghanistan as an adversary and linked the Afghan government to unrest in Balochistan and the NWFP, just as they had seen India playing a role in support of Bengali nationalists. This attention to Afghanistan became more intense later when the Soviet Union became directly involved in Afghan affairs. In years to come, Afghanistan served several purposes for Pakistan's national security establishment. It provided an additional arena in which the army and security services could flex their muscles. Pakistan's military also tested its doctrine of irregular warfare with the help of Islamists in Afghanistan even before the Soviet intervention attracted U.S. involvement there.

In Pakistan's 1970 election, the two provinces bordering Afghanistan had given pluralities to the ethnic nationalist National Awami Party (NAP), led by Abdul Wali Khan. The vote was fractured along tribal lines, and the NAP did not have the same overwhelming support in NWFP and Balochistan that the Awami League had secured in East Bengal.

In 1947, Wali Khan and his family had opposed the partition of British India and had called for an ethnic state for Pashtuns. The Baloch leaders of the NAP also espoused ethnic (as opposed to Pakistani) nationalism, and some had opposed their territory's inclusion in Pakistan. The NAP was avowedly secular and supported close relations with India. In the last stages of his jihad against Bengali ethnic nationalism, General Yahya Khan also banned the NAP for "conspiring to start an insurrection in West Pakistan."[43]

Bhutto lifted the ban when he took over. At the beginning of 1972, he allowed the NAP, in coalition with the Jamiat Ulema Islam (JUI), to form governments in the two provinces. He later dismissed the NAP government in Balochistan amid accusations of the NAP planning a revolt against the central government. It was claimed that a cache of arms found in the Iraqi embassy in Islamabad was intended for use in the rebellion. U.S. diplomats and Pakistani intelligence officials knew that the Iraqi arms were meant for Baloch rebels in the Iranian part of Balochistan—Iraq's response to Iran's support for Kurdish rebels in Iraq. The Pakistani security services had misled Bhutto, leading him into a small-scale civil war along the Afghanistan border. Just days before the discovery of arms in the Iraqi embassy, Bhutto had sought the help of the U.S. chargé d'affaires during political negotiations with NAP's Baloch leadership. Had NAP been part of a conspiracy involving Iraq's relatively new Baathist government, the United States would not have been so sympathetic to rapprochement between Bhutto and the Baloch leaders.

After coming to power, Bhutto gradually became more authoritarian. He used martial law powers to punish several individuals and groups that had crossed his path during his political career. By the time he dismissed the Balochistan government, his critics saw Bhutto as an elected civilian strongman who had little patience for the niceties of parliamentary democracy. For Bhutto's opponents, secular as well as Islamist, the dismissal of the Balochistan government confirmed his dictatorial tendencies.[44] One opposition leader likened Bhutto's decision to place the blame for the smuggled arms on the NAP leaders of Balochistan to Hitler's plot of burning down the Reichstag and using it as an excuse to ban all forms of political opposition.[45]

Immediately after the Balochistan government's dismissal, the NAP government in NWFP resigned in protest. A violent tribal uprising in Balochistan followed.[46] The army was called in to deal with the tribal insurgency, reestablishing the military's credentials as the savior of Pakistan's unity. Under attack from the government, the secular NAP ended up joining an opposition alliance dominated by the religious parties. In effect, Bhutto had weakened his secular rivals and strengthened the position of the Islamists as the focal point of opposition to his government.

The rebellious Baloch tribesmen received some assistance from Afghanistan, which since 1947 had objected to the inclusion of ethnic Pashtun areas in Pakistan. Afghan governments had periodically supported demands for a "Pashtunistan," and, because of its location on the southern border of the Soviet Union's Central Asian states, the Soviet Union maintained a significant political presence in Afghanistan. After the overthrow of the Afghan monarchy in 1973, Soviet influence in Afghanistan increased under the republican regime of Sardar Muhammad Daoud, as did anti-Pakistan propaganda. Afghanistan depended on Pakistan for its transit trade, however, and certainly did not have the military means to force its will on Pakistan.

The Balochistan insurgency presented Pakistan's military and intelligence services with an opportunity to cast Afghanistan as an additional significant threat to Pakistan's security, which justified continued military expenditures and helped maintain Pakistan's status as a garrison state. At a later stage, Bhutto was also persuaded to support the militias of two Afghan Islamist leaders, Burhanuddin Rabbani and Gulbuddin Hekmatyar.[47] Rabbani's Jamiat-e-Islami and Hekmatyar's Hizbe Islami had only limited following in Afghanistan and were ideologically linked to Pakistan's Jamaat-e-Islami and the Muslim Brotherhood in the Middle East. Pakistan had started seeking to expand its influence into Afghanistan with the help of Islamists years before the Soviets invaded that country. Ironically, this covert operation of Pakistan's ISI had been initiated while an ostensibly secular politician, Bhutto, governed Pakistan. According to General Khalid Mahmud Arif:

An Afghan cell had been created in the [Pakistan] Foreign Office in July/August 1973. It met regularly for the next three years, under the chairmanship of . . . Prime Minister Bhutto or Mr. Aziz Ahmad [then Foreign Secretary] and gave out policy guidelines. The Inspector General Frontier Constabulary [a tribal paramilitary force] and the DG ISI [Director General Inter-Services Intelligence] worked in concert to conduct intelligence missions inside Afghanistan. The Afghan leaders, Gulbeddin Hekmatyar and Rabbani came into contact with the Pakistani authorities during this period. The Pakistani intelligence agencies also kept communication channels open with the deposed king, Zahir Shah, who was living in exile in Italy.[48]

The significance of these early forays into Afghanistan under Bhutto's rule can best be understood in the context of subsequent developments, which led to the U.S.-backed Afghan jihad against Soviet occupation.

Soon after initiating Pakistan's involvement in Afghan affairs, Bhutto also tried to seek additional U.S. military supplies on the basis of Pakistan's expanded threat perceptions. In this he was undoubtedly encouraged by Pakistan's security agencies and the military. Bhutto claimed that the tribal revolt in Balochistan was part of an Indian-Soviet grand design to further balkanize Pakistan. The United States, however, did not rise to the bait. State Department talking points for President Nixon, prepared for Bhutto's Washington visit in July 1973, stated:

Bhutto will assert a growing threat to Pakistan from an Indo-Soviet combination. He may claim a Soviet hand in the tribal dissidence in the province of Balochistan . . . We do not perceive the threat to Pakistan with the same sense of alarm as Pakistani officials do. In the short run, neither the Soviets nor the Indians have designs on the integrity of Pakistan. Evidence of Soviet meddling in Balochistan is minimal. Over the longer run, if Pakistan is internally unstable and deeply divided, the Indians, Afghans and Soviets may be tempted to place pressures on Pakistan. In this environment, we see the resolution of Pakistan's security problems primarily in political/psychological and economic terms and only secondarily in military terms.[49]

Bhutto had obviously embraced the Pakistani national security establishment's policy tripod. He continued to see India as Pakistan's eternal enemy and persisted with the previous policy of seeking security through a mix of Islamic ideology and continued building of military power. In addition to confronting India, Pakistan was now also working on plans to seek a sphere of influence in Afghanistan by fomenting Islamist rebellion there. The third element of Pakistan's original policy tripod—getting the United States to pay for Pakistan's economic and military needs—was not working as effectively as the military would have preferred. Pakistan's generals did not like the fact that Bhutto was unable to secure military supplies from the United States.

According to official figures from the U.S. Agency for International Development, Pakistan received $937.3 million in economic assistance between 1972 and 1977, the years that Bhutto governed the country. U.S. military aid during this period, however, stood at a meager $1.7 million, most of it in the form of training for officers and for spare parts for U.S.-made equipment. Although Bhutto secured considerable military assistance from China and was able to purchase equipment from European countries, Pakistan's generals attributed his failure in reopening the U.S. pipeline to his socialist leanings and past anti-American rhetoric.[50]

Despite several hurdles, Bhutto managed to consolidate his populist authoritarian regime within a short time. In the political arena, he allowed little competition. On the economic front, he nationalized banking and several sectors of industry. In the process, certain social and economic groups were hurt by his policies and began coalescing in opposition to these policies. When Bhutto was overthrown in a military coup d'état in 1977 and executed two years later, it was two constituencies—the military and the Islamist groups—that he actively courted after coming to power that caused his downfall.

Bhutto ensured that the military received, in his words, its "fair share of the pie"[51] and gradually both the size of the military and the expenditure relating to it increased. In 1973, he also secured the consensus of all political parties on a constitution that provided for a British-style parliamentary system of government. The religious parties demanded the inclusion of the Objectives Resolution in the preamble of the constitution and the government agreed. Bhutto became prime minister under the new constitution, but the unanimous adoption of the constitution did not translate into Pakistan's transformation into a fully functioning democracy. Bhutto continued to look over his shoulder for signs of what he termed as "Bonapartic tendencies" in the army while he deployed the power of the state to suppress civilian dissent. Bhutto's opponents saw him as an elected dictator. He saw himself as the creator of a "Napoleonic order"—Bhutto's description of a personalized system of governance in a previously inegalitarian country, aimed at benefiting the poor and the dispossessed.[52]

By 1974, Bhutto had gradually phased from power the left wing of the PPP. Socialist intellectuals with middle-class backgrounds made way for traditional landowners who had now joined the party. Bhutto's original political team had been replaced by a new team of ministers and advisers from the civil and military establishment.[53] Under the influence of this team, the PPP's secretary general perceived "Bhutto's tilt toward an obscurantist interpretation of Islam."[54] Three seemingly unrelated developments reflected, and possibly caused, that tilt. The first of these was the decision to declare, through a constitutional amendment, members of the Ahmadi sect to be non-Muslim. The second was the holding of the Islamic summit conference in Lahore. The third related to the secret decision, made in 1972, to develop a Pakistani nuclear-weapons capability, which became an urgent priority after India tested its nuclear device in 1974.

Bhutto had to confront the Ahmadi issue when Islamist groups agitated against the sect after a clash in May 1974 between Islamist and Ahmadi students at the railway station in the town where the Ahmadi sect is headquartered. As mentioned earlier, the Ahmadis are a controversial sect that claims to be Muslim but refuses to recognize the finality of Prophet Muhammad's message or the obligation of jihad. They follow the teachings of Mirza Ghulam Ahmad, who founded the sect in the nineteenth century and is considered a prophet by most Ahmadis. Ahmadis had been the target of orthodox religious groups for several decades, and anti-Ahmadi agitation in 1953 led to Pakistan's first brush with martial law. Herbert Feldman points out, "It is precisely because anti-Qadiani [Ahmadi] agitation is such inflammatory material that it has become, especially in the Punjab, a classic method of embarrassing and undermining authority."[55] The student clash at the Rabwah railway station in May 1974 led to a fresh outbreak of protests against the Ahmadis by religious groups.

Ahmadis had supported Bhutto and the PPP in the 1970 election when they assumed that their secular and liberal agenda would protect them against the bigotry of the orthodox parties. Bhutto was aware of the potential of sectarian and religious agitation to topple governments and knew, from the history of the 1953 anti-Ahmadi disturbances, of the link between religious groups and Pakistan's intelligence services. Instead of taking the risk of confronting the religious agitators, Bhutto decided to concede their demand. The Pakistani constitution was amended to include a provision that effectively declared the Ahmadis non-Muslims. The decision was followed by the creation of the Ministry of Religious Affairs. The new minister for religious affairs was Maulana Kausar Niazi, an erudite former member of the Jamaat-e-Islami, who was believed by left-wing members of the PPP to have close ties to the security agencies.[56] Ironically, Niazi had advised Bhutto against giving in to the religious parties' demand, but Bhutto had apparently been persuaded "by someone else" to take over the religious parties' agenda.[57] Other observers were concerned that by giving in to the Islamists, Bhutto was "encouraging the expression of sectarian opinion."[58] These observers, such as Herbert Feldman, noted that "it is not only Qadianis who excite the wrath of intolerant bigots."[59]

Bhutto's tilt toward religious conservatism was connected to his economic and national security agendas. The Arab oil embargo in 1973 had caused higher prices for oil around the world and a boom in the economies of Persian Gulf Arab countries. Bhutto wanted Pakistan to benefit from the flow of petrodollars, which required emphasizing Pakistan's Islamic identity. Pakistan hosted the Islamic summit conference in Lahore and, under the patronage of Saudi Arabia's King Feisal bin Abdel Aziz, took the lead in creating permanent structures for the Organization of Islamic Conference (OIC). The presence of heads of state and government from all Muslim-majority countries enabled Bhutto to invite President Sheikh Mujibur Rahman of Bangladesh and formally recognize Bangladesh. The Islamic summit's most tangible result was the recognition of Pakistan as a leading power in the Muslim world, something the country's founders had hoped to accomplish since the earliest days of Pakistan's independence. When India tested a nuclear device the same year, Bhutto thought that he could raise money for Pakistan's two-year-old covert nuclear-weapons program from the brotherly Muslim countries he had recently brought together at the Islamic summit.

Bhutto also reopened the discussion of Pakistan's national identity and the country's definition of itself as an ideological state. At a government-sponsored conference on the history and culture of Pakistan, scholars emphasized the Islamic roots of Pakistan.[60] The need to address the roots question was explained by one scholar, Professor Waheed-uz-Zaman:

Sensitive and thinking minds are asking questions which are no longer academic inquiries or theoretical concepts but questions of national continuity and survival. What are the links that bind the people of Pakistan? What is the soul and personality of Pakistan? What is our national identity and our peculiar oneness which makes us a nation apart from other nations?[61]

He then declared:

The wish to see the kingdom of God established in a Muslim territory was the moving idea behind the demand for Pakistan, the corner-stone of the movement, the ideology of the people, and the raison d'être of the new nation-state . . . If we let go the ideology of Islam, we cannot hold together as a nation by any other means . . . If the Arabs, the Turks or the Iranians, God forbid, give up Islam, the Arabs yet remain Arabs, the Turks remain Turks, the Iranians remain Iranians, but what do we remain if we give up Islam?[62]

This revival of an ideological basis for Pakistan echoed the views of the Islamists and negated the prospect of nation building on the basis of geographic identity or even of Muslim self-governance in areas where Muslims form a majority. During the campaign for Pakistan, Jinnah, Pakistan's founder, had emphasized the ideas of Muslim self-governance and overcoming the status of a minority in a united India, but that concept had been superseded by the ideology of Pakistan as an Islamic republic. Now, the loss of Bangladesh had made Pakistan a more compact and relatively homogenous country, presenting the opportunity for exploring an alternative secular vision—geographic unity of the Indus River valley and its adjacent areas. Ethnic, regional, and tribal differences could be subsumed through a democratic polity. The new Pakistan no longer needed to rely on religion, the only bond West Pakistan had had with East Pakistan.

Some secular scholars started looking at "geological, geographic, ethnic and historical grounds for regarding the Indus Valley and its western and northern mountain marches as a distinct national unit separate from the rest of South Asia."[63] But Bhutto did not take that route to complete the circle on his avowed ideal of a progressive Pakistan, and he weakened secular forces in the process.

By the end of 1976, Bhutto had strengthened Pakistan's armed forces and had adopted significant elements of the old Pakistan as part of his new Pakistan. The country was in much better shape than it had been immediately after its division although it remained saddled with a number of unsolved political, social, and economic problems. Bhutto remained personally popular among the masses although his authoritarian ways eroded his support among the urban middle class. One commentator of the time pointed out:

> Institutions—which Bhutto once thought were vital to Pakistan's political development—continued to languish. Political parties, including the ruling PPP, were in a chaotic condition, if not in a shambles; parliament and the provincial legislatures often adjourned for want of quorums, mainly because the prime Minister or the chief minister concerned would not attend, except rarely; and the higher bureaucracy remained demoralized because it had virtually no job security. Student unions and bar associations continued to be vigorous, but they are not institutions of governance. The only institutions, if they can be so called, prospering in Pakistan in 1976, were the security agencies.[64]

Before coming to office, Bhutto had expressed doubts about both the capabilities and intentions of Pakistan's intelligence services. He saw them as an invisible government and was advised by his left-wing colleagues to dismantle them. Once in power, however, Bhutto enjoyed his ability to spy on his political opponents and use the security services for purposes other than gathering intelligence on threats to national security. When Bhutto took over, Pakistan's federal government controlled two spy agencies: the civilian IB and the military ISI. Each arm of the military had its own intelligence service; Military Intelligence (MI), reporting directly to the army chief and focused primarily on defense matters, was most significant. The provincial governments had at their disposal the Special Branch, a domestic intelligence unit tied to each province's police force. Bhutto created a Federal Investigation Agency (FIA) for investigating federal crimes, including corruption. Although ostensibly a crime-investigating agency, the FIA could always be called on to accuse critics and political opponents of financial impropriety ranging from tax evasion to taking of bribes while in office.

The Bhutto government also created the paramilitary Federal Security Force (FSF), which was meant to provide the federal government with special troops for law enforcement but was generally used instead to disrupt opposition meetings and harass government opponents. This expanded political role of the security agencies led to the questioning of Bhutto's credentials as a democrat. It also weakened the political foundations of his elected government, making Bhutto more vulnerable to political blunders:

> People, who have not had the opportunity to watch the operation of a government in Pakistan at close quarters, cannot correctly assess the extent to which the intelligence agencies provide prime ministers and presidents stories of plots and conspiracies against them. A secret and untouchable ring of informants gradually grows around the prime minister. There is no way for him to check [them] out. Gradually he stops listening to other opinions regarding the reliability or otherwise of the "information" supplied to him. Within a few months, he gets totally isolated and is at the mercy of his informants, good, bad, or indifferent but all religiously dedicated to preserving the system which has placed intelligence agencies on such a high pedestal. It has been the tragedy of Pakistan that more than a score of presidents, prime ministers, chief ministers, and elected parliaments have had an unconstitutional ending because of the poli-

cies pursued by a president or prime minister based on the secret information supplied by the intelligence services of the country.[65]

Ironically, after General Zia ul-Haq overthrew Bhutto in 1977 and executed him for plotting the murder of a political opponent, the star witness for the prosecution at Bhutto's trial was the head of the FSF. The FSF chief, granted total immunity by Zia ul-Haq, claimed he had ordered the murder at Bhutto's directive. Bhutto's creation of the new security agency, instead of increasing his political longevity, clearly led to his execution.

Pakistan's intelligence services are not only responsible for providing political intelligence; they also have a role in shaping events through their covert operations. Bhutto's encirclement by the intelligence agencies is relevant to understanding how the mosque-military alliance strengthened even when neither the religious parties nor the military was in power. The ubiquity of the intelligence agencies explains why an ostensibly secular politician, with a mandate for basic change, failed in implementing structural change. When Mubashir Hasan, then secretary general of the PPP, proposed that Bhutto return to his secular roots and rebuild his power base among the people instead of depending on the state security services, Bhutto reportedly told him, "What you want me to do, I do not have the power to do."[66]

On March 1, 1976, Bhutto named General Muhammad Zia ul-Haq as Pakistan's new chief of army staff. General Zia was junior to six other generals and did not have a reputation for military brilliance. One of his predecessors as army chief, Lieutenant General Gul Hassan Khan, claims that a superior officer had once described Zia ul-Haq as being unfit to be a military officer. Most accounts of Bhutto's decision to appoint General Zia as commander of the army suggest that Bhutto did so because of Zia's apparent sycophancy and obsequious behavior while he served as a major general and a lieutenant general.[67] Bhutto himself wrote that his choice of Zia ul-Haq had been influenced by the ISI chief, Lieutenant General Ghulam Jilani Khan.[68] In view of Jilani Khan's and Zia ul-Haq's roles in the military coup that resulted in Bhutto's overthrow and subsequent execution, the reasons for Bhutto's choice of Zia ul-Haq as army chief acquire special significance.

General Zia ul-Haq was both personally religious and closely connected to several Islamists by virtue of his social and family origins; Jilani Khan, however, was secular in his private life. Bhutto was apparently persuaded by General Jilani Khan that a mild-mannered, religiously inclined army chief could not be a threat to the civilian authority. Zia ul-Haq belonged to Punjab's Arain clan, known for its conservatism but not considered a martial group. Bhutto reckoned that an Arain "was unlikely to form deep alliances with the Pathan or the Rajputs, two communities well represented in the armed forces."[69] The explanation for Jilani Khan's advocacy of Zia ul-Haq (and why Jilani Khan and many other personally unobservant military officers remained close to the devout Zia ul-Haq during his eleven-year rule) probably lies in the strategic groupthink of the military's top leadership at the time. They saw the time ripe for projecting the public image of the military as soldiers of Islam, which proved particularly useful when the military took back the reins of power from Bhutto the following year.

Bhutto, who had already been expanding the role of religion in public life, did not object as General Zia ul-Haq changed the credo of the Pakistan army to *Iman, Taqwa, Jihad fi Sabil Allah* (faith, piety, and jihad for the sake of God) soon after taking over as army chief. Even as a corps commander, Zia ul-Haq had distributed books written by Jamaat-e-Islami's founder, Maulana Sayyid Abul Ala Maududi, as prizes to officers who won various competitions in his garrison. Although Maulana Maududi had been a political opponent and the Jamaat-e-Islami was a member of the coalition of opposition political parties, Bhutto apparently did not hold Zia's ideological sympathies against him.[70]

Assured that he was not the man to topple him, Bhutto saw Zia ul-Haq as the right man to take the Pakistani military to the next stage of its evolution as the guarantor of an anti-India, Islamic ideology. He was, of course, wrong in assuming that this extension of the military's ideological function would take place with him in charge of the country.

General Zia ul-Haq's early steps to Islamize the army are identified by Lieutenant General Jahan Dad Khan, who served under Zia ul-Haq as deputy martial law administrator, corps commander, and governor of the province of Sindh:

A devout Muslim, it was a matter of faith with [Zia ul-Haq] to propagate Islam wherever he could. Immediately after his appointment as COAS [chief of army staff] the motto he gave the troops was Eman (Faith), Taqwa (abstinence), Jehad Fi Sabeelillah (war in the way of or for the sake of God). He urged all ranks of the army during his visits to troops as well as in written instructions, to offer their prayers, preferably led by the commanders themselves at various levels. Religious education was included in the training program and mosques and prayer halls were organized in all army units.[71]

At approximately the time that Bhutto appointed General Zia ul-Haq, he started giving thought to renewing his status as an elected leader. As Bhutto pondered an election, analysts recognized his tremendous advantages. The National Awami Party (NAP) had been banned, and its leadership was in jail facing trial for sedition. The NAP's new incarnation, the National Democratic Party (NDP), had found no time to organize itself. Other secular groups had faced repression ranging from periodic imprisonment of their leaders to restrictions on meetings. The media had been only partly free, leaving the public uninformed about many of the government's weaknesses. Above all, Bhutto fully controlled the machinery of state and felt he was in a strong position to fend off any challenge from the religious parties. The situation at this time is described by Professor Anwar Syed:

Most of the parties comprising the opposition are known for their profession of dedication to Islam, which they equate with the "ideology of Pakistan." They will probably accuse the government of being untrue to the national ideology. But even here the Prime Minister is likely to defeat them. He stole their thunder by inviting the Imam of the Prophet's mosque in Madina and later the Imam of the mosque at the Kaa'ba—the two holiest of the holy places of Islam—to Pakistan in the spring of 1976. These dignitaries visited, led prayers, and warmed the hearts of the faithful in major cities. Later in the year his government sponsored and funded an international conference on the life and work of Prophet Muhammad.

For the first time in the nation's history, the central cabinet includes a minister for religious affairs in the person of Maulana Kausar Niazi, a former journalist and an astute politician who keeps sponsoring Islam-related projects and activities, if for nothing else to justify his portfolio. In 1976 copies of the Holy Quran were placed in each room of all first class hotels in the country. Many of the mosques in Pakistan, suffering neglect because of financial insufficiency, have been placed in the charge and care of the provincial Auqaf Departments (which raise many millions of rupees annually from the landed and commercial properties belonging to Muslim shrines taken over by the government in the early 1960s). These departments hire and pay the imams who lead prayers in the mosques. Occasionally such an imam may insist on having a mind of his own but the great majority of them may be relied upon to speak and act as the government's instrumentalities. Thus, Bhutto has plenty of ammunition with which to repel any Islam-related attacks the opposition may choose to launch against him.[72]

In April 1976, soon after Zia ul-Haq's appointment as army chief, the ISI prepared a position paper for Bhutto, recommending that he hold early elections and renew his mandate. In October, Lieutenant General Ghulam Jilani Khan, the ISI chief, sent another paper to the prime minister that spoke of him in glowing terms and repeated the proposal for holding of elections.[73] The ISI's keenness in advising Bhutto to go to the polls is significant in light of subsequent events. Bhutto scheduled the election and was overthrown by the military following mass protests resulting from allegations of rigging the polls. General Zia ul-Haq, the man who overthrew Bhutto and later executed him, kept the ISI's role in planning Bhutto's election strategy a secret. Bhutto's critics dismiss the effect of General Jilani Khan's advice to Bhutto on essentially political matters as an example of the misuse of intelligence services for "personal and political use"—a phrase used by the Zia regime to describe Bhutto's handling of state institutions.[74] In his statement before Pakistan's Supreme Court and in his communications while he awaited execution, Bhutto hinted at the possibility of having been trapped in a conspiracy by the military and intelligence services. This conspiracy, if it existed, would have begun with the ISI proposal for an election, advanced through Pakistan National Alliance (PNA) agitation against the fairness of the election, and finished up with the overthrow of Bhutto in the July 1977 military coup d'état.[75]

Although it is difficult to prove Bhutto's suspicions, they are not completely implausible either. The image of Pakistan's military had been completely rehabilitated by the time the ISI was encouraging Bhutto to hold elections. The army's strength in personnel now exceeded the combined number of troops Pakistan maintained in East and West Pakistan before the 1971 war. Bhutto had used his tremendous diplomatic skills to secure weaponry from a variety of sources. Indigenous production of small arms had been augmented with plants for rebuilding tanks and small aircraft, all acquired with Chinese help. Pakistan's relations with the United States were also stable. The United States had removed all limitations on arms transfers to Pakistan (and India) in 1975,[76] although Pakistan was still unable to buy major weapons systems because of the U.S. desire not to encourage an arms race.

Under such circumstances, it is possible (although by no means a proven fact) that General Zia ul-Haq and at least some of his fellow generals thought it was time to reassert the military's primacy. Coups d'état in Pakistan need political justification, however. Although the country had failed to develop democratic institutions, it still remained part of the South Asian tradition that considers legitimacy an important issue in governance. In the absence of political disorder, it is impossible for a general to simply take over or justify a military coup d'état.

Pakistan's history made it easy to find political disorder or contrive it with the help of the country's megalomaniacal politicians or weak civilian institutions. Zulfikar Ali Bhutto made a number of political mistakes, from interfering with the civil liberties of opponents to isolating himself from his own supporters. Bhutto's legitimacy as a civilian leader derived from his success in a general election; only electoral defeat or an election victory attained by questionable means could render Bhutto's political legitimacy questionable. The military could not topple Bhutto without delegitimizing his leadership position, which explains the ISI's eagerness to advise Bhutto on the holding of elections.

On October 5, 1976, the ISI sent Prime Minister Bhutto a top secret memorandum entitled "General Elections"; it was signed by General Jilani.[77] The memorandum suggested that Bhutto was at the height of his popularity and would sweep the polls in the face of a divided opposition. It also appealed to Bhutto's ego:

> The problems faced by Mr. Bhutto were monumental and of long standing; indeed the nation was splintered into "small pieces." We cannot hope to explore all the revolutionary changes, reforms and achievements of the present government under the leadership of Mr. Bhutto in this brief paper; suffice it to say, his leadership proved to be a breadth [sic] of fresh air in the acrid and suffocating political atmosphere, a dawn of hope in the dark days of economic chaos, a shot in the arm for the revival of the spirit of [the] Pakistan movement. He has given back the "soul" to the people and gave them direction to follow in the new constitution. He has won the admiration of foreign leaders for his astuteness in handling both the Nation's foreign policy as well as reaching a working accommodation with the leaders of the other political parties on the Nation's most pressing domestic problems. It is for the first time in the history of Pakistan that the National aims and objective are clearly defined.[78]

Although the ISI said that it did not intend to "recount, praise or eulogize the massive and monumental achievements of the Chairman or his Ruling Party," the tone of the agency's fifty-three-page paper was sycophantic and clearly aimed at convincing Bhutto to hold elections at a time of the ISI's choosing:

> In so far as the political situation is concerned, the majority of the patriotic intelligentsia still feel that Mr. Bhutto is, and will remain for some time to come, indispensable to the country because: (a) There is no alternative leadership of his standing and stature, or near his standing and stature, available in the field. (b) Mr. Bhutto is the only Pakistani leader with an international standing and image, who has profound knowledge and experience of the

inter-plays of international power politics. He has done a yeoman service to Pakistan. He is the symbol of Pakistan's stability and integrity. (c) He has successfully controlled the secessionist tendencies in the NWFP and Baluchistan, without aggravating the situation. (d) He is the only leader with a middle of the path policy. All others are committed to either complete right or complete left. Both types can create difficulties internally, as well as internationally. (e) Any weakening of his position at this stage will become the strength of anti-state elements against whom he is still waging war. Pakistan can ill afford agitational politics under the prevailing internal situation and international environments.[79]

There has been no significant improvement in the position of the opposition parties . . . The opposition is still in disarray . . . no clear cut and meaningful election alliance have so far emerged.[80]

As of today, a very conservative and a rough estimate of the Party's position on all-Pakistan basis is that in Sindh nearly 75–80% of the people are likely to go along with the ruling party; and in Punjab 70%.[81]

The prime minister appears to have accepted the ISI's suggestion and set a March 7, 1977, date for National Assembly elections. Provincial elections were to follow on March 10. Contrary to the ISI's prediction, two secular parties and the Muslim League joined the religious parties to contest the election as the Pakistan National Alliance (PNA). When the election campaign started, the PNA demonstrated considerable strength, a fact attributed by some analysts to urban middle-class disenchantment with Bhutto's socialist policies. Although the prime minister had tried hard to cultivate the image of deference to Islamist sentiment, the Islamists were not prepared to accept him. They were funded by those who claimed to be victimized by Bhutto's policies of nationalization and income redistribution. Despite the presence of secular parties in the PNA, from the beginning its election campaign took on a religious tone:

For forty-five days, the two political coalitions—the PPP representing the landed interests, rural poor and urban marginals and the PNA standing for the powerful middle class—fought what the

Economist labeled as a campaign "of whiskey, war and Islam." These were indeed the symbols of the confrontation that took place between the two different groups, each determined to impose its will on the other. The opposition's charge that Bhutto drank heavily and indulged in "Bacchanalian orgies" received the response from the Prime Minister that "he drank wine, not people's blood." The PNA in charging the Prime Minister, was defending the middle class's [religious] values; Bhutto's riposte was meant to remind the opposition and the electorate that he stood for the poor.[82]

The strength of the PNA campaign reflected the sentiment of the various constituencies Bhutto had alienated during his five years in power. One U.S. diplomat wrote:

During his five years at Pakistan's helm, Bhutto had retained an emotional hold on the poor masses who had voted overwhelmingly for him in the 1970 elections. At the same time, however, he had made many enemies. The nationalization of major industries during his first two years in office had upset business circles. An ill-considered decision to take over several thousand wheat-milling, rice-husking, and cotton-ginning units in July 1976 had angered small-business owners and traders. The left—intellectuals, students, and trade unionists—felt betrayed by Bhutto's shift to more conservative economic policies and by his growing collaboration with feudal landlords, Pakistan's traditional power brokers. Bhutto's increasingly authoritarian personal style and often high-handed way of dealing with political opponents had also alienated many.[83]

Despite this strong opposition, the support of the poor in a country where the poor constituted an overwhelming majority of the population assured Bhutto an electoral victory. Bhutto did not, however, anticipate that the religious fervor generated during the election campaign would be used later for a campaign of street protests to bring down his government.

American scholar Marvin Weinbaum, who was in Pakistan during the election season, tied Bhutto's decision on the timing of the polls to his economic achievements. The rate of inflation at 6 percent was down from an average of 25 percent between 1972 and 1975. Real GNP was growing at 5 percent, up from 3 percent a year earlier. The agriculture sector was growing after years of stagnation with help from "heavy public investment in tubewells and subsidies for fertilizer, pesticides and other farm inputs."[84]

According to Weinbaum, Bhutto could "rightly claim much of the credit for restoring the nation's self-esteem after the loss of Bangladesh and for a recent easing of tensions in the region." These positive developments were, however, matched by some negative ones. The benefits of most of Bhutto's reforms did not fully reach the people, "nor did government become appreciably more responsive or humane for the average citizen."[85]

Students and the intelligentsia resented the absence of political freedoms, and supported the PNA to manifest their disapproval of the government. Left-wing PPP activists were disillusioned by Bhutto's courting of the old feudal elite and some of them stayed away from the election campaign. Close to Election Day "signs of broad popular support for the PNA suggested a tighter election."[86] The impression of a close race in the absence of opinion polls led to blunders by the PPP, which in turn fed the PNA's allegations of a fraudulent election:

Plainly shaken, the PPP mounted a vigorous counterattack during the last two weeks of the campaign. Organizational efforts were redoubled and the party's principal campaigners intensified their verbal assaults on the opposition . . . [On election day] Polling places were alleged to have been closed for hours, ballot boxes removed at gun point, multiple voting confessed to, and marked ballots found on the streets . . . More probably, the widespread vote fraud resulted not on direct orders by the center but on the local initiatives of party and government officials anxious to demonstrate their efficiency and to protect their jobs and influence. The PPP's majority was, in all likelihood, more padded than stolen.[87]

In the run-up to the election, Bhutto's supporters had bent the rules, which created justification for charges of election rigging. Bhutto was himself elected unopposed in his parliamentary district, as were his provincial chief ministers in similar unopposed elections. In each case, the opposition candidates (mostly from the Jamaat-e-Islami) were abducted by police to prevent them from filing their nomination papers. Although Bhutto and his associates were assured of easy electoral victories in their districts, they resorted to this tactic to establish an aura of being above the political fray. Bhutto's former press secretary, Khalid Hasan, later wrote:

The news of Bhutto's "unopposed" election was released to the national press by the Ministry of Information and Broadcasting. The Secretary, Masood Nabi Noor, [a civil servant], had also supplied the Prime Minister's picture with three captions that had been lifted from Kim il Sung's book. Newspapers had been requested to use one of the three. The *Dawn* turned the tables on the Ministry by printing the picture of the Prime Minister on the front page, underscored by not one but all three captions.[88]

The three captions were "Undisputed Leader," "Supreme Leader," and "Great Leader." An unopposed election carried out in this manner and the description of an elected leader in such exaggerated language was hardly in keeping with the traditions of parliamentary democracy. Even before votes were cast or counted, the foundations had been laid for questioning the integrity of the election process.

On election day, the PPP won 155 seats in the National Assembly, with 58.1 percent of the total votes cast. The PNA secured 36 seats, with 35.4 percent of the votes. The opposition won in NWFP and in all the major cities where they held large rallies, with the exception of Lahore in the Punjab. The PNA's poor showing in Punjab province—only 8 seats out of 116—created the impression in the minds of almost everyone, including Bhutto himself, that the election results may have been altered. To this day there is considerable controversy over who was responsible for the partial rigging of the 1977 poll. Some PNA leaders still blame Bhutto personally for the election irregularities, which was also the position of the generals who overthrew him.[89] But the U.S. ambassador, Henry Byroade, who had been invited by Bhutto on the evening of election day to watch the results on television with him, paints a different picture:

[Bhutto] was losing in Karachi. He was losing in Peshawar. Then the Punjab numbers started coming in and guys who were absolute thugs won by 99 percent . . . Then [Bhutto] became absolutely quiet and started drinking heavily, calling Lahore, and he said, "What are you guys doing? . . ." I saw Bhutto at 8 the next morning, and he wasn't himself. He hadn't had any sleep, obviously drinking. He was just sad.[90]

The PNA and its supporters vociferously questioned the election results and the PPP responded by listing reasons why it had won so overwhelmingly. The PNA allegations were probably exaggerated as was the extent of the PPP's electoral victory. As Weinbaum points out, however, "whatever the extent or origins of the election irregularities, in just a matter of days the legitimacy of the entire electoral exercise had been irretrievably lost."[91]

Bhutto realized that the election results had been tampered with. He immediately contacted the PNA leadership and sought an arrangement that would increase the PNA's representation in the National Assembly. According to Kausar Niazi, Bhutto was informed by his political colleagues the day after the election that thirty to forty seats of the National Assembly had been rigged. He said, "Can't we tell the PNA that if by-elections to these seats are held, we would put up no candidates?"[92] During the three days following the election, the prime minister made at least two contacts with Mufti Mahmood, the cleric who served as the PNA's president,[93] but the PNA leadership had decided to take their battle against Bhutto to the streets.

The alliance boycotted the provincial assembly election on March 10 and called a nationwide strike on March 11. Then a violent protest campaign was launched initially to demand fresh elections. Under the stewardship of the religious parties, the agitation later started calling for Nizam-e-Mustafa (the system of the Prophet of Islam). After a ban on rallies and demonstrations, the PNA used mosques as centers for organizing its protests, which accentuated the religious color of the opposition to Bhutto although secular activists remained part of the PNA. At least two hundred people were killed in clashes between demonstrators and security forces over a period of three months.[94] Bhutto was forced to seek the military's help in quelling the protests. Soon military officers started refusing to obey orders to shoot demonstrators. General Arif, one of Zia ul-Haq's principal staff officers in the GHQ who became his chief of staff, wrote later that the political situation put immense strain on the military:

> The demonstrators accused the army of siding with the administration. They wanted the troops to support their agitation. Through a postal campaign, many letters were received by the military personnel, urging them not to implement the orders given by an "illegal" government. The troops were urged to support the popular public demand for enforcing the Shariah Law in Pakistan. The appeal had a psychological impact. Gradually, it started adversely affecting the soldiers, who, by tradition, were religious-minded. Some of the military commanders expressed apprehensions that a prolonged exposure of troops to public agitation might erode their military discipline.[95]

After Zia ul-Haq's coup d'état, Bhutto and his supporters raised questions over whether the "strains on the military" and the religious color of the protests were mere justifications for return to military rule. If the dispute between the PNA and Bhutto had been about the fairness of the March 7 National Assembly election only, that could have been resolved through a political settlement. Now the demonstrators, small in numbers but ferocious in commitment, were demanding an Islamic system of government. They were also accusing Bhutto of being the antithesis of an Islamic leader. Even before the controversy over the election, the Jamaat-e-Islami's founder, Maulana Maududi, had declared that "only Nizam-e-Islam (Islamic system) would be acceptable in Pakistan."[96] The agitators clearly wanted something more than fresh elections, and their demand for Bhutto's removal could be fulfilled only through a military coup d'état.

In April, after the protests had lasted more than a month, Bhutto announced that Sharia law would be enforced in six months and declared "immediate total prohibition on the use of alcohol, complete ban on gambling in all forms and [on] night clubs."[97] The PNA, which had earlier not responded to offers of compromise on the election results, refused to accept these Islamic measures as sufficient to meet its demand for Islamization; it demanded Bhutto's resignation. At the urging of the ambassador of Saudi Arabia to Pakistan and a member of the PLO Executive Committee, the PNA agreed to a dialogue with Bhutto in June. By now, the Islamists were in full control of the PNA protest campaign and also had a leading role in its negotiating committee. On July 5, 1977, although participants in the parleys stated the two sides were close to agreement over holding fresh elections, the military took over.[98]

The military claimed that it was forced to intervene because Bhutto's talks with the PNA were going nowhere and the country was on the brink of complete breakdown. The Islamic parties, especially the Jamaat-e-Islami, celebrated the takeover by the new military ruler, General Zia ul-Haq, by distributing sweets in the streets of major cities and outside mosques. Zia ul-Haq declared:

> I want to make it absolutely clear that neither I have any political ambitions nor does the army want to be taken away from its profession of soldiering . . . My sole aim is to organize free and fair elections, which would be held in October this year . . . Soon after the polls, power will be transferred to the elected representatives of the people. I give my solemn assurance that I will not deviate from this schedule. During the next three months my total attention will be concentrated on the holding of elections and I would not like to dissipate my energies as Chief Martial Law Administrator on anything else.[99]

But Zia ul-Haq postponed the elections, and one year later included the PNA in his cabinet. He initiated the process of Islamizing the country's laws and institutions. In 1979, Zia ul-Haq executed Zulfikar Ali Bhutto after trying him for plotting to murder a political opponent. General elections were not held until 1985, only after excluding all political parties from the election process.

Several of General Zia ul-Haq's associates and some observers have gone to elaborate lengths to prove that Zia's decision to remove Bhutto from power and impose martial law was forced by circumstances and not premeditated. Zia ul-Haq, they say, intended to hold elections as he promised but was forced to change his mind after he learned of Bhutto's misdeeds and out of fear of retribution in case Bhutto won the election.[100] But Zia's close ties with the Islamists who led the agitation that provided him with the excuse for his coup indicate greater forethought on his part than is often conceded.

Brigadier Tafazzul Hussain Siddiqi, head of ISI public relations, related that Zia ul-Haq had asked him to visit Bhutto's home province, Sindh, in April to assess whether the people would accept martial law.[101] The three service chiefs and the chairman of the joint chiefs issued an unprecedented statement on April 27, 1977, affirming their unity in "support of the present legally constituted government."[102] The statement provided Zia ul-Haq with an alibi of good intentions in supporting the civilian government until it was no longer feasible to do so. On the other hand, it also hardened Bhutto's stance in dealing with the opposition. On May 7, 1977, Zia ul-Haq sent a command communication to all military formations:

In the aftermath of National Assembly elections, the country is unfortunately gripped in the frenzy of agitational politics . . . What is our duty today? We ought to obey the legally constituted government. It is argued that the elections were unfair. Are we in the army justified to pass a judgement? Is there not legally constituted machinery to adjudicate such issues? Are there not the High Courts and the Supreme Court to judge such allegations? Should the army listen to the processionists to decide what is right or wrong . . . ? Let the army not be the judge regarding the legality of the government.[103]

While appearing to be politically correct, Zia ul-Haq also maintained covert contacts with the opposition. According to Nawabzada Nasarullah

Khan, one of the PNA leaders, the ISI had contacted some PNA leaders during the course of PNA negotiations with Bhutto and told the leaders not to trust Bhutto.[104] The PNA secretary general, Professor Ghafoor Ahmad, also confirms this version;[105] the military promised the PNA leaders a fair election and a share in power. For its part, the Jamaat-e-Islami, which had been the driving force in the protests against Bhutto, denies any collusion with Zia ul-Haq before the imposition of martial law although it supported the military takeover once it was effective.[106] It is possible that intelligence operatives in the military let the Islamists manage the violent protests while they permitted another set of politicians to make difficult any deal between Bhutto and the opposition.

Zia ul-Haq apparently misled Bhutto by telling Bhutto that the military would accept the breaking of his stalemate with the PNA if Bhutto held a referendum; Zia's senior commanders, however, had insisted on resolving the deadlock through fresh elections.[107] Several other developments preceding the imposition of martial law by Zia ul-Haq also appear suspicious. Bhutto, citing a conversation of a U.S. embassy official that could only have been intercepted by the Pakistani intelligence services, accused the United States of orchestrating the agitation against him.[108] Bhutto was informed by the intelligence services that his party's left wing was involved in the street protests,[109] which might explain his attempt to balance his rightward policy tilt with a dose of anti-Americanism.

In the middle of his negotiations with the PNA, after a basic compromise had been reached, Bhutto set off in June on an unexplained trip to six Muslim countries, including Saudi Arabia, Iran, and Afghanistan.[110] His sudden departure created suspicion among the opposition about his real intentions, and the terms of the deal between the two parties had to be renegotiated. At one stage of the negotiations, the ISI chief accompanied Bhutto and briefed PNA politicians about "the military threat to Pakistan."[111] In his last days, Bhutto believed that Zia ul-Haq and the ISI chief, Lieutenant General Ghulam Jilani Khan, provided conflicting advice and information to both himself and the opposition, thereby hardening the posture of each side, in an effort to make it impossible for the politicians to overcome their mutual distrust.[112] Soon after the coup d'état, Jilani relinquished command of the ISI and became secretary for defense. Later he was appointed governor of Punjab, a position from which he helped Zia ul-Haq create a patronage-based civilian following.

When Zia ul-Haq took over on July 5, 1977, he claimed he had done so because talks between the government and the opposition had broken down. The military operation for effecting his coup d'état was codenamed Operation Fairplay to indicate that its purpose was to facilitate disengagement between warring political factions and ensure free elections. Zia ul-Haq and his military associates portrayed the coup as a spontaneous response to a difficult situation, but their accounts are replete with contradictions. In an interview with Edward Behr of *Newsweek* soon after the coup, Zia was asked, "How and when did you decide the time had come to take this step [impose martial law]?" He said, "I am the only man who took this decision and I did so at 1700 hours on 4th July after hearing the press statement which indicated that the talks between Mr. Bhutto and the opposition had broken down. Had an agreement been reached between them, I would certainly never have done what I did."[113] However, Zia ul-Haq's chief of staff, General Arif, quotes the ISI's General Jilani as saying that he warned Bhutto of an impending coup d'état on July 3 and asked that he rush the negotiations with the opposition.[114]

By most accounts, the talks had not broken down even though the coup d'état was very much in the offing. Zia ul-Haq also alleged later that the coup had been necessitated by the prospect of civil war and that Bhutto had been planning to distribute weapons to his supporters. General Arif supports the allegation by narrating a June 20 conversation between Zia ul-Haq and Bhutto.[115] After the coup d'état, the generals did not try Bhutto on the charge of planning civil war, and no weapons were recovered from PPP supporters to prove such a plan.

Another of Zia ul-Haq's military colleagues, Lieutenant General Jahan Dad Khan, claims that Zia originally intended to be only an impartial referee but that he changed his mind about holding elections after he came to power:

The General himself told me during a visit to Hyderabad on 14 September 1977 that some of the things which had come to light during the last two months had made him change his mind about his future course of action. He mentioned a number of financial, political and administrative irregularities committed by Bhutto which a patriotic and sincere leader could not even think of.[116]

But Roedad Khan, a civil servant who served as interior secretary under Zia ul-Haq and therefore was boss of the civilian law enforcement agencies, tells a different story. Two decades later he wrote:

The coup against Bhutto and the imposition of martial law were not justified in the circumstances prevailing just before the promulgation of martial law. The resurrection of the murder case against Bhutto, his arrest and subsequent trial were politically motivated. Bhutto did not get a fair trial. He was a doomed man once the army decided to topple him.[117]

In his very first speech as chief martial law administrator, Zia ul-Haq described himself as a "Soldier of Islam." He praised the spirit of Islam that had characterized the PNA protests, adding:

It proves that Pakistan, which was created in the name of Islam, will continue to survive only if it sticks to Islam. That is why I consider the introduction of [an] Islamic system as an essential prerequisite for the country.[118]

By declaring his commitment to building a new political, economic, and social order based on religion, Zia ul-Haq had laid the foundations for reneging on his promise of holding elections. He later asserted that he had come to power not to hold elections, but to enforce Islam. Just as the religious parties in the PNA had gradually shifted their agenda from demanding fresh elections to seeking complete enforcement of Nizam-e-Mustafa, Zia ul-Haq, too, changed course gradually.

Within days of his military takeover, Zia ul-Haq created an election cell comprising two serving generals and two retired generals. Secular politicians could not help but note that one of them—Major General Rao Farman Ali Khan—"had the benefit of a fairly long experience in the field of political manipulation and had been the political adviser to successive governors of East Pakistan, prior to the surrender of the army in Dacca . . . Ostensibly created to establish liaison with political parties to work out a programme for elections, the cell was in fact meant to do precisely the opposite."[119] On September 1, 1977, when Zia ul-Haq held a press conference in Lahore, he suggested that the election date "is not in the Quran,"[120] meaning that it was not sacrosanct. At the same press conference came a hint of the continuity of thought between Zia ul-Haq and the other generals who had ruled Pakistan; Zia said, "This country can be kept together by Armed forces and not by politicians."[121] Just as Yahya Khan had declared at the time of the 1970 election, Zia ul-Haq said, "Parties with manifestos against Pakistani ideology and Islam will not be allowed to take part in the elections."[122]

If Zia ul-Haq had wanted to impose a military-backed theocracy from the beginning, why did he and his military colleagues go to such lengths to claim they had stepped in only to restore democracy? Each of Pakistan's military rulers has made an effort to justify his military coup d'état in terms of the failings of civilians. Pakistan's generals like to be seen as the country's saviors and do not like being viewed as conspirators orchestrating events for personal or institutional power. This tradition was a major factor in Zia ul-Haq's desire to let his dispensation appear improvised, and, indeed, some of his decisions were probably spur of the moment. The timing and circumstances of the 1977 coup d'état also dictated that military rule be presented as a temporary arrangement, at least until all bases were covered.

Operation Fairplay and the story about being gradually sucked into power were necessary to make military rule credible. The military had been out of power for five years, and the events of 1971, which resulted in military defeat, were relatively recent. Zia ul-Haq had ousted a very popular politician. Pakistanis had just gone through a period of intense politics. A cooling-off period was needed to get the nation in a frame of mind that would acquiesce to military rule. The military, too, may not have been of one mind about returning to government, and time was needed to create relative homogeneity within the military's top ranks. Abroad, Jimmy Carter had been inaugurated as president of the United States barely a few months earlier. Carter had emphasized human rights as a plank of his foreign policy platform. Zia ul-Haq needed time to determine the level of U.S. support he could expect for his military dictatorship. Until he knew he would not face a domestic uprising or international isolation, Zia had to keep promising elections and then wriggle out of his promise each time with a new set of reasons and altered circumstances.

In his study of contemporary praetorianism, Eric Nordlinger pointed out that "the military usually act against civilian governments that have evidenced one or more performance failures."[123] Military intervention in politics is often motivated by the military's corporate interests but the Praetorians must appear to be acting in the public interest. According to Nordlinger, "it becomes easier to justify the overthrow of governments whose performance failures have lost them the respect of soldiers and civilians alike . . . the military only act against less than legitimate governments." The coup succeeds mainly because "a large proportion of politicized citizens are not offended by the government's demise, if not positively delighted with its overthrow."[124] In case of Zia ul-Haq's coup against Bhutto, the Islamists were pleased with Bhutto's ouster as were most of his other opponents. Bhutto's resort to emergency laws against critics of his regime amounted to "performance failure" in the eyes of those who expected him to act democratically. The dispute over the March 1977 election, and the delay in attempting to resolve that dispute, eroded the legitimacy of the Bhutto government.

Bhutto, despite his weaknesses and mistakes, had succeeded in creating a new Pakistani order in which secular civilians attained ascendancy. The military could not return to power without undermining the legitimacy of this civilian order, and the military managed to do so with the help of its Islamist allies. Bhutto failed to protect his new Pakistan against this onslaught of the mosque-military combine largely because he accommodated too much of old Pakistan in his new order. It can be argued that Bhutto's downfall was partly the result of his compromises with the forces of obscurantism and his desire for a large military beholden to him. Pakistan reverted to military rule as a result of the religious sentiment unleashed during the PNA campaign against Bhutto, and this time military rule was beholden to Islamists as never before. Zia ul-Haq not only attained power as a result of the mosque-military alliance, he also worked assiduously to strengthen it over the next eleven years.

4

From Islamic Republic to Islamic State

General Muhammad Zia ul-Haq became Pakistan's third military ruler on July 5, 1977, ostensibly to hold elections within ninety days. He ruled for eleven years—the longest tenure of any of Pakistan's rulers to date—until his death in a mysterious plane crash on August 17, 1988. Zia ul-Haq is often identified as the person most responsible for turning Pakistan into a global center for political Islam. Undoubtedly, Zia went farthest in defining Pakistan as an Islamic state, and he nurtured the jihadist ideology that now threatens to destabilize much of the Islamic world; but in doing so he saw himself as carrying forward the nation- and state-building project that started soon after the demise of Pakistan's founder, Muhammad Ali Jinnah.

Like his military and civil service predecessors, Zia ul-Haq did not trust representative institutions to ensure the country's integrity. He believed that Pakistan's survival required it to be an ideological state, carefully run under the guidance of the military and the intelligence services. Like Ayub and Yahya before him as well as several Pakistani leaders before them, Zia ul-Haq hated Hindu India, sought national unity in the name of Islam, and hoped that the United States could be persuaded to foot the bill for Pakistan's security and economic development. He also shared with previous Pakistani rulers the dream of pan-Islamic unity, with a position of leadership for Pakistan within the Muslim world community of believers (*umma*). Whereas Zia ul-Haq's predecessors had seen

Islam only as an instrument of policy, Zia ul-Haq had the fire of a true believer.

 Unlike other Pakistani rulers, Zia ul-Haq was not averse to assigning the ulema and religious parties a significant role in affairs of the state. While Zia ul-Haq's secular critics perceived him as cynically manipulating Islam for the survival of his own regime, some Islamic ideologues felt he was not going far enough in recreating a puritanical state. Exigencies of statecraft required compromises instead of ideology, and Zia ul-Haq compromised. If Zia's predecessors had been totally cynical in using Islam as a unifying ideology for an otherwise disparate populace, Zia was only partly cynical. Part of him actually believed in the notion of Islamic revival through political means.

Most accounts of Zia ul-Haq's life confirm that he came from a religious family and that religion played an important part in molding his personality.[1] His father, Akbar Ali, worked as a civilian official in army headquarters and was known as Maulvi Akbar Ali because of his religious devotion.[2] Maulvi literally means "devoted to God" and is a title normally used for clerics. Zia ul-Haq joined the army before partition, and he occasionally offended his British superiors with his refusal to give up religious and cultural traditions and to adopt the Westernized ways of British Indian officers. Zia attributed his personal resistance to the "lifestyle common among the officers of the British Indian cavalry and the Pakistan armour corps" to "my faith in God and his teachings."[3]

Zia said, "Drinking, gambling, dancing and music were the way the officers spent their free time. I said prayers, instead. Initially I was treated with some amusement—sometimes with contempt—but my seniors and my peers decided to leave me alone after some time."[4] Zia's brother, Amin ul-Haq, noted that when Zia was a junior officer in the Pakistan army, he shut down the mess of his unit during the fasting hours of Ramadan, the Muslim month of abstinence.[5] General Khalid Mahmud Arif, who had known Zia ul-Haq since his days as a captain in the army and had served as his chief of staff as well as vice chief of army staff under his command, ascribes Zia ul-Haq's "religious streak" to his "non-military background" and "humble lineage."[6] According to Arif, Zia ul-Haq's religious devotion "developed with age and experience, and became visibly pronounced as he rose in status."[7] Arif claims that Zia ul-Haq was "not a bigot" because he did not insist on others joining him in prayer and he "never imposed his personal religious beliefs on others, directly or indirectly."[8] Arif acknowledges, however, that "[i]t was a matter of faith with [Zia ul-Haq] to combine politics with religion and [to] govern an Islamic country in accordance with the dictates of the Quran and Sunnah [Prophet Muhammad's tradition]."[9]

In an interview with the British Broadcasting Corporation (BBC) in April 1978, Zia ul-Haq agreed with the assertion that he had a mission "to purify and to cleanse Pakistan."[10] Asked whether he was a puritan, he said, "All I can say is that I try to be a practicing Muslim. If in the process, I can be termed a puritan, it is up to those who judge . . . I am an idealist in all my Islamic beliefs but I don't profess to have all the knowledge . . . [I]f one can bring back Islam in its purity, it would be a good thing."[11] Zia ul-Haq declared himself a "firm believer in God and destiny," and expressed the belief that he would do "something for Pakistan" with the help of "the hand of Providence" that he saw as supporting him.[12] During the next few years, Zia ul-Haq repeatedly expressed his conviction of fulfilling a God-given mission; he even went to the extent of saying that he would stay in power for "as long as Allah wills."[13]

Within days of assuming power, Zia ul-Haq initiated a process of Islamization of laws and society. This detracted from the declared objective of the military coup d'état of July 5, 1977, which was to resolve the impasse between the PPP and the PNA over the fairness of general elections. Some of the earliest actions of Zia ul-Haq's military regime were aimed at settling Pakistan's ideological direction firmly in favor of Islamization. Even if elections had been held within a few months of the coup d'état, the newly elected government would have faced the challenge of undoing extensive lawmaking undertaken by the military authorities soon after the coup. By the end of 1978, a doctrinaire interpretation of Islam became pronounced at the official level, leading a foreign observer to comment:

A general Islamic tone pervades everything, obviously much influenced by the President, who has performed both *Umra* and *Haj* [pilgrimages to Mecca] this year. Government letters are now to begin with "Bismillah," invoking the name of Allah, the merciful and benevolent. A state enterprise advertises for a manager "who should be a God fearing and practicing Muslim." Floggings are common. Television has been greatly changed—to the accompaniment of public protest in the letters-to-the-editors column of the newspapers. Total closure of eating and drinking places between sunup and sunset marked Ramzan, the holy month of fasting, and no tea was served in business establishments or offices, private or public. There has been adverse comment about the Islamization. An Arab observer has called it "petro-Islam," and Hanif Ramay, a former PPP stalwart who has started the Musawat Party, said that the type of Islamic system being introduced was "nothing short of theocracy." Jinnah's stand in favor of a secular state finds its way into letters to the editors . . . On December 2 [1978] (the first of Muharram, the beginning of the Hijri year 1399) came the long promised announcement of the first steps toward Islamization of the laws. Islamic laws on theft, drinking, adultery, and the protection of freedom of belief are to be enforced from the twelfth of Rabi-ul-Awwal (in February 1979), the birthday of the Prophet [Muhammad]. The government will constitute provincial Shariat benches at the High Court level and an Appellate Shariat Bench at the Supreme Court level. These Islamic courts will decide whether any law is partly or wholly un-Islamic, and the government will be obliged to change the law. The period for compliance is not specified in the Ordinance. The Shariat benches will also be able to examine laws even if no case is brought before them . . . Simultaneously with the legal measures, Zia announced the first steps toward an Islamic economy . . . Final steps toward an economy free of "the curse of usury," said Zia, will come as soon as the experts "are able to find a practicable solution."[14]

 Although a number of observers, including some of Zia ul-Haq's colleagues, attribute his Islamizing zeal solely to his personal religiosity, Zia ul-Haq described his policies as the fulfillment of Pakistan's national objective. Zia ul-Haq offered an insight into his motives and thinking in the January 1979 interview with British journalist Ian Stephens, author of *Horned Moon*—a sympathetic account of the emergence of Pakistan.

Stephens, who said he was speaking "virtually as an honorary Muslim," voiced his concern over the attention being paid to Islamization "to the detriment of the basic economic problems" of Pakistan. Zia ul-Haq replied:

The basis of Pakistan was Islam. The basis of Pakistan was that the Muslims of the sub-continent are a separate culture. It was on the two-nation theory that this part was carved out of the sub-continent as Pakistan. And in the last 30 years in general but more so in the last seven years there has been a complete erosion of the moral values of our society. You will hear that Pakistan is full of corruption today. In spite of one-and-a-half years of Martial Law, corruption is at large, people are dishonest; they want to make money overnight. All this is not my feeling but fact. The moral fiber of the society has been completely broken and this was done basically in the last seven and a half years. Mr. Bhutto's way of flourishing in this society was by eroding its moral fiber . . . He eroded the moral fiber of the society by pitching the students against the teachers, sons against the fathers, landlords against the tenants, and factory workers against the mill owners . . . The economic ills of the country are not because Pakistan is incapable of economic production. It is because Pakistanis have been made to believe that one can earn without working . . . Therefore, to my mind the most fundamental and important basis for the whole reformation of society is not how much cotton we can grow or how much wheat we can grow. Yes, they are in their own place important factors; but I think it is the moral rejuvenation which is required first and that will have to be done on the basis of Islam, because it was on this basis that Pakistan was formed . . . We are going back to Islam not by choice but by the force of circumstances. If we had chosen we might as well have stayed with India. What was wrong with that? . . . It is not because of anything other than our cultural and moral awareness that in Islam is our only salvation . . . Islam from that point of view is the fundamental factor. It comes before wheat and rice and everything else. I can grow more wheat; I can import wheat but I cannot import the correct moral values."[15]

Zia ul-Haq then went on to say in the same interview that it was not he or the government that was imposing Islam. It was what "99 percent of the people" wanted. He argued that the street protests against Bhutto reflected the people's desire for Islamic laws, just as the campaign for the creation of Pakistan in 1946–1947 reflected a wish to return to Islamic values. "I am just giving the people what they want,"[16] he argued.

It is significant that Zia ul-Haq identified Bhutto's elected civilian regime with moral degeneration and described its socialist orientation as an attempt to upset the Pakistani order of things. He appeared to equate martial law with rebuilding society's moral fiber, which explains his expression of surprise over the fact that corruption persisted "in spite of one-and-a-half years of Martial Law." Zia ul-Haq clearly thought the Pakistani military superior to its civilians. He was unwilling to criticize his military predecessors, how they ruled for longer than Bhutto and should have received at least some of the blame for the erosion of morals "in the last 30 years." Equally significant was his assertion that Islam was the basis of Pakistan and that Islamization only reflected the people's will. It did not matter if the people had not voted for Islamization of laws. The matter had been settled during the campaign for Pakistan before independence and more recently during the anti-Bhutto protests.

For Zia ul-Haq, Islam was Pakistan's salvation and the characteristic that distinguished the relatively new country from India. He was not alone in that belief. The *New York Times* reported from Islamabad that Zia ul-Haq's Islamization was "being described by some of its advocates as essential therapy to resolve a longstanding national crisis of identity."[17] The newspaper interviewed a "liberal and worldly Pakistani official," who sympathized with the overall aims of Islamization even though he worried about parts of it "like many intellectuals." The official summed up his views in a question, "If we are not Muslims, what are we? Second-rate Indians?"

The support of civilian and military officers who did not personally observe most aspects of Islam was crucial to Zia ul-Haq's project of clearly defining Pakistan as an Islamic state. In the political arena, however, Zia ul-Haq turned toward the organized religious parties, especially the Jamaat-e-Islami, both for political support and ideological inspiration. The Jamaat-e-Islami became "a pillar of the Zia regime and an ardent supporter of the general's Islamic state."[18] Zia ul-Haq also included other sectarian and religious organizations among his regime's civilian supporters. Collaboration with Zia ul-Haq's military regime strained some religious parties internally. During the preceding three decades the Jamaat-e-Islami had emphasized constitutionalism and cultivated its image as a mainstream Islamic political party. A section of the Jamaat-e-Islami leadership was concerned about its political prospects in the event of restoration of democracy if it were seen as aligned with a military regime. Zia ul-Haq understood the need for providing "political cover" to his allies while seeking their support as cover for his own gradual consolidation of power.

Within three months of taking power, General Zia coerced Pakistan's judiciary into approving his extra-constitutional coup d'état and his decision to hold the constitution in abeyance. Basing its judgment on the doctrine of necessity, the court gave Zia broad powers to make new laws and even to amend the constitution.[19] A military regime lacking a constitutional basis had succeeded in creating the legal fiction of constitutionality. Jamaat-e-Islami and others working with Zia ul-Haq could now argue that they were still operating under a constitutional framework.

During his first two years in power Zia ul-Haq publicly maintained the image of his regime as an interim arrangement pending elections. During his first weeks in power, however, Zia promulgated military rules for civil conduct "more thorough and comprehensive than those issued by previous martial law governments."[20] In September 1977, in the middle of the campaign for the election scheduled by Zia for October, Zulfikar Ali Bhutto was arrested on the charge of conspiring to murder a political opponent. The charges stemmed from an assassination bid three years earlier that had resulted in the death of the father of a PPP dissident member of Parliament. Religious parties and the Muslim League celebrated Bhutto's arrest and at their political rallies started demanding his execution.

Bhutto's trial was dragged through the courts for more than eighteen months, but Zia ul-Haq had already decided to portray the man he had overthrown as an evil genius. Islamist media joined Zia in a propaganda campaign similar to that unleashed against Bhutto during the 1970 elections by Major General Sher Ali Khan. Zia ul-Haq's friend, Abdul

Qayyum, has since written that Zia asked him to start preparing a white paper on Bhutto's "misdeeds" in October 1977, within days of Bhutto's arrest and well before he had been convicted.[21] Although Abdul Qayyum did not write the white paper, a four-volume white paper was published before Bhutto's execution in April 1979. The volume on alleged election irregularities alone comprised 405 pages, with 1,044 pages of appendix.[22] During the run-up to Bhutto's execution, state-run radio and television ran a series titled *Zulm ki Dastanein* (Tales of Oppression).[23] Islamist newspapers and magazines ran excerpts from the white paper, subsidized by generous advertisements from public sector enterprises.

Zulfikar Ali Bhutto was convicted of murder by the Lahore High Court in a trial of dubious legality.[24] After confirmation of the conviction by the reconstituted Supreme Court, Bhutto was executed in April 1979. The Jamaat-e-Islami was part of Zia ul-Haq's cabinet during the crucial period of Bhutto's trial and execution, and the party's nominee held the crucial portfolio of information minister. Jamaat-e-Islami joined Zia's cabinet when Zia, claiming that political participation in the government was necessary to pave the way for general elections, included members of the PNA in government one year after the coup d'état. In fact, the inclusion of the PNA in the cabinet was designed to deflect the blame for Bhutto's execution from the military and to share it with Bhutto's opponents.

The PNA remained in government for almost a year. During this period, the Jamaat-e-Islami controlled ministries that allowed it to expand its influence through patronage and provide employment to its younger cadres. In addition to information and broadcasting, Jamaat-e-Islami ministers were in charge of the ministries for production, and water, power, and natural resources. Zia ul-Haq also appointed a Jamaat-e-Islami ideologue, Professor Khurshid Ahmad, to head Pakistan's Planning Commission and draw up plans for Islamizing the economy.

At the end of their year-long association with the government, Jamaat-e-Islami ministers complained that the entrenched bureaucracy wielded greater influence than they did. Zia ul-Haq realized that he had overestimated the Jamaat-e-Islami's ability to run a modern Islamic state.[25] After that year, in an effort to create his own hybrid Islamic system for Pakistan, Zia decided to cast a wider net to find Islamists of different persuasions.

This opened the way for many clerics and Islamic spiritual leaders from all over the world to advise Zia ul-Haq. The general held dozens of conferences and seminars of Islamic scholars and spiritualists (*mashaikh*). He issued numerous decrees, some as banal as prohibiting urinals in public places (because the Prophet Muhammad advised against urinating while standing) and others with significant consequences, such as liberalizing visas for Muslim ulema and students from all over the world. The liberalization of visas for Muslim activists enabled Islamists from several countries to set up headquarters in Pakistan, circumventing restrictions on Islamist political activities in their own countries.

In 1979, Jamaat-e-Islami's support for Bhutto's execution was central to Zia ul-Haq's plan to suppress any resistance from PPP supporters to Bhutto's elimination. Zia ul-Haq met the Jamaat-e-Islami chief, Mian Tufail Muhammad, for ninety minutes the night before Bhutto was hanged.[26] Jamaat-e-Islami members took to the streets to celebrate Bhutto's death, which countered international criticism and domestic disapproval of the ruthless execution of the ruling general's main political rival.

The Jamaat-e-Islami's founder and spiritual leader, Maulana Abul Ala Maududi, set the tone for his party's relationship with Zia ul-Haq's military regime by endorsing Zia's initiatives for Islamization. Maulana Maududi described these steps as "the renewal of the covenant" between the government of Pakistan and Islam[27] and also endorsed Zia's demonization of Bhutto and the PPP by arguing if the PPP were allowed to run in a general election again, the country would face a debacle similar to the one witnessed when East Pakistan separated from West Pakistan.[28] When Maulana Maududi died in September 1979, Zia ul-Haq expressed his admiration for him by attending his funeral.

Although Zia ul-Haq and the Jamaat-e-Islami clearly had a soft spot for each other and enjoyed a close relationship, their ambitions did not always converge. Zia recognized that the Jamaat-e-Islami's base of support was relatively narrow, notwithstanding its impressive organization and its ability to mobilize its cadres. Moreover, the Jamaat-e-Islami was not the only religious political force in the country, and Zia ul-Haq wanted the support of other Islamic groups as well. Once the president declared his intention to Islamize Pakistan, he was confronted with several visions of what an Islamic state should look like. Zia ul-Haq also had to juggle the conflicts of interest between his parent institution, the military, and the various religious parties.

The Soviet military intervention in Afghanistan at the end of 1979 and subsequent U.S. support for his regime greatly bolstered Zia ul-Haq's confidence in domestic matters. The next chapter discusses developments in Afghanistan and the U.S.-Pakistan relationship that evolved once Pakistan became a frontline state in containing Soviet expansion. It would be sufficient to say here that the prospect of renewed American military and economic aid as well as enhanced international support enabled Zia ul-Haq to set aside promises of holding elections.

Parliamentary elections scheduled for November 17, 1979, had been postponed even before Soviet troops occupied Afghanistan on Christmas day. In the run-up to these aborted elections, Zia ul-Haq had repeatedly changed the ground rules under which they were to be conducted. He had introduced separate electorates for Muslims and non-Muslims and required political parties to fulfill registration criteria that excluded most secular political parties, notably Bhutto's PPP, from the arena. The Election Commission was authorized to cancel the registration of political parties for "propagation of any opinions or acting in any manner prejudicial to the ideology of Pakistan or the sovereignty, integrity or security of Pakistan or of views defaming or ridiculing the judiciary or armed forces."[29]

Once international attention was focused on the developments in Afghanistan, Zia ul-Haq had virtually no external or internal compulsions for returning Pakistan to democracy. Most of 1980 was spent in dealing with the influx of refugees from Afghanistan and organizing an expanded anticommunist Afghan resistance. A major step toward Islamization during that year was the introduction of government collection of *Zakat*, the 2.5 percent annual levy on accumulated assets and savings that Muslims are obligated to give to charity. The government announced that it would deduct *Zakat* from bank accounts and distribute it through a central *Zakat* administration.

The *Washington Post* reported that "a network of local committees throughout the country" was being established to distribute *Zakat* among the country's poor. "In Sind province alone, there are 7,644 separate committees, each with seven members who will be distributing funds to the needy," observed the *Post*'s reporter, adding, "This could in effect turn into a Tammany-Hall-type operation with both members of the committees and the recipients grateful to Zia."[30] The "Tammany-Hall-type" patronage network established through *Zakat* expanded the influence of existing Islamist groups and spawned several new ones.

Pakistan's Shiite population opposed the compulsory deduction of *Zakat* on grounds that their sect did not allow compulsion in collection of *Zakat*. Shiites converged in Islamabad and virtually took over the capital. According to the *Washington Post*, "Zia's martial law regime came within hair's breadth of losing power over that confrontation."[31] The Shiites were exempted from the compulsory deduction of *Zakat* as a result of these protests. The success of the protests, coming soon after Iran's Shiite Islamic revolution, contributed to the rise of Shiite radicalism in Pakistan. Shiites compose at least 10 percent of Pakistan's Muslim population. Sectarian issues had played little part in the campaign for Pakistan's creation and Pakistan's official census figures did not report sectarian identities of Muslims in an effort to keep the lid on sectarian differences among Muslims. The demand by Shiites, in the aftermath of the *Zakat* controversy, for effective representation at higher levels of the state and recognition of their sectarian interests laid the foundations of bitter Shiite-Sunni conflict, which later led to the creation of terrorist militias within both sects.[32]

To circumvent having to deal with sectarian issues, Zia ul-Haq briefly attempted to expand his power base by offering to include some influential members of the PPP in his government but "such explorations proved fruitless."[33] The Inter-Services Intelligence (ISI) was assigned the role of buying off or threatening local politicians into cooperating with the military regime. Zia ul-Haq did not, however, give up his efforts to pursue domestic legitimacy through religion. Two American academics noted that Islamic themes occurred in all contexts. "There is talk of an Islamic cargo fleet, an Islamic science foundation and an Islamic newsprint industry, and the All-Pakistan Lawn Tennis Association has instituted the Millat Cup, 'the first big tennis gala of Muslim youth.'"[34]

The ranks of the ISI were expanding considerably as the agency handled the recruitment, training, and operations of Afghan mujahideen.

Over the next eight years, the ISI channeled at least two billion dollars in U.S. covert assistance for the mujahideen and even larger sums from Saudi Arabia and other Gulf countries. The agency's domestic political role of manipulating the regime's allies and intimidating its opponents was now cloaked by the legitimate external function of fighting the evil Soviet empire. The ISI directorate's Internal Wing ran a covert operation of its own, aimed at bolstering Islamist influence at home and undermining support for opposition political parties.

The regime's task was facilitated by the hijacking to Kabul in March 1981 of a Pakistan International Airlines Boeing 727 by members of a group led by late Prime Minister Bhutto's eldest son, Murtaza Bhutto. The group *Al-Zulfikar* described itself as a guerilla group dedicated to avenging the elder Bhutto's death. The hijacking ended after thirteen days with the release of fifty-four political prisoners held by Zia ul-Haq's regime.[35] Although the PPP now led by Zulfikar Ali Bhutto's widow Nusrat and their daughter Benazir disavowed any connection to *Al-Zulfikar*, Pakistani authorities hastened to blame PPP for *Al-Zulfikar*'s actions. PPP leaders, including Benazir Bhutto, have suggested that the ISI's internal wing exaggerated the threat from *Al-Zulfikar* to justify repression of the political opposition. Several acts of sabotage and terrorism were allegedly orchestrated by agents provocateurs acting at the behest of security services and blamed on *Al-Zulfikar*. American analysts had no way of verifying the veracity of either the regime's charges or the opposition's allegations. Some of them did note, however, the advantage to Zia ul-Haq's regime resulting from the guerilla group's emergence. Threats of sabotage and terrorism, wrote Stephen Cohen and Marvin Weinbaum at the time, "amplified Zia's arguments" that "Pakistan's security was threatened from both Afghanistan and India."[36] The threat, whether real or orchestrated, proved the country's need for military rule.

Encouraged by U.S. aid and the image of being a strongman at a time of national crisis, Zia ul-Haq changed Pakistan's constitution by decree on March 24, a few days after the *Al-Zulfikar* hijacking. The provisional constitution promulgated by Zia ul-Haq gave him the authority to amend the constitution further, severely restricting the powers of the judiciary to question his orders and decisions. Members of Pakistan's Supreme

Court and provincial High Courts were required to swear allegiance to the provisional constitution and judges refusing to do so were removed. The Supreme Court Chief Justice and twelve other superior court judges were purged in this maneuver, which consolidated Zia ul-Haq's absolute rule.[37]

The provisional constitution also provided for a nominated Federal Advisory Council, named *Majlis-e-Shura* after the traditional consultative councils that assisted medieval Muslim monarchs and still found in Saudi Arabia and the Gulf Arab monarchies. The *Majlis-e-Shura* was to serve as "an appointive legislative body to be nominated from regular [parliamentary] constituencies, with membership from ten occupation groups, the ulema and ex-military personnel."[38] Although Zia ul-Haq promised that "this council will not smell of any dictatorship," the fact that he had unilaterally changed the country's constitution and opted for a handpicked legislature indicated otherwise. Zia ul-Haq argued that legislators chosen by the military for their "intellect and integrity" were preferable to elected representatives. In the military's view, "elections have given birth only to goons and chaos and confusion."[39]

Zia ul-Haq's *Majlis-e-Shura* comprised a large number of second-tier politicians from mainstream political parties, bribed or coerced into cooperating with the military regime. The discourse within this quasi-legislative body was essentially Islamic and its appointed members included a larger number of ulema and Islamist activists than any elected Pakistani legislature. Members of the *Majlis-e-Shura* debated future laws on the basis of their being Islamic or otherwise. In one year the *Majlis-e-Shura* discussed "a wide range of draconian new laws." These included "death for drug trafficking and prostitution, watchdog committees to safeguard public morals, measures to discourage women from buying jewelry and highly embroidered clothes, a ban on ballroom dancing and 'storm action' against obscene literature, in which offensive books would be burned in bonfires."[40]

Senior commanders of the military included many who did not practice religion in their private lives. They did not mind ruling in the name of Islam, and they accepted greater Islamization of laws and the judicial and economic systems; but they could not accept ceding power to any other organized group. The Jamaat-e-Islami and, later, other religious groups that agreed to cooperate with Zia ul-Haq saw Islamization from the prism of their own political ascendancy. It was not enough for Pakistan to be Islamized; it had to be Islamized by the pious leadership of the Jamaat-e-Islami or another religious party of their affiliation.

Zia ul-Haq's Islamization initiative ended up accentuating sectarian differences and plunged Pakistani society into theological debates over a wide range of issues. The general, as well as a majority of Pakistanis, was Sunni, but one in ten of Pakistan's Muslims was Shiite. Zia ul-Haq looked to Saudi Arabia for inspiration and economic support while Pakistan's Shiites were influenced by developments in Shiite-majority Iran where Ayatollah Khomeini's Islamic revolution was unfolding. The Saudis and the Iranians competed for influence in Pakistan during the Zia ul-Haq years, heightening tensions between Shiites and Sunnis through the funding of rival sectarian organizations and militias.

Islamization under Zia ul-Haq was criticized widely around the world for undermining the status of women through laws that reduced the significance of a woman's testimony to half that of a man in certain trials. Secular democrats and women's groups also opposed the Hudood Ordinance, which covered sexual offenses and prohibitions and restored Islamic punishments such as flogging. Despite their complaints that Islamization was proceeding too slowly, most Islamic groups continued to support Zia ul-Haq until his death in 1988, and they provided legitimacy to his military rule. The military was able to justify its suppression of democratic political forces, notably the PPP, by claiming that it was "building an Islamic order."[41]

Pakistani feminists noted "a particularly anti-female bias"[42] in the Islamization program. Women were ordered to cover their heads in public and the order was implemented in public schools and colleges as well as on state television. Women's sports were severely restricted as was their role in the performing arts. More significant were legal changes that in the eyes of critics "accord[ed] the legal testimony of women half the weight of the testimony of men"[43] and discriminated against women in criminal proceedings. The Law of Evidence was amended to reflect the conservative interpretation of a Quranic verse. Women entering financial contracts were required to have their signatures witnessed by another woman or a man whereas no such requirement applied to men.

Uncorroborated testimony by women was also made inadmissible in case of "Hudood" crimes (crimes specified in the Quran). Clerics supporting these laws argued that "women were emotional and irritable, with inferior faculties of reason and memory" and that courts ought to discount their testimony as well as that of "the blind, handicapped, lunatics and children." The leader of the Jamaat-e-Islami, Qazi Hussain Ahmed, declared that "those who oppose such laws are only trying to run away from Islam." He attempted to justify turning back the clock on women's role in society by saying, "These laws do not affect women adversely. Our system wants to protect women from unnecessary worry and save them the trouble of appearing in court."[44]

Officials, however, claimed that the legal changes were less significant than they appeared. American journalists routinely reported that the new Islamic laws were being put in the law books but not being implemented. "In the past 18 months, no limbs have been severed and no one has been stoned [to death]," wrote one reporter in September 1980, adding "The severest penalties imposed under Islamic law have been lashings, but none of those have been publicized in 11 months."[45] Eight years later, another American reporter said virtually the same thing. "The laws went on the books but no one's hand has been cut off, in part because doctors have refused to perform the operations. One woman convicted of adultery has been sentenced to be stoned but the case is being appealed and many doubt she will ever be punished."[46] The government's attitude was revealed in an exchange between an American journalist and the Secretary of the Ministry of Religious Affairs, I.A. Imtiazi. The official was asked how he could square General Zia ul-Haq's "repeated assertions [of treating women fairly] with the government's refusal to let women compete in the recent Asian Games in New Delhi." He explained that the government did not wish to damage Islamization even if it was occasionally distracted or forced into decisions controversial by contemporary standards. "Is it worth it?" he asked, following up with his own reply. "We have more important things to think about," Imtiazi said, apparently referring to the nation-building function of Islamization.[47]

For most of Zia ul-Haq's eleven years in power, Pakistanis debated what was or was not Islamic. A story typical of the period said:

A Pakistani youth who was sentenced last summer to have his right hand amputated for stealing a clock from a mosque is still in prison while Islamic scholars debate whether just the fingers or the whole hand should be severed and whether the amputated limb becomes the property of the state or the thief . . . A Karachi bus driver who in 1981 was sentenced to death for adultery is still awaiting a review of the piousness of the required witnesses before the sentence can be executed . . . An intense debate is continuing over whether qisas—"eye for eye" retaliation—should be imposed for injurious assault and murder or whether "blood money" compensation should be paid.[48]

Khurshid Ahmad, one of Jamaat-e-Islami's western-educated ideologues, summed up the Islamist position when he said, "A Muslim believes that family law is God-given and no secular authority has the right to fiddle with it."[49] The secular position was articulated by a female activist of the PPP who said, "The issue is whether Pakistan is to be governed by elected representatives of the people or a group of clergymen answerable to no one."[50]

Some of the laws enforced as part of Zia ul-Haq's Islamization program remain controversial to this day. Islamization had less impact on Pakistani society's observance of Islam,[51] however, than it did on the relationship between the military and the religious political groups. At the end of Zia ul-Haq's decade in power, a U.S. academic concluded that Islamization had "only a minor impact upon the political, legal, social and economic institutions of the state."[52] Professor Charles Kennedy, a scholar of Pakistan's institutions of state, said that Zia ul-Haq's rhetoric about making Pakistan "truly Islamic" as well as his critics' arguments about the reactionary character of the laws was primarily "political noise" that changed little in substantive terms.[53]

Implementation of the new Islamic laws varied in different parts of Pakistan.[54] Powerful people used the laws to punish or blackmail individuals and families that challenged their authority. The Islamic legal system that came into being operated parallel to the courts and codified law inherited from the British Raj, and the operation of the Islamic system depended largely on the devotion, or otherwise, of provincial and local authorities and individual judges.

Although Zia ul-Haq's legal reforms may have caused little change for the common Pakistani citizen, they enhanced the share of Islamic political groups within different state institutions and took the relationship between the Pakistani state and Islamic groups to a new level. Lawrence Ziring, who has observed Pakistan's internal political developments since the 1950s, saw the Zia ul-Haq era in terms of a transition from an undefined Islamic Republic to an authoritarian Islamic state:[55]

Pakistan's contemporary experiment with the construction of an Islamic State is a product of the nation's political history. Prior to independence, Islam was not in danger. Rather, many Muslims perceived themselves to be in danger. After independence was granted, it was not the Muslims of Pakistan who were in danger, but Pakistan itself. It was the need to save Pakistan that prompted the armed forces to act in 1977, and to sustain their dominant political role into the mid-1980s. Pakistan was most immediately threatened by internal forces, or at least this was the perception of the military leaders. Domestic strife and division weakened the national fabric and hence permitted external forces to gain advantage. This was the lesson of Bangladesh and it remained the responsibility of the armed forces to inform the nation of its domestic plight as well as protect it from aggressive foreign enemies. The armed forces symbolized national interest and concern . . . They firmly believed they best represented the national interest and were duty-bound to restore stability and order. Moreover, the leitmotif for the resurrection of Pakistan was Islam, and indeed an Islam that emphasized piety, discipline, conformity, and industry. There was no place for debate or differing viewpoints in this design. Pakistan's survival was at stake, and the times called for a rigid adherence to doctrine. In these circumstances and under such pressure, the Islamic State was ushered in.[56]

While Zia ul-Haq's doctrine of an Islamic state presupposed the preeminence of the military, the decision to emphasize piety and religious conformity required the induction of theologians into state institutions. The entire exercise, however, was not whimsical and was not solely the outcome of the army chief's personal beliefs. It was an extension of the Pakistan army's professed belief that a Pakistani nation could be forged only by emphasizing religious identity, and the military's stewardship was crucial to the country's survival. The military leadership justified its power, privileges, and increasing perquisites as just reward for its labor in the course of building a Pakistani nation and state.

Zia ul-Haq's military regime was characterized by much political maneuvering as the military attempted to rid Pakistan of the populist influences of the Bhutto era. According to Ziring, Zia ul-Haq's "purpose was the survival and development of Pakistan."[57] The general "did not expect the political system he had constructed to survive his departure from the scene"[58] because for him politics was ephemeral and the politicians untrustworthy. In Islamization, Zia ul-Haq saw "the realization of the raison d'être of the [Pakistani] state as well as the unity and strength of the nation."[59] Zia ul-Haq considered Islamization to be his primary contribution to Pakistan's nation-building project and thought that he was resolving the issue of Pakistan's identity by asserting the unqualified primacy of Islam.

Although outsiders perceived Zia ul-Haq very differently from the way they saw Ayub Khan and Yahya Khan, for Zia ul-Haq and his military colleagues, his period in power (1977–1988) was the continuation of the Pakistani military's efforts to define Pakistani nationhood as it maintained its patriarchal control over the state. Ayub Khan had concentrated on building ties with the United States as a means of ensuring military modernization and economic development. Yahya Khan confronted India and Indian influence in erstwhile East Pakistan even at the risk of Pakistan's division. Zia ul-Haq focused his energies on trying to create a purer Islamic state to ensure Pakistan's unity. Three elements of policy adopted soon after independence as the recipe for Pakistan's survival and growth guided each of Pakistan's military rulers even as they picked one as their primary focus. They each stuck with their choice although their regimes differed in tactics and emphasis.

Zia ul-Haq increased the role of religious leaders and clerics in the civilian administration without compromising the superior status of the armed forces. To serve alongside Western-educated jurists, Zia nominated representatives of the Islamic parties as judges of the Federal Sharia Court, the first time traditionally educated ulema had held that position since the introduction of English common law under British rule. Several clerics were able to establish large educational institutions, and in some cases even new Islamic parties, after becoming famous through their lectures on Pakistan television. State patronage expanded the influence of Islamist journalists within the government-owned media as well as in terms of the launch of new newspapers and magazines.

Pakistan's educational system also underwent significant change during the Zia ul-Haq years. Since Ayub Khan's military regime, only officially published textbooks could be used in schools from Grade 1 to college level. Pakistani governments used these mandatory textbooks, especially in social studies, to create a standard narrative of Pakistani history. Under Zia ul-Haq, textbooks were rewritten with an Islamist ideological agenda. Pakistani historian K.K. Aziz describes these textbooks as being replete with historic errors and suggests that their mandatory study amounted to the teaching of "prescribed myths."[60] After examining sixty-six textbooks for social studies and Pakistan Studies, mandatory subjects at different levels of schooling, Aziz argued that these textbooks aimed at supporting military rule in Pakistan, inculcating hatred for Hindus, glorifying wars, and distorting the pre-1947 history of the area constituting Pakistan.[61]

According to Aziz, beginning with elementary school, students were now being taught to believe that "Pakistan was a fortress of Islam"; "the advent of Islam reformed Hindu society"; "The nobles and Ulema . . . took part in the selection of a king [during Muslim rule in India]"; "the Muslims came to this country, bringing with them a clean and elegant culture and civilization . . . The Hindus are indeed indebted to Muslim culture and civilization today"; and "The Hindus wanted to control the government of India after independence. The British sided with the Hindus but the Muslims did not accept this decision."

Although Pakistan had emerged through a complex process of negotiations, and between 1858 and 1929 as many as sixty-four different schemes had been proposed for protecting the rights of Muslims in British India, Pakistani students were provided a simplified history. Every

Pakistani textbook "insists and reiterates that Islam was the first premise of the syllogism of the Pakistan demand; Islam cannot co-exist with Hinduism, therefore Muslims must separate from India; ergo, Pakistan must be created."[62] Some books went so far as to suggest that the idea of Pakistan was born the day the first Muslim set foot in India, taking the new country's history back to the eigth-century conquest of a part of modern Pakistan by Umayyad General Muhammad bin Qasim. Traditional ulema, including Jamaat-e-Islami founder Maulana Maududi, were described as being the founders of the ideology of Pakistan even when they had no direct role in the pre-independence history of the country.

The tendentious historic narrative did not end merely with arguing in favor of Pakistan's justification. The communal riots at the time of partition were described as "Hindu and Sikh massacres of unarmed Muslims." The 1965 war with India was described as a Pakistani victory, which ended only when "India sued for peace" because it was "frightened of the Pakistan army and the people of Pakistan." Ayub Khan was described as a virtuous ruler loved by all for "his piety and virtuous deeds." The separation of East Pakistan was explained away as the result of collaboration between Pakistan's "external and internal enemies" and "Indian aggression." The U.S. and the Soviet Union were both presented as enemies of Pakistan's Islamic ideology. Zulfikar Ali Bhutto was demonized as "a dictator" who did nothing "to satisfy public aspirations." Zia ul-Haq was credited with making a valuable contribution toward implementing "the Islamic system dreamed by the founders of Pakistan."[63] This Islamist bias in textbooks ensured that Zia ul-Haq's ideological influence on the hearts and minds of Pakistanis lasted well beyond his period in power.

In addition to expanding the Islamist role in the media and Pakistan's public education system, the Zia ul-Haq regime made the higher echelons of government more accessible to Islamist leaders. He regularly met with ulema and mashaikh (hereditary leaders of Sufi orders) at officially sponsored conferences as well as in well-publicized individual meetings at the President's official residence.

The access of clerics to the presidency increased their influence with the country's bureaucracy. Civil servants sought promotions by demonstrating their religious observances and inviting to religious ceremonies the divines who frequently met the president. Within the military, the culture of the British Raj was supplemented by a new culture of Quranic study groups, *zikr* meetings (prayer sessions presided over by Sufis), *Milad* (celebration of Prophet Muhammad's birth) and *tableegh* (evangelism). A nonpolitical movement, the Tableeghi Jamaat, which sought to purify the souls of Muslims by reminding them of their religious obligations, gained considerable ground.

The roots of the Tableeghi Jamaat lay in the Deoband school of thought among Pakistan's Sunnis. The Deobandis were ultraconservative in their religion, and they had traditionally stayed away from Westernizing influences. Unlike the Jamaat-e-Islami, the Deobandis did not seek a contemporary Islamic revolution and were not serious contenders for political power. They were content with emphasizing social conservatism, a demand that was easier to fulfill for the military than the notion of turning power over to a pious elite. From the military's point of view, the Jamaat-e-Islami and other religious parties had a political agenda, while the Tableeghi Jamaat did not. It was also easier to allow the Tableeghi Jamaat to operate among military officers and civil servants who were not allowed overtly to associate with political parties. Each year while he was in office, Zia ul-Haq personally attended the Tableeghi Jamaat's annual conference, increasing that group's prestige and access within the corridors of power.

A group of Deobandi scholars had participated in politics under the banner of the Jamiat Ulema Islam (JUI, Society of Islamic Scholars), but a large number of Deobandis had participated in politics only minimally until Zia ul-Haq's rise to power. By openly courting the Tableeghi Jamaat and advocating their causes, such as limiting the public role of women and officially encouraging prayer or fasting, Zia ul-Haq secured the support of a large number of previously apolitical Islamist sympathizers. He also politicized them in the process, creating a counterweight to the Islamic political parties in case they decided to withdraw their support from military rule.

Another significant impact of Zia ul-Haq's Islamization was in the sphere of higher education. Zia's military regime favored Islamist student groups and facilitated student-faculty clashes aimed at purging Pakistani universities of secular professors. Professors were penalized for refusing to accept the official view of Pakistan as an Islamic state, and those not purged preferred to resign.[64] The government also declared that the higher *sanad*—a diploma from Islamic seminaries called *madrassas*—was equivalent to a university degree. This paved the way for graduates of traditional seminaries to qualify and compete for government jobs. Thus, the Jamaat-e-Islami expanded its influence in Pakistan's universities and colleges while the Deobandi madrassas thrived with funding from Persian Gulf Arab states and private charities. Zia ul-Haq had enhanced the alliance between the mosque and the military and ensured that it would remain potent for years to come.

Zia ul-Haq's religious zeal extended to the sphere of foreign policy, and it was here that his ambitions intersected with the policies of the United States. After the 1971 military debacle that resulted in the loss of East Pakistan, the Pakistani military avoided confrontation with India and focused on reorganizing and modernizing itself. In 1975, the United States removed the ban it had imposed on military sales to Pakistan during the 1965 war, but Pakistan had not acquired any new U.S. weapons systems by the time of Zia ul-Haq's 1977 coup d'état. In addition to Islamization at home, Zia ul-Haq also paid attention to reviving U.S. military sales to Pakistan as well as securing greater U.S. economic assistance. Like Zulfikar Ali Bhutto before him, Zia sought U.S. support for Pakistan's covert operations in Afghanistan, which had begun in 1974. Although the United States was not interested initially, increased Soviet involvement in Afghanistan finally attracted U.S. attention.

Between 1978 and 1988, the U.S. provided Pakistan with $2.5 billion in economic and $1.7 billion in military aid on a bilateral basis. This was far greater than the $937 million in economic assistance and $1.7 million in military sales during the period of Bhutto's civilian administration. In addition to U.S. bilateral aid, Pakistan received generous assistance from other western donors. Expenditures by the international community on maintaining Afghan refugees in the country, as well as the covert assistance channeled to Afghan mujahideen to Pakistan also boosted Pakistan's economy, thereby extending the longevity of Zia ul-Haq's regime. Saudi Arabia and other Gulf states helped out by employing hundreds of thousands of Pakistani workers, whose remittances back home created an air of prosperity. Pakistani troops were hired by the Saudis to assist in the Kingdom's security, providing an additional source of income for Pakistan.

Parts of Pakistan, however, benefited little from this economic boom. The southern provinces of Sindh and Balochistan felt excluded from the benefits of aid and remittances. The foreign inflows favored Punjab and the North-West Frontier, with some money going to the Pashtun areas of Balochistan. Most of Pakistan's army came from the two Northern provinces as did most Pakistani workers in the Gulf. The economic advantages of Zia ul-Haq's policies muted opposition to military rule in Punjab and the North-West Frontier Province (NWFP). Pakistani workers in the Gulf and their families became either sympathetic or indifferent to Islamization. The expatriate workers were also influenced by Islamist missionaries backed by Saudi Arabia's *Wahabi* religious establishment during the course of their stay in the Gulf States.

The U.S. did not concern itself either with Zia ul-Haq's Islamization or with any of his other efforts to consolidate Pakistan as an Islamic state. The American view of Zia ul-Haq was summed up by Stephen Cohen and Marvin Weinbaum: "Although Zia is actively disliked by many Pakistanis, an increasing number have come to regard him as a necessary evil ... Zia remains a difficult target for his enemies and they have come belatedly to appreciate that whatever his limitations as a charismatic politician, he knows how to retain power."[65]

In 1983, Zia ul-Haq faced his first serious domestic challenge when violent protests against his regime rocked the southern province of Sindh, Bhutto's home region that had benefited little from Zia ul-Haq's rule. The protests were part of a nationwide campaign by the eight-party Movement for Restoration of Democracy (MRD) to force free and fair elections and the end of martial law. Although other parts of Pakistan did not significantly participate in the protests, Sindhis saw this as an occasion to voice their grievances over a wide range of issues, from lack of inclusion in government to the prospect of their becoming a minority in their own province due to emigration from the Northern provinces.[66] The military regime brutally suppressed the protests and blamed India for fomenting unrest in Sindh. The charge of Indian support was substantiated by citing Indian Prime Minister Indira Gandhi's assertion that "Indians would support all democratic movements in Pakistan."[67] Zia ul-Haq's response to the MRD protests provides an insight into the way he connected Islam and military rule to Pakistan's survival:

> Zia claimed that the martial law government was constitutional and Islamic. He went on to argue that it was the duty of Pakistanis as Muslims to obey his government because it was pursuing Islamic principles. He cited the Quran and a *hadith* (saying of the Prophet) in support of the idea that as long as the head of state followed the injunctions of Allah and his Prophet, obedience became mandatory for his subjects. Again, deriving his authority from the Quran, he pointed out that those who opposed or demonstrated against his government could be accused of waging war against an Islamic government and therefore indulging in anti-Islamic activities.[68]

In the aftermath of the protests in Sindh, Zia ul-Haq promised once again to hold elections and to open up the political system. He made it clear, however, that even after the elections he would remain in charge. What he had in mind was sharing of power with elected politicians, not transferring power to them. On December 1, 1984, Zia ul-Haq surprised both Pakistani and foreign observers by announcing a referendum that he said would ensure elections, "would strengthen ideological foundations of the country and would contribute towards national solidarity."[69] The referendum, scheduled for December 20, required voters to answer a single question: "Whether they supported the process initiated by the government for the Islamization of all laws in accordance with the Holy Quran and Sunnah and whether they supported the Islamic ideology of Pakistan."[70] An affirmative vote would automatically elect Zia ul-Haq as president for the next five years. Although Zia ul-Haq campaigned for a "yes" vote with the help of officially controlled media, the opposition was barred from running a "no" campaign.

It was apparent that the referendum was a sham and was intended only as a fig leaf of legitimacy for Zia ul-Haq's continuation in office under the cover of Islamization. The Jamaat-e-Islami officially called for a "yes" vote, arguing that the referendum was the only way toward an election and that the people of Pakistan could not vote against Islamization. Independent observers pointed out massive irregularities in the referendum process and put the voter turnout at no more than 30 percent. The official result, however, declared that more than 60 percent of Pakistan's eligible voters had cast ballots and 97.7 percent had voted yes for Islamization and Zia ul-Haq's continuation as president for the next five years.[71] The referendum demonstrated the relatively small support base for both Zia ul-Haq's military regime and the Islamist parties collaborating with his regime.

Parliamentary elections were held in Pakistan in February 1985, on a nonparty basis. This meant that candidates were not allowed to identify their political affiliation and ran as individuals in each district. Opposition parties, led by the PPP, boycotted the election, leading some of their members to resign from the parties and contest the polls.[72] Zia ul-Haq had hoped that the absence of party labels would favor personally pious individuals backed by the military as well as candidates affiliated with religious parties.[73] But his wish was not fulfilled. Most of Zia ul-Haq's cabinet ministers, running as individuals, were defeated and the elected parliament comprised mainly locally influential politicians, some of whom had been members of the PPP until recently. The Islamists failed to significantly increase their numbers in the new national assembly.

The momentum for Islamization declined after Zia ul-Haq appointed a conservative Sindhi politician, Mohammed Khan Junejo, as prime minister. Zia ul-Haq had chosen Junejo because he lacked stature and popular support and was expected to toe the military's line. Junejo, however, decided to build popular support and enhance his stature as a national politician by demanding the end of martial law in his first speech to parliament as prime minister. Junejo, his cabinet, and the national assembly refused to be a rubber stamp for Zia ul-Haq's decisions and "demonstrated an ability to chart an independent course without coming into direct confrontation with the military."[74] Parliament watered down the constitutional amendments decreed by Zia ul-Haq, martial law ended, and the pace of Islamization legislation slowed down. Junejo also revived political parties and himself became president of the Pakistan Muslim League.

Zia ul-Haq persisted with the rhetoric of Islamization even though elected politicians were reluctant to expand the sphere of Islamic laws. Junejo said he wanted to revert Pakistan to the days of the vague Islamic Republic and considered Zia ul-Haq's Sharia-based Islamic State divisive and impractical.[75] On May 29, 1988, Zia ul-Haq dissolved the National Assembly and dismissed Junejo from the office of prime minister. Within a fortnight he decreed an overarching law that required every judicial decision in the country to be based on Sharia law.[76] This marked a departure from the gradual approach to Islamization that had been practiced for over a decade. Instead of new legislation to cover specific subject areas, the new Sharia law required individual judges to rule according to Sharia and to consult theologians in determining what the Sharia required.

Zia ul-Haq's death in a mysterious plane crash on August 17, 1988, marked the end of his era, described in his obituary by the *New York Times* as the "era of Atom and Islam"[77] for Pakistan. Before Zia ul-Haq, Pakistan's establishment and the Islamists were divided by culture even when their political worldviews coincided. Pakistani generals and civil servants did not share the strong opinions of theologians and Islamists on issues such as segregation of the sexes, enforcement of Sharia laws, adherence to conservative dress codes, and public observance of religious rituals.

For the civil-military combine, Islam was a rallying cry for Pakistani nationalism and an important instrument in the conduct of foreign policy. The consequence of this cultural divide was the inability of the State to fully tap the fervor of Islamists for the policies of state relating to confronting India or expanding Pakistan's influence westwards toward Central Asia and the Middle East. Although the civil-military combine was not averse to using the Islamists, it showed little respect for them. Zia ul-Haq made it possible for the Islamists to feel empowered by the Islamic State of Pakistan. Members of the Pakistani civil and military elite, too, were now more accepting of Islamic clerics and Islamist ideologues.

The Soviet invasion of Afghanistan enabled Zia ul-Haq to play the great game of espionage and subversion that had been played between Czarist Russia and Imperialist Britain during the nineteenth century, albeit with U.S. assistance and full Islamist participation. The Afghan jihad marked the unfolding of a wider plan for global Islamic revival under Pakistani leadership that continued well beyond Zia ul-Haq.

5

Afghan Jihad

Pakistan, long wanting to extend its influence into Afghanistan, willingly accepted U.S. help and became the staging ground for the guerrilla war against the Soviet Union in Afghanistan. After Soviet troops withdrew from Afghanistan, Pakistan continued to support hard-line Islamist mujahideen in the ensuing civil war, leading to the rise to power of the Taliban, but Pakistan's involvement in Afghanistan was not just the inadvertent consequence of America's proxy war against the Soviet Union.

Although Pakistan's leaders after independence had assumed that the country would inherit the functions of India's British government in guiding Afghan policy, Afghanistan responded to the emergence of Pakistan by questioning the rationale of Pakistan. Afghanistan's initial reluctance to recognize Pakistan and Afghanistan's claim on Pakistani territory inhabited by Pashtun tribes along their shared border added to the psychological insecurity of Pakistan's leaders, who already believed that India sought to undo partition. The prospect of Afghanistan, with Indian backing, stirring the ethnic cauldron in Pakistan became part of the list of challenges that the country's leaders had to deal with to forge Pakistan's identity as an independent state. Pakistan's Afghan policy was fitted into the overarching policy tripod. Pakistan emphasized its Islamic ideology with the hope of blunting the challenge of ethnic nationalism supported by Afghanistan, tied Afghan aspirations for a Pashtunistan to an Indian plan to break up Pakistan, and sought U.S. assistance in pursuing an agenda of regional influence.

Pakistan's attitude toward Afghanistan was partly the result of historic developments that took place long before the demand for Pakistan was raised. During the nineteenth century, Britain and Russia competed for influence in Central Asia in what came to be known as the "great game" of espionage and proxy wars. Britain's great fear was the southward expansion of the Russian empire that might threaten its control over India, the "jewel in the British crown" progressively acquired during more than a century at great expense. Concerns about security against Russia pushed the frontier of British India westward. Both the Russians and the British encountered fierce resistance from Muslim tribes described by Russian Prince Alexander Gorchakov as "lawless"[1] and by British historian Arnold Toynbee as "anti-barbarian."[2] The British had lost precious lives in their effort to directly control Afghanistan. Recognizing Afghanistan as a buffer between the two empires saved the Russians and the British from having to confront each other militarily. By accepting a neutral and independent Afghan kingdom they sought to pass on the burden of subduing some of the lawless tribes to a local monarch, albeit with British economic and military assistance.

Afghanistan's frontier with British India was drawn by a British civil servant, Sir Mortimer Durand, in 1893 and was accepted by representatives of both governments. The border, named the Durand Line, intentionally divided Pashtun tribes living in the area in order to prevent them from becoming a nuisance for the Raj. On their side of the frontier, the British created autonomous tribal agencies, controlled by British political officers with the help of tribal chieftains whose loyalty was ensured through regular subsidies. The British used force to put down sporadic uprisings in the tribal areas but, in return for stability along the frontier, generally left the tribes alone.

Adjacent to the autonomous tribal agencies were the settled Pashtuns living under direct British rule in towns and villages. Here, too, the Pashtuns were divided between the NWFP and Balochistan, which did not enjoy the status of a full province under British rule. Although Muslim, Pashtuns generally sided with the cause of anti-British Indian nationalism and were late, and reluctant, in embracing the Muslim separatism of the All-India Muslim League's campaign for Pakistan. Pashtun leader Abdul Ghaffar Khan launched the Khudai Khidmatgaar (Servants of God) movement, known as Red Shirts because of their uniform, and supported the Indian National Congress. So close was the association between the Red Shirts and the Congress that Ghaffar Khan became known as the "Frontier Gandhi." Even in the 1946 election that led to the emergence of the Muslim League as the representative of Muslims throughout British India, Ghaffar Khan's Red Shirts and the Congress remained the dominant political force among Pashtuns and controlled the elected provincial government in NWFP.

When the creation of Pakistan appeared inevitable, Ghaffar Khan demanded that the Pashtun areas be allowed independence as Pashtunistan, a demand that was not accepted by the British. A referendum on whether to join Pakistan was subsequently held in NWFP—a referendum that Ghaffar Khan and his supporters boycotted—and participating voters chose inclusion in Pakistan.

Soon after Pakistan's independence, Afghanistan voted against Pakistan's admission to the United Nations, arguing that Afghanistan's treaties with British India relating to Afghan borders were no longer valid because a new country was being created where none existed at the time of the signing of these treaties. Afghanistan demanded the creation of a Pashtun state, Pashtunistan, that would link the Pashtun tribes living in Afghanistan with those in the NWFP and Balochistan. Ambiguous demands were also put forward for a Baloch state "linking Baloch areas in Pakistan and Iran with a small strip of adjacent Baloch territory in Afghanistan."[3] The most outspoken advocate of this irredentist claim was Sardar Muhammad Daoud, a cousin of Afghanistan's king, Zahir Shah, who also served as Zahir Shah's prime minister for several years.

From Pakistan's perspective, Afghanistan's claims amounted to demanding the greater part of Pakistan's territory and were clearly unacceptable. The Afghan demand failed to generate international backing, and Afghanistan did not have the military means to force Pakistan's hand. At the time, Afghanistan had a population of twelve million and a small military that could not constitute a threat to Pakistan.[4] Its claim received no support from the international community. Britain insisted that its treaties with Afghanistan remained valid for the lawful successor state— Pakistan—and Afghanistan did not formally take its claim to the United Nations.[5] In light of the overall feeling of insecurity on the part of

Pakistan's leadership about the future of their fledgling state, Afghanistan and its demand for Pashtunistan became part of the combination of perceived security threats that required Pakistan's military buildup backed by great-power alliances.

Although India publicly did not support the Afghan claim, Pakistan's early leaders could not separate Afghan skepticism of Pakistan's borders from their perception of an Indian grand design against Pakistan. Ian Stephens, a pro-Pakistan British author, explained Pakistani fears when he wrote, "if on Pakistan's birth coordinated movements opposed to her could be produced in Kashmir and Afghanistan, both of them predominantly Muslim territories and near to one another, the new state might be still-born, sort of crushed by a sort of pincer movement."[6]

Pashtuns who opposed the creation of Pakistan were thus cast in the mold of traitors by Pakistan's early leadership, which prevented the Muslim League from cutting a deal with Ghaffar Khan's political grouping soon after independence and unsettled the politics of NWFP for several years. Ghaffar Khan's brother, Dr. Khan Sahib, was dismissed from the office of chief minister of NWFP soon after Pakistan's independence, and his suggestion that the NWFP be renamed to reflect its Pashtun character within Pakistan was rejected. The two brothers, other family members, and several of their supporters were imprisoned, thereby prolonging the preindependence conflict among Pakistan's Pashtuns. Several years later, Dr. Khan Sahib was finally included in the governing coalition when the West Pakistan provinces were merged into a single entity. By then, however, the damage had been done, for Afghanistan's backing for Pashtunistan had poisoned Pakistan's relations with its smaller and weaker northwestern neighbor.

In addition to the Pashtunistan issue, Pakistan's pursuit of alliance with the United States during the 1950s also affected its relations with Afghanistan as well as Afghanistan's own subsequent direction. The lure of Pakistan as a security partner in its Cold War containment strategy led to the neglect of Afghanistan in U.S. diplomacy and foreign assistance. The Pakistanis developed an interest in painting a menacing picture of Soviet influence in Afghanistan to bolster their own position as the first line of defense against Soviet expansion into South Asia. The Pakistan army needed weapons to maintain its ascendancy at home and to face India, and military officers realized that the United States would be willing to modernize Pakistani forces to face the menace of communism. Because a threat from India did not qualify as a communist threat, Pakistani officials thought they could make a case for securing U.S. aid by invoking geopolitics and the history of southward invasions from across the Hindu Kush. Aslam Siddiqi, an official with Pakistan's Bureau of National Reconstruction, published in 1960 what Pakistani interlocutors had been telling their U.S. counterparts since the early 1950s:

> Pakistan inherited almost all the burden of the external land defense of United India. This mainly meant the defense of the northwest frontier where was normally stationed about eighty percent of the Indian Army. But in December 1947, movements of the Indian armed forces became such a menace to its security that Pakistan withdrew all its forces from the northwest frontier and posted them near the Indo-Pakistan border. So the overall burden of defense [that] Pakistan has got to carry is much heavier than that of United India ... Pakistan has to look ahead in the North and watch the trends there. The first line of defense of the Indo-Pakistan subcontinent lies in the Hindukush ... In Afghanistan, the Hindukush spreads out and dominates the entire country in a series of subsidiary ranges, branching off to north and south . . . It is crossed by several passes and routes, which though difficult are open for about six months in a year . . . Several of these passes are difficult in themselves or lie through barren countries. But some of them are regular highways. Alexander and Timur [Tamerlane] crossed the Hindukush through the Khawak Pass. Chengiz Khan chose the Shibar Pass and Babur, the Kipchak Pass. The Soviets have now chosen the Salang Pass to link the Oxus valley with Kabul.[7]

[handwritten margin note: proof that this was a geo-pol move ... in Paki politics]

Siddiqi also claimed, "After the death of Stalin, Afghanistan was selected as the first target of Soviet economic penetration," and he added:

> This penetration has almost become a stranglehold. The Soviets have virtual control of the Afghan army. They train and equip the Afghan soldiers. They have provided Afghanistan with jet fighters

and bombers and substantial military equipment. A road of great strategic importance which links Mazar-i-Sharif with Kabul is nearing completion . . . These roads should bring Afghanistan from the Soviet periphery right into the Soviet orbit.[8]

While Pakistan portrayed itself as the first line of defense against Soviet expansion into South Asia, Afghanistan was engaged in clumsy diplomacy of its own, seeking an external patron to substitute for the British. The British Indian empire had helped Afghan rulers maintain control and manage whatever little development Afghanistan had seen in the first half of the twentieth century. With Britain's withdrawal from South Asia, Afghanistan's royal family needed someone else to carry the burden of military and economic assistance.

The Afghan search for an alternative foreign source of support was undermined partly by Afghanistan's confrontation with Pakistan and partly by inadequate attention from Washington. The United States, seeking alliance with much larger Pakistan, chose to neglect Afghanistan and "inadvertently pushed Afghanistan toward rapprochement with the U.S.S.R."[9] Until 1953, the United States "dominated Afghanistan's external trade, aid and cultural contacts,"[10] with Afghanistan's elite showing a marked preference for Western ties. The value of these exchanges was small, less than $1 million a year.[11] Afghan modernizers sought higher levels of aid for their country's development and were frustrated by the U.S. view that Afghanistan was not ready for industrialization. U.S. aid was confined to an irrigation project that was never completed as well as some agricultural and education projects.

Border clashes with Pakistan in 1949–1950 and an embargo by Pakistan on oil supplies to Afghanistan caused serious hardship for landlocked Afghanistan, which had hitherto imported virtually everything through the Pakistani port of Karachi. In 1950, the Soviets offered, and the Afghans accepted, a barter agreement that provided for the exchange of Soviet oil for Afghan wool and cotton. Advocates of closer ties with the Soviet Union began winning the argument at the royal court in Kabul by pointing out that the Soviets were willing to finance Afghanistan's modernization while the Americans were not. The United States began providing Afghanistan an aid package only after Soviet aid had already started flowing in 1956. By 1968 Afghanistan had received $550 million in Soviet aid compared with $250 million in U.S. assistance.[12]

The Afghan leader accepting Soviet assistance was none other than the principal advocate of Pashtunistan, Sardar Muhammad Daoud, who became prime minister in 1953. It was easy, therefore, for Pakistan to claim a link between the demand for Pashtunistan and Soviet penetration. Pakistan had already positioned itself as the critical U.S. ally in the region, and its perceptions of Afghanistan began to influence the U.S. view of developments there. Because Pakistan's military elite saw Afghanistan as a potential sphere of influence for Pakistan, Pakistan's security services highlighted Soviet inroads into Afghanistan to prove Pakistan's usefulness to U.S. containment strategy instead of helping roll back Soviet influence in Afghanistan by befriending its royalist regime.

Securing U.S. assistance was not the only reason for Pakistan's early focus on Afghanistan. Soon after independence, Pakistan's military had become concerned about the lack of depth in Pakistan's land defenses. Pakistan's early military leaders had been trained as part of the British Indian army, with strategic doctrines that suited the Raj. The British empire was global, and plans for its defense could rely on one part of the empire springing into action to protect another. Furthermore, the empire's defense strategy for India envisaged a single unit stretching from the frontier with Afghanistan in the west to Burma in the east. Pakistan's generals applied their training for defending the British empire to developing a strategy to defend a much smaller country, divided until 1971 into two wings and threatened from what was originally the heartland of the British empire—the postpartition state of India. The Pakistani generals' notion that East Pakistan could be defended against India from a strong and impregnable base in West Pakistan proved deeply flawed, especially when put to the test during the India-Pakistan wars of 1965 and 1971. The generals' other strategic belief—about the fusion of the defense of Afghanistan and Pakistan—led to Pakistan's complicated role in Afghanistan, a role that began well before the Soviet invasion of 1979 and lasted through the rise and fall of the Taliban.

For many years, Pakistan's open conflict with India overshadowed its ambitions regarding Afghanistan. Most people believe that Pakistan developed an interest in creating a client regime in Afghanistan after the country played a key role in the anti-Soviet jihad during the 1980s. Pakistan's pursuit of strategic depth in Afghanistan began soon after independence, however. The early view of Pakistan's military-bureaucratic leadership toward Afghanistan is summarized by Siddiqi:

Afghanistan . . . has a very great and special importance for Pakistan. It has throughout history been the gateway of forces, mostly from beyond the Hindukush on their way to the Indo-Pakistan subcontinent. A series of invasions, beginning with the Greeks (Alexander and Demetrius), Kushans, Mongols and Turks, continued right up to 1526 when Babur set up the Mughal Empire . . . All this clearly points out that the safety of the Indo-Pakistan subcontinent has depended on the degree of influence, which its rulers could wield on the areas round about the mountains of the Hindukush . . . Mr. Fraser Tytler is so much impressed by the danger from beyond the Hindukush that, in his opinion, nothing but concerted action by Afghanistan and Pakistan can prevent it. He writes: "the remedy is the fusion of the two states of Afghanistan and Pakistan in some way or other. It may be argued that, given the differences in mental and political outlook of the two states, such fusion is impossible. This may be so. But history suggests that fusion will take place, if not peacefully, then by force . . ." Fusion by force will mean confusion, which will inevitably lead to the ruination of both the states. Such possibilities in fact are tied up with the controversy of racialism versus ideology within the Islamic civilization. If Islam is again to become a force, Islamic ideology must triumph over racialism.[13]

Echoing the thinking of Pakistan's security establishment, Siddiqi cited the history of various invasions of India and argued that, because most invaders of India came through Afghanistan and because historically the land that now constituted West Pakistan was closely linked to Afghanistan, Pakistan's defense could be ensured only by integration of the two contemporary states. By this reasoning, Afghanistan would have to join Pakistan in staving off penetration from the Soviet Union although

Pakistan, being the bigger country, obviously would have the greater role. Citing history again, Siddiqi made the case that "toward the West, Pakistan can have depth in defense,"[14] and Afghanistan and Iran could provide depth in Pakistan's defense against India.

But Pakistan's strategic vision did not appeal to Afghans who were beholden to ethnic or racial nationalism. Only Afghans convinced of Islamic ideology, and Pakistan's special place in the revival of Islam's glory, would transform their country into Pakistan's allies. By the early 1960s, Pakistan's intelligence agencies were encouraging Pakistan's Islamist political groups to pursue a forward policy of seeking ideological allies in Afghanistan.[15]

Pakistan's preoccupation with India relegated Afghanistan to a secondary position until 1971, when the separation of East Pakistan to become Bangladesh freed Pakistani strategic planners from having to think about the defense of Pakistan's eastern wing. Pakistan had been clashing with Afghanistan sporadically since 1947 over Afghan propaganda on behalf of Pashtunistan. Episodic tribal insurgencies in Balochistan and NWFP provided Afghanistan with an opportunity to create difficulties for Pakistan and, instead of dealing with the local factors giving rise to the revolts, Pakistan blamed these insurgencies on India and Afghanistan. In Pakistan's tribal regions, Pakistani officials emphasized Islam as the unifying force "in spite of foreign attempts at subversion,"[16] and the government deployed ulema and *mashaikh* to combat tribal sentiment among the Baloch and the Pashtun. Pakistani repression drove Baloch and Pashtun nationalists to ally with left-wing intellectuals and activists, gradually making Pakistani claims of communist influence along the Durand Line a self-fulfilling prophecy. During this period, Soviet influence had also grown among the urban Afghan political class unhappy with Afghanistan's monarchy.

In 1973, the Afghan monarchy was overthrown in a coup d'état by Zahir Shah's cousin, Sardar Muhammad Daoud, who was backed by Soviet-trained military officers. Daoud abolished the monarchy and proclaimed a republic, of which he became president. On Moscow's direction, a major faction of the Afghan Communist Party, the People's Democratic Party of Afghanistan (PDPA), supported Daoud; and some PDPA members even served in cabinet positions. The PDPA was not a party with a base among the masses; one observer wrote that it probably did not have "more than five or six thousand members all told."[17] It represented a well-organized group within the Afghan elite, however, and it maintained close ties with the Communist Party of the Soviet Union.

Daoud's coup d'état reflected the dissatisfaction of educated urban elites with the pace of modernization and reform in Afghanistan:

> By the time Daoud seized power for the second time in 1973, Soviet aid at 1,500 million dollars between 1953 and 1973 was more than three times that of America (450 million dollars) and there were probably some three to four thousand Russian technicians working at all levels in Afghanistan.[18]

Daoud wanted to speed up Afghanistan's development and was initially keen to accept Soviet assistance. Within two years of taking power, Daoud's government had signed up seventy new projects involving Soviet help. Hastening Afghan development was only one part of Daoud's

agenda. The 1973 coup d'état had, at least in part, also been precipitated by the failure of Zahir Shah to respond vigorously to events in Pakistani provinces bordering Afghanistan.[19] Daoud, and Pashtun nationalists and communists backing him, felt that active engagement by Afghanistan's government on behalf of Baloch and Pashtun groups in Pakistan might force Pakistan's hand in reopening discussion about the Durand Line.

In Pakistan at this time, Pakistan's military had retreated from power following its 1971 defeat in Bangladesh and was backing the civilian government of Zulfikar Ali Bhutto. The 1970 election that provided Bhutto the mandate to rule West Pakistan had also given a plurality in Balochistan and NWFP to the ethnic-based National Awami Party (NAP). The leader of NAP, Abdul Wali Khan, was the son of the Pashtun nationalist, Abdul Ghaffar Khan, and was therefore vulnerable to charges of seeking a Pashtunistan.

Bhutto had overcome his authoritarian tendencies and had begun initially to share power with the Baloch and Pashtun leaders, but within months of the commencement of the power-sharing arrangement, ISI informed Bhutto of NAP's plans for a revolt in Balochistan against the central government. The ISI chief, Lieutenant General Ghulam Jilani

Khan, produced intelligence that a cache of arms had arrived at the Iraqi embassy in Islamabad, and he asserted that the arms were meant for use in the rebellion in Balochistan.[20] Bhutto, backed by Jilani Khan, decided to dispense with diplomatic niceties and recover the arms from the Iraqi embassy in full view of television cameras. Bhutto dismissed the Balochistan government, accusing it of planning the rebellion, an action that prompted the NWFP government to resign in protest. Soon Balochistan was up in arms, and the army moved in to suppress the rebellion. The NAP was banned, and Wali Khan and his colleagues in the party imprisoned.

Baloch and Pashtun nationalists interpreted the Pakistani military action along the Afghan border as a provocation motivated by the desire of both Bhutto and the Pakistan army to centralize authority. Pakistan justified its army action in Balochistan by pointing at the weapons in the Iraqi embassy. U.S. diplomats and Pakistani intelligence officials had known all along, however, that the Iraqi arms were meant for Baloch rebels in the Iranian part of Balochistan and were Iraq's response to Iranian support for Kurdish rebels in Iraq. Pakistan's opposition parties, always suspicious of Bhutto's motives, believed that he had used the discovery of Iraqi arms as the pretext for getting rid of an opposition-led provincial government.[21] One of Bhutto's close associates, Rafi Raza, acknowledged that Bhutto had intended to remove the NAP government in Balochistan "even without the Iraqi arms incident."[22] The charge of armed rebellion followed by military action against Baloch tribal leaders incited a wider tribal revolt. The Pakistan army undertook a large-scale counterinsurgency operation along the Afghan border, losing thirty-three hundred soldiers in battle; the Baloch suffered fifty-three hundred casualties.[23]

The Pakistani operation in Balochistan lasted four years. Subsequent events indicate that it may have been part of a strategic design to subdue Pakistan's Baloch and Pashtun provinces before a planned effort to extend Pakistani influence into Afghanistan. When Bhutto's military successor, General Zia ul-Haq, assumed power in 1977, he released the Baloch and Pashtun leaders who had been accused by Pakistan of rebellion, and he ended the army operation in Balochistan. The "rebels" were forgiven and, in some cases, were offered compensation. Had the

ι the real threat to Pakistani security it was made out to be, army action against it would not have been so readily terminated. Sardar Daoud's republican regime in Afghanistan supported the Baloch tribal leaders with propaganda and small arms during the Baloch miniwar against Pakistan's army. Several Baloch and Pashtun leaders who were escaping the military crackdown were officially hosted in Kabul, which provided Pakistan the justification it needed to escalate its engagement in Afghanistan. In addition, Daoud's opening of Afghanistan to greater levels of Soviet aid and the inclusion of Afghan communists in his government alarmed the United States. Soon the U.S. Central Intelligence Agency (CIA), the ISI, and the secret service of the Shah of Iran (Savak) were running clandestine operations in Kabul, making it an arena for Cold War rivalries and intrigue. Selig Harrison wrote, "As factionalism, corruption, and political uncertainty grew, externally backed forces began to jockey for position in preparation for the power struggle expected to follow the elderly Daoud's death."[24]

Pakistan's allies as well as its instruments of influence in this game of intrigue were Afghan Islamists. Religious sentiment had always been strong in Afghanistan and had been a crucial factor in Afghan opposition to British influence through much of the nineteenth century. Conservative religious leaders had successfully opposed attempts at Westernization by King Amanullah (who ruled from 1919 to 1929) and had supported the short, nine-month reign of the Tajik, Bacha-e-Saqqao, on the basis of his promise to rule according to Islamic law. When Pashtun ascendancy was restored under King Muhammad Nadir Khan in 1929, Pashtun tribes secured the ulema's support for him by granting the religious establishment considerable influence.

Afghanistan's 1931 constitution created a dual legal system—Sharia courts alongside Islamic ones. Zahir Shah established the Faculty of Theology at Kabul University in 1950 and counted theologians among his advisers. Afghanistan's 1964 constitution established the primacy of secular law but recognized Islam's sacred status and stipulated that Sharia law would be the law of last resort "where no existing secular law applied."[25] Political factions emerged in Afghanistan with the introduction of an elected parliament in the 1960s. Among the factions were the communist PDPA and the Islamist groupings that "set out to establish a political movement that would work for the creation of an Islamic state based on Sharia law."[26]

Pakistan's Jamaat-e-Islami served as both model and mentor for some Afghan Islamist leaders. By the 1960s, Jamaat-e-Islami had established links with Islamist groups in most parts of the Muslim world. The writings of Jamaat-e-Islami's founder, Maulana Abul Ala Maududi, were being translated into several languages and their arguments were particularly effective in mobilizing Islamist networks in several countries. As Pakistan's next-door neighbor, Afghanistan was among the first countries to receive Persian and Pashto language translations of Maududi's writings. Jamaat-e-Islami also received financial assistance from Saudi Arabia and the Saudi-sponsored Rabita al-Alam al-Islami (Muslim World League) for global outreach, particularly in areas under communist control or influence. The Muslim-majority regions of Central Asia attracted the Jamaat-e-Islami's attention, and the group started a project to establish contact with Muslims in the region as well as to tell the story of communist oppression to the world.

Alongside the Jamaat-e-Islami's headquarters in Lahore was established the *Darul Fikr* (Center for Thought), which published numerous accounts of oppression of Muslims by communists during the late 1960s. Magazines and newspapers associated with the Jamaat-e-Islami, notably the popular monthly *Urdu Digest* (modeled on *Reader's Digest*) amplified the theme that Muslims around the world had an obligation to free their coreligionists from Soviet communist occupation. Muslims in Eastern Turkistan—China's Xinjiang province—were also initially identified for liberation, but the development of close ties between China and Pakistan made their liberation a lesser priority. Afghanistan was a crucial link in the Jamaat-e-Islami's broader Central Asia plan.

In 1972, Jamiat-e-Islami Afghanistan (Islamic Society of Afghanistan) emerged from among the informal Islamist groupings that had existed since the 1960s. Led by Burhanuddin Rabbani, a professor of theology at Kabul University, Jamiat-e-Islami Afghanistan resembled Pakistan's Jamaat-e-Islami in more than just its name. The party, inspired by Maulana Maududi and the thinkers of Egypt's Muslim Brotherhood, sought to radically restructure all aspects of society in accordance with a particular interpretation of Islamic principles.[27] Rabbani was an ethnic

Tajik. His Pakistani supporters considered him suitable not only for influencing Afghanistan but also for igniting the flames of Islamic revolution among fellow Tajiks inside the Soviet Union. Rabbani's early followers included two Kabul University students, Ahmed Shah Massoud and Gulbuddin Hekmatyar, both of whom played a significant role in subsequent events in Afghanistan.

Jamiat-e-Islami's conservative vision of an Islamic state did not find favor with the segment of Afghanistan's elite that sought to sideline religious traditions, especially in areas such as women's participation in national life. The Islamists soon clashed with communists on the campus of Kabul University. After Daoud's coup in 1973, Jamiat-e-Islami questioned communist influence in the Afghan republic and resisted Daoud's secular orientation. Daoud ordered the arrest of Rabbani, who fled to Pakistan with most of his key supporters. In Pakistan, Rabbani's group was initially hosted by the Jamaat-e-Islami.

Although it is difficult to find hard evidence of prior collusion between Pakistani Islamists and the state regarding Rabbani and the members of the Jamiat-e-Islami Afghanistan, Jamaat-e-Islami and the Pakistani security services had common objectives in Afghanistan and Central Asia. Just as the Jamaat-e-Islami had wanted to instigate an Islamic awakening in Soviet Central Asia, Pakistani intelligence services had also recognized the potential for a major Pakistani role in combating communism with religious fervor. The ISI and the IB also watched developments in Afghanistan closely. In both Afghanistan and Central Asia, the Jamaat-e-Islami's contacts and protégés were also the ISI's likely collaborators even if, at that stage, the Islamists and the ISI did not always act in tandem.

Soon after their arrival in Peshawar in 1973, Rabbani was provided financial support by the ISI, and some of his associates received military training. To maintain deniability in case the Pakistan army and the ISI were blamed for destabilizing Afghanistan, management of the covert operation was initially assigned to the paramilitary Frontier Scouts. Until recently, serving and retired Pakistani officials have played down Pakistan's role in support of the Afghan Islamist insurgency in the pre-Soviet days. Later, in the aftermath of the Soviet invasion of Afghanistan in 1979, the Pakistan-sponsored Islamist rebellion became the U.S.-backed jihad against Soviet occupation. The massive covert operation in support of the Afghan mujahideen enhanced Pakistan's value as a U.S. ally. After the Soviet withdrawal, when the United States walked away from Afghanistan and terminated aid to Pakistan in retaliation for its nuclear program, Pakistan claimed it had been betrayed by the United States after being used as the staging ground for a decisive battle against their rival superpower. The official Pakistani argument, supported occasionally by American scholars, has been:

> Pakistan played a critical role in the historic defeat of the Soviet Union in Afghanistan. It risked its own stability by accepting 3.5 million Afghan refugees and by serving as a conduit for arms shipments from the United States to the Mujahideen. It has not yet recovered from the aftershock of this enterprise. Much of the drug traffic, smuggling, and terrorism can be attributed to this role in the Afghan crisis. In a nation whose religious ideology places a premium on the loyalty and steadfastness of friends, whether personal or political, Pakistan finds it difficult to comprehend the United States indifference to the Kashmir issue, its double-standard toward nuclear proliferation in South Asia.[28]

By emphasizing Pakistan's role as the conduit for U.S. arms for Afghans fighting Soviet occupation, the Pakistanis are able to divert attention away from their ambitions in Afghanistan. The fact remains, however, that Pakistan did not merely oblige the United States by launching resistance to the Soviet occupation of Afghanistan in 1979. With U.S. money and weapons, and with support from other Western and Arab governments, Pakistan was able to expand the scope of an operation that had been ongoing since 1973.

After arriving in Peshawar and signing up for Pakistani support, the Afghan Islamists found dissension in their ranks. In 1976, Hekmatyar split off from Jamiat-e-Islami Afghanistan to form the Hizbe Islami (Islamic Party), which also operated from Pakistan. Rabbani wanted to move cautiously and gradually, building broader support before seeking power. Like Maulana Maududi, Rabbani's original scheme for Islamic revolution did not envisage armed struggle or certainly anything that could be described as terrorism. Although Maulana Maududi's followers have been involved in militant struggles for the past several decades, none of his writings openly advocated violence. Rabbani, too, in the initial stages was reluctant to convert Jamiat-e-Islami into a militia or a guerrilla army although later, after the Soviet occupation, the party became a leading band of mujahideen.

Gulbuddin Hekmatyar, on the other hand, from the beginning was willing to embrace radical methods. His militancy soon made him a favorite of the ISI, which was at that stage more interested in generating military pressure on Daoud's regime than in laying the foundations of a sustainable Islamic revolution in Afghanistan. The ISI also had an eye on identifying future leaders for an Afghanistan more closely linked to Pakistan. As an ethnic Pashtun, Hekmatyar seemed qualified for that role.

Between 1973 and 1977, Afghanistan and Pakistan fought what can best be described as a low-intensity proxy war. Sardar Muhammad Daoud supported Baloch rebels in Pakistan while Pakistan backed the Afghan Islamist insurgents based in Peshawar. Accounts by Pakistani officials from that period also suggest that Pakistan's decision to back the Afghan Islamists was initiated by Bhutto in retaliation for Daoud's support to Baloch and Pashtun groups in Pakistan.[29] The Pakistani covert operation was not merely retaliatory, however; it reflected the longer-term Pakistani interest in the affairs of Afghanistan.

The insurgency in Balochistan started soon after Bhutto's dismissal of the provincial government in February 1973. Sardar Daoud's coup d'état against Zahir Shah took place on July 17, 1973, and it was followed immediately by the arrival in Peshawar of Rabbani, Massoud, and Hekmatyar. The Baloch were fighting the Pakistan army before Daoud took power, and Pakistan was playing host to Afghan Islamists almost simultaneously with the proclamation of an Afghan republic. After coming to power, Daoud established training camps for Baloch rebels, training between ten and fifteen thousand tribesmen for war against Pakistan.[30] He also renamed one of Kabul's central squares as Chowk Pashtunistan (Pashtunistan Square).[31]

Daoud's actions on behalf of the Baloch tribesmen and his revival of propaganda for Pashtunistan may have added another reason for the

ISI's support for Rabbani and Hekmatyar, but it was certainly not the primary instigator. Pakistan had thought hard about expanding its influence in Afghanistan, and the plan for the Islamist insurgency took shape as a result of this evaluation. General Khalid Mahmud Arif, who served in Pakistan's GHQ at the time and who later served as the principal lieutenant to General Zia ul-Haq has described the "Afghan cell" that was created in the Pakistan Foreign Office as early as July/August 1973. He has also described the role of the ISI in conducting "intelligence missions inside Afghanistan" during that time and its contacts with Hekmatyar, Rabbani, and the exiled Afghan king, Zahir Shah.[32]

The Pakistan-trained Afghan insurgents were able to accomplish little against the Kabul regime.[33] More effective were the efforts by the Shah of Iran to offer Daoud economic assistance comparable with that provided by the Soviets. Anticommunists within Daoud's inner circle opposed sharing power with Afghan communists, leading to the purge of communists from Daoud's regime beginning in 1975. Daoud reached out to traditional Islamic leaders at the same time. At the Shah's prodding, Daoud and Bhutto began a dialogue to resolve the differences between Pakistan and Afghanistan, a dialogue that was interrupted by Bhutto's ouster from power in July 1977 but was resumed with General Zia ul-Haq a few months later.

After distancing himself from the Soviet Union and Afghan communists, Sardar Daoud proceeded to build a new relationship with conservative Arab regimes, Iran, and the United States. Afghanistan was now more dependent on foreign aid than ever, with aid being the source of 60 percent of Afghanistan's budget expenditures for 1977–1978.[34] By reaching out to the West and pro-Western neighboring states, Daoud was gradually diversifying the sources of aid and backing away from Afghanistan's special relationship with the Soviet Union. During a visit to Pakistan in March 1978, Daoud came close to concluding a deal with Pakistan that would have recognized the Durand Line and ended Afghanistan's support for Pashtunistan in return for Baloch and Pashtun autonomy within Pakistan.[35] These foreign policy changes were accompanied by significant changes on the domestic front as well. Daoud cracked down on the PDPA and informed the Baloch and

Pashtun activists from Pakistan that Afghanistan would no longer be their sanctuary.[36]

On April 27, 1978, Daoud was overthrown and killed in a coup d'état carried out by procommunist military officers who had not yet been purged. The coup d'état was led by some of the same officers who had helped Daoud come to power almost five years earlier. Several accounts of the coup suggest that "it was a last-minute operation, orchestrated by Afghans, in which support from Soviet intelligence agencies and military advisers, if any, came only after they were confronted with a virtual fait accompli."[37] The military officers involved in the coup d'état released the PDPA leaders who had been imprisoned by Daoud, and leading figures of the PDPA assumed top positions in the new, revolutionary government.

Pakistan recognized the new regime and maintained diplomatic relations with it, but the coming to power of communists in Afghanistan accelerated the Pakistan-backed Islamist insurgency. During a meeting between General Zia ul-Haq and the new Afghan president, Nur Muhammad Taraki, in September 1978, both leaders saw the contrast in their fundamental beliefs. General Arif wrote, "the two Muslims disagreed on the interpretation of Islamic philosophy."[38] Taraki was introduced to Zia ul-Haq as "comrade," and he began by sharing his view of Afghan history with the Pakistani leader. He told Zia that the Afghan royal family "had exploited the Afghan nation for 200 years. Now everything belongs to the people. The revolution has given land to eleven million people." This caused Zia ul-Haq to remind Taraki that Muslims must consider all property as belonging to Allah and should see man only as His custodian. Taraki responded by saying, "All land belongs to the tiller."

Zia ul-Haq's invitation to be fearful of God and to recognize obligations toward God were met with Taraki's comment that "God is *aadil* (just). We don't have to fear a just God." After saying "To serve the people is to serve God," Taraki poked fun at Pakistan's membership in CENTO, pointed out that Pakistan had not got what it wanted from the United States, and was sarcastic about Zia ul-Haq's deference to the Shah of Iran. Although both leaders spoke of the need to resolve their differences peacefully, Zia ul-Haq felt no obligation to make life easier for a man whose beliefs and interests were diametrically opposed to his own Islamist convictions. Pakistan continued supporting the Afghan Islamist parties operating out of Kabul and formally transferred responsibility for them from the paramilitary Frontier Scouts to the ISI.

Zia ul-Haq calculated that it was only a matter of time before Pakistan's Islamist protégés would become more than a mere nuisance in Afghanistan. As the PDPA regime implemented its radical social and economic policies, resentment against the new order in Kabul spread through the Afghan countryside. Land reform limited landholding to five acres, which made a large number of Afghan landowners into enemies of the regime. Disrespect toward clerics and traditional tribal leaders coupled with efforts to change conservative social norms by decree created a larger pool of disgruntled Afghans from which Islamists could now recruit insurgents. In addition to the Jamiat-e-Islami and Hizbe Islami, which were already active, several new Afghan groups began to organize. These anticommunist parties were led by conservative politicians and tribal leaders excluded from, or persecuted under, the new political order in Afghanistan.

Soon after the April 1978 coup d'état, Pakistan revived its Afghan cell. General Arif recalled that the task of the cell was "to analyze the available information and suggest policy options. The defense plans were updated as a destabilized Afghanistan had adversely affected the security of Pakistan."[39] But the Afghan cell's primary functions were to coordinate the resistance to communist rule in Afghanistan as well as secure international backing for Pakistan and the resistance. In December 1978, when the PDPA government in Afghanistan signed a treaty of friendship with the Soviet Union, the Pakistanis tried to ring alarm bells in Washington by reviving Pakistani requests for U.S. aid. The Carter administration was unmoved. Even the assassination of the U.S. ambassador in Kabul in February 1979 was overshadowed by the fall of the Shah in Iran and the return to Tehran of Ayatollah Khomeini. Pakistani officials complained about Washington's lack of interest in developments in Afghanistan. "The Carter administration continued business as usual as if these were routine events,"[40] General Arif lamented, echoing the sentiment of the Zia ul-Haq regime at the time.

The revolution in Iran did serve to revive intelligence cooperation between Pakistan and United States, paving the way for Pakistan getting what it wanted in Afghanistan later. The United States had lost its listening posts in Iran because of the revolution. When U.S. officials contacted Zia ul-Haq for "collaboration in the collection of communications intelligence,"[41] Zia readily agreed. Although U.S. specialists were not immediately stationed in Pakistan, the CIA worked with Pakistani intelligence to "improve Pakistan's electronic intercept capabilities."[42] Data collected by these intercept installations were then passed on to U.S. intelligence, laying the foundation for close ties between the Pakistani ISI and the CIA. By July 1979, President Carter had approved a modest program of covert assistance to the Afghan Islamist resistance, which was routed through Pakistan. Robert Gates, then deputy director (later, director) of the CIA narrated in his memoirs the sequence of events leading to this initial covert operation:

The Carter Administration began looking at the possibility of covert assistance to the insurgents opposing the pro-Soviet, Marxist government of President Taraki at the beginning of 1979. On March 5, 1979, CIA sent several covert action options relating to Afghanistan to the SCC [Special Coordinating Committee]. The covering memo noted that the insurgents had stepped up their activities against the government and had achieved surprising successes. It added that the Soviets were clearly concerned about the setbacks to the Afghan communist regime and that the Soviet media were accusing the United States, Pakistan, and Egypt of supporting the insurgents. The SCC met the next day and requested new options for covert action . . . Meanwhile, in Saudi Arabia, a senior official also had raised the prospect of a Soviet setback in Afghanistan and said that his government was considering officially proposing that the United States aid the rebels. The DO [Directorate of Operations] memo reported that the Saudis could be expected to provide funds and encourage the Pakistanis, and that possibly other governments could be expected to provide at least tacit help. The memo conceded that the Soviets could easily step up their own resupply and military aid, although "we believe they are unlikely to introduce regular troops." Further, if they decided to occupy the country militarily there was no practical way to stop them, but such a move would cause them serious damage in the region . . . On March 30, 1979, [David] Aaron [Deputy National Security Adviser] chaired a historic "mini-SCC" as a follow-up to the meeting some three weeks earlier. At the mini-SCC, Under Secretary of State for Political Affairs David Newsom stated that it was U.S. policy to reverse the current Soviet trend and presence in Afghanistan, to demonstrate to the Pakistanis our interest and concern about Soviet involvement, and to demonstrate to the Pakistanis, Saudis, and others our resolve to stop the extension of Soviet influence in the Third World . . . Walt Slocombe, representing Defense, asked if there was value in keeping the Afghan insurgency going, "sucking the Soviets into a Vietnamese quagmire?" Aaron concluded by asking the key question: "Is there interest in maintaining and assisting the insurgency, or is the risk that we will provoke the Soviets too great? . . ." The day before the SCC meeting on April 6 to consider Afghan covert action options, Soviet NIO Arnold Horelick sent Turner a paper on the possible Soviet reactions. Horelick said if the Soviets were determined to keep Taraki in power, covert action could not prevent it, and external assistance would be used to justify their own deepening involvement. But, he added, they would take this line anyway and were already making such charges. His bottom line: covert action would raise the costs to the Soviets and inflame Muslim opinion against them in many countries. The risk was that a substantial U.S. covert aid program could raise the stakes and induce the Soviets to intervene more directly and vigorously than otherwise intended.[43]

According to Gates, a wide range of options to support the Afghan resistance were considered by the Special Coordination Committee at its meeting of April 6, 1979, and "there was a general preference for an active role, but only for nonlethal assistance."[44] The CIA had meanwhile learned that the Chinese "might supply arms to the Afghan Mujahideen."[45] The close ties between Pakistan and China make it safe to assume that Pakistan had persuaded the Chinese to support their initiative. Gates confirms that President Jimmy Carter signed the first authorization "to help the Mujahideen covertly" on July 3, 1979, "almost six months *before* the Soviets invaded Afghanistan."[46] But Carter's first authorization covered only

> support for insurgent propaganda and other psychological operations in Afghanistan; establishment of radio access to the Afghan population through third-country facilities; and the provision either unilaterally or through third countries of support to the Afghan insurgents, in the form of either cash or nonmilitary supplies. The Afghan effort began relatively small. Initially, somewhat more than half a million dollars was allocated, with almost all being drawn within six weeks.[47]

General Zia ul-Haq was not satisfied with the relatively low levels of U.S. support for his Afghan operation. He recognized the nervousness of U.S. policy makers resulting from the fall of the Shah of Iran, and he wanted to rebuild the U.S.-Pakistan alliance in more or less the same way that Ayub Khan had joined the anticommunist treaties of the 1950s. Zia ul-Haq also faced serious legitimacy problems at home after executing popular Prime Minister Bhutto and abandoning promises of free elections within ninety days of his coup d'état. Funding from the United States to expand an Islamist jihad in Afghanistan would solidify support for Zia ul-Haq's rule among Pakistani Islamists, and U.S. military assistance would help Zia retain the support of Pakistan's military; however, U.S. opinion about Pakistan was now more divided than it had been when Ayub Khan won over the U.S. national security establishment in the early 1950s. Pakistan's track record vis-à-vis India, the persistence of military domination in Pakistan's politics, and the emerging intelligence about Pakistan's incipient nuclear program all caused concerns among various constituencies in Washington.

Zia ul-Haq had to overcome the skepticism of his U.S. critics. He focused on Americans who were concerned with containing the Soviet Union, and he pitched the insurgency in Afghanistan as having the potential to halt the expansion of communism; in other words, communism in Afghanistan could be rolled back and Soviet prestige would diminish provided the Pakistani and U.S. intelligence services undertook a joint venture. Pakistan had decided to try to generate support within the United States for higher levels of aid by allowing U.S. journalists to report on Pakistani efforts to train anticommunist Afghan guerrillas even as Islamabad officially denied such operations from Pakistani soil. The *Washington Post* was thus able to report on February 2, 1979, that at least two thousand Afghans were being trained at Pakistani bases guarded by Pakistani troops.[48] By leaking word of a substantive effort by Pakistan to roll back communism in Afghanistan, Zia ul-Haq justifiably expected to rally anti-Soviet hard-liners in the United States to his cause.

On the one hand, Pakistan was eager to secure U.S. support for its Afghan venture; on the other, Pakistani officials spoke of the "risk" of "Soviet wrath" unless there was a firm, large-scale U.S. commitment to Pakistan's security. Zia ul-Haq wanted U.S. support not only for the insurgents, whom he was already backing, but also for Pakistan's armed forces. Expanding the insurgency in Afghanistan was the service Pakistan would provide for the United States. Greater economic and military aid was the reward it sought for this service. Gates records how Zia ul-Haq lobbied for U.S. aid during the months preceding the Soviet invasion:

> By the end of August [1979], Pakistani President Muhammad Zia ul-Haq was pressuring the United States for arms and equipment for the insurgents in Afghanistan. He called in the U.S. ambassador to make his pitch and indicated that when he was in New York for the UN General Assembly session in September, he would raise the issue at higher levels in the Department of State. Separately, the Pakistani intelligence service was pressing us to provide military equipment to support an expanding insurgency . . . When [CIA Director Stansfield] Turner heard this, he urged the DO to get moving in providing more help to the insurgents. They responded with several enhancement options, including communications equipment for the insurgents via the Pakistanis or the Saudis, funds for the Pakistanis to purchase lethal military equipment for the insurgents, and providing a like amount of lethal equipment ourselves for the Pakistanis to distribute to the insurgents.[49]

Despite the cooperation between the CIA and the ISI, Pakistan's relations with the United States at the political level were, at this stage, not particularly warm. On November 21, 1979, students affiliated with the Jamaat-e-Islami's student wing burned down the U.S. embassy in Islamabad on the basis of rumors that the United States had had a hand in the seizure of Islam's holiest shrine, the Grand Mosque in Mecca. Several embassy officials were trapped in the burning building, and it took the Pakistan military four hours to arrive at the site and several more to restore order despite the fact that Zia ul-Haq's residence as military chief and the Pakistan army's headquarters in Rawalpindi were less than a half hour's drive from the U.S. embassy in Islamabad. Two Americans and two Pakistani employees of the embassy died in the incident.[50] A similar effort to attack the U.S. consulate in Karachi was foiled by cooperation between more moderate student leaders and police.

Although Pakistan later agreed to pay for the reconstruction of the embassy, the incident alerted U.S. diplomats to anti-Americanism among Pakistan's Islamists and the possibility of the government's complicity in it. The government's role in the episode was the subject of much controversy among U.S. officials, who wondered why it took so long for the Pakistan army to come to the embassy's rescue. By way of comparison, in 1999, when the Pakistan army decided to stop Prime Minister Nawaz Sharif from announcing the removal of General Pervez Musharraf from his command, it took the army less than 35 minutes to move troops between the two same general areas. Dennis Kux summed up the various U.S. views of the 1979 sacking of the U.S. embassy:

Although Pakistani officials attributed the slow reaction to bureaucratic snarls, lack of preparedness, and plain incompetence, the less charitable views of U.S. officials on the scene appear closer to the mark. Some Americans thought that the Pakistanis were hesitant about intervening lest the rumors of U.S. involvement in [Mecca] prove true. Others felt that the Pakistanis found it not a bad idea to let the Americans "sweat a bit." Still others believed that Pakistani intelligence had instigated the embassy demonstration (U.S. facilities in Rawalpindi, Lahore, and Karachi were also attacked), which then had gotten out of hand.[51]

Zia ul-Haq privately cited the incident as further evidence of why the United States needed a military strongman like himself to control an emotional and volatile Pakistani nation and to channel the religious fervor of Pakistanis against the Soviets instead of allowing it to run against the United States.[52] Zia ul-Haq portrayed himself as a friend of the United States, willing to defend U.S. interests in a turbulent region despite the hostility of his countrymen toward the United States. He was not the first Pakistani general to do so and, as we will see later, certainly not the last.

Meanwhile, events in Afghanistan took a course that helped Zia ul-Haq in his ambition to secure massive U.S. assistance for Pakistan as well as to qualitatively expand the jihad that Pakistan was already supporting in Afghanistan. For as long as it had existed, the PDPA had comprised two major factions, which were named after their respective publications—the Khalq (masses) and the Parcham (flag). In addition, clashes of personalities existed within each faction. Within a few months of the April 1978 coup d'état that brought the PDPA to power, the Khalq faction managed to exile Parcham leaders, sending them abroad as ambassadors. A power struggle within Khalq led to the rise to power of Hafizullah Amin, "an intensely nationalistic, independent man who exuded a swaggering self-confidence."[53]

Amin got rid of President Taraki in September 1979 and consolidated his own position by becoming president of Afghanistan. The PDPA government was, by now, less mindful of Soviet advice. It was also provoking greater opposition to its policies among conservative Afghans, and the Pakistan-backed insurgents were beginning to have some impact. The fratricidal warfare within the PDPA, accentuated by Amin's tendency to concentrate power in his own hands, was also weakening the Kabul regime. At the same time, Amin was giving out mixed signals, including some that he might reduce Soviet influence in Kabul.[54] The Soviet Union was led by an ailing Leonid Brezhnev who, along with other Soviet leaders, suspected that Amin might make it easy for the United States to avenge the fall of the Shah's regime in Iran by intervening in Afghanistan.

Concerned by these developments, and not willing to allow a satellite to leave the Soviet constellation, the Soviet Union intervened militarily in Afghanistan on Christmas Eve of 1979.[55] Amin was killed; Babrak Karmal, leader of the Parcham faction of PDPA and at the time serving as ambassador to an East European country, was installed by the Soviets as Afghanistan's new leader. The Soviets claimed they had intervened in response to Karmal's request for military assistance under the friendship treaty signed a year earlier. Because Karmal was installed through their military intervention, that claim was nothing more than a fig leaf. The Soviet invasion caused great consternation around the world because it raised questions about the future intentions of the Soviet Union. Earlier, opinion in Washington had been divided between those who saw the Afghan communist regime as a Soviet cat's-paw and those who considered developments in Afghanistan independent of superpower rivalry.[56]

Given the global environment at the time and the all-too-real threat of Soviet expansion, some experts concluded that, by invading Afghanistan, the Soviets were planning to extend their influence in Southwest Asia. The ultimate Soviet goal, they argued, was to control the Persian Gulf. With Iran already in the throes of a revolution, Pakistan was now the pivotal state in Western security strategy for the region. Zia ul-Haq's moment had arrived. Publicly he gave the impression of being fearful for Pakistan's security, but he asked his close confidant and ISI chief, Lieutenant General Akhtar Abdul Rahman, to draw up plans for a large-scale guerrilla war against the Soviet occupation of Pakistan's neighbor. He was certain he would now be able to persuade the United States to seek alliance with Pakistan on Pakistan's terms.[57]

Some former ISI officials who worked with General Abdul Rahman insist that the idea for expanded resistance against the Soviets came from the Pakistani intelligence chief, and Zia ul-Haq endorsed it only after being assured of its viability as a military proposition. Brigadier Mohammad Yousaf, who ran ISI's Afghan operation between 1983 and 1987, credited Abdul Rahman with planning a guerrilla war that would hurt the Soviets but not to a point where they might lash out at Pakistan:

[Akhtar Abdul Rahman] argued that not only would [support for the Afghan resistance] be defending Islam but also Pakistan. The resistance must become a part of Pakistan's forward defense against the Soviets. If they were allowed to occupy Afghanistan too easily, it would then be but a short step to Pakistan, probably through Balochistan province. Akhtar made out a strong case for setting out to defeat the Soviets in a large scale guerrilla war. He believed Afghanistan could be made into another Vietnam, with the Soviets in the shoes of the Americans. He urged Zia to take the military option. It would mean Pakistan covertly supporting the guerrillas with arms, ammunition, money, intelligence, training and operational advice. Above all it would entail offering the border areas of the NWFP and Balochistan as a sanctuary for both the refugees and guerrillas, as without a secure, cross-border base no such campaign would succeed. Zia agreed.[58]

According to Brigadier Yousaf, General Zia ul-Haq's motives in agreeing to make Afghanistan a Soviet Vietnam were not exclusively related to global security. Regime survival and Pakistan's traditional policy paradigm of seeking leadership in the Muslim world, securing national unity through Islam, and obtaining Western economic and military assistance were also factors that weighed in his decision:

In 1979 Zia had just provoked worldwide consternation and condemnation by executing his former prime minister; his image both inside and outside Pakistan was badly tarnished, and he felt isolated. By supporting a jihad, albeit unofficially, against a communist superpower, he sought to regain sympathy in the West. The US would surely rally to his assistance. As a devout Muslim he was eager to offer help to his Islamic neighbors. That religious, strategic and political factors all seemed to point in the same direction was indeed a happy coincidence. For Zia, the final factor that decided [the matter for] him was [Lieutenant General] Akhtar's argument that it was a sound military proposition, provided the Soviets were not goaded into a direct confrontation, meaning the water must not get too hot. Zia stood to gain enormous prestige with the Arab world as a champion of Islam and with the West as a champion against communist aggression.[59]

Although Pakistan had been backing Afghan Islamists since 1973 and U.S. covert assistance had begun several months before the Soviet military intervention, Zia ul-Haq gave an impression to his U.S. interlocutors that he was fearful of a Soviet threat to Pakistan. He said, in effect, that an opportunity existed to create a Vietnam-like quagmire for the Soviets, but for it to be successful the United States would have to commit itself to Pakistan's security and pay the right price for Pakistan's cooperation. Zia ul-Haq also asked for assurances that would cover the possible threat of attack from India. President Jimmy Carter's national security adviser, Zbigniew Brzezinski, publicly reassured Pakistan that "the United States stands behind them"[60] and reiterated the terms of the 1959 U.S.-Pakistan mutual defense treaty, which committed the United States to come to Pakistan's aid in case of communist attack. Brzezinski wrote later that "the Pakistanis were rather concerned that they might be the next target of Soviet military aggression,"[61] but he stated plainly that the United States could not guarantee support in the event of an Indian attack.

The purported fear of Soviet military action did not keep the Pakistanis from escalating their support for the mujahideen. During a visit Brzezinski made to Pakistan and Saudi Arabia, discussions were held on "an expanded covert action program."[62] Brzezinski noted that Zia ul-Haq had asked him to emphasize the importance of Saudi-Pakistan cooperation and that the Americans had secured the Saudi undertaking "to facilitate Pakistani arms purchases, in return for a Pakistani military input to Saudi security."[63] An arrangement was made whereby "the Saudis would match the U.S. contribution to the mujahideen."[64] The CIA's Robert Gates wrote, "By July 1980, the covert program had been dramatically expanded to include all manner of weapons and military support for the Mujahideen ... [T]he insurgents were becoming ever more dependent on Pakistan, which had agreed to step up arms deliveries."[65]

Within a few months of the Soviet invasion of Afghanistan, the Pakistanis had managed to receive significantly higher levels of U.S. support for their covert operations. Saudi Arabia had started matching the U.S. contribution. General Zia ul-Haq also wanted economic assistance and military aid for his government—the reward from the United States for taking on the Soviets directly. Pakistan had invested heavily in its intervention in Afghanistan, and all along Zia ul-Haq had been increasing the level of intervention with the expectation of high levels of U.S. aid. He never doubted that the Americans would support his covert operation, and in fact the United States had begun its support even before the Soviets sent troops into Afghanistan. Zia also wanted the benefits for Pakistan's economy and its military that Pakistani military leaders expected from an alliance with the United States. He coveted the respect and legitimacy he would acquire as the military ruler of a frontline state in the struggle against Soviet expansion.

The Carter administration offered an initial package of $400 million in economic and military aid, which fell short of Pakistan's expectations. Brzezinski attributed the relatively modest size of the aid package to "budgetary stringencies as well as Pakistan's dubious record both on human rights and on non-proliferation."[66] General Zia described the offer as "peanuts" in a briefing for journalists on January 18, 1980. The amount was inadequate to ensure Pakistan's security, he declared, adding that it would "buy greater animosity from the Soviet Union, which is now much more influential in this region than the United States."[67] With his January 18 statement, Zia ul-Haq was bargaining for an offer of far greater levels of aid from the United States.

Even after describing the public offer of aid as inadequate, Zia ul-Haq continued to accept U.S. covert assistance. Cooperation between the CIA and the ISI in support of the Afghan mujahideen increased progressively. Within a few months, Saudi funding added to the size of Pakistan's Afghan jihad. Had Zia ul-Haq really been concerned about upsetting the Soviets, he would probably not have deepened Pakistan's involvement with the mujahideen before resolving the issue of U.S. security assistance. Zia had clearly calculated that covert cooperation would build support for Pakistan's position within the U.S. national security apparatus and pave the way for more aid down the road.

Zia ul-Haq's plan came to fruition in 1980 with the election of Ronald Reagan as president of the United States. The Reagan administration was less concerned than the Carter administration about Pakistan's human rights record or, for that matter, the question of Pakistan's nuclear program. Within its first few months, the Reagan administration put together a package of $3.2 billion in economic and military aid to be allocated over a five-year period. A State Department memorandum described the purpose of the aid as "to give Pakistan confidence in our commitment to its security and provide reciprocal benefits in terms of our regional interests."[68] Secretary of State Alexander M. Haig Jr. even told Pakistani officials that U.S. reservations over Pakistan's nuclear program "need not become the centerpiece of the U.S.-Pakistan relationship."[69] The new U.S. administration appeared to have communicated tacitly that it "could live with Pakistan's nuclear program as long as Islamabad did not explode a bomb."[70]

The U.S. Congress waived sanctions against Pakistan, imposed earlier because of Pakistan's nuclear program, soon after President Reagan came to office. The Pakistan government soon began receiving U.S. aid once again. The five-year aid package was followed in 1986 by a commitment of $4.02 billion in aid to be distributed during the next six years.

U.S. military assistance pleased the Pakistan army and solidified support for the continuation of Zia ul-Haq in power. The United States also rescheduled and wrote off part of Pakistan's outstanding debt. The flow of U.S. aid was accompanied by economic support from other Western and Arab donors. The U.S.-brokered security relationship with oil-rich Arab states like Saudi Arabia generated an additional benefit: large numbers of Pakistani workers were employed in the Persian Gulf states, where massive infrastructure development projects were then under development. Workers' remittances, coupled with the inflow of aid, contributed to Pakistan's enjoyment of a period of rapid economic growth.[71]

Zia ul-Haq considered the Afghan jihad as the core of his regime's policies. Once the security relationship with the United States had been consolidated, the quantum and quality of Pakistan's support for the mujahideen increased dramatically. The inflow of refugees escaping the fighting in Afghanistan provided an opportunity for Pakistan to recruit a much larger number of Afghans for the resistance organizations that had been organized in Peshawar. Although the CIA provided money and arms for the mujahideen, their recruitment, training, and political control was in the hands of the ISI. Tracing the history of the CIA's involvement in Afghanistan, journalist Steve Coll explained the terms of the arrangement between the United States and Pakistan:

> Zia sought and obtained political control over the CIA's weapons and money. He insisted that every gun and dollar allocated for the Mujahideen pass through Pakistani hands. He would decide which Afghan guerrillas benefited. He did not want Langley setting up its own Afghan kingmaking operation on Pakistani soil. Zia wanted to run up his own heart-and-minds operation inside Afghanistan ... For the first four years of its Afghan jihad, the CIA kept its solo operations and contacts with Afghans to a minimum ... To make his complex liaison with the CIA work, Zia relied on his chief spy and most trusted lieutenant, a gray-eyed and patrician general, Akhtar Abdul Rahman, director-general of ISI. Zia told Akhtar that it was his job to draw the CIA in and hold them at bay ... Akhtar laid down rules to ensure that ISI would retain control over contacts with Afghan rebels. No American—CIA or otherwise—would be permitted to cross the border into Afghanistan. Movements of weapons within Pakistan and distribution to Afghan commanders would be handled strictly by ISI officers.[72]

By the end of 1980, almost one million Afghans had come to Pakistan as refugees. By 1988, the number of refugees reached three million. These refugees had fled Afghanistan because of the upheaval following the Soviet invasion. As the mujahideen's guerrilla attacks made Afghanistan unsafe for Russian and Afghan communist forces, security in small towns and the countryside became fragile. Some of the refugees were religiously minded subsistence farmers escaping the godlessness of communism at the urging of village clerics. Middle-class professionals, landowners, small shopkeepers, civil servants, royalist military officers, and businesspeople also joined the flood of refugees headed toward Pakistan and Iran.

Pakistan housed Afghan refugees in tented villages, mainly in the NWFP and Balochistan. The refugees' expenses were paid primarily by the Office of the UN High Commissioner for Refugees. A Pakistani civil servant was also appointed commissioner for Afghan refugees, to administer the provision of basic services to the refugees. Pakistani officials gave the mujahideen groups an unofficial role in registering refugees upon their arrival in Pakistan, which created a linkage between access to refugee aid and membership in one of the seven mujahideen parties that Pakistan recognized. In addition to the Jamiat-e-Islami and Hizbe Islami that had been active since 1973, two other fundamentalist parties had emerged by the time U.S. and Arab aid started flowing through Pakistan. One was the Ittehad-e-Islami (Islamic Union) led by the Wahhabi cleric, Abdur Rab Rasool Sayyaf. The other was the faction of Hizbe Islami led by an elderly Pashtun theologian, Yunus Khalis, who broke away from Hekmatyar's group in 1979. In addition, there were three moderate groups led by conservative leaders who did not share the radical Islamist worldview of the Islamists. Although Pakistan allowed all seven groups to operate, it clearly favored the two factions it had worked with the longest—Jamiat-e-Islami and Hekmatyar's Hizbe Islami. Sayyaf managed to secure the sponsorship of Saudi Arabia by virtue of his affiliation with Wahhabi theology. The three moderate groups were preferred by Western diplomats and journalists, but the size of their political and military following was limited by Pakistan's refusal to give them more than a small percentage of money and arms.

One of the earliest Pakistani refugee commissioners, Abdullah, was closely linked to Pakistan's Jamaat-e-Islami. In a pattern similar to that followed by the ISI in dealing with the mujahideen, Abdullah worked to minimize donor influence in refugee camps. Although in principle the refugee administration had nothing to do with the jihad or military activities, the refugee camps became recruitment centers for mujahideen groups. In addition to making use of the refugees' religious and political sentiments, mujahideen recruiters could also take advantage of refugees' need for survival. Most young refugees could not find work, but they could be offered jobs as mujahideen soldiers. Over time, Pakistani officials set up the education system for refugees in a manner that converted young Afghans to the cause of jihad and the Islamist worldview. Zia ul-Haq also encouraged Islamist charities from Saudi Arabia and the Gulf states to build mosques and madrassas both for Afghan refugees and Pakistan's own population.

As the scope of the Afghan jihad expanded, so did the influence of Islamist ideology in Pakistan. Ever mindful of the need to retain control, Zia ul-Haq made sure that Jamaat-e-Islami was not the only Pakistani party involved with the Afghan refugees and militants. One faction of the Jamiat Ulema Islam comprising clerics from the influential Deobandi school joined in the distribution of charity received from Arab countries and in the setting up madrassas. In his pan-Islamic zeal, Zia ul-Haq allowed volunteers from all over the world to come and train alongside the Afghan mujahideen. By 1984, Islamists from Morocco in North Africa to Mindanao in South Philippines had arrived in Pakistan. Some enrolled in Pakistani madrassas and at the International Islamic University at Islamabad. Others, like the Moro Islamic Liberation Front (a group dedicated to an Islamic state in the Muslim areas of the Philippines) and the Rohingya Muslim Liberation Front (which sought autonomy for Burma's Muslim minority), opened offices, albeit small ones, to raise funds and issue statements for their respective causes.

These global mujahideen received grants from the Saudi-based Rabita al-Alam al-Islami. Rabita enabled members of the Arab Muslim Brotherhood to travel to Pakistan and work with both the refugees and the mujahideen. The Motamar al-Alam Islami (Muslim World Congress), another pan-Islamic network that had been founded in Pakistan in 1949 under the leadership of the former grand mufti of Palestine, Al-Haj Amin al-Husseini, established a liaison relationship with Muslim communities in Southeast Asia. Since Motamar's founding, the Pakistan government had provided it with a small annual grant. Now, with U.S. and Arab aid flowing for the Afghan jihad, Motamar's funding could be increased, and Pakistan's government handed over a large mosque in Islamabad to serve as headquarters for the Motamar. From its new headquarters, Motamar al-Alam Islami aided efforts to spread the message of jihad and of Pakistan's support for Islamic causes around the world.

The most significant person to arrive in Pakistan at the time was the Palestinian scholar Abdullah Azzam, who created the Maktab al-Khidmaat (Services Bureau) to facilitate the participation of foreign mujahideen in the Afghan jihad. Azzam cited the Quran and Hadith to remind Muslims of their obligation to assist the jihad. Osama bin Laden, scion of a prosperous Saudi business family, was one of many who were moved by Azzam's call. Azzam moved to Pakistan in 1984 and started funding the Maktab al-Khidmaat. His contributions increased the number of foreign recruits for mujahideen activities.

Western journalists reporting on Afghanistan at the time often saw only the side of the Afghan refugee relief effort that involved Western governments and nongovernmental organizations. In their reporting of the jihad, described widely as the Afghans' freedom struggle, the CIA's role was highlighted. Parallel to the U.S.-led effort on behalf of the Afghans was the operation run by the Islamists. To this day, no one knows how much money the Islamist charities raised or spent. Reliable figures are also not available for the number of foreign mujahideen who went through Pakistan at the time. The ISI was the only organization that dealt with both Western and Islamist participants in the anti-Soviet jihad.

Although Zia ul-Haq had been keen to obtain U.S. funding and weapons for his venture in Afghanistan, he had always known that U.S. objectives were different from those he had defined as Pakistan's goals. For Zia, Afghanistan marked an important turning point in Pakistan's quest for an Islamic identity at home and for leadership of the Islamic world. Although he publicly voiced his Islamist sentiments, Zia shared the full extent of what he hoped to accomplish only with a small group of confidants, one of whom, journalist Ziaul Islam Ansari, explained Zia's overarching vision:

As a Pakistani soldier and practicing Muslim, General Muhammad Zia ul-Haq believed that Islamic precepts should be influential in Pakistani social life to such an extent that those seeking to move Pakistan in the direction of secularism and socialism should fail in their designs . . . [In Zia ul-Haq's view] Pakistan would be turned into a self sufficient, stable and strong country with a strong position within the Islamic world, South Asia and West Asia, capable of providing strength to Islamic revivalist movements in adjoining countries and regions. This includes that region of the Far East that has become distant from us because of the loss of East Pakistan. [This Pakistani sphere of influence] comprises the region encompassing the area from Afghanistan to Turkey, including Iran and the Muslim majority states of the Soviet Union in Central Asia.[73]

Ansari's description shows a Zia ul-Haq who believed that his policies of Islamization at home would strengthen Pakistan against those conspiring to move Pakistan away from Islam. By codifying Islamic principles in the country's constitution and legal system, Zia ul-Haq was paving the way for the day when "the lower rungs of society are mobilized in favor of greater Islamization."[74] At the same time, the Afghan jihad would make Pakistan "the instrument for the creation of an Islamic ideological regional block that would be the source of a natural Islamic revolutionary movement, replacing artificial alliances such as the Baghdad Pact. This would be the means of starting a new era of greatness for the Muslim nations of Asia and Africa.[75]

While Zia ul-Haq pursued an ideological dream in Afghanistan, U.S. objectives were more specific and somewhat limited. In Afghanistan, the United States hoped to roll back what had been an expanding Soviet influence in the third world. For the United States, Afghanistan was just the largest in a series of covert wars—others were being fought in Nicaragua and Angola—that were meant to punish the Soviet Union and inflict a heavy cost in men, money, and prestige. The CIA estimated that Soviet costs between 1981 and 1986 in Afghanistan, Angola, and Nicaragua amounted to about $13 billion.[76] Soviet casualties in Afghanistan amounted to eighteen thousand dead and numerous wounded. By contrast, the United States spent $2 billion in covert aid to the Afghan resistance between 1980 and 1989 and lost no soldiers in its proxy engagement with the Soviets.

Once the United States decided to supply sophisticated ground-to-air missiles to the mujahideen in 1986, the Soviet Union's one major advantage—airpower—against the mujahideen became ineffective. The mujahideen were described as "freedom fighters" in the international media, and their successes were a symbol of Soviet humiliation. By 1987–1988, the United States had achieved its objective in Afghanistan, and the Soviets, now led by the reformer Mikhail Gorbachev, were willing to negotiate a way out of their Afghan quagmire.

In Pakistan, Zia ul-Haq held parliamentary elections in 1985 and appointed a civilian prime minister whom he expected to be weak and compliant. The new prime minister, Muhammad Khan Junejo, slowly extended press freedom and demanded the removal of martial law. Although Zia ul-Haq kept Junejo away from briefings about Afghanistan for almost a year,[77] Junejo intervened in the conduct of Pakistan's foreign policy. During an official visit to the United States in 1986, Junejo indicated to his American interlocutors that he would follow the U.S. lead in a negotiated settlement of the Afghanistan issue. He also directed his Minister of State for Foreign Affairs, Zaim Noorani, to forward cables from Pakistani embassies abroad to him first, before routing them to the president.[78] Noorani, a politician like Junejo, agreed with the need to assert the civilian government's role in international relations. Zia ul-Haq was not always informed first of routine diplomatic developments.

In 1986, Junejo also allowed Benazir Bhutto—daughter of former prime minister Zulfikar Ali Bhutto, the man Zia ul-Haq had overthrown and executed—to return to Pakistan from exile. The younger Bhutto returned home to a rapturous welcome. During her exile she had made a favorable impression on Western journalists, diplomats, and some members of the U.S. Congress. Although she was careful not to criticize the United States upon her return to Pakistan, Bhutto publicly questioned the wisdom of Pakistan's Afghan policy.

Pakistani public opinion against the Afghan war had never been a factor in Zia ul-Haq's calculation while he kept the lid on dissent; in the new environment, however, the support of Islamist parties was no longer sufficient to deal with the overt manifestation of public opinion against Pakistan's role in the Afghan war. Afghan refugees, now numbering some three million, were upsetting the political balance in Pakistan and causing considerable social strains. Pakistan was officially training an average of 20,000 Afghan mujahideen per year. Pakistan's Islamist parties were getting their cadres trained alongside the Afghans as well, leading to a flexing of muscle in political clashes, especially on college campuses. Vast amounts of weapons, destined for use by the mujahideen but finding their way into the open market, were being brought into Pakistan from several countries. The Pakistan-Afghan border area had become a haven for smuggling of all kinds of goods, including opium poppy and heroin. Allegations were widespread that ISI officials, now numbering in the tens of thousands, were freelancing in the weapons and drug trades. Law and order in many Pakistani cities had deteriorated, for which many Pakistanis blamed the Afghan war. By the time the United States and the Soviet Union came close to a deal on Afghanistan, ordinary Pakistanis were ready for a settlement.

Prime Minister Junejo, encouraged by U.S. diplomats, in April 1988 accepted a deal negotiated through the UN for the withdrawal of Soviet troops from Afghanistan. Zia ul-Haq and the ISI insisted that any agreement for Soviet withdrawal should also address the issue of who would rule Afghanistan after the departure of the Soviets. The accords signed at Geneva, however, left that question unresolved. U.S. officials maintained that the PDPA regime in Kabul would fall to the mujahideen within weeks of the withdrawal of Soviet military protection. Zia ul-Haq was certain that the mujahideen would end up fighting among themselves.

At the heart of Zia's concern was the fear that, after the Soviet military presence was gone, the United States would no longer support Zia's vision of an Islamic fundamentalist Afghanistan closely tied to Pakistan. Zia ul-Haq had "hoped to force a political settlement while the superpowers were still engaged."[79] He wanted the United States to pay him his due for helping defeat the Soviets by installing his preferred Afghan leader, the Islamist Gulbuddin Hekmatyar, at the head of an Afghan mujahideen coalition government. The United States wanted to do no such thing and was content with declaring victory now that the Soviets were leaving Afghanistan.

In the end, Zia ul-Haq publicly went along with the Geneva accords, which provided for the withdrawal of Soviet troops from Afghanistan, the return of refugees, and the end of Soviet and U.S. intervention in Afghanistan. The accords set a deadline for both the withdrawal of Soviet forces and the final shipments of arms by the two superpowers to their respective clients in Afghanistan. The stated deadline meant the ISI could receive additional shipments of weapons from the CIA; these weapons would be used to help the mujahideen get rid of the Soviet-installed regime in Kabul, headed by Najibullah.

After the large shipment of arms for the post-Soviet phase of the Afghan jihad had been received, Zia ul-Haq in May 1988 dissolved Parliament and dismissed Prime Minister Junejo, acts that divided the conservative political coalition Zia had put together during the decade. Even some Islamist groups, notably the Jamaat-e-Islami, did not publicly agree with what they saw as Zia ul-Haq's final power grab. Zia was politically isolated at home and unsure of U.S. support. With the ISI's help, Zia planned to hold a referendum that would give him absolute power to complete Pakistan's Islamization.[80]

On August 17, 1988, General Zia ul-Haq and several of his key generals died in a mysterious plane crash. Those killed included the U.S. ambassador to Pakistan and the architect of the Afghan jihad, General Akhtar Abdul Rahman, who had been promoted to chairman, Joint Chiefs of Staff, some time earlier and whom some considered Zia ul-Haq's possible successor. Those who shared Zia ul-Haq's vision of an Islamized Pakistan and a forward policy of Islamic revival felt that at one stroke the Afghan mujahideen had lost their two most influential champions.[81]

With the death of Zia ul-Haq, Pakistan's military and ISI did not give up jihad or the pursuit of strategic depth in Afghanistan. If anything, the divergence of Pakistani and U.S. interests during negotiation of the Geneva accords on Afghanistan made Pakistan's security establishment more suspicious than ever before of U.S. intentions. The numerous conspiracy theories about who killed Zia ul-Haq invariably included the United States as a possible suspect. One former ISI official wrote:

[T]he US government shed few genuine tears at Zia's death. It was the State Department's belief that Zia had outlived his usefulness. With the Soviets leaving Afghanistan, the last thing the US wanted was for communist rule in Kabul to be replaced by an Islamic fundamentalist one. U.S. officials were convinced that this was Zia's aim. According to them his dream was an Islamic power block stretching from Iran through Afghanistan to Pakistan with, eventually, the Uzbek, Turkoman and Tajik provinces of the USSR included. To the State Department such a huge area shaded green on the map would be worse than Afghanistan painted red.[82]

The massive covert operation and aid packages that had formed the basis of close relations between Pakistan and the United States also drove the two countries apart. Islam as a factor in Pakistan's national security policy grew severalfold during the period of jihad against the Soviet Union. The much enlarged ISI—its covert operations capability enhanced tenfold—became a greater factor in Pakistan's domestic and foreign policies. Pakistan's military and security services were deeply influenced by their close ties to the Islamist groups. Islamists staunchly adopted the Pakistani state's national security agenda and, in return, increasing numbers of officers accepted the Islamist view of a more religious state.

Pakistan still wanted U.S. economic and security assistance as it had since its inception, but its military leaders were more convinced than ever that they needed to chart their own course and that the only practical basis for Pakistan's relations with the United States would be for both sides to use each other. Pakistan's military leadership believed the Americans would have to learn to live with Pakistan saying one thing and doing another. Pakistan would not settle for anything less than the major role it sought as a leader in its region and the Muslim world.

6

Military Rule by Other Means

At the time of his death, General Zia ul-Haq wielded absolute power. He was president of Pakistan as well as the chief of army staff. No one had planned for the contingency of his sudden death. The 1973 constitution, as amended by Zia ul-Haq, provided for succession to the office of president by the chairman of Pakistan's indirectly elected senate. The incumbent of that office at the time of Zia's death was Ghulam Ishaq Khan, an elderly bureaucrat who had been the late general's most trusted civilian associate. The vice chief of the army staff, General Mirza Aslam Beg, invited Ishaq Khan to army headquarters soon after confirmation of Zia ul-Haq's death. Both men represented Pakistan's permanent establishment although the fact that the meeting was held in military headquarters indicated Ishaq Khan's understanding of the general's preeminence. Immediately after that meeting, Ishaq Khan became president and Beg took over as army chief.[1]

After an elaborate state funeral for Zia ul-Haq, at which a large number of his supporters and Afghan refugees demonstrated their admiration for him, Ishaq Khan and Beg attended to the challenges facing Pakistan.[2] The instinct of both establishment figures was to persist with Pakistan's traditional policy although they gave a lot of thought to the changed circumstances in which they operated. With impending Soviet withdrawal from Afghanistan, U.S. aid could not be guaranteed to continue beyond 1992—the last year of the $4.02 billion aid package negotiated in 1986. Differences between the United States and Pakistan over

199

what kind of government should replace the communist regime in Kabul were unresolved. With its interest in Afghanistan waning, the United States would most likely resume pressure on Pakistan over the twin issues it had chosen to ignore for the preceding several years—nuclear proliferation and absence of democracy.

Ishaq Khan and Beg decided to continue with Zia ul-Haq's policy of backing the Islamists in Afghanistan, hoping that over time they would be able to persuade the United States to let Pakistan have its way. Islam as a cornerstone of Pakistani identity was not in question for either of them although Beg was less devout in his personal life than Zia ul-Haq or, for that matter, Ishaq Khan. The issues that most concerned the two conjoined successors of Zia ul-Haq related to security policy. Beg had argued even during Zia ul-Haq's life that "Pakistan needs to show its spine"[3] to the United States. The Americans could not afford to ignore Pakistan, their only ally in a turbulent region, he maintained.

General Beg also believed that Pakistan's nuclear capability was its greatest strategic asset.[4] Instead of postponing the development of nuclear weapons to avert U.S. sanctions, Beg proposed accelerating the nuclear program and going public about it. He believed that the United States would not abandon a nuclear-armed Pakistan; in fact, a demonstrated nuclear capability could become the new reason for continued U.S. interest in supporting Pakistan. The United States was more likely to accept Pakistan's choice of leaders for Afghanistan if Pakistan stayed the course. In Beg's view, Pakistan could compensate for crossing the nuclear Rubicon by simultaneously taking steps toward democracy.[5]

Beg also realized that the military, as an institution, had become unpopular after eleven years of dictatorship under one of its generals. Only a few days before Zia ul-Haq's death, an incident had occurred not far from army headquarters that had involved the outpouring of antimilitary sentiment. An impromptu crowd first beat up a uniformed junior officer responsible for an automobile accident and then had shouted slogans against the army's domination.[6] If such incidents were to be avoided, the implications of further direct military rule would have to be addressed. The army could keep power, but with extreme repression of a type that Pakistan had not experienced and most probably would not have accepted. The alternative would be to create a civilian facade that would allow the army to rule without causing the hatred that invariably results from intrusion into civilian life by men in uniform.

The army's charisma was fading. Major General Sher Ali Khan had advised General Yahya Khan in 1969 that the army's ability to rule lay in its being perceived by the people as "a mythical entity, a magical force, that would succor them in times of need when all else failed."[7] It was in the army's interest, Beg concluded, to give the impression of civilian rule. Beg decided to operate from the shadows while he allowed Ishaq Khan to announce upcoming parliamentary elections. The ISI assembled a coalition—Islami Jamhoori Ittehad (IJI—Islamic Democratic Alliance)—of Islamist and promilitary parties to serve as the military's proxy in a controlled political process. While Pakistan's civilians contested elections, Beg started work on plans to restore the military's standing in the eyes of the Pakistani people.

As soon as campaigning for the 1988 elections began, it became obvious that Benazir Bhutto and the PPP had wide support. The PPP was seen as the party of change after eleven years of military rule under Zia ul-Haq. The IJI, on the other hand, was seen as an alliance of individuals and parties that had by and large supported Zia ul-Haq and who were likely to continue his policies. The ISI funded the IJI and ran a dirty tricks campaign on its behalf.[8] Beg established contact with Bhutto and assured her that elections would be free and fair.[9] The government, however, announced that only voters with national identity cards would be allowed to vote, which effectively disfranchised one-fifth of registered voters who had not yet been provided with these cards; Beg then prevailed upon the courts to uphold the restriction. Those excluded from voting by this ruse were usually poor farmers and urban workers, both classes that generally favored the PPP.

The military wanted to influence the outcome of the election but was not willing to rig the polls. Their best case would have been the election of an IJI government; in the worst case the military hoped to keep the PPP in check with a slim majority or at the head of a weak coalition.

The lead role in the IJI's election campaign was assigned to the Jamaat-e-Islami. Jamaat-e-Islami's new leader, Qazi Hussain Ahmed, initially refused to join the IJI. He wanted to break from Jamaat-e-Islami's image as a party with limited appeal, and he sought to cast himself as a leader of the masses. Qazi Hussain Ahmed reckoned that his party's interests would best be served by participating in the democratic process as an alternative to the PPP instead of trying to block the PPP in collusion with the military. Lieutenant General Hamid Gul, who had succeeded Akhtar Abdul Rahman as director general of the ISI, told Qazi Hussain Ahmed that membership in the IJI was not optional; if the Jamaat-e-Islami did not help the army and the ISI in their domestic political strategy, their role as partners in Afghanistan and future jihad operations could suffer.

General Gul also made an emotional argument about how the Islamists cause would suffer if Bhutto were not restrained. Gul and his deputy, Brigadier Imtiaz Ahmed, told Islamists, "The ISI has intelligence that Benazir Bhutto has promised the Americans a rollback of our nuclear program. She will prevent a mujahideen victory in Afghanistan and stop plans for jihad in Kashmir in its tracks."[10] Although jihad had not yet started in Kashmir, the ISI was apparently preparing for it. The domestic political struggle had become intertwined with the army's ideological national security agenda.

The Jamaat-e-Islami not only came on board with the IJI; it even decided to campaign against Bhutto with arguments put forward by the ISI. Soon the IJI was accusing Bhutto of advancing America's interests and planning to sell out Pakistan's nuclear program. General Gul also encouraged other Islamist groups, notably the pro-Zia faction of the Deobandi group, the Jamiat Ulema Islam, to advance the argument that Islam did not allow a woman to become the leader of an Islamic state. The campaign on the nuclear issue enabled Islamists to claim that they were guardians of Pakistan's nuclear capability. Although voters were not significantly swayed by the arguments against a woman becoming prime minister, the issue soured Bhutto's relations with Pakistan's clergy. The ISI had effectively made it difficult for Bhutto to mend fences with some religious groups for a long time to come.

The 1988 election gave Bhutto's PPP 92 seats out of 215 in the lower house of Parliament. The IJI won 54. Even after these results, the ISI tried to patch together a coalition led by the IJI. The IJI had gone into the election with a dual leadership. Its president was Ghulam Mustafa Jatoi, an elder, senior politician from Bhutto's home province of Sindh who had served in her father's cabinet. The IJI's most resourceful leader, however, was Nawaz Sharif, a young industrialist whom Zia ul-Haq had appointed chief minister of Punjab. Sharif was vying for control of the Pakistan Muslim League, the largest party within the IJI, nominally still headed by former Prime Minister Junejo. In the election, Jatoi lost his own seat in Parliament to a PPP candidate, as did Junejo. Sharif, on the other hand, managed to use his position as Punjab chief minister to gain a plurality in the provincial legislature. The ISI could no longer push Jatoi's candidacy as prime minister, but appointing Sharif would have further alienated Sindhis who were already aggrieved by Punjabi domination during years of military rule.

Working with the parliamentary arithmetic, military leaders found a way to resolve the problem. They would let Bhutto become prime minister, and they would help elect Sharif as chief minister of Punjab, the largest province, once again. Sharif, as de facto opposition leader, would then keep Bhutto on her toes as he simultaneously controlled the levers of patronage in the provincial government. Confrontation between Bhutto and Sharif would provide the army and the ISI with additional leverage for influencing domestic politics.

President Ishaq Khan waited to nominate Bhutto as prime minister for fifteen days after her party had emerged as the largest parliamentary bloc in general elections. Behind-the-scenes bargaining during that fortnight had involved Bhutto, on the one hand, and Ishaq Khan, General Beg, and the U.S. ambassador, Robert Oakley, on the other. Bhutto promised to support Ishaq Khan in presidential elections due to be held soon. She promised the United States continuity in Pakistan's foreign policy. Sahibzada Yaqub Khan, the retired general who had served as foreign minister from 1982–1987 and re-appointed to that position by Zia ul-Haq a few months before his death, was retained in that position to signal that continuity. The army was given a say in the choice of defense minister while a senior civil servant continued as economic adviser. Bhutto also agreed to maintain existing levels of defense spending and assured General Beg that she would not interfere with the military's privileges and perquisites.[11] One of Bhutto's advisers at the time wrote later:

The establishment had only accepted Benazir as Prime Minister on sufferance. General Aslam Beg did not always miss the opportunity of drawing attention to his king maker role. "Had *we* made such conditions (as the Afghan interim government was being asked to fulfill), *Mohtarma* [Benazir Bhutto] would not be Prime Minister today," was one of his refrains. On another occasion, reacting testily to a press comment that [the army] had hijacked foreign policy from the Foreign Ministry, he said, "We have bigger things to hijack, if we want to."[12]

Bhutto was sworn in as prime minister on December 1, 1988, and declared that she would "free political prisoners, revive student and labor unions and remove government controls on the press."[13] She gave credit to Ishaq Khan and the military leadership for accepting her as prime minister after years of opposing her. Reporters and observers noted the irony that "those who had tortured her and rounded up her supporters"[14] were now saluting her and pledging to protect her. Some also asked the question, "Would they let her govern?"[15] Difficulties between the civil-military bureaucracy and the political leadership began to surface within a few days of Bhutto's inauguration. "Phone calls were being misdirected, files going missing, her own servants blackmailed by General Hamid Gul's ISI,"[16] British journalist Christina Lamb wrote of the atmosphere in the prime minister's house. To show how they did not take the change in government seriously, senior civil servants allowed a hijacked Soviet plane to land in Pakistan without consulting the prime minister on the day she took office.

In addition to sharing power with Ishaq Khan and General Beg, Bhutto also had to contend with the election of Nawaz Sharif as chief minister of Punjab. This was the first time in Pakistan's history that the government at the center did not also control the government of Pakistan's largest province. Sharif adopted a confrontational attitude toward Bhutto, demanding greater provincial autonomy and defying the authority of the federal government.[17] Provincial autonomy had historically been demanded by Pakistan's smaller provinces, which did not like the dominance of Punjab, and this was the first time that a Punjabi provincial government was confronting the central authority and seeking greater autonomy under the constitution.

Sharif attacked Bhutto's government at two levels. On the one hand, he worked with the Islamist parties, which were already allies within the IJI, in questioning Bhutto's ideological credentials. On the other, Sharif unleashed provincial sentiment among Punjabis who resented Bhutto for being a Sindhi. With the help of the ISI, Sharif also forged alliances with ethnic political parties from other Pakistani provinces, claiming that the cause of provincial autonomy was more likely to succeed now that a Punjabi leader had embraced it.

Bhutto attempted to get rid of Sharif's provincial government by accepting the suggestion from her party to move a vote of no confidence in the Punjab legislature against Sharif.[18] The IJI government in Punjab depended on several independents for its majority and the PPP tried to win over some of these independents with inducements. Sharif fought off the attempt successfully as he "was good at the game himself and had more patronage, money and menace at his disposal."[19] The federal government then attempted to break Sharif's confrontational resolve by hurting the economic interests of his family's vast industrial empire. One-hundred sixty charges of tax evasion, loan default, and other felonies and misdemeanors were brought against Sharif, his family, and business or political colleagues.[20] State-controlled Pakistan Railways "suddenly discovered that it could spare no wagons for transporting imported scrap iron from Karachi port to the Sharif foundries in Lahore."[21]

Sharif withstood these threats and challenges, comfortable in the knowledge that he enjoyed the military's backing. He periodically appealed to the president or the army chief publicly to seek protection, which provided justification for the military's behind-the-scenes political maneuvers. This clearly served the purpose of those within the civil-military establishment who had reluctantly accepted the idea of sharing power with civilian politicians but who were eager to prove that the politicians simply did not possess any talent for governance.

The confrontation hurt Bhutto's prestige while raising Sharif's stature. American scholar Lawrence Ziring commented thus on the situation:

> The political infighting that has characterized the Pakistan scene since Bhutto was selected to lead the government has been nasty

and bitter, and not without cost. Although there is considerably more political expression, there is also increasing difficulty in tackling the problems at hand. The Prime Minister's shaky majority and her dependence on the army as a stabilizing influence have deflected attention and energies from pressing national and regional issues. Matters of social justice remain to be addressed and the repeal of fundamentalist laws considered degrading to women has yet to be attempted. The economy has been allowed to drift and economic dislocation has burdened the middle class along with the poor . . . The inability to act on these fronts is attributed to backdoor politics wherein the Pakistan Peoples Party (PPP) must satisfy different constituencies lest it lose its slim majority, but the failure to confront these matters is also due to structural limitations and financial constraints.[22]

Ziring observed that "Nawaz Sharif's performance reminded too many Pakistanis of the authoritarian patterns experienced during the Zia period" and noted his "seemingly open call to the president and the armed forces to intervene in domestic political affairs."[23] Although Bhutto had risen to power because of her mandate from the people, a year after her coming to office Ziring pointed to her "apparent reliance on the armed forces."[24]

The 1988 election and its aftermath determined the pattern of Pakistan's domestic politics for the next eleven years. When Benazir Bhutto became prime minister in December 1988, she had no experience in government. She was at college when her father was prime minister, and the younger Bhutto had been in prison or in exile for most of the Zia ul-Haq era. The PPP had been in opposition for eleven years, and most of its rank and file in Pakistan had been persecuted. Politicians from the generation of Bhutto's father either hated her for being his daughter or did not treat her with respect because of her youth. Many members of the PPP with experience of government had been co-opted by the military, which left only inexperienced radicals or idealists to serve at Bhutto's side. To make matters worse, President Ishaq Khan, General Beg, General Gul, and Nawaz Sharif saw Bhutto as an adversary from her first day in office. Islamists sniped at her, questioning her faith and her patriotism, and they were regularly provided fresh material for new attacks by the security services.

While planning for general elections after Zia ul-Haq's death, the ISI had already identified Islamic issues as one of Bhutto's "greatest vulnerabilities."[25] Although the Pakistan Muslim league (PML) accounted for 80 percent of the IJI's electoral candidates, care had been taken to ensure that the alliance comprised nine parties to generate comparisons with the nine-party Pakistan National Alliance (PNA) that had campaigned against Zulfikar Ali Bhutto in 1977. Six of the nine alliance partners were religious parties. In addition to the Jamaat-e-Islami and a faction of Jamiat Ulema Islam (JUI), these were Jamiat-e-Mashaikh (Society of Spiritual Leaders), Jamiat-e-Ahl-e-Hadith (Society of the Followers of the Prophet's Tradition), Nizam-e-Mustafa Group (Group for the System of the Prophet), and Hizb-e-jihad (the Party of Jihad). The participation of these groups, however small, ensured that religious issues could be kept alive and "the Islamic spirit that brought people out in the streets against [the elder] Bhutto could be revived to meet the challenge posed by his daughter."[26]

During the election campaign, some of the clerics in the IJI had denounced Bhutto and her mother as "gangsters in bangles."[27] In an effort to paint her as a westernized woman, who would corrupt the morals of Pakistanis once in power, leaflets purporting to show Bhutto and her mother in swimsuits were airdropped in major Pakistani cities.[28] Training aircraft from the Lahore Aero Club had been rented for this purpose by a Lahore businessman with close ties to General Beg after Sharif and his team refused to use the material in their election literature. The Islamist weekly *Takbeer* ran photos of Bhutto's mother dancing with President Ford when she visited Washington as First Lady. ISI's Brigadier Imtiaz Ahmed had made these photographs available to several Islamist publications.[29]

Soon after Bhutto's election as prime minister, several ulema issued a fatwa (religious edict) declaring that a woman could not be head of government in an Islamic country.[30] The fatwa was followed by ulema conferences at madrasas (Islamic seminaries) known for their ties with the Afghan jihad. The Jamaat-e-Islami leader, Qazi Husain Ahmed, advised against both the attacks on Bhutto as a decadent western woman and the campaign against a woman's right to lead the country.[31] He argued that Bhutto had just won an election, which showed that the people were not affected by these issues. Bhutto's real vulnerability, he argued, lay in her "lack of credibility" on national security issues. According to Ahmed, the IJI's focus should have been on criticizing Bhutto as a security risk, someone that could not be trusted with the country's nuclear program and the jihad in Afghanistan. The smaller clerical parties preferred sticking to the line of attack on cultural issues. In the end, the IJI engaged in both.

As part of an opening up of the media, Pakistan television started popular music programs. Women singers and actresses could now appear on TV without covering their head, ending the restrictions imposed under Zia ul-Haq. Bhutto herself was always careful to cover her head in public but that did not seem to make a difference to the Islamists. They demonstrated outside television stations against the introduction of a new permissive culture and accused the government of spreading obscenity and undermining Islamic morality.[32]

These campaigns by the Islamists did not have a major impact on the political situation until February 12, 1989, when a protest in Islamabad against British author Salman Rushdie's book *Satanic Verses* turned violent. The book parodied the prophet of Islam and was deemed offensive by most Muslims once their attention was drawn to some of its passages. But the book had been published a year earlier, in 1988, and no one in the Muslim world had taken notice of it until Pakistani cleric-politician Maulana Kausar Niazi wrote a series of articles about it in the Pakistani press. Niazi said that a copy of the book, with offensive passages duly highlighted, had been sent to him by a senior official in the ISI.[33] Niazi had been minister for religious affairs in Zulfikar Ali Bhutto's government and had split from the PPP soon after Zia ul-Haq's coup d'état in 1977. He was in the political wilderness at the time he wrote the articles about Rushdie's book. The ISI did him a political favor by providing him an issue to revive his political fortunes. As for the ISI's motives, the agency was repeating what Pakistani intelligence services had successfully done in the past: It was hoping to embarrass a civilian government over an emotive religious issue.

After the publication of Kausar Niazi's articles in the Urdu press, another veteran of similar campaigns, Maulana Abdul Sattar Niazi, called a conference of ulema to demand action against Rushdie. As a young man Sattar Niazi had been part of the campaign for Pakistan's creation. After independence, he had been part of almost every religious-political campaign that helped the military's intervention in politics starting with the anti-Ahmedi protests of 1953. The government had already banned *Satanic Verses* and officials in Bhutto's administration did not know what else to do in response to the ulema's fresh campaign.[34] For their part, the Islamist organizers of the anti-Rushdie protests took the position that the publication of the book was an American-Zionist conspiracy against Islam. When a major demonstration led by the two Niazis against *Satanic Verses* was organized in Islamabad on February 12, 1989, the protesters attacked the U.S. Information Service building. They were carrying signs that read, "America and Israel: Enemies of Islam."[35] Police had to shoot at the mob to disperse demonstrators and protect the lives of Pakistanis and Americans inside in the building. Five demonstrators were killed.[36]

The news of the violent Pakistani protests drew international attention to Rushdie's book and led to Ayatollah Khomeini's *fatwa* against the author as a blasphemer. In Pakistan, it exacerbated the religious parties' hatred of Bhutto and her fledgling pro-western administration. Rushdie's American publishers had earlier published Bhutto's autobiography *Daughter of the East*, enabling her detractors to link the two, however tenuous that connection.[37] The storming of the U.S. Information Service in the presence of CNN cameras brought images of the burning of American flags in Benazir Bhutto's Pakistan into U.S. homes, undermining Bhutto's credentials as America's friend. The ISI managed to keep its role in the affair hidden. The U.S. ambassador, Robert Oakley, spoke of "outside influence" on the protesters but voiced no suspicion about sabotage of Bhutto's government by powerful domestic forces.

"There is the smell of money around," Oakley said, "but it is too soon to say for sure. There is a tradition of Libyan and Iranian money here. We will look. The Russians aren't happy about either the Pakistanis or us not backing down on Afghanistan either."[38] Given the IJI's role in the violent protests, and the ISI's support for the IJI, the U.S. embassy should at least have examined the possibility of a home-grown plot. Even if the Libyans, Iranians, or Russians had been involved, they would have had to exercise their influence through clerics forming part of the IJI and with ties to the ISI.

Bhutto started out with tremendous disadvantages, which compounded with the passage of time. The system of governance that emerged after Bhutto's election as prime minister did not make her as powerful as other prime ministers in countries with a parliamentary form of democracy. Bhutto clashed sporadically with the president and the army chief until she was dismissed from office in August 1990. As one observer put it, "the Bhutto government operated against the backdrop of a hostile military establishment that was prepared to use any opportunity to remove her from power. The actual behavior of her government provided a number of such chances."[39] Bhutto's mistakes can be listed in summary as follows:

From the start the federal government failed to establish a workable relationship with the provinces. Relations with the Baluchistan provincial government were tense throughout Bhutto's regime; growing political confrontation with Nawaz Sharif brought relations with Punjab to a low point; and the major cities in Bhutto's home province of Sindh suffered from the worst violence since independence. In addition, frequent allegations of corruption surrounded both the PPP and the Bhutto family. But more important, Benazir Bhutto frequently challenged the military either directly or indirectly. General Hamid Gul, who had been directing the all-powerful Inter-Services Intelligence (ISI), was replaced by a retired general, and later Bhutto pre-empted the president by announcing that the chairman of the Joint Chiefs of Staff, Admiral Sirohey, was due to retire.[40]

There was, however, a more fundamental conflict between Bhutto and the civil-military combine. The young prime minister was seen as "the symbol of a democratic Pakistan."[41] Her success would have marked the end of the Pakistani establishment's control over the country. Bhutto was widely admired and accepted in the United States, which meant that she could develop relations with the U.S. independent of the military's model of aid seeking. Bhutto called for foreign direct investment in addition to aid. She also spoke of the need to "set an example in Asia" and to "encourage the spread of democracy" together with the United States.[42] Bhutto's liberal instincts could mark the end of the decades-old policy paradigm of Pakistan's permanent establishment. Instead of looking at conservative interprétations of Islam as the national unifier, Bhutto emphasized democracy. For her, the United States was more of a long-term friend than mere supplier of arms and aid on a quid pro quo basis. More important, Bhutto seemed seriously committed to "a new era in relations"[43] with India.

Indian Prime Minister Rajiv Gandhi visited Islamabad within a few days of Bhutto's inauguration as prime minister to attend a summit meeting of the South Asian Association for Regional Cooperation (SAARC). According to Iqbal Akhund, then Bhutto's adviser on foreign affairs:

> Rajiv Gandhi himself was now all too keen to come to Pakistan in order to meet Pakistan's charismatic young prime minister and readily agreed to the proposal that a bilateral visit should be dovetailed with his visit for the SAARC summit. The PPP was committed to mending fences with India and making a new start toward settling the disputes between the two countries. The Indian prime minister's visit, coming so soon after Benazir's advent, seemed to provide just the occasion to set the ball rolling. The Foreign Office and other ministries and departments concerned were asked to dust up any proposals and draft agreements that could be concluded or moved forward on the occasion in order to give the process a start. The Americans told us that Rajiv had also instructed the Indian External Affairs Ministry and others concerned to look into their files for any agreements that could be reached.[44]

When Bhutto and Gandhi met in December 1988, observers thought that this new generation of leaders was better suited to "bury the bitter past and start over."[45] Bhutto was thirty-five years old and Gandhi was forty-four. Neither had lived through the bitterness of partition and both were perceived to be committed to their nations' prosperity and modernity.

The Bhutto-Gandhi meeting resulted in the two sides agreeing not to attack each other's nuclear facilities. A joint ministerial committee was created to promote cooperation in science and technology. There was also an agreement on boosting bilateral trade. Gandhi also responded positively to Bhutto's suggestions regarding the reduction of conventional arms and reviving negotiations on the dispute over Siachen glacier.[46] Bhutto was trying to proceed cautiously, given the Pakistani military's sensitivity to accommodation with India. For the military and its Islamist allies, however, even her cautious moves signaled loss of control.

At the time Bhutto was unaware that the ISI had been planning a guerilla insurgency in Indian controlled parts of disputed Jammu and Kashmir involving Islamist militants.[47] Bhutto's initiatives for normalization of relations with India interfered with the military's strategic plans, in addition to disrupting the traditional formula of keeping the Pakistani people's attention focused on the external enemy.

As soon as plans for Gandhi's visit to Islamabad were finalized, the president of Pakistan-controlled Azad Kashmir, Sardar Abdul Qayyum, announced that he would organize a demonstration "against Indian occupation of Kashmir."[48] Qayyum was an IJI ally and was known for close links to Pakistan's military and intelligence services. If the government refused his request for permission to demonstrate, it would have given the IJI another reason to charge Bhutto with being soft on India. A potentially violent demonstration, however, would have vitiated the atmosphere for Bhutto's talks with Gandhi.

In the end, Qayyum and his IJI supporters were allowed to organize a demonstration far from the venue of the Bhutto-Gandhi talks.[49] This did not prevent the IJI from denouncing Bhutto for seeking close ties with India instead of demanding resolution of the Kashmir dispute. Domestic unrest in Kashmir began within months of the Bhutto-Gandhi summit, followed by Pakistani support for the insurgency (discussed in detail in Chapter 7). By the beginning of 1990, while Bhutto was still Pakistan's prime minister, relations between India and Pakistan had deteriorated again and were, in the words of an American scholar, "the worst since the 1971 war."[50] Islamist criticism of Bhutto's India policy coupled with the ISI's covert operations in support of the Kashmiris had made it impossible for Bhutto to fulfill her plans for normal relations with India.

Bhutto maintains that she did not have prior knowledge of the ISI's support for the insurgency in Kashmir. "When the unrest in Kashmir began almost everyone agreed that it was indigenous," she said, adding "I was told by the ISI and General Beg that they were supporting the Kashmiris in non-military ways,"[51] possibly with money. This was consistent with Bhutto's public stance at the time that Pakistan only provided moral and diplomatic support to Kashmiris demanding self-determination. Covert plans for a Kashmiri insurgency were probably afoot when Bhutto changed the command at the ISI in May 1989, a move seen at the time as part of "her struggle to assert control."[52] The potential disruption of the insurgency plans was most likely the reason why the army had been displeased by Bhutto's decision to remove General Gul from command of the ISI and replace him with a retired general. The army's suspicions about her stance on the nuclear issue and Afghan policies persisted. On Afghanistan, Bhutto deferred to the views of Pakistan's Ministry of Foreign Affairs, but that ran contrary to the military's partiality to Islamist factions.

By the time Bhutto came to office, the Soviet Union had started withdrawing its troops from Afghanistan according to the terms of the April 1988 Geneva Accords. The Soviet withdrawal was completed by February 1989, leaving the Afghan communist regime propped up by the Soviets, headed by Najibullah, in control of the capital, Kabul, and other major cities. After the Soviet withdrawal, U.S. and Pakistani policy makers had to deal with the question of what to do with Najibullah's regime. Most U.S. and Pakistani diplomats felt that it was time for a negotiated settlement that would allow the various anticommunist mujahideen factions and the Afghan communists to share power. Bhutto supported this political solution.[53] The ISI, publicly supported by Pakistani Islamists, favored military means to establish "Afghan Muslim fundamentalists— particularly a group led by radical anti western rebel chieftain Gulbeddin Hekmatyar—as the dominant political force"[54] in post-Soviet occupation Afghanistan.

The ISI encouraged the mujahideen to launch "frontal attacks on major cities"[55] in Afghanistan without success. Although the U.S. initially went along with the ISI's plans, European and some American diplomats saw the Pakistani policy of trying to dictate the future shape of Afghanistan's government as dangerous.[56] At one stage in early 1989, the ISI forged an Afghan interim government in the Pakistani city of Peshawar in the hope of securing recognition for it by the international community. Bhutto, however, refused to extend diplomatic recognition to the Afghan interim government before it gained control of a major Afghan city, which led to a failed ISI-backed assault on the city of Jalalabad.[57] The interim government was backed by Pakistan's Jamaat-e-Islami, which held rallies in its support. The IJI government in Punjab ignored Pakistan's constitution, which reserves conduct of foreign policy exclusively for the federal government, and hosted a civic reception for the Afghan interim government leaders in Lahore.

As ISI chief, General Hamid Gul declared that he did not like the "Foreign Ministry's 'interference' in Afghan policy" and that "the Mujahideen had no time for Foreign Minister Yaqub Khan's gentrified ways."[58] From his point of view, an Islamist government in Kabul beholden to Pakistan was the logical reward for Pakistan's decade-long involvement in the Afghan jihad. General Gul's view was widely shared by senior military officers and the ISI rank and file.

The military's frustration with Bhutto's handling of Afghan policy is thus described by General Khalid Mahmud Arif:

The Bhutto administration had a different policy on Afghanistan. She spoke of the futility of the Mujahideen operations and sought a quick end to the conflict, without evolving an alternative action plan. With wavering political support and a lack of professional guidance, the ISI directorate was left alone to handle the workload. In early 1989, egged on by the CIA, the ISI directorate committed the Mujahideen to a conventional military attack for the capture of Jalalabad. The mission failed. The half-trained guerilla fighters were incapable of launching a set-piece attack against a well defended city . . . For inexplicable reasons, high level meetings on Afghanistan in which policy decisions were taken were also attended by the US ambassador in Islamabad, Mr. Robert Oakley, who earned the nickname of 'the Viceroy of Pakistan.' Zia had suspected that at some stage America might undercut Pakistan. He had ordered the ISI directorate to prevent Americans from meeting the Mujahideen leaders and commanders on their own on Pakistani soil. The policy was fully implemented during his lifetime. The situation underwent a change after his death. The Benazir [Bhutto] administration was too weak to resist American pressure. The American officials started meeting the Mujahideen leaders directly, to the exclusion of the Pakistani officials. The Americans had their own policy objectives to achieve. Leaning toward the moderates they told Afghan leaders, who in turn informed Pakistani authorities, to distance themselves from Pakistan as [Pakistan] had a soft spot for the fundamentalist Afghan leaders.[59]

From the military's point of view, Bhutto was too close to the Americans and wanted to see the end of conflict in Afghanistan without ensuring the emergence of a pro-Pakistan Islamist regime in Kabul. Bhutto's ouster made it possible for the military's views on Afghanistan to prevail. Instead of influencing the Pakistani military to subordinate itself to the elected civilian leadership, the United States leaned in the military's favor. Only with the benefit of hindsight did Oakley and other U.S. officials of that period acknowledge that "the United States made a mistake in continuing to support the largely ISI-driven Pakistan policy on Afghanistan."[60] Richard Armitage, assistant secretary of defense for international security affairs at the time, said, "We drifted too long in 1989 and failed to understand the independent role that the ISI was playing."[61]

Something similar happened in relation to Pakistan's nuclear program, which was effectively controlled by the military and not the civilian prime minister. Pakistan's nuclear program and the U.S. failure to stop or control it is not the subject of this book, which is why the nuclear program is referred to only in the context of its relevance to the covert alliance between Pakistan's military and Islamist groups. Although Pakistan's nuclear program began in 1972 while Zulfikar Ali Bhutto was prime minister, it took shape during the Islamizing regime of General Zia ul-Haq. In the post–Zia ul-Haq phase, as the program reached the stage where it was no longer possible for Pakistan to conceal its possession of nuclear weapons, Pakistan's military and intelligence services turned increasingly toward the Islamists to demonstrate support for a nuclear Pakistan. During this period, any suggestion that Pakistan should accept international restraints on its nuclear weapons capability was described by Pakistani Islamists as treason.

During Zia ul-Haq's regime, the U.S. looked the other way while Pakistan proceeded with its ambition to develop nuclear weapons on the basis of Zia ul-Haq's assurances that he would not embarrass the United States.[62] The embarrassment Zia ul-Haq hoped to avoid was public disclosure that Pakistan possessed nuclear weapons or was on the threshold of having them. The U.S. Congress had legislated that aid to Pakistan would be cut off whenever the U.S. president failed to certify that Pakistan did not have nuclear weapons. The Reagan administration and Zia ul-Haq reached an agreement whereby Pakistan would not "enrich its uranium above 5 percent"[63] but that threshold had been crossed by the time Benazir Bhutto visited Washington as Pakistan's prime minister in June 1989. The George H. W. Bush administration that took office earlier that year believed that Pakistan was "pressing ahead with some aspects of a weapons program"[64] and hinted that the U.S. president could withhold certification of Pakistan not possessing nuclear weapons if new assurances were not given.

After intense negotiations, the U.S. dropped the demand for adherence to the condition of not enriching uranium beyond 5 percent and accepted Bhutto's promise that Pakistan would not produce "weapons-grade uranium."[65] Bhutto was given a briefing by then CIA Director William Webster, detailing "what Washington knew about the Pakistani program," possibly in the hope that the civilian prime minister would exercise some restraint on Pakistan's nuclear scientists and the military.[66] The compromise on limiting uranium enrichment enabled President Bush to certify in October that "despite continuing nuclear activity in secret plants Pakistan does not today 'possess a nuclear explosive device.'"[67] U.S. aid to Pakistan continued but so did Pakistan's nuclear weapons program.

Instead of recognizing Bhutto's successful negotiations in Washington as an achievement, the hard-line Islamists and generals saw it as the beginning of a gradual caving in to American demands. At an IJI meeting, Jamiat Ulema Islam leader Maulana Sami ul-Haq said, "Pakistan's nuclear weapons capability simply cannot be safe under the leadership of a westernized woman. She cares more for American approval than for ensuring the *Umma's* first nuclear bomb."[68]

In September, the military held large-scale exercises code-named Zarb-e-Momin (blow of the believer) with extensive media coverage. The purpose of the exercise was to improve the military's public image and wash away the negative impact of over a decade of military rule. During the course of the exercise, General Beg and some his closest lieutenants provided unprecedented access to Pakistani journalists and spoke openly of Pakistan's access to a nuclear option. Beg displayed Pakistan's missile capability for the first time and said, "Both the nuclear option and the missiles act as deterrence and these in turn contribute to the total fighting ability of the army."[69] This open acknowledgement of a nuclear weapons capability ran contrary to the official Pakistani position of denying that Pakistan wanted or was on the verge of possessing nuclear weapons.

In the area of nuclear proliferation, Bhutto was unable to provide General Beg the political cover he sought when Pakistan crossed the threshold of nuclear enrichment beyond the level agreed under Zia ul-Haq. When the United States confronted Ishaq Khan, Bhutto, and Beg with evidence of Pakistan breaking its word, Beg expected Bhutto to help him with denials or take responsibility for the decision. Bhutto did neither. This also displeased the United States because it had expected Pakistan's pro-Western, democratically elected prime minister to stop her generals from putting together a nuclear weapon. Once the U.S. government learned that the civilian prime minister could not stay the military's hand and had, in fact, acquiesced to its decisions, the prospect of the United States protesting Bhutto's dismissal diminished.

The Pakistani establishment was, however, sensitive to the possibility of the United States reacting to Bhutto's removal from office. Some observers noted that "the decision to remove Bhutto was carefully timed"[70] in case Washington chose to speak up in her favor. Bhutto was dismissed on August 6, 1990, four days after the Iraqi invasion of Kuwait. President Ishaq Khan also declared a state of emergency. Ishaq Khan later said that the demand for dismissal had come from the military.[71]

General Beg claimed that he "was not instrumental" in Bhutto's removal and that "it was the president's decision."[72] The U.S., distracted by the prospect of war in the Persian Gulf, accepted Bhutto's ouster as Pakistan's internal matter.

At the time of her dismissal, Bhutto was accused of corruption and incompetence—reasons that Zia ul-Haq had cited to dismiss Prime Minister Junejo two years earlier even though the real reasons related to Junejo's differences with Zia ul-Haq over Afghan policy. Junejo's dismissal on those grounds had surprised most Pakistanis because no scandals had implicated him and his alleged incompetence had not been apparent. In Bhutto's case, the ISI prepared for her dismissal from the day she took office. The Bhutto government was vulnerable to ISI machinations because it extended patronage to PPP members who had endured persecution and now, after a long time, had come close to power. Bhutto's husband, Asif Ali Zardari, continued his business while she was in office and took an active interest in government contracts involving his friends. Despite the absence of conflict-of-interest laws in Pakistan, there was sometimes a clear sense of impropriety. The ISI orchestrated leaks to the media of every incident of alleged corruption. The IJI followed up with accusations of its own, which helped build the perception of widespread corruption by the time Bhutto's government was dismissed.

As in several other third world countries, corruption and nepotism are endemic in Pakistan. The civil service and military officers enjoy vast amounts of perquisites and privileges and are not above corruption. Politicians, because they are out of power (and occasionally in prison) for long periods of time and are insecure about their tenures in office, tend to line their pockets with money from graft and kickbacks. There is no excuse for corruption, and many officials in Pakistan—whether political appointees or permanent employees of the state—remain incorruptible and are recognized in society for their honesty. It must be said, however, that as part of its justification for its own intervention in politics, Pakistan's military has made a concerted effort since the 1950s to paint politicians and political activists as corrupt. In the period of partial civilian rule beginning in 1988, corruption charges were frequently bandied about, making it easier to get rid of politicians who did not otherwise see eye to eye with the security establishment.

It is relevant to note that several cases were filed against Bhutto and her husband after her removal from office in 1990. Roedad Khan, a retired civil servant, was appointed head of a special accountability cell to process the filing of these cases. None of these prosecutions had resulted in convictions by 1993, when Bhutto's elected successor Nawaz Sharif was dismissed from office on similar charges and the proceedings against Bhutto and her husband were dropped.[73] In a speech to the Asia Society in New York a few months after Bhutto's dismissal, U.S. ambassador Robert Oakley acknowledged the political nature of corruption allegations in Pakistan. He said that Bhutto had been singled out for corruption while others were being overlooked. The Pakistani establishment responded to Oakley's comments by accusing him of acting like a viceroy.[74]

After Bhutto's dismissal, Ishaq Khan and the military installed IJI President Ghulam Mustafa Jatoi as caretaker prime minister. In the 1990 election that followed, the ISI brokered a deal among all political parties opposed to the PPP, thereby creating a grand anti-Bhutto coalition. As a result of this arrangement, only one candidate stood against the PPP in almost every parliamentary seat. The ISI also distributed large amounts of cash, some of it raised from a Karachi banker who was later jailed for swindling account holders. The banker's arrest in 1995 led to the revelation of an election slush fund amounting to 150 million rupees (approximately $3 million) created at the ISI by General Beg. ISI chief Lieutenant General Asad Durrani admitted in an affidavit that he distributed "a total of [Pakistani rupees] 60 million to 20 anti-Bhutto politicians"[75] for the 1990 elections.

In 1997, Beg's response to the Pakistan Supreme Court, where a petition had been brought about the matter, showed the army's attitude toward its behind-the-scenes role in Pakistani politics after the death of General Zia ul-Haq. Beg told the court that he "was not answerable to [the court] regarding his actions as the chief of army staff"[76] and that the sitting army chief was "the only competent and proper person" to ask him what he did and why. Beg and the ISI chief at the time, Lieutenant General Asad Durrani, claimed that they had raised and disbursed the money in the national interest. The refusal of Beg's successor army chiefs to question his operation of the slush fund confirms that his decision reflected the collective choice of Pakistan's military to not allow politics to take its course.

Although Beg wanted to install Jatoi as prime minister after the IJI won the 1990 elections, Nawaz Sharif managed to rally the support of several other generals, notably General Hamid Gul, on ethnic grounds. The IJI had ostensibly swept the polls in the Punjab province, and Sharif asserted that he was the man Punjabis wanted as prime minister. The Punjabi generals tended to agree. In November 1990, Nawaz Sharif took over as prime minister of Pakistan.

The IJI's 1990 campaign had been directed almost entirely by General Hamid Gul, who was now a corps commander, and his former subordinates at the ISI. Nawaz Sharif and the Jamaat-e-Islami accused Bhutto of being a security risk, alleging that she had revealed to India the identities of Sikh insurgents with links to Pakistani intelligence.[77] This charge was unusual because Pakistan had always denied any role in the Sikh insurgency in India's Punjab state that had begun in 1983. Charges were also repeated that, had Bhutto remained prime minister, she would have effectively terminated Pakistan's nuclear-weapons program by opening it to international inspection. Sharif promised the liberation of Kashmir by arms and vowed that Pakistan would become a nuclear power at all costs.[78] After the polls closed and the results began to come in, General Gul called journalists who were commenting on the results on Pakistan television and asked them to describe the vote as a rebuff to the United States.[79] Beg and Gul still believed that Pakistan's strategic importance and possession of nuclear weapons would persuade the United States to withdraw the sanctions it had imposed a few weeks before Pakistan's 1990 election. The generals wanted to use the election result to improve their bargaining position with their superpower patron.

The tone of the IJI's campaign had been set by Jatoi and the caretaker Information Minister, who accused Bhutto and the PPP of "strong Zionist links."[80] According to one commentator, "Questioning Benazir's patriotism [the Information Minister] asked why [Bhutto] had hired the services of the American public relations expert Mark Siegel"[81] who was identified as a "well-known Zionist." The caretaker government, whose job according to the constitution was only to supervise a free election, described Bhutto as "'a great danger to the security of Pakistan' because they opposed the president, the military establishment and the country's judiciary."[82]

The Washington-based National Democratic Institute (NDI), which had sent an international delegation to observe the elections, described them as "controversial" and listed several criticisms of the pre-election environment as well as the actual conduct of the polls.[83] The NDI could not, however, detect "systematic fraud" in the polls and accepted its result as reflecting the will of the Pakistani people. In its report the NDI also summed up the IJI's campaign:

Members of the IJI criticized not only Bhutto's abilities but also her right as a woman to rule a Muslim state . . . The most contentious element of the election campaign, and perhaps the most successful from the IJI perspective, was the IJI's strategy of tying Benazir and Nusrat Bhutto to the United States and the so-called "Indo-Zionist lobby" in the U.S. The lobby was portrayed as having close ties to India and Israel and opposing Pakistan's development of a nuclear capability. In particular, the Bhuttos were accused of "selling-out" Pakistan's nuclear program . . . The IJI ran a nationalistic campaign and repeatedly accused Bhutto of being unpatriotic. The former Prime Minister was called the conduit for American influence into Pakistan and her efforts to influence Congress on her behalf were criticized. Articles were also published in the government-controlled papers alleging her links to India and other reportedly anti-Pakistan groups. One of these articles was based on what was evidently a forged letter from Bhutto to a staff member of the U.S. Senate Committee on Foreign Relations.[84]

Reports of the military's funding of the IJI and the IJI's religiously oriented and anti-Semitic, anti-American campaign had little impact on the U.S. government attitude toward Nawaz Sharif, once he had formed his government. Just days before the election, President Bush had refused to certify to Congress that Pakistan did not possess a nuclear weapon. After October 1, 1990, the flow of U.S. aid to Pakistan froze although USAID could still continue to implement ongoing programs, amounting to $1 billion.[85] U.S. officials were working on the assumption that aid was America's main leverage with Pakistan. They found solace in Sharif's "pro-business" promises and felt that they could live with his Islamic orientation just as they had dealt with "his political godfather, Zia ul-Haq."[86]

For his part Sharif also tried to sound more businesslike and less ideological after his election. In a statement he promised "a strong government, which will play a vital role in the development of Pakistan, bringing it out of economic backwardness and ushering in an era of industrial and agricultural revolution."[87]

Sharif's first term as prime minister was an era of contradictory policies and priorities. As a businessman, Sharif's heart lay in economic reform and reducing the role of government. He wanted to privatize and deregulate as fast as he could. These probusiness policies also made Sharif generally pro-United States. He was eager to bring an end to sanctions so that aid would start flowing in again and investment, facilitated by U.S. credit, would become easier. Sharif sent out feelers to the Indian prime minister, Chandra Shekhar, to begin a process of normalization of relations, which he felt would help Pakistan jump-start its economy. At one point he asked a lobbyist in Washington to form the outlines of a deal that would secure a debt write-off and other economic benefits for Pakistan in return for meeting U.S. objections to the controversial nuclear program. While thinking and talking boldly about casting Pakistan in the same mold as the fast-growing "Tiger" economies of Southeast Asia, Sharif also carried the baggage of his links to the Pakistan army and the ISI.

The ISI continued to push for an Islamist government in Afghanistan and launched its guerrilla operations in Indian-controlled parts of Jammu and Kashmir. President Ishaq Khan and General Beg wanted to hear nothing of a nuclear rollback. Sharif agreed to both the ISI policy in Afghanistan and the new venture in Kashmir. Before long, he also started contemplating the option of a nuclear test. Only on the occasion of the 1991 Gulf War did he resist his army chief. General Beg wanted Pakistan to tilt in Iraq's favor and spoke of the need for "strategic defiance" against U.S. hegemony. Islamists marched in Pakistani cities, protesting U.S. actions, and Sharif's closest associates suspected that General Beg wanted to take over in a military coup d'état after massive anti-U.S. protests.

The Gulf War was especially sensitive because it involved the interests of Saudi Arabia, a longtime benefactor of Pakistan.

A majority of Muslim countries took part in the U.S.-led coalition against Iraq, and Pakistan itself sent a military contingent to Saudi Arabia after the Iraqi occupation of Kuwait. For Sharif and generals other than Beg, defying the United States was one thing, but annoying the leadership of major Islamic countries was quite another. With the acquiescence of other generals, Sharif announced the appointment of General Beg's successor as army chief several months before Beg's scheduled date of retirement, which made Beg a lame duck and bought Sharif a few months without much interference from the army chief. Sharif was unable, however, to implement major policy changes because he still had to contend with the influence of President Ishaq Khan.

Sharif initially made no effort to interfere with the basic policy tripod upheld by Pakistan's civil-military complex. Instead, he focused on trying to maximize his own influence and power. He appointed Brigadier Imtiaz Ahmed, who had helped to create the IJI while working as head of ISI's internal politics wing, as head of the civilian Intelligence Bureau. Brigadier Ahmed was now retired from the military but retained his contacts from his days at the ISI. He worked at building new political alliances for Sharif, aimed at isolating the president.[88] Brigadier Ahmed did not seek to upset existing policies on Afghanistan or Kashmir and was willing to be more aggressive in dealing with the United States. His plan for Sharif, however, was to exercise full control over the execution of these policies. With Ahmed's help, Sharif also persisted with the persecution of Bhutto and the PPP.

The result of Sharif's effort to increase his influence with the help of the Intelligence Bureau, and the Intelligence Bureau's rivalry with military intelligence services, was what American reporter Steve Coll described as Pakistan's "political culture of shadow games." "Here, the acronyms of intelligence agencies, such as MI (Military Intelligence), ISI (Inter-Services Intelligence) and IB (Intelligence Bureau), are part of everyday vocabulary," Coll reported. "Unproven reports abound of secret wiretappings, videotapings and sexual blackmail schemes. And nearly everyone of prominence believes his or her telephone is bugged." Coll cited Pakistani newspaper reports about Sharif "crooning love songs to a girlfriend in Bombay who may be an Indian spy" based on the intelligence agencies' wiretaps of the prime minister's phone. A separate newspaper report, attributed to a different intelligence service, accused Bhutto of "using her Karachi home as the secret headquarters of a terrorist organization backed by India."[89] The result of these intrigues was continued weakness of the political system and empowerment of the military and intelligence services as Pakistan's kingmakers.

Pakistan's progress in its nuclear weapons program and the ISI's support for the Kashmiri insurgents increased tension with the United States. The Sharif government tried, at one point, to break the stalemate over the nuclear question by admitting on record that "Pakistan had the capability to make a nuclear bomb." Foreign Secretary Sheheryar Khan made that admission in an interview with the *Washington Post* and said he did so to "avoid credibility gaps" caused by earlier Pakistani statements.[90] This did not lead to a change in U.S. policy. The United States was losing interest in Pakistan now that the cold war had come to an end. Sharif's ambassador to Washington, Abida Hussain, observed that at this stage American interest in Pakistan was no more than Pakistani interest in the Maldives.

The Sharif government was ideologically wedded to certain positions, as was Pakistan's military. The U.S., however, maintained more cordial relations with the Pakistani military than it was willing to maintain with the civilian government. Sharif failed to get officially invited to Washington whereas Pakistani generals continued to travel to the U.S. for meetings with the U.S. Central Command. The Bush administration's defense department thought that Pakistan "could play a helpful role in support of U.S. interests in the Persian Gulf."[91] This enabled the Pakistani military to project itself as a force for moderation to their American counterparts, leaving the civilians with all the blame even for policies that were actually being conducted by the military or the ISI. The military now had the option of keeping dialogue with the U.S. going by forcing a change of civilian leaders and following that change with the promise of a different policy.

Beg's successor as chief of army staff, General Asif Nawaz, attempted to bring about a reconciliation between Nawaz Sharif and Benazir Bhutto so that the venality introduced in Pakistan's politics after the 1988 election campaign would come to an end. Like all Pakistani generals, Asif Nawaz recognized the army's dominant role in Pakistani life but was also aware of the military's limitations. He was alarmed by the increasing influence of Islamists and wanted to restore to the army some semblance of professionalism, which politics and ideology had eroded. Asif Nawaz was also convinced that Pakistan needed to cut its losses in Afghanistan and rebuild relations with the United States. These objectives could be fulfilled only if the civilian government were effective and politics functioned sufficiently well for the military's gradual withdrawal from nonprofessional matters. Asif Nawaz believed that compromise between the leaders of the two major parties was necessary to lay the foundations of a functioning parliamentary democracy.[92]

Asif Nawaz set up a meeting between Nawaz Sharif and Benazir Bhutto, but Sharif backed out at the last minute.[93] Sharif's many contacts in the military and intelligence services had told him that a deal with Bhutto would deprive him of his status as the military's political protégé. Asif Nawaz was army chief for the moment, they said, but he was not the army. Convinced that the army's institutional opinion was against a "patriotic" Sharif working within Parliament with the "treacherous" Bhutto, Sharif passed by an opportunity to strengthen the civilian polity.

Asif Nawaz died in 1993 of a heart attack, and Sharif and Ishaq Khan disagreed vehemently over naming his successor. Ishaq Khan nominated General Abdul Waheed, a fellow Pashtun, as army chief and set about getting rid of Nawaz Sharif. Like Asif Nawaz, Abdul Waheed hoped to reduce the military's political involvement, but the wishes of the army chief did not translate into a command for his men. The army continued to play a political role, and, more often than not, it was aided by Pakistan's Islamists.

Sharif appeased the Islamists on cultural issues by ordering women to cover their heads on television just as Zia ul-Haq had done. During the 1992 Olympic games, "the government refused to allow women's swimming events to be shown on television because the swimsuits were considered too immodest for Islamic sensitivities."[94] The Islamists, however, kept up the pressure for more. On at least three occasions Sharif's relatively moderate views on international affairs clashed with the radical pan-Islamism of his Islamist allies. During the 1991 Gulf war, the

Islamists backed Saddam Hussein's Iraq while Sharif continued to support Saudi Arabia and the United States. When Hindu nationalists in India destroyed a historic mosque at Ayodhya, Pakistani Islamists attacked Hindu temples in retaliation. Sharif's government cracked down on the Islamists for attacking the temples. In the case of Afghanistan, too, Sharif's government started tilting in favor of the moderate mujahideen groups though the Islamists and the ISI continued to support the fundamentalists.

Notwithstanding Asif Nawaz's personal views, Pakistan's support of the Kashmiri militants escalated while he was army chief and Sharif was prime minister. This led to Pakistan being warned by the U.S. that it might be declared a state sponsor of terrorism, a subject discussed in greater detail in Chapter 7.

In Afghanistan, Najibullah's communist regime survived without the presence of Soviet troops for four years, until 1992. The United Nations had failed to negotiate a power-sharing arrangement that would bring the mujahideen into a coalition with former communists while infighting between mujahideen factions prevented their military victory. The ISI had persistently tried to promote the cause of Pashtun Islamist Gulbeddin Hekmatyar and his Hizb-e-Islami but the Islamists had failed to wrest control of Afghan cities. An ISI-sponsored effort to overthrow Najibullah in a coup had fizzled out in March 1990 when six of the seven mujahideen groups refused to help Afghan General Shahnawaz Tanai in his effort to seize power.[95] The mujahideen factions were torn apart by ethnic and ideological rivalries and were not willing to help the ISI secure a major share in power for its protégé, Hekmatyar.

By the beginning of 1992, Sharif's foreign minister indicated the civilian government's willingness to support "a United Nations plan to bring together all factions, including representatives of the former Communist government in Kabul to form an interim government"[96] in Afghanistan. This meant that Pakistan would no longer insist on installing an Islamic government and its Afghan Islamist proxies would have to settle for a smaller share in power than the ISI had envisaged for over a decade.

In February 1992, one of Najibullah's commanders, General Abdul Rashid Dostum, defected to an alliance of non-Pashtun mujahideen led by Tajik commander Ahmed Shah Massoud. Although Massoud had been part of Burhanuddin Rabbani's Jamiat-e-Islami, he differed with Pashtun leaders such as Hekmatyar over the future division of power among Afghan ethnic groups. Pashtuns had traditionally dominated the Afghan power structure and the ISI's vision of a future Afghanistan, obviously shared by Hekmatyar and other Islamist Pashtun leaders, was to continue that domination albeit under Islamic law. Massoud, on the other hand, wanted a new arrangement that empowered ethnic minorities like the Tajiks. Dostum, an ethnic Uzbek, decided to make common cause with Massoud. Dostum's militia comprised forty thousand troops and controlled tanks, artillery, and aircraft.[97] The combination of Massoud's mujahideen and Dostum's militia enabled them to reach the outskirts of Kabul as Najibullah called for a "joint struggle against fundamentalism" and appealed for U.S. assistance.[98]

The ISI had never considered Massoud as trustworthy as Hekmatyar on account of Massoud's ethnicity and independence. Massoud was looked upon with suspicion for his refusal to be dragged into ISI's wider agenda for Pakistani influence in Afghanistan and beyond. As Massoud's troops positioned themselves outside of Kabul with the help of Dostum, Hekmatyar made his own plans for taking the city. Advised by ISI officers who flew on Pakistani helicopters to his base outside of Kabul, Hekmatyar negotiated with a different faction of the Communist Party to surrender to him.[99] Sharif, helped by American and Saudi diplomats, tried to negotiate an arrangement among the mujahideen group for an interim government and an accord was reached with great difficulty. Although both of them pretended to accept that agreement, Massoud and Hekmatyar moved their respective militias into Kabul. Massoud won. As Steve Coll observed, "Hekmatyar and the ISI might have a reputation for ruthless ambition but they had yet to prove themselves competent."[100]

The fall of Kabul to the combined forces of Massoud and Dostum marked the beginning of the civil war among mujahideen factions that devastated Kabul and subsided only with the rise to power of the Taliban. Mujahideen leaders signed and violated several agreements. Field commanders made temporary alliances and, in the absence of a strong central government, became warlords. Kabul was divided into a "checkerboard of ethnic and ideological divisions."[101] Pakistan's Afghan policy became a shambles. Sharif and the foreign ministry continued to engage with the leaders of the mujahideen factions that had fought the Soviets. In the field, however, ISI operatives continued to support Hekmatyar and other fundamentalist groups. Sharif's failure to put his government's full weight behind the Afghan Islamists proved to be the last straw in his already deteriorating relationship with his own Islamist allies. By the beginning of 1993, IJI had ceased to exist and Sharif led the government under the banner of his Pakistan Muslim League (PML).

The sudden death of army chief General Asif Nawaz in January 1993 resulted in "months of political turmoil."[102] General Nawaz's wife alleged that he did not die a natural death and hinted that the prime minister might have been involved in a conspiracy to poison her husband.[103] Although a judicial commission found no evidence of conspiracy or of poisoning, the episode was part of intensified shadow games that resulted in Sharif accusing President Ishaq Khan in a televised speech of undermining his government. Ishaq Khan dismissed Sharif the next day, "accusing him of corruption and mismanagement,"[104] appointed a caretaker prime minister, and dissolved parliament.

After being dismissed as prime minister by Ishaq Khan, Nawaz Sharif managed a brief comeback when Pakistan's Supreme Court declared unconstitutional the president's decision to fire him. Confrontation between Ishaq Khan and Sharif persisted, exacerbated by Sharif's failure to make peace with Bhutto, and eventually the army stepped in to convince both Sharif and Ishaq Khan to resign.[105] A caretaker government comprising technocrats selected by the army was formed. The caretaker prime minister, Moin Qureshi, was a senior official of the International Monetary Fund who had not lived in Pakistan for almost three decades. Given the neutrality of Qureshi and General Abdul Waheed, Pakistan experienced a relatively fair election.

The Jamaat-e-Islami contested the 1993 elections with some independent Islamists under a new formation, Pakistan Islamic Front (PIF) and fared poorly. In fact, the four Islamic parties managed only nine seats in the 207-member National Assembly. It seemed that Pakistan had moved toward a two-party polity, with Sharif's center-right PML taking 39.7 percent of the vote and securing seventy-two seats and Bhutto's center-left PPP capturing eighty-six seats with 38.1 percent of the popular vote.[106]

Benazir Bhutto returned as prime minister, at the head of a coalition government.

Farooq Leghari, a Baluch tribal chief from Punjab, became president. Although Leghari had been a PPP member since the 1970s, he had also been a civil servant and was close to the establishment. He resigned from the PPP in accordance with the tradition of parliamentary democracy, which requires the head of state to be politically neutral. Bhutto "fully trusted Leghari"[107] as he had stood by her through the Zia ul-Haq years and throughout her political career. As it turned out, Leghari allied himself with the establishment and used presidential powers to dismiss Bhutto's government three years later.

During her new term, Bhutto had hoped to focus on economic and social issues while avoiding confrontation with Pakistan's civil-military complex. For its part, the military and the ISI were keen to create the impression that the civilian authorities were in full control even as they continued with their efforts to set the government's strategic direction. The ISI had existed since 1948 and had managed to operate invisibly for decades. Even under Zia ul-Haq, ISI officials were told to be unobtrusive while organizing the Afghan jihad and controlling domestic politics. But the ISI's overt involvement with the IJI during 1988–1993 and the high profile role of General Hamid Gul and his key operatives had made the ISI a household name by the time Bhutto became prime minister for the second time. The Military Intelligence Directorate (MI) had also been dragged into public view as successive MI Directors played a role in the dismissal of civilian governments and went on to become heads of ISI.[108]

When Lieutenant General Javed Ashraf Qazi was appointed chief of the ISI in May 1993, he declared that his prime objective would be "to make ISI invisible again."[109] The military's charisma was suffering from its image as a kingmaker and behind-the-scenes manipulator. The shadow games that characterized Pakistani politics at the time would continue to be played but with greater subtlety. For each of their covert actions, the Intelligence services would now make sure there was a civilian to blame.

Within the first year of becoming prime minister for the second time, Bhutto launched a significant Social Action Program (SAP) with funding from international financial institutions. SAP was aimed at the "provision of basic social services, primary education, healthcare, family planning and rural water supply and sanitation"[110] Privatization of Pakistan's massive public sector enterprises was undertaken with some vigor. A plan to open up the energy sector for foreign private investment resulted in investment commitments of $16.5 billion in 1994 alone[111]—the largest commitment of foreign investment in Pakistani history.

Bhutto also proceeded to improve Pakistan's relations with the United States, which had reached a low point with the U.S. threat to declare Pakistan a state sponsor of terrorism in 1992. The threat had subsided with Sharif's ouster and the change of guard at ISI. Bhutto's administration entered negotiations with the Clinton administration to end U.S. sanctions imposed in 1990 because of Pakistan's nuclear program. At one stage, President Clinton proposed withdrawing the "1985 law that cut off military aid to Pakistan because of that country's development of a nuclear arsenal, arguing that U.S. foreign policy should not be constrained by sanctions that target individual nations."[112] The Clinton administration plan was to deliver Pakistan the F-16 fighter aircraft that Pakistan had paid for but did not receive because of sanctions in return for a verifiable Pakistani freeze on its nuclear program. In doing so, the U.S. was "shelving the unrealistic goal of rolling back the Pakistani capability and signaling its willingness to live with a freeze in the program—something that the Pakistanis had previously offered."[113]

The proposal was, however, opposed by Congressional opponents of Pakistan's nuclear program as well as the Pakistani military. According to Dennis Kux, "On the Pakistani side, the chief of army staff, General Abdul Waheed, who was visiting the United States, made clear his opposition. The army chief declared that the military would not 'bargain away Pakistan's nuclear program for F-16s or anything else.' Were the country's political leadership willing to compromise, the army would certainly make its views known, Waheed declared threateningly."[114]

Bhutto's government was still able to secure an easing of sanctions. Pakistan helped U.S. officials in arresting Ramzi Yusuf, the fugitive mastermind of the 1993 terrorist attack on New York's World Trade Center.[115] The arrest was well timed, coming just before Bhutto paid her second official visit to Washington in April 1995. The Republican Senate resulting from the 1994 Congressional elections approved an amendment to the Foreign Relations Act moved by Colorado Senator Hank Brown, allowing Pakistan to "take possession of the military equipment frozen in the United States, except for the F-16s and allowed the resumption of training to Pakistani military personnel."[116]

The Brown amendment also paved the way for economic assistance, Export-Import Bank lending, and loan guarantees from the Overseas Private Investment Corporation. Pakistan could now receive military equipment worth $368 million, which it had bought before the imposition of sanctions, as well as a refund of $120 million "for items paid for but not produced before the 1990 sanctions took effect."[117]

The United States also continued its parallel interaction with Pakistan's military. Defense Secretary William Perry visited Islamabad in January 1995 and "agreed to revive regular high-level military discussions."[118] The U.S. hoped to engage the Pakistani military with a package of "joint exercises, military educational exchanges and extensive talks about peacekeeping operations." At that time Pakistan had large contingents of 3,000 troops in Bosnia and 6,000 in Somalia serving as U.N. peacekeepers, which led the U.S. military to look upon Pakistan as a potential partner in its Middle Eastern and Central Asian strategies. The Pakistani military liked peacekeeping operations because they brought money for its officers and men. Soldiering abroad also kept global attention away from the Pakistan military's intrigues at home.

The positive aspects of Bhutto's term were, however, overshadowed by political developments and violence. In her effort to cultivate the establishment that had undermined her first government, Bhutto ignored the need for political accommodation with her civilian opponents. The establishment's acceptance of Bhutto proved only to be tactical, and one segment of the intelligence apparatus continued to work against her while the other assured her of its loyalty. Bhutto's refusal to accommodate her political foes, including Sharif, enabled the establishment to play the civilians against one another.

The two challenges that weakened Benazir Bhutto most were violence in Pakistan's commercial center and largest city, Karachi, and bickering with her brother Murtaza Bhutto, who returned to Pakistan after sixteen years in exile. Murtaza Bhutto had been identified by the Zia ul-Haq regime as the mastermind of the terrorist organization Al-Zulfikar, which had sought vengeance for the execution of Zulfikar Ali Bhutto through violent acts between 1980 and 1984. Murtaza Bhutto had, for some time, been based in Kabul and had lived in Damascus under Syrian protection until his return to Pakistan.

The ISI had established contacts with Murtaza Bhutto by the late 1980s.[119] When Benazir Bhutto became prime minister for the first time in 1988, she could not allow her brother's return to the country in view of her political difficulties. The siblings had disagreed over politics since the last days of their father, with Benazir Bhutto opting for parliamentary politics and Murtaza Bhutto choosing the label of radical and revolutionary. As prime minister, Bhutto felt that she must uphold the law and that Murtaza Bhutto should clear his name through Pakistani courts before returning to the country.[120] This led to further estrangement between the siblings.

In the 1993 election, Murtaza Bhutto ran against the official PPP candidate in the family's home district. Murtaza Bhutto's faction failed to make any inroads even though he got elected to the Sindh provincial assembly while still in exile. After his sister's election as prime minister, Murtaza Bhutto continued to challenge her in harsh statements leading to what the media described as "the battle of the Bhuttos."[121] Murtaza Bhutto returned from exile, was arrested and released on the orders of a court. He failed to divide the PPP significantly but did succeed in creating a media spectacle that distracted his sister from governing effectively.

Since the heyday of Al-Zulfikar, the ISI had accused Murtaza Bhutto and his followers of links with the intelligence services of foreign countries, notably India. Once the brother challenged her authority, Benazir Bhutto's government was advised that "there were RAW (Indian Intelligence Agency) agents among Murtaza's followers."[122] On September 20, 1996, Murtaza Bhutto was shot to death by the police outside his residence in Karachi.[123] That incident proved to be a double tragedy for Prime Minister Bhutto. Not only did she lose her sole surviving brother, her husband was accused of murdering Murtaza Bhutto when Leghari dismissed her from office in November 1996.

Continuing violence in the port city of Karachi had even greater consequences for Pakistan and Bhutto's government than Bhutto's conflict with her brother. Since the mid-1980s, political leadership in Karachi had been taken over by the Muhajir Qaumi Movement (MQM), a group claiming to represent the interests of migrants from India and their descendants known as Muhajirs (migrants or refugees). The MQM had rallied the Muhajirs by arguing that the Urdu-speaking Muslims of Northern India had been the driving force in Pakistan's creation but their share in political power and economic benefits was shrinking.

MQM leader Altaf Hussain was a fiery orator who railed against Punjabi domination of Pakistan and Sindhi domination of Sindh, where most of Pakistan's Muhajirs are concentrated. Since 1988, the MQM had become a powerful bloc in parliamentary politics, winning most seats in the federal and provincial legislatures from Karachi and other urban centers in Sindh province. The MQM had alternately aligned itself with Bhutto and Sharif in 1988–1990, at the ISI's behest,[124] influencing the parliamentary balance of power. The party also maintained a militant wing, which was reputedly involved in ethnic violence, robberies, and kidnapping for ransom witnessed in Karachi's urban sprawl. In 1992, Altaf Hussain went into exile and the military started an operation in Karachi against the MQM. A rival MQM faction was created and pitted against the one led by Altaf Hussain. The MQM alleged that the military operation was not aimed at restoring order but rather "was directed against the Muhajirs."[125]

The MQM supported the PPP in securing Leghari's election as president in 1993 but the two parties could not agree on sharing power in Sindh. Within a few months of Bhutto's inauguration as prime minister for the second time, a Pakistani scholar noted:

In Sindh, the absence of an agreement on power-sharing between the Muhajir Qaumi Movement (MQM) and the PPP, internecine civil war between the two factions of the MQM fueled by the covert role of civil and military intelligence agencies, and sectarian conflict between extremist Shia and Sunni organizations and possibly Indian Intelligence Agency (RAW) agents all worked together to create a proverbial Hobbesian condition of 'war of all against all' in Karachi. This resulted in approximately 800 dead during 1994, including some very prominent personalities.[126]

A year later, an American observer described the situation in the city as "near anarchy" and explained its several dimensions: "(1) ethnicity (Muhajirs, Pathans, Afghans, Sindhis and Biharis pitted against each other); (2) Sectarianism (Sunnis versus Shias); (3) Islamic fundamentalism versus secularism; (4) economics; (5) the struggle for power and the absence of power-sharing; and (6) drugs and drug trafficking."[127]

Bhutto decided to deal with the violence in Karachi with an iron hand. Her policy was to "combine the power of the state with the PPP's support base" to ferret out "criminals and insurgents."[128] PPP workers in various Karachi neighborhoods identified criminals and MQM militants and police and paramilitary arrested them. In many cases, the individuals with the worst reputations were not captured alive, giving rise to the charge of extrajudicial murders. As a result of the government's efforts, a semblance of peace returned to Karachi after months of unabated violence but the government's violent methods embittered the city's residents. Karachi is the pivot of Pakistan's economy. Violence in the city disrupted the country's economy and undermined investor confidence.

The military and the ISI had been firmly behind Bhutto's plans for restoring peace in Karachi through military means. The military saw the violence in Karachi as India's retaliation for its troubles in Kashmir. Taking its cue, the government closed down the Indian consulate in Karachi in 1994, citing "covert Indian involvement in inciting"[129] the city's troubles.

Pakistan's support for insurgents in Indian-controlled Kashmir spiked during Bhutto's second term. Jamaat-e-Islami and other organizations were now openly recruiting volunteers for jihad in Kashmir. Pakistani media regularly reported on the "martyrdom" of Pakistanis fighting in Kashmir even though the government continued to claim that the freedom struggle there was being waged by Kashmiris. "Unlike the Indian stereotype of ISI-trained commandos," wrote the Pakistani news magazine *Herald*, "Pakistani fighters in the [Kashmir] valley are ordinary middle class people. They grow up in completely controlled conditions where there are few differences of opinion. In their world, religion is the basic identity and everything else is secondary. Their bedtime stories invariably comprise tales of brave Muslims fighting against Christians or Hindus in faraway lands. Every day, they listen to the tales of brutalities by Indian forces. By the time they reach secondary school, Kashmir has become an integral part of their thinking."[130] The insurgency in Kashmir was rooted in the ideology of Pakistani Islamists, carefully nurtured for decades by the Pakistani military.

The level of military support for elected civilian leaders depended on their willingness to support the jihad in Kashmir. For her part, Bhutto was now competing with Sharif to show her resolve in supporting Kashmiri self-determination. The ISI helped the Islamists recruit and train militants on a large scale primarily to fight and tie down the Indians in Kashmir. The global agenda of the Islamists was, in the eyes of those military officers that did not agree with Islamist views, the price that had to be paid to maintain pressure on India. For Islamist military officers, pan-Islamism was an integral part of Pakistan's external relations.

An American observer noted that "Pakistan has put itself in the difficult position . . . of allowing the [Islamist] groups to operate in the country for the purpose of fighting Indian troops in the disputed region of Kashmir and at the same time trying to prevent the groups from using Pakistan as a base of operations against other countries."[131] The Philippines government protested during Bhutto's visit to Manila that "Pakistanis were fighting alongside Muslim extremists battling for autonomy" in Mindanao; Russia alleged that Pakistanis had been among Islamists fighting in Chechnya. Arab governments in Egypt, Algeria, and Jordan also identified their foes among those living in Pakistan since the anti-Soviet Afghan jihad.

Pulitzer-prize winning journalist John F. Burns reported in the *New York Times* in March 1995 that Peshawar and its adjacent areas had "emerged as one of the most active training grounds and sanctuaries for a new breed of international terrorists fighting a jihad—a holy war—against governments and other targets they see as enemies of Islam."[132] Citing diplomats and intelligence reports, Burns said that Muslims trained in Pakistan "have fought in places including Mindanao, the largest of the Philippine islands, where [Ramzi Yusuf, the mastermind of the World Trade Center bombing of 1993] is said to have had links with a Muslim insurgency; the Indian-held portion of the state of Kashmir, where 500,000 Indian troops and police officers are tied down by a Muslim revolt; Tajikistan; Bosnia; and several countries in North Africa that face Muslim rebellions, including

Egypt, Tunisia and Algeria . . . Like previous Pakistan governments, Ms. Bhutto has responded to Western pressures cautiously, fearing a backlash from powerful Muslim groups within Pakistan."[133]

The reason for Bhutto's caution in cracking down on the Islamist militants was not the fear of an Islamist backlash as much as the prospect of her own intelligence service turning against her. Bhutto was, at the time, convinced that the military and the ISI would leave her alone if she did not interfere with their national security policies. The ISI chief, Lieutenant General Javed Ashraf Qazi, had a plausible explanation for most of his actions and he went to great lengths to convince Bhutto that he was favorably disposed toward her.

In 1995, terrorism in Kashmir became an international priority when one of the Kashmiri militant groups, Harkat-ul-Ansar, took six western tourists hostage and demanded the release of twenty-two militants from Indian jails in return for their safe return. One of them, an American, managed to escape from his captors' custody while the beheaded body of another was found over a month later. A previously unknown organization, Al-Faran, belatedly claimed responsibility and said that three of the tourists had been taken by Indian authorities during a military encounter while the fourth was missing. The incident worried Bhutto, who asked JUI leader and Chairman of the National Assembly's Committee on Foreign Affairs, Maulana Fazlur Rehman, to visit India and try to mediate with the Islamist militants. The Pakistani government tried to deflect international condemnation of the incident as an example of India's "dirty tricks."[134]

The United States declared Harkat-ul-Ansar a terrorist organization, making it the first Kashmiri group to be put on the State Department's list of global terrorist organizations. Bhutto ordered the arrest of Harkat-ul-Ansar leaders. The ISI told Bhutto that it had no contact or connection with the organization and failed to arrest anyone.[135] A few days later, most of Harkat-ul-Ansar's known leaders surfaced as leaders of a new formation, Harkat-ul-mujahideen.[136] After American demarches and media reports about the participation of Arabs, Afghans, and Pakistanis in the Kashmiri insurgency, Bhutto told army chief General Jehangir Karamat and ISI's General Qazi that such reports contradicted Pakistan's claims that the insurgency in Kashmir was indigenous. General Qazi retorted that the insurgency was originally indigenous but now non-Kashmiris had to carry it on because the Indians had killed all Kashmiri men above the age of sixteen.[137] Instead of questioning the veracity of her generals' claims before her, Bhutto accepted them and repeated them to her foreign interlocutors. In the public eye, Bhutto had to take responsibility for actions of the ISI that she did not actually control.

Bhutto's efforts to appease the military with a tough line on Kashmir and Karachi did not bring to an end the attacks on her patriotism that had been launched during her first term. Once in an interview with the BBC, she tried to make a distinction between insurgencies in Indian Punjab and Kashmir. She said that during her first administration, Pakistan had helped India control the Punjab insurgency because that was India's internal matter. Kashmir, on the other hand, is an international dispute and Pakistan could not forgo its claim here. The mere suggestion that a Pakistani government might have helped India led to the opposition, led by Sharif, describing Bhutto as "'soft' on India, 'disloyal' and a 'security risk' to the country."[138]

Toward the end of 1994, a group of unidentified ISI officers approached several prominent non-political Pakistanis to join a future government of national unity that would follow Bhutto's ouster. One of those contacted by the would-be coup planners was Pakistani social worker Abdul Sattar Edhi, who fled the country to avoid becoming entangled in "political machinations."[139]

The Islamists also continued their sniping at Bhutto's heels. There was a violent revolt in Malakand, a remote part of the North-West frontier Province, where Tehreek-e-Nifaz-i-Shariat-i-Mohammadi (TNSM, or Movement for the Enforcement of Muhammad's Sharia) demanded enforcement of Sharia laws.[140] The TNSM took civil court judges and government officials hostage, captured an airport and blocked highways.[141] The TNSM had "some outside support—Arab and Afghan mercenaries left over from the Afghan civil war."[142] The army refused to intervene, leaving civil authorities to deal with the crisis on their own.[143] In October 1995, several army officers including a Major General with Islamic fundamentalist leanings were arrested for plotting to overthrow the Bhutto government.[144] This led Robert LaPorte Jr., a well-informed observer of Pakistan affairs, to write:

[The plotters] belonged to a Muslim fundamentalist group allegedly patronized by Lieutanant General (retd.) Javed Nasir, the
former Inter-Services Intelligence chief. In the first press reports,
the officers were to be forced to retire from active duty, but in November [1995] it was announced that they would be court martialed,
largely because their plans involved the elimination of the nine
army corps commanders. This was the first widely publicized incident of Islamic fundamentalism in the military. The character of
the Pakistan military is changing but its impact on the command
structure and discipline has not yet been documented.[145]

The development with the most far-reaching consequences in Bhutto's
second term was the rise to power in Afghanistan of the Taliban. At the
end of 1993, Afghanistan's civil war was in full swing and Pakistan's
ambition of installing its favorite Pashtun Islamist leader, Gulbeddin
Hekmatyar, as Afghanistan's ruler was nowhere near fulfillment. Although Hekmatyar had been named Prime Minister in a mujahideen
government under the terms of an agreement negotiated by the Saudis
and the Pakistanis, Commander Massoud's forces would not allow him
to enter the capital, Kabul. Hekmatyar's forces and Massoud's troops
routinely lobbed rockets at each other on the capital's outskirts. Regional
warlords ran various parts of Afghanistan. The Pakistanis saw Massoud
as an impediment to peace as well as a Pakistan-friendly Afghanistan.
Massoud, on the other hand, was so fed up with the ISI's opposition to
him that he had started befriending Pakistan's arch-rivals, the Indians.
This made it difficult for a Pakistani government to accommodate
Massoud's concerns, even if it wanted to. The balance of forces was such
that neither ISI and Hekmatyar nor Massoud were able to force the other's
hand militarily despite several attempts.

The stalemate in Afghanistan made life for ordinary Afghans very
difficult. The once respected mujahideen had now become dreaded soldiers in the armies of warlords who looted and raped unarmed Afghans.
In such circumstances, a group of religious students challenged the warlords in the southeastern province of Kandahar. According to Steve Coll:

The birth and rise of the Taliban during 1994 and the emergence of
the movement's supreme leader, Mullah Mohammed Omar, were

often described in the United States and Europe as the triumph of a naive, pious, determined band of religious students swept into power on a wave of popular revulsion over Kandahar's criminal warlords. As they constructed their founding narrative, they weaved in stories of Mullah Omar's visionary dreams for a new Islamic order for Afghanistan. They described his heroic rescue of abducted girls from warlord rapists. They publicized his yearning for popular justice, as illuminated by the public hanging of depraved kidnappers. "It was like a myth," recalled the Pashtun broadcaster Spozhmai Maiwandi, who spoke frequently with Taliban leaders. "They were taking the Koran and the gun and going from village to village saying, 'For Koran's sake, put down your weapons.'" If the warlords refused, the Taliban would kill them. "For us it was not strange," Maiwandi recalled. Religious students had meted out justice in rural Kandahar for ages. "We knew these people existed."[146]

Most accounts of the Taliban's emergence acknowledge that they were a local phenomenon reflecting frustration with the mujahideen leaders and warlords, which was later backed by Pakistan's ISI. In his book *Taliban*, Ahmed Rashid explains that most leaders of the movement were "part-time or full-time students at madrasas [Islamic seminaries]," which led them to choose the name *Taliban* for themselves. "A *talib* is an Islamic student, one who seeks knowledge compared to the mullah who is one who gives knowledge. By choosing such a name the Taliban (plural of *talib*) distanced themselves from the party politics of the mujahideen and signaled that they were a movement for cleansing society rather than a party to grab power."[147] The Taliban declared their aims as being to restore peace, disarm the populations, enforce Sharia law and defend the integrity and Islamic character of Afghanistan.[148]

Rashid suggests that Pakistan may have been involved in the rise of the Taliban from the beginning though he attributed that support to "the frustrated Pakistani transport and smuggling mafia, the [Jamiat Ulema Islam] JUI and Pashtun military and political officials"[149] seeking to open a land route from Pakistan to the Central Asian Republics. Jamiat Ulema Islam was the only Islamist faction that was part of Bhutto's coalition government. Its leader, Maulana Fazlur Rehman, had been made Chairman of the National Assembly's standing committee on Foreign Affairs. JUI's support base was in the Pakistani provinces bordering Afghanistan and Fazlur Rehman had developed close ties with Pashtun business interests through his access to government patronage.

According to this account, the Pakistanis seeking access to Central Asia through Afghanistan were encountering difficulties in securing the cooperation of warlords in Kandahar. Around this time, Mullah Omar had established his reputation as a "Robin Hood figure" in Kandahar by standing up for helpless women and children. The Pakistani trucking interests donated "several hundred thousand Pakistani rupees and promised a monthly stipend to the Taliban, if they would clear the roads of chains [put up by warlords to collect taxes] and bandits and guarantee the security for truck traffic."[150]

Two Pakistani accounts, one by Lieutenant General Kamal Matinuddin[151] and the other by journalist Imtiaz Gul,[152] suggest that Pakistani officials came into contact with the Taliban well after they had already established themselves as a significant presence in Kandahar. Whether ISI officials helped create the Taliban or simply enlisted them as allies after the movement had already become influential, Pakistani support for the Taliban was crucial.

Bhutto was "slowly, slowly sucked into" supporting the Taliban by the ISI.[153] Initially, the U.S. was not particularly perturbed by the emergence of a peaceful Afghanistan under the Taliban. American oil company Unocal negotiated a gas pipeline from Turkmenistan to Pakistan through Afghanistan and the State Department was not averse to Pakistan bringing the Taliban and other Afghan factions to the peace table.[154] Later, however, the Taliban's human rights violations and their hosting of Osama bin Laden and his Al Qaeda network made the U.S. and the Taliban implacable foes. In March 1996, Bhutto's government was reported as having second thoughts about supporting the Taliban even though Interior Minister Nasirullah Babar continued to support them.[155] Civilian officials expressed concerns "about the consequences for Pakistan of a Taliban government in Kabul, which might foment Muslim fundamentalism, and possibly even secessionism in Pakistani-ruled tribal areas bordering Afghanistan."[156] Curiously, around the same time Bhutto was mired in a controversy with Pakistan's judiciary. The Jamaat-e-Islami started a campaign to demand Bhutto's resignation and her replacement by an interim government headed by the judiciary.[157]

By the summer of 1996, Jamaat-e-Islami's campaign against the government became violent, leading to the death of three party activists in clashes with police in June. In July, nine opposition parties, including Sharif's PML and the Jamaat-e-Islami, called for a strike that paralyzed industry in Karachi. The opposition alliance expanded to fourteen parties, including the MQM and increased agitation for Bhutto's removal. A series of unexplained bomb blasts and sectarian killings followed. Murtaza Bhutto's death in an alleged exchange of fire with the police aggravated the impression of Bhutto not being in control of the domestic situation.[158]

Bhutto's government came to an end on November 5, 1996, when President Farooq Leghari dismissed the prime minister and dissolved Parliament. Leghari's decision was backed by the military, which reportedly "warned Leghari about growing unrest in its ranks and had provided him with evidence of corruption involving [Bhutto's husband] Zardari."[159] Bhutto was briefly detained and her husband was taken away by military intelligence, to be imprisoned later on corruption charges. Bhutto had not expected to be removed from office a second time though the president had told her that the military wanted her out and the army chief warned her that the president was about to dismiss her from office.[160]

Leghari accused Bhutto of failing to "put an end to extra-judicial killings," "undermining the independence of the judiciary," and "corruption, nepotism, and violation of rules in the administration of the affairs of government."[161] The *Friday Times*, whose editor, Najam Sethi, was appointed a presidential adviser by Leghari, voiced the sentiment of Bhutto's many critics at the time in its editorial. It said, "Benazir Bhutto had it coming. She was an arrogant, reckless, capricious and corrupt ruler who surrounded herself with sycophants, lackeys and flunkeys and squandered away a second opportunity to serve the people of Pakistan."[162]

Bhutto clearly made mistakes in her confrontation with the political opposition and the judiciary as well as in running the government. Her greater mistake, however, might have been to trust the Pakistani establishment to support her elected government through its full term. By the time of her dismissal, Bhutto was no longer useful to the civil-military combine in bringing additional American aid or glossing over their covert operations in Afghanistan and Kashmir. After Bhutto's dismissal, the Taliban consolidated their control over most of Afghanistan and Pakistan extended diplomatic recognition to their regime.

Massoud and his non-Pashtun allies in the Northern Alliance managed to hold on to ten percent of Afghanistan's territory until the United States helped them drive the Taliban out of power in 2001.

The ISI moved its training facilities for Kashmiri mujahideen into Afghanistan, where anti-American terrorists and Kashmiri jihadists trained together.[163] The change of governments in Islamabad had ensured that there would be no civilian obstruction or delay in carrying out these policies.

The second Benazir Bhutto government lasted a little longer than the first. Wiser from her experience, Bhutto avoided conflict with the army and the ISI as much as possible. She took a hard line toward India, supported the Kashmir insurgency, and even acquiesced to the rise to power of the Taliban in Afghanistan, orchestrated by the ISI. Bhutto was unable to control the perception of corruption at the highest levels of government, however, and she failed to end her acrimonious confrontation with Nawaz Sharif. Amid calls for accountability from Islamist parties, Bhutto's second government was dismissed like the first.

Before holding new elections, Leghari conceded the military's longstanding demand for the creation of a "National Defense and Security Council" to "advise the government on everything from national security to economic issues."[164] The ten-member Council, headed by the president, was to include the prime minister, four cabinet ministers, the chairman of the Joint Chiefs of Staff, and three armed services chiefs. Pakistan's political parties opposed the creation of the council, which they saw as an effort to institutionalize the military's political role. It resembled Zia ul-Haq's proposed National Security Council that had been excluded from the constitution by the National Assembly in 1985. Only Nawaz Sharif's PML "welcomed the creation of the council as a 'stabilizing' presence,"[165] obviously to curry favor with the military.

Leghari also created an Accountability Commission, also at the military's behest, "to root out corruption."[166] Six weeks after the commission's creation, however, the government admitted that it had "not been able to gather enough evidence to act against top politicians, including Ms. Bhutto and her husband, Asif Ali Zardari."[167] The failure to prove corruption allegations disrupted the establishment's plans to disqualify both Bhutto and Sharif before fresh elections. Elections were held on February 3, 1997, with the PPP and PML, still led by Bhutto and Sharif respectively, as the main contenders.

This time, the Jamaat-e-Islami "decided not to participate because the caretaker government had not disqualified corrupt politicians from seeking reelection."[168] The role of a third force in the elections was played by Pakistan's cricket idol, Imran Khan, who led a new formation called Pakistan Tehrik-e-Insaf (PTI, or Movement for Justice). The PTI "promised to purge Pakistan of corruption and establish a government of 'fresh faces.'"[169] The ISI had hoped that the balance of power in the new Parliament would be held by MQM and Khan's PTI as well as several influential landowners close to Leghari who ran as independent candidates.[170] But the military's favored political scenario failed to materialize once again.

Fewer voters than ever cast their ballots in the election, with nationwide turnout at around 30 percent. Less than 41 percent of the eligible voters exercised their franchise in Punjab, 31.2 percent in Sindh, 29.6 percent in the North-West Frontier Province, and 22.84 percent in Balochistan.[171] The electorate was clearly tired of electing governments that faced dismissal within a couple of years. The low turnout favored the PML, which secured two-thirds of the seats in the new National Assembly.[172] Leghari and the military had to choose between scrapping the election, on grounds of low turnout, or to accept Nawaz Sharif as Prime Minister. They opted for the latter and Sharif returned as Prime Minister, this time with a parliamentary majority sufficient to amend the constitution.

Bhutto and Sharif cooperated briefly to amend the constitution and remove the provision that enabled Pakistani presidents to dismiss elected governments.[173] Sharif continued, however, with proceedings initiated by Leghari against Bhutto and her husband. The accountability commission was transformed into an accountability cell within the Prime Minister's secretariat and expanded its role with the passage of time to hound politicians, businessmen, and journalists opposing Sharif.

Having secured his position vis-à-vis a presidential dismissal, Sharif secured another amendment to the constitution authorizing "leaders of parliamentary parties to expel from the legislature any member who violates party discipline, that is, who speaks or votes against his/her party, and the expulsion cannot be challenged in court."[174] This meant that members of Sharif's parliamentary group could neither speak nor act against him and if they did, they would lose their seats in Parliament. Leghari and the military were alarmed at the prospect of "prime ministerial dictatorship."[175] In the absence of presidential powers, the only remaining civilian check on Sharif's authority was the judiciary. Leghari and General Karamat encouraged the Chief Justice of Pakistan's Supreme Court, Sajjad Ali Shah, to confront Sharif.

The clash started over the appointment of five new Supreme Court justices Sharif had wanted to block and subsided only after the intervention of the military. In November 1997, the *New York Times* reported the fear of an army takeover in Pakistan:

Nine months after the election in which Nawaz Sharif won a landslide victory and became Prime Minister again, his bruising drive to entrench his authority has raised fears that Pakistan could be headed for another cycle of upheaval . . . Since he regained the office from which he was ousted by presidential decree in 1993, Mr. Sharif, 47, has sought to insure that he cannot be unseated again before completing a full five-year term. To that end, he has set out to curb the powers of the President, army commander, Parliament and judiciary . . . With newspapers warning that he was risking a new takeover by the armed forces, which have ruled Pakistan directly or indirectly for nearly 30 of its 50 years as a nation, Mr. Sharif staged a last-minute retreat from the latest in a series of power struggles. This time, the dispute was over the appointment of five new Supreme Court justices Mr. Sharif had wanted to block . . . Mr. Sharif maintained that the 12-member Supreme Court had no need for the extra judges, but his critics say that he viewed several of the nominees as potential adversaries who might vote against him if old corruption accusations resulted in attempts to remove him from office . . . According to accounts circulating in Islamabad, Mr. Sharif agreed to the judges' appointments only after the army commander, Gen. Jehangir Karamat, told him that he would not tolerate a constitutional crisis . . . Although the military leadership issued a statement saying that it was acting "without being partisan in any way," General Karamat's role in the dispute was seen by many as a reminder that the army remains the final arbiter of power here . . . But many newspapers today carried warnings that Mr. Sharif, who earned a reputation for being impulsive in his first term as Prime Minister, might return to the offensive.[176]

Sharif did fight back. Chief Justice Shah was deposed by his fellow judges after "about 100 men and women of Sharif's Muslim League party swamped the Supreme Court and interrupted the Prime Minister's trial on charges of contempt of court."[177] Leghari resigned from the office of president on December 2, 1997.[178]

The changes did not bring stability to Pakistan, however. The Islamists who had minimal representation in the elected assemblies threatened to "launch mass movements to overthrow the present parliamentary system and replace it with a true Islamic government."[179] Sharif's authoritarian ways antagonized virtually every political force in the country. The PPP allied with fourteen smaller political parties to demand the end of political persecution and fresh elections for Parliament. The consolidation of Taliban rule in Afghanistan encouraged Pakistan's Islamists, who demanded a similar regime in Pakistan. Sharif attempted to increase the powers of the prime minister "at the expense of the parliament, the judiciary and the provinces under the pretext of introducing *Sharia.*"[180] This mobilized "orthodox Islamic groups to counterbalance his political adversaries"[181] but also increased the leverage of the Islamists.

When Sharif spoke of "easing relations with India," the Islamists opposed him with greater vehemence. The Islamists and the ISI were now running large-scale jihad operations in Afghanistan and Kashmir that could be jeopardized by Sharif's ideas of trade with India. "Sharif wanted to expand trade, partly because Pakistan could buy raw materials and finished products from India at lower prices than in more distant international markets," wrote an expert on Pakistani politics. "There was some serious talk of Pakistan selling electric power to the Indian states of Punjab and Haryana."[182]

Before Sharif's initiatives for expanding trade with India could reach fruition, India carried out tests of its nuclear weapons on May 11 and 13, 1998.[183] Pakistani public opinion overwhelmingly favored Pakistan conducting its own tests despite President Bill Clinton's promise of "economic, political and security benefits"[184] for all in case of Pakistan's show of restraint. Immediately after India's nuclear tests, the United States and other developed nations had imposed sanctions on India. Similar sanctions, if applied to Pakistan, would have been debilitating for Pakistan's economy. The Karachi Stock Exchange lost one third of its value after India's tests and the business community, in particular, did not look forward to new international sanctions.

Sharif discussed the political and economic consequences of testing with Pakistani economists, businessmen, and foreign policy experts and did not take a decision to test for over a week. Any chance that Sharif would heed Clinton's advice was lost when Pakistan's Islamist parties brought tens of thousands of demonstrators in the streets demanding nuclear tests and the military weighed in favor of testing.[185] Bhutto joined other opposition leaders in taunting Sharif over his hesitation.

On May 28 Pakistan "exploded five nuclear bombs"[186] and Pakistan became a declared nuclear power. "We have nuclear weapons, we are a nuclear power,"[187] said Pakistani Foreign Minister Gohar Ayub Khan whose father, Ayub Khan, had been Pakistan's first military ruler. "We have an advanced missiles program," he added and warned that Pakistan now had the capacity to retaliate "with vengeance and devastating effect" against Indian attacks. Sharif has apparently told the Americans that he went ahead with the tests out of fear of "an alleged Israeli plot to destroy Pakistan's nuclear facilities in collusion with India."[188] Bruce Riedel, President Clinton's Special Assistant for Near Eastern and South Asia Affairs at the National Security Council, says he "had the Israeli Chief of Staff deny categorically to the Pakistani Ambassador in Washington any such plan the night before the tests but that fact mattered little to Islamabad."[189]

Pakistanis celebrated their nation's new nuclear power status but the celebration for affluent and middle-class Pakistanis was marred, not by international sanctions, but by a government decision made in panic. The night after the nuclear tests, Sharif's government froze over $11.8 billion in private foreign currency deposits in Pakistani banks. Ordinary Pakistanis had maintained these deposits to protect themselves from fluctuations in the value of Pakistani currency and for years the government had guaranteed that balances in these deposits could be withdrawn in foreign currency. Successive governments had, however, used these deposits to finance Pakistan's trade imbalance and the banking system would not have been able to cope with demands for hard currency withdrawals expected after the nuclear tests.[190] On the day of the nuclear tests, Pakistan's Central Bank only had $1.26 billion in foreign exchange reserves.

The freezing of the foreign currency deposits depressed any prospect there might have been of overseas Pakistanis and local investors sustaining Pakistan's economy once international sanctions went into effect. It lost Sharif support of the business community and the middle class, which coupled with his already strained relations with the Islamists and the political opposition, paved the way for overt military intervention.

Initially, Pakistan faced suspension of economic assistance from the IMF, World Bank, and Asian Development Bank, creating the specter of default on the country's external debt, which stood at $32 billion at the time. Sharif's government was, however, able to secure financial support from oil-rich Arab countries. Within a few months of the tests, the Clinton administration relaxed sanctions to the extent of the U.S. not opposing IMF funding for Pakistan, which eased Pakistan's economic crisis.[191] The American decision was based on Sharif's commitment to renew dialogue with India.

The military decided to make known its unhappiness with Sharif's confrontational style of governance and the perennial air of domestic crisis it generated. The deteriorating economic situation affected what Hasan-Askari Rizvi terms as "the professional and corporate interests of the military."[192] The army chief, General Jehangir Karamat, made several statements on the domestic situation and in October 1998, proposed the creation of a National Security Council backed by "a team of credible advisors and a think tank of experts" to "institutionalize decision-making."[193] In proposing an NSC, Karamat was only repeating what the Pakistani military, as an institution, had sought for years. Zia ul-Haq had included the NSC in his package of constitutional changes and Leghari had created a similar council after his dismissal of Bhutto's second administration. From the military's point of view, civilian politicians could hold office only as long as they ensured continuity in policies preferred by the military and ceded some of their constitutional authority to technocrats and army generals.

Sharif, however, was in no mood to heed Karamat's advice to avoid "polarization, vendettas and insecurity-driven policies."[194] The Prime Minister asked his army commander to either resign or take over. Karamat was, by temperament and personal conviction, not a coup-maker. He decided to step down from his position three months ahead of his scheduled retirement date.

Sharif had already been in contact with his choice as army commander through a mutual friend in anticipation of Karamat's retirement.[195] Sharif's choice was Pervez Musharraf, "an Urdu-speaking Muhajir from Karachi"[196] who was third in seniority among three-star generals at that time. Musharraf became army chief on October 28. The mutual friend who brought Sharif and Musharraf together was banker Hamid Asghar Kidwai, who had been a key player at Mehran Bank when the bank helped the ISI fund Sharif's 1990 election bid as the head of IJI. Sharif had appointed Kidwai as Pakistan's ambassador to Kenya, a position he retained even after Musharraf overthrew Sharif in a coup d'état a year later.

In appointing Musharraf, Sharif calculated that "a Muhajir Army chief presiding over a predominantly Punjabi-Pashtun high command would be weak and thus not able to build pressure on the government."[197] This proved to be a blunder similar to the one made by Zulfikar Ali Bhutto when he designated General Zia ul-Haq as Chief of the Army Staff, based on the assumption that an obsequious and pious general would pose no threat to the civilian order. It is significant that both Bhutto and Sharif were encouraged in their choices by individuals tied to Pakistan's military intelligence apparatus.

Having placed an ally in the army's top slot, Sharif proceeded to initiate a peace process with India with American blessings. Sharif first met Indian Prime Minister Atal Bihari Vajpayee on the sidelines of the SAARC summit in Colombo two months after the two countries' nuclear tests and proposed reduction of tensions.[198] Then, notwithstanding occasional public rattling of sabers, the two sides engaged in official talks coupled with track-two diplomacy. In November, they agreed to resume passenger bus service across their border.[199] When the bus service started in February 1999, Vajpayee announced his plan to ride the first bus from India into Pakistan.

Vajpayee's bus diplomacy led to "a summit filled with symbolism and hope of warmer relations"[200] between the two nuclear-armed adversaries. The two prime ministers agreed to a "composite dialogue" covering all disputes between their countries, including Kashmir. Sharif voiced the hope first, expressed by Pakistan's founder Muhammad Ali Jinnah days before partition, that "Pakistan and India will be able to live as the United States and Canada."[201] Vajpayee made a symbolic visit to the monument in Lahore marking the Indian Muslims' demand for a separate homeland in a bid to reassure Pakistanis that even Hindu nationalists in India no longer question Pakistan's right to exist.[202]

The public mood in both India and Pakistan seemed to favor the peace process.[203] Pakistan's Islamists and the military did not. The Jamaat-e-Islami threatened to block Vajpayee's bus route, described the Indian leader as Pakistan's "national enemy" and held street demonstrations against India to highlight the Kashmir problem. The Islamists also called for a general strike in Lahore on the day of the summit meeting. Several ambassadors invited to a state dinner for Vajpayee "were turned back after demonstrators banged on their vehicles and blocked the road."[204] Sharif had planned to arrest Jamaat-e-Islami leader Qazi Hussain Ahmed ahead of the demonstrations. Ahmed, however, could not be found as he stayed at the homes of military intelligence officials to avoid arrest.[205]

The demonstrations did not interrupt the peace process but the threat of war did. India-Pakistan talks came to an abrupt halt with the intrusion of Pakistani troops into a part of Indian-controlled territory along the Line of Control in Kashmir. In the summer of 1999, the two countries became embroiled in what came to be known as the "Kargil crisis," named after the mountainous region in the Himalayas where the conflict took place. According to U.S. officials, the conflict had the potential to escalate into nuclear war based on "disturbing evidence that the Pakistanis were preparing their nuclear arsenals for possible deployment."[206]

Shaukat Qadir, a retired Pakistani brigadier, has written the most comprehensive account of developments on the Pakistani side during the Kargil crisis, basing it on his "not inconsiderable personal knowledge" of the area, the principal Pakistani actors in the crisis, and "the collective character of the Pakistan army."[207] According to Brigadier Qadir, the Indian army found in May 1999 that "intruders had occupied the heights close to the Dras region in Kashmir." Until then, the area known as Kargil was controlled by the Indians during summer but left unoccupied during the harsh winters. Four Pakistani generals, led by Musharraf, had planned "sometime around mid-November 1998" to occupy the terrain in Dras-Kargil during the winter absence of Indian troops. The plan was kept secret from other military commanders and "preparations proceeded in secret." Musharraf "casually broached" the subject with Sharif at some point in December 1998 but the army "has not presented a complete analysis of the scale of the operation or its possible outcome." Musharraf and the other three generals saw the occupation of Indian-controlled territory as a means of providing "a fillip to the Kashmiri freedom movement."[208]

Brigadier Qadir believes that Musharraf's operation in Kargil was "not intended to reach the scale that it finally did. In all likelihood, it grew in scale as the troops crept forward to find more unoccupied heights, until finally they were overlooking the [Kashmir] valley. In the process, they had ended up occupying an area of about 130 square kilometers over a front of over 100 kilometers and a depth ranging between seven to fifteen kilometers. They were occupying 132 [Indian] posts of various sizes."[209] The occupying troops belonged to Pakistan's Northern Light Infantry and numbered around one thousand, with four times that number providing logistical support. These troops were supported by "some local mujahideen assisting as labor to carry logistical requirements."[210]

Qadir describes the plan as envisaged by the Pakistani military leadership:

The political aim underpinning the operation was 'to seek a just and permanent solution to the Kashmir issue in accordance with the wishes of the people of Kashmir.' However, the military aim that preceded the political aim was 'to create a military threat that could be viewed as capable of leading to a military solution, so as to force India to the negotiating table from a position of weakness'. The operational plan envisaged India amassing troops at the LOC [Line of Control] to deal with the threat at Kargil, resulting in a vacuum in their rear areas. By July, the mujahideen would step up their activities in the rear areas, threatening the Indian lines of communication at pre-designated targets, which would help isolate pockets, forcing the Indian troops to react to them. This would create an opportunity for the forces at Kargil to push forward and pose an additional threat. India would, as a consequence, be forced to the negotiating table.[211]

Little attention was paid in the plan to international reaction or the prospect of India's deployment of different battlefield tactics.

From India's perspective, Pakistan's military incursion into Kargil was not a small matter. Pakistani forces now occupied "mountaintops overlooking the Kargil highway" and were "threatening to weaken Indian control over a significant (yet barren) part"[212] of Kashmir. Moreover, it violated the spirit of the peace process that Sharif and Vajpayee had agreed upon barely a few months ago and amounted to treachery on Pakistan's part. India fought the Kargil intruders with a large force including heavy artillery. The Indian Air Force was brought in to bomb Pakistani soldiers on mountains as high as 17,000 feet above sea level. Initially, the intruders held on to their positions. The induction of Swedish-made Bofors guns and laser-guided aerial bombardment reversed the situation by the middle of June.[213]

India also mounted a major diplomatic campaign and received support from, among others, the United States and China. The international community almost unanimously demanded Pakistan's withdrawal from Kargil. Instead of helping focus on the Kashmiri freedom struggle, Musharraf and his three fellow generals had managed to unite the international community against Pakistan.

Pakistan first denied that the military operation in Kargil involved government troops and tried to blame Kashmiri militants, the mujahideen, for the incursions. India released a tape-recorded conversation between Musharraf and the Pakistan army's Chief of General Staff, Lieutenant General Aziz Khan, that left no doubt about Pakistan's military presence in Kargil. The conversation between Musharraf and Aziz Khan took place while Musharraf was in Beijing and Aziz Khan at army headquarters in Rawalpindi. It remains a mystery to this day how the Indians got hold of a tape of their conversation. Pakistani intelligence suspected that American intelligence taped the conversation and gave it to the Indians to embarrass Pakistan and force its withdrawal from the Kargil heights.[214]

Unable to deny Pakistan's role any longer, and faced with the prospect of India defeating Pakistan militarily for the first time under civilian rule, Sharif started looking for a face-saving settlement. India offered Sharif a chance to distance himself from actions in Kargil by suggesting that "the Pakistani army had undertaken the operation without political sanction."[215] Sharif did not want to take on the military leadership publicly and was also reluctant to show the world that he did not control the affairs of Pakistan as prime minister. Ironically, these were the same fears that had prevented Bhutto from going public over her differences with the generals during both her terms. Like Bhutto, Sharif paid a heavy price for pretending to go along with out-of-control generals. He lost the power he tried to hold on to and also the credibility that might have survived had he exposed Musharraf's strategic miscalculation once the world turned against Pakistan during the Kargil crisis.

Sharif called President Clinton on July 2 and "appealed for American intervention immediately to stop the fighting and to resolve the Kashmir issue,"[216] followed by a more desperate call the next day. The Pakistani prime minister traveled to Washington for a July 4 summit with Clinton. He was seen off at Islamabad airport by Musharraf and the two were shown together on Pakistan television to indicate that Sharif's mission had the support of the army. Clinton and Sharif met at Blair House on U.S. Independence Day. Bruce Riedel, who was present at the meeting, gave this account of their discussions:

The Prime Minister told Clinton that he wanted desperately to find a solution that would allow Pakistan to withdraw with some cover.

Without something to point to, Sharif warned ominously, the fundamentalists in Pakistan would move against him and this meeting would be his last with Clinton . . . Clinton asked Sharif if he knew how advanced the threat of nuclear war really was? Did Sharif know his military was preparing their nuclear tipped missiles? Sharif seemed taken aback and said only that India was probably doing the same. The President reminded Sharif how close the U.S. and Soviet Union had come to nuclear war in 1962 over Cuba. Did Sharif realize that if even one bomb was dropped . . . Sharif finished his sentence and said it would be a catastrophe . . . The President was getting angry. He told Sharif that he had asked repeatedly for Pakistani help to bring Osama bin Laden to justice from Afghanistan. Sharif had promised often to do so but had done nothing. Instead the ISI worked with bin Laden and the Taliban to foment terrorism. [Clinton's] draft statement would also mention Pakistan's role in supporting terrorists in Afghanistan and India. Was that what Sharif wanted, Clinton asked? Did Sharif order the Pakistani nuclear missile force to prepare for action? Did he realize how crazy that was? You've put me in the middle today, set the U.S. up to fail and I won't let it happen. Pakistan is messing with nuclear war.[217]

At the end of that meeting, Sharif agreed to announce a Pakistani withdrawal from Kargil and restoration of the sanctity of the Line of Control in return for Clinton taking a personal interest in resumption of the India-Pakistan dialogue.

On returning to Pakistan, Sharif asked the army "to proceed against the principal actors in this episode and get rid of them."[218] Musharraf knew that "if heads were to roll, his would be the first."[219] The army chief went on a tour of Pakistan's garrisons to explain his position to his troops and galvanize support for his position as their commander. The Islamists hit the streets, again, with a vengeance, this time with banners that read, "'Remove Nawaz, save the country' and 'Kargil retreat is betrayal.'"[220]

On October 10, 1999, the *Washington Post* reported that Sharif's hold on power was growing tenuous and "Army leaders, humiliated by his decision to withdraw from a border conflict with India in July, have come close to breaking with his government."[221] The *Post* article said Army spokesman Brigadier Rashid Qureshi "acknowledged 'dissatisfaction' in the army over Sharif's decision to pull back from the border, but he insisted the military is eager to work with civilian officials to save Pakistan from disaster."[222] In conversations with Pakistanis, however, Qureshi was asking, "What is the worst the Americans can do if the army takes power directly?"[223]

Musharraf had started planning a coup d'état and, as part of that plan, had appointed some of his closest friends in the army as commanders in positions critical during a coup. On October 12, the coup was executed as soon as Sharif tried to fire Musharraf and replace him as army chief with the head of ISI, Lieutenant General Ziauddin while Musharraf was out of the country. Official accounts, however, projected the coup as the military's spontaneous reaction to Musharraf's ouster. "I wish to inform you that the armed forces have moved in as a last resort to prevent further destabilization," Musharraf told the Pakistani people at 3:00 a.m. the morning after the coup, adding, "The armed forces have been facing incessant public clamor to remedy the fast-declining situation from all sides."[224]

According to the official account, Sharif's firing of Musharraf resulted in an institutional decision by the army to depose him. Later Sharif was put on trial for trying to "hijack" the plane on which Musharraf was traveling back from a trip to Sri Lanka. A reporter summed up the official version:

> Unaware that he had been ousted, General Musharraf was returning to Pakistan from Sri Lanka on a commercial flight. Air traffic controllers, reportedly under Mr. Sharif's orders, refused to allow the plane to land as scheduled in Karachi. Vehicles blocked the landing strips. Runway lights were turned off. The airliner, nearly out of fuel, was finally able to land only after army officers loyal to General Musharraf had seized the airport.[225]

In other words, the army had seized power only after being provoked to do so by Sharif's decision to replace Musharraf.

The Pakistani military always insists on an immediate provocation as the trigger of its coups. This narrative presents every Pakistani military ruler as a reluctant coup-maker: Ayub Khan came to power after a violent scuffle in the East Pakistan legislature; Yahya Khan took over after months of rioting against Ayub Khan and the failure of Ayub Khan's round table conference with politicians; Zia ul-Haq's coup was the result of Zulfikar Ali Bhutto's inability to compromise with politicians protesting a rigged election and the possibility of civil war; and now the army had deposed Sharif because he was trying to replace their commander and was possibly endangering his life. The army's ability to swiftly execute a military takeover within hours of a supposed provocation is often attributed to its having contingency plans for such occasions. Closer scrutiny, however, reveals a pattern of careful prior planning, including disorder in the streets orchestrated with the help of the reliable street power of Islamist political parties.

Initially, the international community condemned Musharraf's coup d'état but Musharraf gained acceptance as a moderate "likely to pursue foreign policies that are acceptable and even pleasantly surprising to the Clinton administration."[226] Within days of Musharraf taking power, the leading Republican contender for the U.S. presidential nomination expressed his belief in Musharraf's ability to bring stability to South Asia. Although George W. Bush could not name Musharraf, he said, "the new Pakistani general, he's just been elected—not elected, this guy took over office . . . It appears this guy is going to bring stability to the country and I think that's good news for the sub-continent."[227]

Bush's Communications Director, Karen Hughes, explained that Bush was only agreeing with State Department officials "who welcome Musharraf's pledge to work for return to democracy."[228] In an article titled "Pakistan: Democracy Is Not Everything," Richard N. Haass argued:

> The coup that brought Army Chief of Staff Pervez Musharraf to power . . . should not be condemned out of hand. And it may well bring stability to a country and a region where stability is in short supply . . . The greatest danger is a Pakistan that fails, a Pakistan where the central government loses effective control over much of

the county and, in the process, becomes a safe haven for terrorists and drug traffickers and zealots.[229]

There was no recognition that Musharraf's institution, the Pakistani military, had contributed to the rise of terrorists and religious zealots in Pakistan.

Pakistan's generals are aware that most people, especially American policy makers, remember the failings of Pakistani politicians far more readily than the overall context of Pakistani politics. The Pakistani military makes a special effort to maintain close institutional ties with the U.S. military. The Pentagon looks upon the Pakistan army leaders as soldiers and that image enables Pakistani generals to cover up their role as petty political intriguers. It is perhaps for this reason that immediately after the coup, Musharraf telephoned General Anthony Zinni, Commander of the U.S. Central Command. According to Zinni, Musharraf told him "what had led to the coup and why he and the other military leaders had had no choice other than the one they took."[230] Zinni also mentions Musharraf's help, two months later, in arresting some terrorists sought by the United States, which led Zinni to tell Washington, "Now do something for Musharraf."[231]

In his memoirs, General Tommy Franks, the commander of U.S. Central Command during the Afghan war of 2001, writes of his efforts to forge strategic ties with General Musharraf. "Musharraf's a soldier," General Franks says he told CIA Director George Tenet in 2000. "So are most of the key players in his government. You have to see their world from the military perspective."[232] The American general offered help to Pakistan "to modernize her conventional forces, thus reducing her reliance on nuclear arms" even before the events of September 11, 2001, led to Pakistan's renewed alliance with the United States. In a January 2001 meeting Musharraf, according to Franks, summarized the complex information for him like the general that he had been "before leading an Army coup against Pakistan's corrupt civilian government in 1999."

It is unlikely that Musharraf summarized unsavory details of civil-military relations or that Franks remembered the chronology of internal and external developments in Pakistan's history. According to Franks, "Musharraf added that the only reason Pakistan had invested so much wealth and energy into developing ballistic missiles was that their air force had been crippled by America's arms embargo."[233] In fact, Pakistan had gone public with its missile program in 1989, which it described then as being in an advanced stage, long before U.S. sanctions interrupted the delivery of F-16 fighter jets in 1990.

For General Franks, dealing with General Musharraf was a soldier-to-soldier matter. "His military needed help; so did we. Maybe we could make a deal," Franks believed. "It struck me that it was appropriate we both wore uniforms. For years, American officials and diplomatic envoys in business suits had hectored soldier-politicians such as Pervez Musharraf about human rights and representative government. Of course I believed in these with equal conviction, but at this point in history we needed to establish priorities. Stopping Al Qaeda was such a priority and Musharraf was willing to help."[234] American generals such as Zinni and Franks see military sales in return for Pakistani operational assistance for the U.S. military as major successes of negotiation. They are often unaware that the prospects of such deals are an integral part of the Pakistani military's calculus.

Much has been said or written about the reasons for Pakistan's failed experiment with democracy between 1988 and 1999. No doubt the alternating civilian governments of Benazir Bhutto and Nawaz Sharif were flawed. The two civilian leaders made numerous wrong choices; the greatest were their refusals to compromise and work with each other. Notwithstanding the military's role in amplifying the charges of corruption and the selectiveness with which these charges were made, civilian politicians failed to keep graft in check. Allegations against top politicians of personal enrichment at the expense of the people are particularly unfortunate and disturbing. In many spheres, the civilians simply had to pay the price for their pride, which prevented them from admitting that they were hardly free agents. Pakistan's civilian leaders might not have blundered into many of their bad decisions if they had not had the mullahs and the military narrowing their options.

Hasan-Askari Rizvi, one of Pakistan's foremost scholars of civil-military relations, has described the Pakistani political system after the death of Zia ul-Haq:

The Army Chief is a pivot in Pakistan's post-1988 power structure. Together with the President and the Prime Minister, he constitutes one-third of the "Troika"—an extra-constitutional arrangement for civilian-military consensus-building on key domestic, foreign-policy and security issues. The Troika meets periodically; senior military and civilian officials are summoned to give briefings relating to the issues under discussion. The Army Chief also holds meetings separately with the President and Prime Minister on political and security affairs. Another institution that has gained prominence is the Corps Commanders' meeting. Presided over by the Army Chief, this conference includes top commanders, Principal Staff Officers at the Army Headquarters and other senior officers holding strategic appointments. Its members not only discuss security and organizational and professional matters, but also deliberate on domestic issues such as law and order, and general political conditions—especially when the government and the opposition are engaged in intense confrontation. These discussions are intended both to underline senior officers' political concerns and to develop a broad-based military consensus. Executing the consensus decisions is left to the Army Chief, thereby strengthening his position when he interacts with the President and the Prime Minister.

A smooth interaction among the Troika members ensures the military's support for the Prime Minister, which contributes to general political stability. If serious differences develop among these key players, political uncertainty and instability are likely. The Prime Minister—the civilian side of the power-equation—can find him or herself in a difficult situation. The military is well placed to exert pressure on him. Furthermore, the 1973 Constitution, as amended by Zia in 1985, greatly strengthened the position of the President vis-à-vis the Prime Minister, making it difficult for the latter to emerge as an autonomous power. The Prime Minister's position was boosted somewhat by an April 1997 Constitutional amendment curtailing the President's powers so that he cannot dismiss the Prime Minister. However, so long as the Prime Minister presides over divided and mutually hostile political forces, he will have to work in harmony with the President—and the Army.[235]

In 2002, Musharraf amended Pakistan's constitution to reintroduce the idea of a National Security Council and to enhance presidential powers, before holding parliamentary elections. Bhutto and Sharif were barred from participating in these polls, as were several other politicians disqualified by a National Accountability Bureau (NAB) headed by a Lieutenant General. Before the election, Musharraf held a referendum to seek a five-year mandate as president. British academic Ian Talbot described the referendum's many flaws:

The Election Commission announced a 70 percent turnout, with 98 percent of those voted providing a mandate for General Musharraf to serve the nation as President for a further five years. Voting irregularities, coupled with the absence of formal identification requirements and of electoral rolls, tarnished the result and invoked memories of General Zia ul-Haq's rigged referendum that 'legitimized' his power as president . . . Moreover, the *Nazims* or district administrators, the cornerstone of the vaunted devolution of power [by Musharraf] had been inducted into a partisan role similar to that of the Basic Democrats under Ayub Khan. The regime's 'bubble of good governance' had been burst. Musharraf publicly admitted on television that he had been informed about cases of vote rigging, for which he expressed regret.[236]

The 2002 parliamentary election was officially said to have a voter turnout of 40 percent but most political parties said less than 25 percent voters cast their ballots.[237] Only thirty-nine days were given for the election campaign, with additional restrictions on the manner of campaigning. The ISI had created a "King's Party" by engineering defections from Sharif's PML well ahead of the polls. Called the PML (Q), this faction forged alliances with other pro-government parties and independents. The PPP and the PML faction loyal to Sharif ran as the opposition parties, as did Muttahida Majlis-e-Amal (United Action Committee), an alliance of Islamist parties led by the Jamaat-e-Islami and Jamiat Ulema Islam. Although the alliance of pro-government parties emerged with a plurality of seats in the new National Assembly, the biggest gains were made by the MMA. The Islamists had run an anti-

...ign,[238] and their success was aided by the fact that ...e the only major party spared government restrictions on campaigning or choosing candidates.

It took the military forty days after the election to put together a coalition of its supporters and a PPP faction threatened with prosecutions under corruption charges and bought off with promises of ministries. The PML (Q) candidate, Zafarullah Jamali, a lackluster tribal politician from Balochistan, was elected prime minister with 170 out of 342 National Assembly votes.[239] Musharraf succeeded in diluting the political strength of Bhutto and Sharif.

Musharraf's package of constitutional changes needed the support of a two-thirds majority in the National Assembly, which was difficult to secure in view of the assembly's makeup. The Islamists in Parliament postured against Musharraf and made him promise that he would step down as a serving general at the end of 2004 before voting for the constitutional changes. Musharraf later reneged on that promise to continue as president and army chief.

Jamali lasted as prime minister only for eighteen months. As a politician, albeit a very weak one, he was still not trustworthy for Pakistan's generals. In August 2004, Shaukat Aziz, who had been a Citibank executive until Musharraf appointed him finance minister immediately after the 1999 coup, took over as Pakistan's prime minister. The military's desire for a civilian government fully under its control, with only a marginal role for popular or electable politicians, was now fulfilled. The MMA's enhanced profile served an important function in convincing Musharraf's American backers that Pakistan faced the threat of an Islamist takeover if the military did not retain the levers of power. The military's alliance with Pakistan's Islamists had once again thwarted the prospect of democratic rule in the country. Having used the Islamists in the previous decade to undermine civilian authority, Pakistan's generals now cite them as the threat against which the international community, especially the United States, should help the Pakistani military maintain its control over the country.

7

Jihad without Borders

On February 4, 2004, Pakistan's military ruler, General Pervez Musharraf, told Pakistan's newspaper editors in Islamabad, "Pakistan has two vital national interests: Being a nuclear state and the Kashmir cause."[1] The statement represented continuity in Pakistani strategic thinking almost twenty-nine months after Musharraf revived Pakistan's alliance with the United States in the aftermath of the September 11, 2001, terrorist attacks in New York and the Washington area. For American consumption, however, Musharraf claimed that he was leading Pakistan through a "major strategic reorientation."[2] U.S. officials seemed to accept that claim at face value.

The immediate price Musharraf paid to qualify for U.S. support in September 2001 was to end Pakistan's support for the Taliban regime in Afghanistan and to sign up as a member of the U.S.-led coalition against terrorism. As time passed, Musharraf was coerced or persuaded by the United States to expand intelligence sharing against jihadi groups linked to Al Qaeda, shut down the infiltration of militants across the Line of Control into Indian-controlled Kashmir, and join a peace process with India. Toward the end of 2003, after information surfaced about Pakistan's covert sales of nuclear technology to Iran, North Korea, and Libya, Musharraf also had to shut down the clandestine nuclear sales network headed by Pakistani scientist Dr. A. Q. Khan and share intelligence about the network with the United States.

Musharraf believed he was restructuring Pakistan's priorities with a view to retain and rebuild the relationship with the United States. His statement about Pakistan's "vital national interests" was meant to reassure his military and Pakistan's religious conservatives that the alliance with the United States was not the policy U-turn it appeared to be. Musharraf was in effect saying that he had not abandoned the core policies that had guided Pakistan's direction as an independent state almost since its inception; he was only making adjustments in some areas to regain U.S. trust and support, something that was as integral to Pakistan's conventional strategic thinking as the commitment to Islamic nationalism and defiance against India's regional influence.

As a result of Musharraf's reassurances, U.S. sanctions, imposed in retaliation for Pakistan's covert nuclear program and Musharraf's 1999 military coup d'état, came to an end. Pakistan was declared a frontline state in the global war against terror. President George W. Bush restored U.S. economic and military aid for Pakistan and announced a five-year bilateral aid package of $3 billion. Pakistan's outstanding debt to the United States and other Western nations was also forgiven or restructured. The new U.S.-Pakistan relationship and renewed U.S. aid commitments brought back memories of the favored treatment given to the Zia ul-Haq regime during the Afghan jihad. By acting against terrorists, reducing the emphasis on Islam in official discourse, and going through the motions of a peace process with India, Musharraf was trying to accommodate immediate U.S. concerns. Musharraf's predecessors as military rulers—Ayub Khan, Yahya Khan, and Zia ul-Haq—had also acted to please the United States in some crucial area of policy, only to advance on the side other agendas contrary to U.S. interests. At the same time, Musharraf wanted to convince Pakistani hard-liners that the army would continue to run the country and protect what the army had declared to be Pakistan's vital national interest.

In the years between 1988 and 2001, Pakistan's military and national security apparatus had defined Pakistan's vital national interests as maintaining and expanding its nuclear capability, forcing India out of Kashmir, and securing strategic depth in Afghanistan. Pakistan's Islamists had wholeheartedly embraced this strategic paradigm. Later, after abandoning the Taliban in the face of U.S. pressure, Musharraf held on to the other two elements of national interest as defined by him and his fellow generals and said so in his February 4, 2004, briefing of newspaper editors. The Islamists, and many Pakistani military officers, were visibly irked by Musharraf's turn away from Pakistan's dream of influence in Afghanistan and, beyond that, in Central Asia. Musharraf claimed that Pakistan's interests in Afghanistan had to be "sacrificed" to save even more important interests: a nuclear-weapons capability and the claim to Kashmir. Musharraf told Pakistanis on September 19, 2001, that if Pakistan did not accept U.S. demands after the September 11 attacks, "[o]ur critical concerns, our important concerns can come under threat. When I say critical concerns, I mean our strategic assets and the cause of Kashmir. If these come under threat it would be a worse situation for us."[3]

In the years of partial civilian rule following General Zia ul-Haq's death, the military's definition of national interest was cited as the major reason for its open intervention and behind-the-scenes political role. Identifying the six reasons—reasons based on interviews with military officers and analysis of their views—why Pakistan's military wanted to remain dominant in the country's affairs, Hasan-Askari Rizvi described "national interest" as the first:

During the Zia era, the military directly controlled nuclear policy and the conduct of the Afghan War. Nuclear policy has remained their close preserve, even under civilian rule. Benazir Bhutto complained in September 1991 that she was denied information about highly sensitive aspects of the country's nuclear program during her first term as Prime Minister. The role of the Foreign Office and the civilian leadership in formulating and implementing the Afghanistan policy increased after the 1989 withdrawal of Soviet troops, but senior Army commanders and the Inter-Service Intelligence (ISI) continue to have a significant input. Similarly, the Army maintains deep interest in policy toward India, including Kashmir. The military elite are not opposed in principle to Indo-Pakistani rapprochement, but they are concerned that the civilian government not ignore what they see as New Delhi's "hegemonic" agenda. Strong and credible conventional defence and nuclear weapons capabilities are considered vital to ward off Indian pressures and to enable Pakistan to conduct independent foreign and domestic policies. Unless the military is satisfied that there are credible guarantees against India's efforts to interfere, it will resist surrendering its nuclear-weapon option and advise caution on normalizing relations. Furthermore, the military—like most civilian policymakers—will not want to improve bilateral relations unless India addresses the issue of Kashmir.[4]

The desire to force India's hand over Kashmir led Field Marshal Ayub Khan into the 1965 war with India. With the help of trained insurgents, Ayub Khan in 1965 had hoped to ignite a massive uprising by Muslim Kashmiris against Indian rule. Pakistan's alliance with the United States was expected to help bring sufficient international pressure on India to force talks that would alter the territorial status quo in Jammu and Kashmir. With its consolidated military position, especially after the 1971 war, India showed no interest in negotiating the Kashmir dispute, let alone considering outcomes that might be deemed favorable to Pakistan. Although Indian leaders no longer spoke of undoing partition, their acceptance of Pakistan was seen by Pakistanis as conditional to Pakistan's subservience to India. Pakistan's elite, particularly the military, was unwilling to accept the Indian view that Pakistan could not be India's equal owing to the disparity in the sizes of the two countries.

Despite the failure of the 1965 effort to militarily wrest Kashmir from India and the setback of the 1971 Bangladesh war, Pakistan's planners did not give up thinking of ways to liberate Kashmir from Indian rule. Although diplomatic relations between India and Pakistan were restored after the 1972 Simla accord, the two countries maintained only a cold peace; trade and travel between the countries were limited. Within days of taking over as leader of a diminished Pakistan, Zulfikar Ali Bhutto ordered the expansion and reorganization of the Pakistan army. Pakistan's nuclear-weapons program was also under way, with the clear aim of defending Pakistan against Indian hegemony. Although the international community, including the UN, showed no interest in tackling the issue, Pakistan continued to raise the question of Kashmir whenever it was diplomatically feasible. Beginning in 1973, a national day of solidarity with the Kashmiri people was observed every year to remind Pakistan's people of the unfinished business of partition.

The tendency of Indian leaders and intellectuals to belittle Pakistan and question the validity of partition at every available opportunity contributed to the perception among Pakistanis of India as an existential enemy. After the separation of Bangladesh in 1971, Pakistani Islamists and military officers spoke consistently of the need to inflict military defeat on India to avenge the humiliation of Pakistan's breakup as well as to ensure that India accepts Pakistan's existence. Pakistan's ambitions were constrained, however, by the absence of military supplies from the United States[5] because the embargo on arms sales imposed by the United States during the 1965 war continued until 1975, only to be reimposed in 1979 in retaliation for Pakistan's covert nuclear-weapons program. The resumption of Pakistan's security relations with the United States in the aftermath of the Soviet invasion of Afghanistan gave Pakistan the confidence to consider seriously the military options for securing Jammu and Kashmir.

General Zia ul-Haq had seen his two military-rule predecessors, Ayub Khan and Yahya Khan, stumble into war with India. Both lost power at home after failing to win the wars along the country's borders. More than once, Zia ul-Haq observed that he would never let India-Pakistan relations collapse to the point of war while he ruled Pakistan.[6] Zia ul-Haq understood the paradox that had emerged from Pakistan's simultaneous pursuit of hostility toward India and military ties with the United States. The semblance of good relations with India had become a prerequisite for Pakistan's security relationship with the United States, which in turn was necessary if Pakistan could even think of military competition with India.

Soon after Zia ul-Haq took power in the military coup d'état of July 1977, there occurred what an Indian diplomat characterized as "a surrealistic thaw in relations" between India and Pakistan.[7] In parliamentary elections a few months earlier, the Congress party that had led India to independence was voted out of office for the first time since 1947. The new ruling alliance, the Janata (Peoples) Party, was eager to prove itself different from the long-ruling Congress. India's foreign minister, Atal Bihari Vajpayee (who later became prime minister as head of a Hindu nationalist offshoot of the 1977 Janata Party) visited Pakistan in February of 1978 and spoke of the need for normalizing relations. Zia ul-Haq, who was still struggling with his lack of legitimacy at home and abroad, saw an easing of tensions with India as politically useful. Direct sporting contacts between India and Pakistan were resumed, and official discussions relating to cooperation in commerce, railway transport, and agriculture began. Indian diplomatic representation in Pakistan was expanded to include a consulate in the port city of Karachi.[8] The process did not last long. Indian observers pointed out that the two governments had danced a "minuet of manifesting good intentions and giving some content to it at the public level, while in terms of realpolitik neither the concerns nor the attitudes underwent any change in India or Pakistan."[9]

The Congress party returned to power in India in 1979, and Pakistan's security relationship with the United States resumed soon thereafter with the Soviet invasion of Afghanistan. India's prime minister, Indira Gandhi, had presided over Pakistan's dismemberment in 1971, and her government did not see any need for befriending Pakistan. Zia ul-Haq, on the other hand, had gained the confidence that comes to Pakistan's military leaders from the assurance of U.S. support. Gandhi was a firm believer in India's status as the preeminent power in South Asia. She disapproved of Pakistan's alliance with the United States, recognized the Soviet-installed communist regime in Afghanistan as legitimate, and interpreted the Simla accord as a virtual settlement of the dispute over Kashmir. Pakistan perceived that India wanted Pakistan to "exercise its sovereignty according to Indian desires,"[10] which was unacceptable for Pakistan. Zia ul-Haq, backed by Pakistan's Islamist and military ideologues, felt that India was constantly pressuring Pakistan to renounce the two-nation theory that had led to partition in 1947. Zia sought a long-term solution to the disparity in power between India and Pakistan.[11]

Dealing with the Soviets in Afghanistan, Zia ul-Haq had already adopted a policy that would bleed the Soviets without goading then into direct confrontation with Pakistan. Pakistani intelligence officers said "the water must not get too hot"[12] to describe Zia's approach. After U.S. economic and military aid began to flow, Zia ul-Haq asked that a forward policy be developed to deal with India. A biography of Zia ul-Haq's confidante and intelligence chief, General Akhtar Abdul Rahman, authorized by Abdul Rahman's family, refers to a conversation between the two generals that ostensibly took place sometime in 1981–1982:

A worried Zia ul-Haq asked General Akhtar, "What is the solution to Indian pressure?" General Akhtar was convinced that the Indians would never understand the language of decency. They do not recognize the existence of Pakistan in their hearts and their objective is still the creation of Akhand Bharat (Undivided India). [General Akhtar Abdul Rahman] presented a plan to the President . . . The President remained quiet and then said, "This requires a lot of forethought" but Akhtar had already thought things through . . . The plan was put into effect. ISI spread its tentacles deep inside India. Several files from [Indian Prime Minister] Indira Gandhi's office were brought to Pakistan. Indian troop movements were kept under constant observation. The conditions in Kashmir were studied and a search was launched for [Kashmiris] possessing the capability of leading the freedom struggle. Simultaneously, President [Zia ul-Haq] launched a peace offensive.[13]

Pakistan's two-track policy—clandestine operations to weaken India while simultaneously appearing to seek a durable peace—remained in operation throughout the period Zia ul-Haq was in power as well as in subsequent years. This strategy was determined by the Pakistan military's analysis of India's strengths and weaknesses. One Pakistani general, then head of the army's Command and Staff College, wrote:

India has its limitations and serious ones at that. There was a post-1971 tendency to view India as the dominant regional power. The media, both national and international, played its dubious role in building up this image. But we, as level headed, cool, calculating, military analysts, must keep the objective realities in mind while assessing India as a regional power. Analysis of the objective realities will lead us to a more balanced view of India, a blend of its weaknesses and genuine strengths. A one-sided view of either can lead us to faulty conclusions. If only its strengths are counted we will be closer to the propagandist view of India as a mini super power. Taken in its totality, including its limitations, India will be cut to its proper size and dimension, that is, only quasi powerful and very much a manageable military power.[14]

"Cutting India down to size" was not a mere figure of speech. It was also to be an active policy based on a tendentious and ideological analysis by the Pakistani military of Indian society and politics. Although similar analyses had been undertaken since Pakistan's independence, the arguments were refined and more clearly defined during and after the Zia ul-Haq years. Islamist periodicals popularized the view that Pakistan could, over time, restrain India with a mix of religious fervor and military moves. Critics of the U.S.-backed jihad in Afghanistan were told that the revival of the spirit of jihad for Afghanistan was only a precursor of Pakistan's grand design to meet the Indian challenge.

Lieutenant Colonel (later Lieutenant General) Javed Hassan researched more than two thousand years of Hindu and Indian history to write *India: A Study in Profile* for the army's Faculty of Research and Doctrinal Studies. The book, distributed by the military's book club, reflects the mind-set that was evolving among military officers. It claimed that "India has a poor track record at projection of power beyond its frontier and what is worse a hopeless performance in protecting its own freedom and sovereignty," but its history bears testimony to "the incorrigible militarism of the Hindus":[15]

Nations are characterized by the key elements of their national character. As an illustration it is the "elementary force and persistence" of the Russian, the "individual initiative and inventiveness" of the American, the "common sense" of the British and the "discipline and thoroughness" of the German. How does one characterize a Hindu? The Hindu is a more complex personality and displays a combination of key traits based on varying power equations. For those that are weak the Hindu is persistently exploitative and domineering. If the weak shows an inclination for defiance the Hindu becomes persistently intolerant and violent. With those of equal power the Hindu patiently persists in deceit and should a weakness be observed does not fail to capitalize. In the case of a more powerful adversary it is patience, passivity, deceit and a persistent attempt to corrupt the powerful to his own outlook. If forced to summarize the key traits then the most appropriate (though an oversimplification) would be a "presumptuous, persistent and devious" Hindu.[16]

The description of Hindus as devious justified dealing with them with similar deviousness. More significant, Pakistani military officers were told that "India was hostage to a centrifugal rather than a centripetal tradition"[17] and that India had a "historical inability to exist as a single unified state."[18] Equating the modern Indian state with ancient Brahmanical civilization, three circles of Indian states were identified. India's northern and western states represented its Hindu core. The second circle comprised states with a regionalist impulse but with insufficient momentum for secessionism. The outermost circle, comprising Indian Punjab, Jammu and Kashmir, the southern state of Tamil Nadu, and the six northeastern tribal states, was seen as completely alienated from the Indian mainstream.[19] With some encouragement, the alienated regions of India could become centers of insurgencies that would, at best, dismember India and, at least, weaken India's ability to seek regional domination for years to come.[20]

The Pakistanis were correct in their identification of tensions between some Indian regions and the central government, but their beliefs in India's tendency toward fragmentation as well as the concept of predetermined Hindu traits and their relevance to contemporary statecraft were grossly exaggerated. The history and racial origin of Pakistanis from across the Indus were not different from the history and racial origin of the Indians. If India's Hindus were historically or racially determined to behave in a certain way, why should those whose ancestors converted to Islam be significantly different? The difference was explained by religion or ideology. The notion of a Hindu character distinct from a Muslim character further emphasized Islam as Pakistan's raison d'être, and Pakistani military officers were trained to see themselves through the prism of Islamist ideology. Islamist reasoning helps explain the dynamic at work within and between India and Pakistan: Hindu India would fragment because of the historic character weaknesses of

Hindus; Islam, however, would protect Pakistan because the Pakistani character was shaped by the religion of its people, not their ethnic or racial origins.

During the 1980s and 1990s, India battled insurgencies in different parts of the country and routinely blamed its neighbors, especially Pakistan, for arming and training insurgents. Some of the rebellions, such as those in the tribal regions of northeast India, started long before General Zia ul-Haq's rise to power. Pakistan could not, and most likely did not, instigate every rebellion against central authority in India, especially ones far from Pakistan's borders. Moreover, most challenges to Indian rule came from non-Muslim populations that were unlikely to be swayed by Pakistan's calls to jihad. That does not mean, however, that no external support existed for India's internal conflicts. The governments of Prime Minister Indira Gandhi and her son, Rajiv Gandhi, were ham-handed with some of India's regions, which paved the way for revolt by violent opposition groups. India's attitude toward its smaller neighbors was seen as arrogant and high-handed by those countries.

Zia ul-Haq forged close ties with the governments of South Asian states that had grievances of their own against India. In an effort to encircle India, the ISI set up operations in Nepal, Bangladesh, Sri Lanka, and Nepal[21] that enabled Pakistan to monitor, and possibly assist, the separatist movements in India. The presence of Pakistani clandestine operatives in these countries proved valuable when a major Pakistani-backed insurgency began later in Jammu and Kashmir.[22] Zia ul-Haq also visited Burma in 1985 and created a special relationship with Burma's internationally isolated military regime. Pakistan's relations with Burma have since remained strong, and Burma merited a second head of state visit when General Musharraf arrived in Rangoon in 2000. These relations are not based on significant trade exchanges and are part of the strategy to create covert operational bases in countries adjoining India.

Soon after the ISI and the CIA became partners in their massive anti-Soviet covert operations in Afghanistan beginning in 1980, violence erupted in India's Punjab state bordering Pakistan. Complex local reasons had led to the insurgency in Punjab, including attempted manipulation of state politics by the central government that had spun out of control, but Indian officials could not help but notice the fact that in

1978–1980 Pakistan had entertained unusually large numbers of Sikh pilgrims at Sikh shrines in Pakistan.[23] Most of the communal violence directed against Muslims in Punjab at the time of partition in 1947 had involved Sikhs, and the two communities felt bitterly toward each other ever since. Pakistan under Zia ul-Haq went forward and restored Sikh holy places and opened them for religious pilgrimage. The demand for an independent Sikh homeland, Khalistan, was raised by Sikh leaders from England and North America, most of whom had been among the pilgrims visiting Pakistan. Some of these pilgrims had been personally received by General Zia ul-Haq.

As violence flared in Punjab, the Indian government accused Pakistan of arming and training the Sikh insurgents. The ISI chief, General Abdul Rahman, created a desk at his agency headed by a brigadier "to analyze the situation in East Punjab where Sikhs had started their freedom struggle against India."[24] Abdul Rahman's colleagues took pride in the fact that, despite the deployment of large numbers of Indian security personnel, "the Sikhs were able to set the whole province on fire. They knew who to kill, where to plant a bomb and which office to target."[25]

For his part, Zia ul-Haq simply denied a Pakistani role in supporting the Sikhs. "These allegations are false and baseless," he told an Indian news magazine. Zia ul-Haq insisted that "Pakistan is a state which does not believe in Machiavellian practices." But in the same interview, Pakistan's ruler declared, incredibly, "Your assumption that the CIA is involved in arming the mujahideen in Pakistan is wrong. If this is correct it is not within my knowledge. If it is not with my knowledge, no weapons can pass to the Afghan mujahideen through Pakistani territory."[26] Zia ul-Haq was speaking at a time when hundreds of millions of dollars had already been spent on the joint CIA-ISI operation in support of the Afghan mujahideen, and the mujahideen were about to be armed with Stinger antiaircraft missiles. Zia's statement marked the early phase of total denial that characterized Pakistan's policy about charges of supporting terrorism.

India used brutal methods to suppress the Punjab insurgency. Sikhs in England, the United States, and Canada built a strong lobby that criticized India's human rights violations and ignored Sikh terrorism in Punjab. The United States, which was not interested in embarrassing its

Cold War ally, did not find the proof offered by India of Pakistan's role in the Sikh rebellion convincing at the time. Only after the Soviet withdrawal from Afghanistan and the termination of covert U.S. assistance to Afghan mujahideen did the United States acknowledge Pakistani support for the Sikh insurgency. The State Department's 1991 report on global terrorism said, "There were continuing credible reports throughout 1991 of official Pakistani support for Kashmiri militant groups engaged in terrorism in Indian-controlled Kashmir, as well as support to Sikh militant groups engaged in terrorism in Indian Punjab. This support allegedly includes provision of weapons and training."[27] Reports for subsequent years also spoke of Pakistani support for Sikh insurgents. Pakistan's role in terrorism in Indian Punjab had been ignored by U.S. officials at the peak of the Sikh insurgency, however, which led Pakistani officials to conclude that U.S. responses to Pakistan's support for militants in India would be determined by the degree of warmth in Pakistan's relations with the United States rather than by U.S. concerns about terrorism against India.

The stakes in the Punjab insurgency proved to be exceptionally high when a Sikh bodyguard assassinated Prime Minister Indira Gandhi in 1984. At around the same time, Pakistan's southern province of Sindh became embroiled in ethnic and sectarian violence. The port city of Karachi, in particular, was the epicenter of turmoil for years to come. Pakistan accused India's overseas intelligence service, the Research and Analysis Wing (RAW), of instigating the violence in Karachi. Both sides probably interpreted their own actions as retaliation for the subversion by the other. The Khalistan insurgency did not lose momentum until 1989, when the Indians fenced off part of the Punjab border with Pakistan and Pakistan's civilian government headed by Benazir Bhutto agreed to joint patrols of the border by Indian and Pakistani troops. Sporadic violence continued until the insurgency died out in the mid-1990s. Peace in Indian Punjab did not, however, mean peace between India and Pakistan.

Insurgencies in Punjab and other parts of India undoubtedly created security problems for India and contributed to the project of making India a manageable military power. It was in Jammu and Kashmir that Pakistan believed it could prove the sustainability of the two-nation theory. Jammu and Kashmir had been in dispute since partition and had a Muslim majority population. Kashmiris had never been at ease within the Indian union and, with minimal Pakistani prodding, had periodically questioned their state's 1947 accession to India. The political process in Indian-controlled Kashmir had been carefully orchestrated from New Delhi, limiting the benefits for Kashmiris of Indian democracy. From the perspective of Pakistan's generals and their Islamist allies, Kashmir was the perfect place to transfer the experience of jihad they had acquired in Afghanistan with U.S. help.

On Zia ul-Haq's orders, in 1984 the ISI had drawn up a plan for Kashmir that was to mature in 1991.[28] Unlike in Afghanistan, where the ISI had trained rank-and-file mujahideen, the initial plan for rebellion in Kashmir was limited to the training of group leaders and trainers. It was expected that these potential leaders would be able to recruit disaffected young Kashmiris and form parties or guerrilla groups. The pattern that Zia ul-Haq had in mind was similar to the one adopted in Afghanistan in the early years preceding Soviet intervention when Burhanuddin Rabbani and Gulbuddin Hekmatyar had been provided a base in Pakistan and, with ideological training and material support, were encouraged to organize their Jamiat-e-Islami and Hizbe Islami in Afghanistan.

ISI officers met regularly with representatives of the Jammu and Kashmir Jamaat-e-Islami and the secular nationalist Jammu and Kashmir Liberation Front (JKLF) during the mid-1980s. In a clandestine meeting with Jamaat-e-Islami and JKLF leaders in 1987, Zia ul-Haq himself explained his design for gradually weakening Indian control over Kashmir.[29] But events in Kashmir, badly managed by Indian authorities, created unrest in the region earlier than the D-day envisaged by the ISI. There was little room for Zia ul-Haq's stage-by-stage plan to go into action, and the Pakistanis had to respond to a developing situation in Indian-controlled Kashmir.

In an effort to reelect a state government allied with New Delhi, India's central government and its ally in the state had rigged the 1987 election for the Kashmir assembly. The most aggrieved contender in that election was the Muslim United Front (MUF), an Islamic alliance led by the Jammu and Kashmir wing of the Jamaat-e-Islami. Protests and agitation began in Srinagar and other towns in Indian-controlled Kashmir, initially without any outside instigation. Large segments of the Kashmiri population embraced the slogan of *azadi* (liberation or freedom). India dealt with the situation with an iron hand and deflected criticism of its human rights violations by blaming Pakistan:

> The grievances amongst the Kashmiris, which had been allowed to fester, the steady erosion of the "special status" promised to the state of Jammu and Kashmir in 1947, the neglect of the people by their leaders, were clearly India's responsibility. Tavleen Singh believes that Kashmir would not have become an issue "if the valley had not exploded on its own thanks to Delhi's misguided policies." Over a period of time, "the LOC [Line of Control] would have been accepted as the border and we could have one day forgotten the dispute altogether." Instead, as the decade of the 1980s drew to a close, the valley of Kashmir became "the explosive situation" of which [Kashmiri leader] Shaikh Abdullah had so often warned.[30]

The uprising in Kashmir was still in its initial phase when Zia ul-Haq and several key Pakistani generals, including his intelligence wizard, General Akhtar Abdul Rahman, died in a plane crash in August 1988. Zia ul-Haq's death came soon after the conclusion of the Geneva accords that provided for the withdrawal of Soviet troops from Afghanistan. The Soviet withdrawal would mark the end of Pakistan's status as a frontline state in the U.S. war against communist expansion, which in turn meant a reduction in U.S. interest in Pakistan. Converging at that time were a number of factors that made Pakistan more openly involved in jihad in Kashmir and beyond, invited U.S. sanctions, and expanded Islamist influence over military strategy.

In his lifetime, Zia ul-Haq combined the offices of army chief and president and governed secretively with the help of a few chosen aides. Zia ul-Haq's iron-fisted rule also enabled the ISI, which by then employed tens of thousands of operatives, informants, and contractors, to operate in the shadows in both controlling domestic politics and managing foreign operations. Zia ul-Haq also personally managed relations with Pakistan's various Islamist groups and personalities, who deferred to his appeals for secrecy in matters involving statecraft. Their

deference enabled Zia to juggle relations with the United States and India and to cover his tracks in the pursuit of clandestine operations that
would have offended both.

Pakistan's critical role in the anti-Afghan jihad meant that the United
States not only provided Pakistan with economic and military assistance;
it was also willing to overlook several aspects of Pakistani policy. The
United States ignored Zia ul-Haq's pan-Islamic aspirations even when
they took on a clearly anti-Western dimension because Zia was such a
staunch ally against the Soviet Union. U.S. officials tended to think of
anti-Western Islamist sentiment as mere rhetoric. Zia ul-Haq's India
policy, too, received scant attention in Washington, where there was little
sympathy for an India widely perceived to be pro-Soviet.

In its post–Zia ul-Haq phase, Pakistan became less crucial as a U.S.
ally—something Pakistan's military had not planned. Successive generals after Zia still continued to juggle among their desire for aid from the
United States, hostility toward India, and military domination of decision making within Pakistan. Islamist ideologues remained the military's
reliable allies in confronting India and seeking regional pre-eminence
for Pakistan. Gradually, elements of Pakistan's policy that had been tol-
erated or ignored in the preceding decades became irritants in U.S.-
Pakistan relations. Pakistani officials resented what they perceived as
the undependability of the United States as an ally; the United States
went from indulging the Pakistanis under Zia ul-Haq to imposing sanctions, which were insufficiently effective, under his successors. U.S. hopes
for a change in Pakistan's stance were raised with every change in
Pakistan's army and civilian leaderships during the next eleven years,
but Pakistan did not budge from the Islamist strategies that had evolved
during several decades and were refined during the Zia ul-Haq era.

Zia ul-Haq's death marked the end of his personalized rule and resulted in changing the context, though not the substance, of Pakistan's
security policies. The offices of president and army chief were now occupied by two separate individuals—President Ghulam Ishaq Khan and
General Aslam Beg—making tactical disagreements unavoidable even
when the two shared similar views. After the parliamentary elections of
1988, an elected prime minister, Benazir Bhutto, also entered the picture.
Domestic power plays now clouded the scene and a relatively freer

media made the extreme secretiveness and outright denials of the Zia ul-Haq era more difficult. The national security apparatus responded to the new situation by manipulating the existence of contending power centers to its advantage. The gap between Pakistan's stated and actual policies became wider; for example, the prime minister or president could promise international interlocutors one thing while the military and security services worked toward a different end. It also became possible for the military to pin blame for some of its decisions on civilians and for the ISI to create public distractions for its covert operations.

Benazir Bhutto's preferred policies toward Afghanistan and India were different from those favored by the military:

> [Bhutto] favored a negotiated settlement in Afghanistan while the army and the ISI wanted to enable the mujahideen to defeat the [communist] Kabul regime on the battlefield. She wanted to moderate her government's support for the insurgency in Kashmir, but the army, entertaining a sense of enhanced capability vis-à-vis India, wished to escalate it. The army regarded Benazir's advocacies as unpatriotic.[31]

The military, through the ISI, had helped create the Islami Jamhoori Ittehad (IJI) precisely to obstruct Bhutto from advocating reversal of the strategic direction they had already adopted. Although the IJI's political leadership was made up of conservative politicians, most of whom were not Islamists, its ideology was defined by the ISI and the Jamaat-e-Islami. Islamists taunted Bhutto's PPP with the jingoistic (and historically inaccurate) slogan "You lost Dhaka, we won Kabul,"[32] a reference to the perceived success of jihad in Afghanistan.

Demands for declaring Pakistan a nuclear-weapons power, defying India and the United States, and openly assisting Kashmiri mujahideen were part of the IJI's election rhetoric. When Bhutto finally took office on December 2, 1988, she possessed little latitude in seeking an early end to the war in Afghanistan, normalizing relations with India, or accepting U.S. limitations on Pakistan's nuclear program.[33] Islamists in the IJI and the military were acting in tandem. Policies proposed by General Mirza Aslam Beg and his intelligence chief, Lieutenant

General Hamid Gul, in the councils of government were backed by pressure from the IJI in the media and through street demonstrations. Islamists were helping build momentum for the military's strategy, creating the impression that public opinion supported jihad in Afghanistan as well as in Kashmir.

By the end of 1989, Bhutto was under attack for, among other things, being soft on India, which made her practically give up on her efforts to normalize relations with India. The process of dialogue that Bhutto had initiated during a brief visit to Islamabad by the Indian prime minister, Rajiv Gandhi, had already stalled partly because of deterioration in the situation in Kashmir. By then, violent street protests, coupled with attacks by armed militants on symbols of Indian authority, had become the norm in Indian-controlled Kashmir. Officials in the Pakistan-controlled part of Kashmir, known as Azad Kashmir (Free Kashmir), reported the arrival of refugees escaping the retaliation of Indian military and paramilitary forces.

Bhutto was informed by the ISI that it would be providing some support to indigenous Kashmiri groups that were demanding a plebiscite on the disputed state's future.[34] She approved Pakistan government funding for refugee rehabilitation as well as for an international media and government relations campaign on behalf of the Kashmiris.[35] Given the strong sentiment in Pakistan over Kashmir, and her political need to overcome the opposition's criticism over her alleged softness toward India, Bhutto might have also agreed with the need to provide material support to Kashmiri militant groups. On February 4, 1990, the Bhutto government invited all political parties for a meeting to develop a national consensus over Kashmir. By doing so, she hoped to "pre-empt any mischief her political adversaries might try to create for her government on its Kashmir policy."[36]

But the ISI and its political front, the IJI, went farther than the prime minister in supporting the protests in Kashmir, with the clear objective of destabilizing Bhutto's government. The ISI hastened the process of setting up training camps for guerrillas who would wage an armed insurgency inside Indian-controlled territory. IJI leader Nawaz Sharif called for a nationwide general strike to show sympathy for the Kashmiri people. Iqbal Akhund, then serving as Bhutto's adviser on foreign affairs, recalled the IJI's efforts to cast itself as the greater champion of the Kashmir cause:

Shaikh Rashid, another opposition Assembly member, got into the act by setting up a so-called "training camp" and calling for volunteers who would be lodged, fed and trained to fight in Kashmir. This was a challenge to the government either to try to stop him and be accused of accepting "Indian hegemony," or to do nothing and be seen by the world as providing sanctuary to "terrorists" . . . More foolhardy were attempts by sundry groups to cross the Line of Control (cease-fire line) in Kashmir. On the same day as Nawaz Sharif's strike, a crowd, 4000-strong, of students, workers, farmers etc. got fired up by Jamaat-e-Islami speakers and started moving across the Line [of Control] near Sialkot. Some were carrying Pakistani flags that they intended to plant on the other side in place of Indian flags. At the first attempt, Indian border guards scuffled with the crowd, took away the Pakistani flags, and sent the boys back across the Line. The crowd regrouped and made another foray, to which the Indians responded by firing into the air. At the third attempt, [the Indians] fired into the crowd, killing one boy on the spot and wounding about a dozen, some seriously. Six days later, another attempted crossing of the Line, near Uri, resulted in six deaths by Indian fire.[37]

Domestic maneuvers established the IJI as the party more committed to the liberation of Kashmir from Indian rule. Bhutto, too, was forced to harden her posture. During the next several months, Sharif and Bhutto competed in making rhetorical statements supporting Kashmiri self-determination and Pakistan's resolve to secure Kashmir. Bhutto did not want to sound too bellicose because as prime minister her words reflected official policy even if she did not completely control the making or execution of policy. Bhutto had received warnings from V. P. Singh, who had replaced Rajiv Gandhi as India's prime minister, that "if there was war, it would not be confined to Kashmir."[38] Bhutto felt responsible for defusing tension with India, even as she needed to respond to the strong sentiment over Kashmir building up within Pakistan. Sharif, on the other hand, was not held back by such considerations. Egged on by his Islamist allies, he spoke belligerently about settling scores with India. The Jamaat-e-Islami, meanwhile, raised funds and trained volunteers—both Kashmiris and Pakistanis—for jihad in Kashmir.

The dismissal of Bhutto's government in August 1990 and the election of Nawaz Sharif as prime minister three months later paved the way for more extensive and more open support for the militancy in Kashmir. For one thing, the Jamaat-e-Islami was now part of the ruling IJI coalition even though its representation in Parliament was nominal compared with Sharif's Pakistan Muslim League (PML). During the 1990 election campaign, Sharif promised to liberate Kashmir, and he allowed his IJI allies to speak of India's destruction. During IJI election rallies, Sharif called Bhutto "a security risk" for her failure to sufficiently support covert operations against India, and Sharif's colleagues accused Bhutto of jeopardizing the lives of Pakistani agents operating inside Indian Punjab. Sharif's campaign also alleged that Bhutto was selling out to U.S. nuclear "imperialism, blackmail and exploitation."[39] Privately, however, Sharif spoke to his advisers of the need for a peace process with India "so that we can get on with Pakistan's economic development."[40] While making belligerent speeches on the campaign trail, Sharif sought out Indian journalists for interviews and off-the-record conversations, which he hoped would convey to Indians his willingness to engage in quiet diplomacy once he was in office.

The military supported Sharif during the 1988 and 1990 elections because the military wanted its security agenda to be perceived as having popular support. During the 1990 election, the ISI channeled funds to the IJI and provided advice on electioneering. After the election, Bhutto and other Sharif critics alleged that the ISI had, in fact, helped steal the election for Sharif and the IJI.[41] The ISI's funding of the IJI campaign was later admitted by General Beg and the ISI head at the time, Lieutenant General Asad Durrani, before the Supreme Court of Pakistan. Although they had clearly violated the law by using the military to influence parliamentary elections, the generals claimed that they had acted in the national interest.[42]

Nawaz Sharif's tenure as prime minister reflected the dichotomy between Sharif's desire for policies centered on economic growth and his deal with the military on allowing them a free hand in national security matters. Sharif allowed the ISI to expand its support for the insurgency in Indian-controlled Kashmir, but he was circumspect about retaining a publicly anti-U.S. posture, which General Beg considered useful. Sharif also initiated back-channel diplomacy to explore alternatives to the deadlocked positions of India and Pakistan over Kashmir. For example, during a 1991 visit to Tehran, he told an Iranian journalist that Pakistan was willing to consider the option of an independent Kashmir if India would rescind its position that Kashmir's status could not be negotiated. Although Sharif had discussed the "offer" with the Pakistani Ministry of Foreign Affairs, the ISI expressed concern that it signaled a softening of Pakistan's stance on Kashmir. Sharif backed off from his statement within twenty-fours hours of making it.

The Jamaat-e-Islami's position during this period usually followed closely the line taken by General Beg in public and the ISI in intragovernment discussions. The Jamaat-e-Islami argued that, notwithstanding the size of its representation in Parliament, it had the right to define policies of the Sharif government because the IJI's electoral victory was a mandate for the Islamist worldview. Jamaat-e-Islami leader Qazi Hussain Ahmed publicly disagreed with Sharif on a number of issues, notably the war to liberate Kuwait from Iraqi occupation. Sharif aligned himself with Saudi Arabia and the United States in the war, and he sought to fulfill the commitment of troops for the anti-Iraq coalition that Pakistan had made soon after the occupation of Kuwait. The Jamaat-e-Islami and other Islamist groups held public demonstrations of support for Iraq, however, arguing that the introduction of U.S. troops in the region would install U.S. imperialism in the Muslim heartland.

Ironically, the Islamists' support for Iraq against the United States was in harmony with the public stand of the army chief, General Mirza Aslam Beg, and with Pakistani public opinion, which showed overwhelming support for Saddam Hussein. On January 28, 1991, General Beg told an audience of Pakistani military officers that the Gulf War was part of Zionist strategy.[43] Beg spoke of the need for "strategic defiance" by medium-sized powers such as Iraq, Iran, and Pakistan, with the help of China, against the dictates of the United States. Such defiance, he argued, would protect the sovereignty of smaller nations. The argument was later expanded by Professor Khurshid Ahmad in an article in Jamaat-e-Islami's monthly journal, *Tarjuman-al-Quran* (Interpretation of the Quran).[44] Ahmad asserted that the new world order sought by the United States would pose a threat to "Pakistan, Islamic revival and the Muslim Umma."[45] The Islamist recipe for dealing with the challenge of U.S. unipolar dominance was to seek the unity of Muslim nations as well as concerted action with other nations opposed to U.S. hegemony.

Despite the congruence of views of the Islamists and the army chief, Nawaz Sharif's policy of supporting the United States prevailed. Pakistan's generals did not want a break with the United States regardless of the country's difficulties with the United States over nuclear policy. With the backing of President Ishaq Khan and other generals, Sharif named a successor to General Beg two months ahead of his scheduled retirement date.

The change of commanders in 1991 helped maintain military-to-military relations between Pakistan and the United States even though the special relationship resulting from the anti-Soviet war in Afghanistan was coming to an end, and it fed the impression in the United States that institutionally the Pakistan military sought to remain a U.S. ally but was periodically pulled in the opposite direction by individual generals with Islamist leanings. Beg's successors—General Asif Nawaz, General Abdul Waheed, General Jehangir Karamat, and General Pervez Musharraf—all presented themselves as pro-Western in the mold of pro-U.S. generals of the Cold War era such as Ayub Khan and Yahya Khan. None of them, however, was averse to presiding over jihadi policies aimed against India but occasionally spilling beyond South Asia. The successor generals differed from General Beg in their not speaking out against the United States and in their appearance of being willing to help with U.S. military and intelligence-gathering plans. Although Pakistan would not terminate its nuclear program or end its effort to "cut India to size," the Pakistani generals continued to see the United States as the country's superpower patron of choice.

Pakistan's nuclear program became the major irritant in its relationship with the United States after 1989. Until 1989, Pakistan's nuclear program had evaded sanctions mandated by the U.S. Congress because the Reagan administration had certified annually under the Pressler Amendment to the Foreign Assistance Act of 1961that Pakistan did not as yet possess a nuclear weapon.[46] Pakistan did, however, assemble a nuclear device in 1987,[47] which meant that the U.S. president could either issue a certification he knew to be incorrect or impose sanctions on Pakistan. The United States warned Pakistan that certification was no longer possible without Pakistan rolling back its nuclear program to an earlier stage. Until 1990 the United States had, in the words of Dennis Kux, "threatened frequently that trouble lay ahead but in the end had always found a way to avoid punishing Pakistan."[48] When President George H. W. Bush withheld certification, thereby triggering sanctions that suspended aid beginning on October 1, 1990, Islamabad reacted with "disbelief, shock and anger."[49]

By achieving nuclear-weapons capability, Pakistan had crossed the threshold. Pakistan could no longer carry on with a nuclear program without inviting U.S. sanctions. Pakistanis did not see their own violation of commitments as the source of disruption in U.S.-Pakistan relations; from Pakistan's point of view, the imposition of sanctions was another example of the United States being a fair-weather friend. Pakistani officials believed that the United States was willing to tolerate their violation of U.S. law over nuclear proliferation as long as the United States needed Pakistan for the anti-Soviet war in Afghanistan. Now that U.S. involvement in the Afghan war was tapering off, with the withdrawal of the Soviets, U.S. indulgence of Pakistan's nuclear program had ended. In an interview with the Urdu weekly, *Awaz,* in 1993, General Beg said, "The United States continued issuing a certificate that Pakistan had not crossed the line in its atomic program but as soon as the Soviet Union was defeated in Afghanistan the situation changed immediately."[50]

A possible explanation, reconciling the U.S. and Pakistani accounts, is offered by Dennis Kux:

Conceivably, the Pakistanis were simply dissembling and, as the Americans alleged, had reactivated the program to machine bomb cores in 1990. It is also possible that the capability was achieved earlier (as Pakistanis claim) but the U.S. analysts did not reach a firm conclusion about this until 1990. Since the intelligence community assessments were based on information collected clandestinely rather than firsthand knowledge, such a time lag is not implausible.[51]

The one thing that gives credence to the Pakistani account, however, is the interview of Pakistani nuclear scientist Dr. A. Q. Khan by Indian journalist Kuldip Nayar in 1987. In that interview, Khan declared that Pakistan possessed a nuclear-weapons capability: "America knows it. What the CIA has been saying about our possessing the bomb is correct and so is the speculation of some foreign newspapers . . . They told us that Pakistan could never produce the bomb and they doubted my capabilities but they now know we have done it."[52] Khan said in the same interview that his laboratories were producing highly enriched uranium. "We have upgraded it (the uranium) to 90 percent to achieve the desired results," he was quoted as saying. Khan said that Pakistan had tested its bomb "through a simulator" and explained that the country had to evade U.S. and Western embargoes to purchase the equipment necessary for its nuclear-weapons program.[53]

Khan's 1987 interview coincided with a massive Indian military exercise, code-named Operation Brasstacks, and served the purpose of threatening India in case the exercise led to actual military operations along the Pakistan border.[54] Soon after the Khan interview was published, Pakistan's Ministry of Foreign Affairs denied that the interview had taken place, clearly trying to cover tracks to avoid the potential for U.S. sanctions. Nayar, however, had definitely met A. Q. Khan in the presence of Pakistani editor Mushahid Hussain, and the military had approved the granting of the interview.[55] The refusal of the United States to take the interview into account at the time indicates willful blindness on the part of the Reagan administration. The war against the Soviets in Afghanistan was obviously more important at that moment, and the public pronouncements of the father of Pakistan's nuclear bomb could be conveniently ignored as posturing. President Reagan twice certified that Pakistan did not possess a nuclear bomb after Khan had publicly acknowledged that Pakistan did. President Bush issued a similar certification in 1989 although he made it clear, through U.S. ambassador to Pakistan Robert Oakley, that future certification would not be possible if Pakistan did not freeze its nuclear program at a certain level.[56]

Soon after the imposition of proliferation sanctions in 1990, the ISI prepared an assessment of U.S. resolve to punish Pakistan, which was discussed among senior military commanders as well as generals then serving in the GHQ.[57] The assessment concluded that the United States wanted to pressure Pakistan over the nuclear issue but that this was a temporary threat to U.S.-Pakistan relations resulting from "the political maneuvers of Indian and Zionist lobbies" in the United States.[58] If Pakistan remained engaged with the United States without giving in to U.S. demands, the ISI assessment said, it was only a question of time before the United States came to terms with Pakistan's nuclear program as a fait accompli. The period of sanctions was expected to be brief. The ISI believed that the U.S. military and intelligence community had pockets of goodwill for Pakistan that could be maintained by cooperating in areas where the United States needed Pakistan's cooperation. At the same time, it was important to maintain the impression of widespread anti-U.S. sentiment in Pakistani society, which could be assured by periodic demonstrations by Islamists. This would create sympathy for Pakistani military and intelligence officials among their U.S. counterparts, who would recognize their difficulties in swimming against the national tide in befriending the United States.

During the course of internal discussions among Pakistan's generals and civilian officials, a strategy evolved to move toward ridding Pakistan of sanctions without giving in to U.S. demands over matters of national interest—Afghanistan, nuclear weapons, and Kashmir. Just as the legislative branch of the U.S. government had imposed sanctions on Pakistan while the executive branch had said it sought Pakistan's friendship, Pakistan decided that it, too, could play the game of different branches of government having different attitudes toward the United States.

This proposed strategy for dealing with the United States emphasized the need for Pakistan's military commander, intelligence chief, and prime minister to interact with U.S. officials; they would all have somewhat different talking points. Each individual would give the impression of wanting more than the others to resolve Pakistan's differences with the United States. Minor modifications of policy would be highlighted as major breakthroughs. Above all, just as General Beg's verbal excesses at the time of the Gulf War had been explained away as his personal views, actions objectionable in U.S. eyes could be described as the personal follies of high-ranking officials. During the decade of the 1990s, Pakistan implemented this strategy of dealing with the United States, thereby avoiding aggravated sanctions and periodically raising hopes on the U.S. side of improved relations without any substantive changes in Pakistani policy.

The Pakistani assessment was incorrect in predicting a brief period of sanctions, but it was not entirely off the mark in recognizing U.S. reluctance to punish Pakistan. President George H. W. Bush had been "genuinely sad"[59] when he could no longer certify that Pakistan did not possess a nuclear device. The administration made attempts to delay sanctions "to give the government the Pakistanis would elect in October 1990 a chance to deal with the nuclear problem."[60] Congressional opposition prevailed, however; it was based on the argument that lowering standards for Pakistan would lead to erosion of nuclear proliferation standards for all nations. At the time of imposition of sanctions, Pakistan was the third-largest beneficiary of U.S. aid. In response to Pakistan's protests that the sanctions amounted to a U.S. abandonment of Pakistan, the United States softened the blow by continuing to disburse $1 billion in economic assistance for ongoing projects. Pakistan lost approximately $300 million in annual arms and military supplies but received the remaining portion of the economic aid package for another three years after the sanctions went into effect. Pakistan was also allowed commercial purchases of military equipment until 1992.[61]

The United States initially wanted to jolt the Pakistanis into realizing that they could not break their nonproliferation commitments with the United States with impunity, but the United States still intended to give Pakistan a way out rather than punish it. In an information paper for the Pakistani prime minister's office, dated February 6, 1991, Brigadier John Howard, the U.S. defense representative in Islamabad, explained the U.S. desire to continue military cooperation:

It is apparent that while security assistance to Pakistan suffers under the suspension, it is still a viable short-term program, and would be a very significant program once the problems with Pressler were resolved—even at the reduced level of about 100 million dollars per year. Significant actions are being worked out. However, if the policy decision were made by the USG [U.S. government] to close all the "valves," for one reason or another, there would be further adverse impact on Pakistan's armed forces. To date, the USG has made every effort not to be harsh in the application of the suspension guidelines. Nor has it reacted or responded to the anti-American statements of Pakistani politicians or senior officials.[62]

The nuclear proliferation sanctions did not obligate the United States to use its clout against Pakistan in the International Monetary Fund and the World Bank, which meant that the Pakistanis were able to borrow from the international financial institutions to make up for the lost benefit of U.S. economic aid. Sanctions resulting from the Pressler Amendment undoubtedly hurt Pakistan but not enough to force any significant change in Pakistani policy. More comprehensive sanctions would have resulted if the United States had declared Pakistan a state sponsor of terrorism on the basis of Pakistan's role in Indian Punjab and Kashmir. Initially, Pakistan's support for militants was ignored; when the subject finally did come up, the United States did not back up its threats with specific sanctions.

As the Pakistan military's relationship with the U.S. Department of Defense endured through the Pressler sanctions, Pakistan's generals had rising expectations that they could retain the friendship of the United States while staying their course in security policy. The United States military fondly remembered Pakistan's cooperation during the Cold War. The U.S. military had invested heavily in modernizing the Pakistan army during the 1960s. The intelligence community had also benefited from Pakistani cooperation, even before the war against the Soviets in Afghanistan. U.S. strategists looked upon military assistance to Pakistan as an instrument of influence even though Pakistan had taken aid in the past and still pursued policies independent of U.S. influence. Memories of the Cold War era, coupled with Pakistan's strategic location and the favorable disposition of its generals during their interaction with Americans, convinced the Pentagon of the need to keep Pakistan on the U.S. side. Diplomatic historian Dennis Kux wrote:

The Pentagon was especially sorry about the rupture in cooperative security ties. The U.S. military liked its counterparts and was unhappy with the strain in relations . . . [They] thought that Islamabad could play a helpful role in support of U.S. interests in the Persian Gulf and regarded Pakistan as a force for moderation in the Islamic world.[63]

Pakistan's military remained engaged with the Pentagon and the U.S. Central Command, whose area of operations included Pakistan. Despite the pro-Iraq statements by General Mirza Aslam Beg, Pakistani troops participated in the 1991 Gulf War as part of the U.S.-led coalition. Pakistan also responded later to U.S. requests for troops for peacekeeping operations in Somalia and Bosnia. While the U.S. military saw this cooperation as a sign of moderation on the part of Pakistan's military compared with Islamist extremism, the Pakistan military's role within Pakistan and in its immediate neighborhood was far from a moderating influence.

Soon after the beginning of the unrest in Indian-controlled Kashmir during 1988–1989, Pakistan's ISI expanded its support for Kashmiri groups opposing Indian rule. The ISI had been in contact with the Jammu and Kashmir Jamaat-e-Islami and the secular nationalist Jammu and Kashmir Liberation Front (JKLF), the two significant indigenous Kashmiri groups, for several years. Now the unrest in Kashmir enabled the ISI to transfer the experience it gained during the orchestration of anti-Soviet resistance in Afghanistan to the Kashmir insurgency. A Kashmir cell within the ISI was assigned the tasks of recruiting, training, and arming of Kashmiri militants. Pakistani support tilted away from the JKLF and toward Jamaat-e-Islami and its militant organization, Hizbul Mujahideen. Once India started cracking down inside Kashmir, punishing rebels as well as their family members, the ISI concluded that it could not leave the insurgency to the Kashmiris only. By the end of 1991, the ISI was helping Pakistani and international volunteers, including veterans of the

Afghan jihad, to cross over into Indian-controlled Kashmir and mount guerrilla attacks against Indian forces.[64] Thus, Kashmir's indigenous struggle for self-determination became linked with the global jihad of the Islamists.

The JKLF had been formed in 1977 by Kashmiris living in Britain and was an offshoot of the Jammu and Kashmir National Liberation Front that had been active during the 1960s. Although the JKLF accepted Pakistani assistance, its demand for Kashmiri self-determination extended to those parts of the pre-1947 Jammu and Kashmir state that were now controlled by Pakistan. The JKLF demanded that Kashmiris be given the option of independence from both India and Pakistan, a position that did not sit well with Pakistan's decision makers. JKLF's history of representing Kashmiri self-determination made it, according to one Indian writer, "the most important, most indigenous and most acceptable in Kashmir out of all secessionist and underground organizations."[65]

The JKLF secured a major victory in 1989 when its militants kidnapped the daughter of the home minister of Indian-controlled Kashmir and secured the release of six of their colleagues from an Indian prison in exchange of the release of their hostage.[66] However, the JKLF's stance in favor of independence, as well as its desire for operational independence, did not appeal to Pakistani officials. The ISI was already having difficulty handling the contestation for power among the mujahideen groups in Afghanistan following the Soviet withdrawal, and because it did not want what one ISI officer described as "a Kashmiri PLO"[67] on its hands, it sought to exercise greater control over the Kashmiri resistance from its earliest phase.

Indigenous Kashmiri commanders belonging to groups based in Kashmir were considered less reliable than those affiliated with a group rooted in Pakistan. Pakistani officers argued that Indian intelligence could manipulate Kashmiris and make them into double agents. The ISI felt that it could better control foreign jihadis and Pakistani fighters because the Pakistanis had more at stake and would have to think harder before diverging from the path determined by the ISI. In addition, most of the foreign fighters were Islamists from countries to which they could not return, and they could be trusted to fight to the death on the battlefield or remain part of jihad forever out of religious conviction.

One other consideration played a role in the Pakistan military's decision to make Kashmir an arena for global jihad instead of merely an indigenous insurgency. Pakistan's plan for liberation of Kashmir comprised two parts. The first was to make Kashmir ungovernable for the Indians and to raise the cost of continued Indian occupation to an unbearable level. A guerrilla struggle and terrorist campaign was expected to achieve this objective. The other component of Pakistan's plan was to internationalize the Kashmir issue once again by securing the involvement of the international community in determining the future of Kashmir. When the Indians were forced by the militants to negotiate with Pakistan, international support for Pakistan's position would ensure that the negotiated settlement was favorable to Pakistan. The participation of mujahideen from around the world would ensure wide support for the Kashmiri cause within the Islamic countries. The United States and Western nations could not ignore the jihad against India in Kashmir so soon after supporting a similar struggle against the Soviets in Afghanistan. The Pakistanis reasoned that if the mujahideen in Afghanistan were recognized as freedom fighters, the Kashmiri mujahideen, too, could gain similar recognition.[68]

The ISI moved swiftly to organize and centrally control the Kashmir insurgency soon after the removal of the Bhutto government in August 1990. The IJI government headed by Nawaz Sharif had mobilized public support for the liberation of Kashmir during the election campaign. The Jamaat-e-Islami's inclusion in the IJI made it easy for the civilian and military branches of the Pakistan government to act in a coordinated manner. Within the first year of Sharif's tenure, the Jamaat-e-Islami's group, the Hizbul Mujahideen, had muscled its way to dominate Kashmiri militant groups:

As the [Kashmiri] freedom movement transformed into religious Jihad, its first target was the JKLF, which had struggled for the Kashmiri people's right of self determination. Jamaat-e-Islami's Hizbul Mujahideen started "Jihad" against JKLF in addition to fighting the Indian forces. This fact is now admitted by some Hizbul Mujahideen leaders. The JKLF leader, Amanullah Khan, told a Press Conference in Islamabad in 1991 that "Hizbul Mujahideen not only liquidates JKLF fighters, it also informs the Indian army of our hideouts. As a result 500 important JKLF commanders have already been martyred." In Muzaffarabad, a leader of JKLF who wanted to remain anonymous because he held a government job, said, "The ISI had actually given Hizbul Mujahideen the task of completely liquidating JKLF from [Indian] occupied Kashmir. This was because the JKLF demanded an autonomous Kashmir and also because it was the largest Kashmiri organization [independent of the ISI]. Several JKLF leaders were bought over; leading to the organization's splintering into at least 20 factions."[69]

In subsequent years, the ISI's desire for control led it to shift its support from the Hizbul Mujahideen to other religious factions with fewer Kashmiri members. Although the Hizbul Mujahideen was affiliated with the Jamaat-e-Islami and therefore more amenable to the ISI's control, its leadership was still Kashmiri. Hizbul Mujahideen was reluctant to carry out some of the more radical ISI plans, such as "communal cleansing" of Kashmir, by attacking non-Muslim indigenous Kashmiris.[70] Moreover, the Nawaz Sharif government and some elements of the Pakistan army were concerned at the prospect of Pakistan's Jamaat-e-Islami getting all the credit for the struggle against India in Kashmir.[71] By organizing new jihadi groups with few Kashmiri members and no agenda for domestic Pakistani politics, the ISI hoped to control fully the conception and execution of militant operations.

As Pakistani-backed insurgents escalated their attacks inside Indian-controlled territory, India responded by stepping up its brutal repression of Kashmiri dissent. Indian repression only increased the alienation of Kashmiris and damaged India's international prestige, which in turn led Pakistan to believe that its strategy was working. Priding itself on being the world's largest democracy, India was now confronted with charges of being a major human rights violator. Amnesty International wrote a typical critique in its 1992 report:

Widespread human rights violations in the [Jammu and Kashmir] state since January 1990 have been attributed to the Indian army, and the paramilitary Border Security Force (BSF) and Central Reserve Police Force (CRPF) . . . Cordon-and-search operations are frequently conducted in areas of armed opposition activity . . . Torture is reported to be routinely used during these combing operations as well as in army camps, interrogation centers, police stations and prisons. Indiscriminate beatings are common and rape in particular appears to be routine . . . In Jammu and Kashmir, rape is practiced as part of a systematic attempt to humiliate and intimidate the local population during counter-insurgency operations.[72]

But Pakistan could draw little comfort from the criticism of India over human rights violations because international pressure on India was still insufficient to cause it to acquiesce to Pakistan's demand for a plebiscite. The international community still did not see Kashmir as an issue of self-determination, as Pakistan desired; and, after the first few years, condemnation of Islamabad over its support to the militants outweighed international pressure on India to address the Kashmiris' concerns.

The Kashmir militancy tied down large numbers of Indian troops in counterinsurgency operations, which Pakistan's military planners took to be a success. The insurgency in Kashmir did not, however, drive India toward a resolution of the issue Pakistani officials described as the "core" of tensions between the two nations. As time went by, the Pakistanis simply increased the tempo of militancy in Indian-controlled territory. As Indian counterinsurgency operations became more sophisticated, the plans for militant attacks became more elaborate. Attacks on Indian troops and Hindu civilians in Kashmir were supplemented by planned attacks beyond Kashmir. Within a few years, suicide attacks were planned. Plans for a more ferocious insurgent war against India required larger numbers of insurgents, and jihadi groups soon sprang up throughout Pakistan, raising funds and seeking recruits. Pakistan was now in the grip of what came to be known as "jihadi culture."

The expansion of the jihadi culture in Pakistan coincided with the appointment in 1992 of Lieutenant General Javed Nasir as director general of the ISI. General Nasir was, by his own admission, a member of the evangelical Tableeghi Jamaat, and the "first general officer with full grown beard," a symbol of Islamic piety.[73] The Tableeghi Jamaat is a nonpolitical religious movement associated with the orthodox Deoband school of Sunni Islam, which seeks to purify the souls of Muslims by reminding them of their religious obligations. Its members support jihad, believe in pan-Islamism, and share the concern of political Islamists about the ascendancy of non-Muslims in the international order.

General Nasir invited several Deobandi religious scholars to organize jihadi groups and extended the ISI's patronage to these groups. When the Soviet-installed regime in Afghanistan finally collapsed in 1992 and the civil war among mujahideen factions got under way, some Deobandi groups such as the Harakat-e-Jihad-e-Islami recruited and trained volunteers to fight in both Afghanistan and Kashmir. Nasir widened the ISI's covert operations against "the enemies of Islam," including the "USA, Hindu leadership of India, the communists, [and] the Zionists."[74] Under Nasir's direction, the ISI violated the UN embargo on supplying arms to the warring parties in Bosnia-Herzegovina and "airlifted sophisticated anti-tank guided missiles" for the Bosnian Muslims.[75] When communal riots broke out in India after the razing of the historic Babri mosque at Ayodhya by Hindu fanatics, Nasir authorized ISI collaboration with Dawood Ibrahim, a Muslim leader of the Bombay underworld, who organized an attack on the Bombay Stock Exchange on March 12, 1993, resulting in the death of at least 250 people and injury to more than one thousand others.

Although some of General Nasir's actions and methods were not approved by either the civilian leadership or the Pakistan army high command, his overall plan of expanding the jihadi network beyond Afghanistan, Pakistan, and Kashmir clearly had wider support. Nasir was prematurely retired from his ISI position on May 13, 1993, after U.S. pressure, but he resurfaced as head of an organization responsible for the upkeep of Sikh shrines in Pakistan. Nasir served in that position until 2002, almost three years after General Musharraf's military coup d'état and well after September 11, 2001. After retirement, Nasir also occasionally published hard-hitting articles against enemies of Islam and

Pakistan in Pakistani newspapers and, like General Hamid Gul, continues to be popular among the military and ISI rank and file.

The ISI's support for Deobandi and Wahhabi groups as part of the
jihadi movement remained part of official policy even after Nasir's removal from the ISI. By the time General Nasir officially left the ISI, the
liberal English-language Pakistani weekly *Friday Times* had started to
parody the ISI as the "Invisible Soldiers of Islam," and the agency made
every effort to live up to that reputation.

The United States did not express alarm at Pakistan's involvement
with the jihadi movement, especially the Kashmir insurgency, until some
time after the withdrawal of Soviet troops from Afghanistan. The last
Soviet troops left Afghanistan on February 15, 1989, and the United States
continued to help the Afghan mujahideen and Pakistan for almost one
additional year in an effort to install a stable, noncommunist government in Kabul. During the post-Soviet phase, the United States generally deferred to the "largely ISI-driven Pakistani policy on Afghanistan,"[76]
which handed the ISI an opportunity to extend its jihad to Kashmir without serious objections from the United States. Years later, U.S. officials
who had been involved admitted that the United States had made a
mistake "in failing to shift gears sooner after the Soviet pullout."[77] U.S.
direct involvement with the Afghan jihad ended after September 1991,
when the United States and the Soviet Union agreed not to support any
of the warring parties in Afghanistan. By then, Pakistan's breach of its
promises on nuclear proliferation had led to U.S. sanctions. With the
blinders of collaboration in Afghanistan finally off, the United States
also began noticing Pakistan's support of Islamist terrorism.

A new U.S. ambassador, Nicholas Platt, arrived in Islamabad at the
end of 1991 with the earliest warnings of U.S. concern over terrorism.
During meetings with Platt and the State Department's coordinator of
the office of counterterrorism, Peter Burleigh, Pakistani officials flatly
denied any official Pakistani involvement in support of terrorist activities. The ISI advised civilian officials dealing with official Americans to
ask for evidence from the Americans of Pakistani activities supporting
terrorism. The answers would give the ISI an idea of the means the United
States was using for intelligence gathering in Pakistan and would en-

able it to restructure its effort to evade U.S. detection.[78] Pakistani diplomats and civilian officials blamed private individuals and Islamist parties, such as the Jamaat-e-Islami, for organizing support for Kashmiri militants. The government officially promised to close down training camps for Kashmiri militants set up by individuals and political parties and to halt "the training which outsiders, including Kashmiris, previously received alongside the Afghan mujahideen in Pakistan."[79]

Despite these promises, the situation on the ground did not change, and in May 1992, the Bush administration threatened to designate Pakistan a state sponsor of terrorism. In a letter dated May 10, 1992, from Secretary of State James A. Baker to Prime Minister Nawaz Sharif, the U.S. government acknowledged Pakistani claims that support for the Kashmiri militants came from private groups and Islamist parties. It also appreciated Sharif's promises that "Pakistan will take steps to distance itself from terrorist activities against India," but it added, "We have information indicating that ISID [ISI] and others intend to continue to provide material support to groups that have engaged in terrorism. I must take that information very seriously; U.S. law requires that an onerous package of sanctions apply to those states found to be supporting acts of international terrorism and I have the responsibility of carrying out that legislation."[80]

While delivering the letter, Ambassador Platt made it clear that the United States did not believe official Pakistani claims about the Islamists acting on their own. His talking points, handed for effect to the prime minister in writing, said:

We are very confident of our information that your intelligence service, the Inter-Services Intelligence Directorate, and elements of the Army, are supporting Kashmiri and Sikh militants who carry out acts of terrorism . . . This support takes the form of providing weapons, training, and assistance in infiltration . . . We're talking about direct, covert Government of Pakistan support. There is no doubt in our mind about this . . . This is not a case of Pakistani political parties, such as Jamaat-e-Islami, doing something independently, but of organs of the Pakistani government controlled by the President, the Prime Minister and the Chief of Army Staff . . . Our information is certain. It does not come from the Indian government. Please consider the serious consequences to our relationship if this support continues . . . If the situation persists, the Secretary of State may find himself required by law to place Pakistan on the U.S.G. state sponsors of terrorism list . . . We would not want to take such a drastic step but cannot ignore the requirements of the law . . . You must take concrete steps to curtail assistance to militants and not allow their training camps to operate in Pakistan or Azad Kashmir.[81]

The scope of sanctions Pakistan would face as a state sponsor of terrorism was far wider than the ones that had been imposed because of its nuclear program. U.S. law forbade the slightest indirect assistance to terrorist states. The new sanctions would mandate the shutdown of funding from the International Monetary Fund, the World Bank, and other international financial institutions as well as bar bilateral trade. Designation as a state sponsor of terrorism would also mean the end of Export-Import Bank financing for projects in Pakistan.

A few days after the U.S. ambassador delivered the warning, Prime Minister Sharif presided over a meeting of senior officials from his secretariat, the Ministry of Foreign Affairs, and the armed forces to discuss the new U.S. threat. The army chief, General Asif Nawaz, and the ISI director general, Lieutenant General Javed Nasir, participated. Nasir began by blaming the "Indo-Zionist lobby" in Washington for the changed U.S. attitude toward Pakistan and insisted that Pakistan demand evidence from the United States confirming its allegations. He argued that the jihad in Kashmir was at a critical stage and could not be disrupted. "We have been covering our tracks so far and will cover them even better in the future," General Nasir said, adding "These are empty threats. The United States will not declare Pakistan a terrorist state. All we need to do is to buy more time and improve our diplomatic effort. The focus should be on Indian atrocities in Kashmir, not on our support for the Kashmiri resistance."[82]

Nawaz Sharif agreed with General Nasir's assessment, which reflected the consensus of the meeting. With the exception of two participants, no one saw anything wrong with Pakistan's strategy of supporting the Kashmiri militants. The highest levels of Pakistan's government saw the problem as one of managing the country's relations with the United States, not a substantive problem of adopting an incorrect policy. Sharif said that, as long as Pakistan could be useful to the United States, the United States would remain favorably disposed toward Pakistan and would not want to disrupt the relationship built during the Afghan jihad. "We have a problem only with the American media and the Congress," he said. "This problem can be resolved by a stronger lobbying effort."[83] Sharif approved an additional allocation of $2 million "as the first step" toward improving Pakistan's relations with the U.S. media and lobbying Congress. The secretary for foreign affairs, Sheheryar Khan, disagreed, arguing that Pakistani support for Kashmiri groups should be curtailed. Sheheryar Khan said that Pakistan would "probably be more successful by focusing on diplomacy and political action" in favor of the Kashmiris, instead of "setting off bombs." General Nasir's response was that "the Hindus do not understand any language other than force." General Asif Nawaz said that it was not in Pakistan's interest to get into a confrontation with the United States, but "we cannot shut down military operations against India either." The army chief suggested that Pakistan could get off the hook with the United States with some changes in its pattern of support for Kashmiri militancy without shutting down the entire clandestine operation. That is precisely the policy Pakistan adopted over the next year.

Nawaz Sharif responded to the U.S. warning with assurances that any covert support to militants fighting India would be discontinued. He also listed Pakistan's grievances with India over Kashmir and asked for an active U.S. role in resolving that dispute. The United States did not carry out its threat to list Pakistan as a state sponsor of terrorism although Pakistan was subjected to numerous sanctions over its nuclear tests in 1998 and for its lack of democracy after Musharraf's coup d'état in 1999.

Sanctions against Pakistan were, however, watered down frequently as Pakistan convinced Washington of improved behavior. Thus began a long period of Pakistan's proverbial glass being half full in the eyes of American policy makers, a view that was set aside periodically only to be embraced again.

During the decade following the American threat to declare Pakistan a state sponsor of terrorism, Pakistan repeatedly promised to crack down on Islamist militant groups operating from its territory. Each time, some measures were taken to create the impression that the task of uprooting the jihadists was a difficult one and that the Pakistani government was struggling to deal with the problem. In April 1993, while the U.S. threat still lingered, Pakistan arrested nine Arabs belonging to militant Islamist groups and announced that this was the beginning of a "crackdown on Islamic extremists."[84]

Pakistani officials also described the problem as a holdover from the anti-Soviet jihad in Afghanistan and suggested that the jihadists had come to Pakistan "with the connivance of the world."[85] The official explanation also featured the difficulty of the mountainous terrain along Pakistan's border with Afghanistan, where the foreign militants (who later became Al Qaeda) were said to be hiding. "The Pakistani-Afghan border area is the mountainous homeland of the fiercely independent Pashtun ethnic group," wrote the *Washington Post*. "Afghanistan maintains no control over its own sector and Pakistani government authority is weak outside of major towns."[86] Another reason given for why the U.S. should not pressure Pakistan's government of the day was that it would "throw Pakistan into the hands of mullahs."[87] That argument was first made in 1993 and continues to be made today.

In the end, the U.S. withdrew its threat over terrorist listing after the ouster of Prime Minister Sharif and the replacement of General Javed Nasir as ISI chief. The new government promised a purge in the ISI. "Even though the change was to some extent cosmetic," Kux explains, "it proved sufficient for the State Department not to take the extreme step of pinning the 'terrorist state' label on Pakistan."[88] Pakistani support for the militants in Kashmir continued unabated and became stronger with each change of government in Pakistan. U.S. pressure on the subject never again touched the level it had reached during the last several months of Sharif's first tenure as prime minister.

During Bhutto's second stint as prime minister (1993–1996), Pakistan's official position on Kashmir hardened as the ISI insisted that the government stop apologizing for the freedom struggle in Kashmir. Pakistani

Islamist groups organized openly for jihad in Kashmir and raised funds from the public.[89] The ISI demanded special programs on state-owned Pakistan Television to highlight Indian atrocities in Kashmir and describe the courageous deeds of the mujahideen.

In the summer of 1995, a group of Jamaat-e-Islami militants was besieged in a shrine at Charar Sharif in Indian-controlled Kashmir. After days of fighting and the burning down of the shrine, Indian forces allowed these militants safe passage to the Pakistani side. The militants' commander, Must Gul, was a Pakistani citizen, who was given a hero's welcome upon arrival in Rawalpindi.[90] At ISI's insistence, the welcome rally was shown on the government television network even though Jamaat-e-Islami leaders condemned the Bhutto government at the rally.

Bhutto could not stop the ISI and the Islamists but she appealed to the U.S. for help in dealing with the jihadis. She told American reporters to convey a message to their government, "You are a fair nation. You have been our allies. Help us to overcome militancy and terrorism."[91] One of the reporters present at her briefing for U.S. journalists wrote, "Ms. Bhutto hinted that powerful forces are arrayed against [her] government when she said that Pakistan could not move on its own against terrorists."[92] The Islamists retaliated with public condemnation of the prime minister.

At a rally in Rawalpindi after Must Gul's release, Jamaat-e-Islami chief Qazi Hussain Ahmed demanded that the government should officially declare jihad against India. Hussain Ahmed took Pakistan's Foreign Office to task for criticizing receptions organized for Must Gul and observed that the Foreign Office was infected by the "American virus."[93] The Islamists also claimed that "public money is being used to fill the treasury of Asif Ali Zardari and not spent on Defence, arms and development" and that the government "was trying to create obstacles in the way of jihad."[94]

When Sharif returned as prime minister (1997–1999), he made little effort to curb the jihadi militants until the beginning of the Lahore peace process with India. The jihadi groups became more brazen, collecting funds in mosques and bazaars and publishing the lists of foreign and Pakistani martyrs in their newspapers and magazines. Official deference to the jihadi groups was demonstrated by the visit in April 1998 of the Governor of Punjab and the Pakistani Information Minister to the headquarters of Lashkar-e-Taiba (Army of the Pure), a Wahhabi militant group. The Lashkar headquarters, known as Markaz Al-Dawa wal-Irshad (Center for the Call to Righteousness), was widely known as a training facility for militants. Lashkar-e-Taiba later played a crucial role in the Kargil conflict and its members were involved in suicide missions against Indian military garrisons.[95] The group was among the first to be put on the State Department's list of global terrorist organizations after the September 11, 2001, terrorist attacks in the United States.

At the April 1998 event attended by high-ranking Pakistani officials, as reported by the official Associated Press of Pakistan, "The Governor [of Punjab] . . . lauded the spirit of jihad and sense of sacrifice among the students of the Markaz which it had waged for supporting Kashmiri freedom fighters."[96] The Pakistani Information Minister was quoted as saying that the "government had strengthened the national defence by launching [the nuclear-capable] Ghauri missile . . . Now [the] country's fate was not decided by superpowers."

The jihadi activities of the ISI and Pakistan's Islamists were greatly helped by the establishment of the Taliban regime in Afghanistan. The Pakistan-Afghan border was now open for militants and a significant portion, but not all, of the training infrastructure for Pakistani jihadis was shifted across the border into Afghanistan. This gave Pakistani officials greater deniability. Moreover, deteriorating security in Pakistani cities and fatal attacks on American officials (1995) and oil company employees (1997) had created security concerns that limited the American presence in Pakistan. The U.S. could no longer extensively monitor militant activities in Pakistan and intelligence on Pakistani camps in Afghanistan was also limited. For these reasons, U.S. protests about Pakistani support for Kashmiri militants became less specific than they had been at the time when Pakistan was threatened with designation as a state sponsor of terrorism.

U.S. attention on Pakistan and Afghanistan increased after terrorist attacks on American embassies in Kenya and Tanzania in August 1998. The U.S. retaliated with cruise missile attacks against what it believed were command and control facilities run by Osama bin Laden's Al Qaeda, which was responsible for the terrorist attacks in East Africa. The cruise missiles overflew Pakistani territory and an American general visiting

Pakistan at the time informed Pakistan's army chief that they were aimed at Afghanistan. But the missiles did not kill bin Laden, who reportedly left the targeted camps shortly before the missiles landed. Instead, at least eleven Pakistani members of Harkat-ul-Ansar were killed, pointing at a Pakistani connection with bin Laden.[97] The rumor that bin Laden left the targeted camp moments after the missiles were fired from U.S. navy warships led to speculation that he was warned by members of the ISI once Pakistan knew the missiles were on their way to Afghanistan.

By the time Sharif was deposed by the military, Pakistan had become a fully militarized society. Citing the study of militarism and society by Stanislav Andreski, Stephen Cohen wrote in his book *The Pakistan Army*, "[There are] four kinds of 'militarism.' There is idolization of the military, rule by the military, the peacetime militarization of society (even under civilian leadership), and the gearing up of a society for war. Pakistan has seen only the first two, and even those on a sporadic basis."[98] That was in 1984. The mass mobilization for jihad throughout the 1990s had geared up Pakistani society for war and the nation was militarized even under civilian rule. General Musharraf's military regime was less apologetic than any previous Pakistani military government and initially openly committed to continuing the militarization of society.

General Musharraf's October 1999 coup d'état, coming as it did in the background of his role in the Kargil crisis, was generally welcomed by Pakistan's jihadis. An anti-India Islamist web site published an article attributed to Maulana Masood Azhar, a leader of the Harkat-ul-Mujahideen who was then in prison in India. It said, "The government in Pakistan has changed. The tyrannical rule of Nawaz Sharif has reached its natural conclusion. We congratulate our fellow country-men. The honorable armed forces of Pakistan have taken a necessary step at an extremely critical time and saved the country from a grave disaster and frightening turmoil, thus discharging their . . . duty. We pay glowing tribute to them."[99]

Masood Azhar went on to make the argument that the Pakistan army and the ulema were the guardians of Pakistan and the Islamic faith and they had to guard against internal and external enemies. He identified a long list of Pakistan's enemies, including the politicians, those seeking to make Pakistan a "colony of America or Russia," ethnic political parties working at the behest of the Indian intelligence service RAW, and those connected to the Jewish lobby.

Within two months of the coup, Masood Azhar was freed from Indian captivity when an Indian Airlines plane was hijacked from Katmandu, Nepal, and diverted to Kandahar, Afghanistan, in December 1999. Five hijackers, armed and wearing ski masks, took over the plane and held its 155 passengers and crew hostage for eight days. The hijacking came to an end on New Year's Eve only after India released three prisoners, including Masood Azhar.[100] India blamed Pakistan for the incident and Pakistan denied any involvement. Within a couple of days, however, the prisoners released as a result of the hijacking surfaced in Pakistan. Masood Azhar went on to organize Jaish-e-Muhammad (Army of Muhammad), which quickly became one of the most effective militant groups in Kashmir. The other prisoner released in exchange for hostages, Omar Saeed Shaikh, was convicted of kidnapping *Wall Street Journal* reporter Daniel Pearl in 2002.[101]

Although Musharraf spoke of ending religious extremism in Pakistan from the day he took power, it soon became obvious that he made a distinction between Kashmiri freedom fighters and domestic Islamists. In 2000, at least eighteen militant organizations devoted to the jihad in Kashmir operated from Pakistan.[102] Musharraf's military regime did not take action against any of them in its first two years even as it moved swiftly to arrest politicians and businessmen accused of corruption. The attitude of Pakistan's military leaders was reflected in their response to the beheading of Indian troops by a group of militants on New Year's Eve 2001. The mujahideen beheaded three Indian soldiers during a foray into Indian-controlled territory and brought their heads with them, which they displayed at a public crossing on the Pakistani side.[103] The Pakistan army spokesman, Major General Rashid Qureshi, said the incident did not disturb him per se but he was concerned that it should not be published in any English-language newspaper. "It would be bad for Pakistan if western diplomats read about it," he said.[104]

Al Qaeda's terrorist attacks in the United States on September 11, 2001, changed Pakistan's relationship with the United States but did not immediately alter the Pakistani establishment's position on Kashmir. Like Sharif in 1992, Musharraf continued to link the end of militancy to the resolution of the Kashmir question even after becoming an American ally in the aftermath of 9/11.[105] American generals turned to Pakistan for crucial logistics and vital intelligence support when they went to war in Afghanistan. Musharraf gave that support in return for U.S. assurances of revived military and economic aid.

Initially, Musharraf had hoped for a role for some Pakistani clients in the new government in Kabul and the ISI floated the idea of "moderate Taliban" joining the future Afghan government. For its part, the U.S. held out the hope that the Northern Alliance would invest but not enter Kabul until the U.N. had agreed on the composition of Afghanistan's government.[106] President George W. Bush did not push Musharraf on Kashmir at this stage.[107] The Islamists demonstrated in the streets against alliance with the United States, which only strengthened Musharraf's bargaining position with the United States. Musharraf told Pakistanis he had given up support for the Taliban to save Pakistan's nuclear program from possible [American] attack and he expected the Kashmiri resistance to continue without too much pressure from the United States.

The American Central Command felt indebted to Musharraf because he had allowed "basing, staging and overflight support"[108] for the war in Afghanistan. According to Central Command General Tommy Franks, "Musharraf had also agreed to a detailed list of seventy four basing and staging activities to be conducted in Pakistan, from Combat Search and Rescue, to refueling and operating communications relay sites, to establishing a medical evacuation point near the Afghan border."[109] His only request in return had been the exclusion of India from military operations in Afghanistan even though India, too, was part of the anti-terrorism coalition assembled by the U.S. after 9/11. By doing so many operational favors for the U.S. military, Musharraf hoped to revive Pakistan's relations with the United States to where they were under Ayub Khan and Zia ul-Haq.

The United States could not ignore Kashmiri militancy in return for Pakistani cooperation against Al Qaeda for long. The Pakistan-based Islamist groups continued their attacks inside Indian-controlled Kashmir as if the Pakistani relationship with the U.S. were not their concern. On October 1, militants attacked the Kashmir legislature in Srinagar, killing thirty-eight people, mostly civilians. Immediately after the attack, "men who said they were from Jaish-i-Muhammad phoned newspaper offices in Srinagar to claim responsibility."[110]

The day after the attack, *Jang*, the largest Urdu newspaper in Pakistan, reported that it had contacted Masood Azhar, the leader of the group, who confirmed that the attack had been carried out by Jaish-e-Muhammad. Masood Azhar was quoted in the paper's first edition as saying, "We will continue to respond to Indian terrorism with terrorism. This is a major historic achievement."[111] But the paper's second edition did not carry the story. The next day, Jaish-e-Muhammad denied responsibility for the Srinagar attack. The group's ISI handlers had obviously persuaded Masood Azhar to tone down the rhetoric while Musharraf negotiated for economic and military aid from the United States.

A second attack on December 13, this time on the Indian Parliament in New Delhi, had more serious consequences. India considered this attack, in the heart of its capital, as a provocation grave enough to threaten war. Within a few days, India had moved several divisions along its 1,800-mile border with Pakistan, with "missile batteries and air force squadrons"[112] ready for battle. Musharraf responded first by announcing the arrest of fifty members of Lashkar-e-Taiba, the group Indians held responsible for the Parliament attack but India described the measure as "entirely cosmetic."[113] Then the arrests of Lashkar-e-Taiba leader Hafiz Muhammad Saeed and Jaish-e-Muhammad's Masood Azhar were announced.[114] But Indian Prime Minister Vajpayee still refused to "take part in any talks [with Pakistan] until he was satisfied that Pakistan had shut down Islamic militant groups."[115]

Musharraf made a policy speech on January 12, 2002, banning some militant groups and declaring that he would not allow terrorism, even in the name of Kashmir.

That speech, coupled with American diplomacy, was expected to defuse tensions with India. Pakistani authorities arrested several hundred militants only to release them a few days later. Hafiz Saeed and Masood Azhar, too, were back in circulation after only short periods of detention. It was clear that the ISI was not keen to offend its jihadi partners by keeping them in prison for too long. "Even if General Musharraf is sincere about wanting to crack down on the groups," wrote an American reporter, "it is not clear whether he can exert full control over them or whether the militants will continue to receive backing of parts of Pakistan's intelligence service that hold the Kashmir cause dear."[116]

Although Musharraf was building his image as America's dependable ally against terrorism, he was unwilling to turn away completely from the Pakistani military's consistent support of jihad against India. Musharraf made his views clear in an interview with the *Washington Post*, in which he made a distinction between various elements of Pakistan's militant problem and stressed that the militants fighting in Kashmir were freedom fighters:

> There are three elements of terrorism that the world is concerned about. Number one, the Al Qaeda factor. Number two is what [the Indians] are calling cross-border terrorism and we are calling the freedom struggle in Kashmir. Number three is the sectarian [Sunni vs. Shia] extremism and sectarian terrorism in Pakistan ... the third one is more our concern, and unfortunately, the world is not bothered about that. We are very much bothered about that because that is destabilizing us internally.[117]

Musharraf promised that Pakistan was "flushing out anyone who comes from outside" and took pride in the fact that Pakistan had arrested more Al Qaeda members than the United States. Pakistan had impressed the United States by arresting and handing over Abu Zubaydah, "a top commander under Osama bin Laden"[118] in March 2002 and Musharraf thought that was sufficient to avert American scrutiny of activities across the Line of Control in Kashmir. "There is nothing happening across the Line of Control,"[119] he said, flatly denying that there was any Pakistani support for terrorism against India. Musharraf also made it clear that his government's priority was controlling sectarian terrorism within the country.

Musharraf also made it plain that he did not trust or like India. According to Musharraf, India wanted "to destabilize Pakistan" and "to isolate Kashmir and then crush whatever is happening with all their force." Asked if India wanted "a stable modernizing Pakistan as its neighbor," he replied, "Not at all. They want a subservient Pakistan which remains subservient to them."[120] Musharraf's views had not changed from what they had been at the time of the Kargil war. He was still committed to balancing India's might with the low-cost option of unconventional warfare. He was still denying Pakistan's support for the mujahideen primarily to maintain respectability in the eyes of the international community, especially the United States.

Pakistan's relations with India deteriorated further in May 2002, when India expelled Pakistan's ambassador to protest a terrorist attack.[121] Artillery duels between the two armies followed.[122] India demanded that the U.S. declare Pakistan a terrorist state as militant attacks escalated during summer,[123] when milder weather made it easier for militants to cross the mountainous Kashmir frontier.

The United States intervened to create détente in South Asia. Pakistan had by now been promised a five-year aid package of $3 billion and the U.S. considered it necessary to use its leverage with Musharraf to pull India and Pakistan from the brink. U.S. Deputy Secretary of State Richard Armitage traveled to the region in June and extracted a promise from Musharraf to permanently end incursions across the Line of Control. In return, India would wait for the promise to be fulfilled and avoid escalation of tensions. Two and a half months later Armitage had to go back to New Delhi and Islamabad because militant attacks in Indian-controlled Kashmir had not completely ceased.[124]

Despite Pakistani promises of controlling the jihadis, they simply did not go out of business. Musharraf's critics said that he was "warehousing some extremists and leaving others untouched for fear of alienating the religious right whose support he needs."[125] The government banned militant groups with much fanfare and even detained their leaders only to allow their re-emergence under different names. "Several of the jihadi organizations have reconstituted under different names and are once again raising money and proselytizing for jihad against India and the West,"[126] reported the *Washington Post*.

The pattern was similar to promises of crackdowns, and occasional action, followed by free rein for the jihadis that emerged ten years ago.

The U.S. was more engaged in Pakistan, however, and the Musharraf regime enjoyed greater support in Washington than either Sharif or Bhutto in their interrupted tenures. Pakistan had managed to arrest a significant Al Qaeda figure every few months, usually at a critical moment. In September 2002, Ramzi bin al-Shibh, wanted by the U.S. in connection with the September 11 terrorist attacks, was caught in Karachi.[127] Then on March 1, 2003, Pakistan announced the capture in Rawalpindi of Khalid Shaikh Mohammed, the man who had planned many Al Qaeda attacks including the ones on the World Trade Center and the Pentagon.[128] Both high-profile arrests came at times when reports of Pakistan's continued support for Kashmiri insurgency or sheltering of Taliban remnants along the Afghan border were causing concern among U.S. policy makers. When the two senior-most members of the U.S. Senate Foreign Relations Committee expressed concern over the presence of Taliban fighters in Pakistan, they pointedly expressed their belief that Musharraf could not be "involved in the destabilizing activities."[129]

Musharraf apparently kept his promise with Armitage and militant forays into Indian-controlled Kashmir started declining significantly after the summer of 2003. It was now up to India to fulfill its end of the bargain and revive bilateral talks. Two assassination attempts against Musharraf in December, eleven days apart, jolted the Pakistani establishment.[130] At least some of the militants protected by ISI because of their contribution to jihad in Kashmir are more closely aligned with Al Qaeda than Pakistani officials had previously admitted. These harder-line jihadis had been responsible for several terrorist attacks in Pakistan since September 2001. Now, as these uncontrollable militants attempted to kill the chief of Pakistan's army, the need to target them became more obvious. Pakistani authorities have, since then, killed or arrested several sectarian or out-of-control militants.

Most militants, however, remain at large. The ISI paid substantial amounts in "severance pay" to jihadi leaders such as Hafiz Muhammad Saeed of Lashkar-e-Taiba, Maulana Masood Azhar of Jaish-e-Muhammad, and Maulana Fazlur Rehman Khalil of Harkatul Mujahideen in return for their agreement to remain dormant for an unspecified duration.[131]

The case of Fazlur Rehman Khalil is particularly interesting. Khalil was one of the signatories of Osama bin Laden's 1998 fatwa against the United States and was reportedly in the camp struck by U.S. cruise missiles in Afghanistan in 1998. In January 2004, the *Los Angeles Times* reported that Khalil remained openly active despite government-imposed bans on him and his organizations:

A barrage of U.S. cruise missiles several years ago didn't sap Fazlur Rehman Khalil's devotion to holy war, and two subsequent bans issued by Pakistan's government haven't silenced his invective against Jews and Americans . . . But Khalil, who co-signed Osama bin Laden's 1998 edict that declared it a Muslim's duty to kill Americans and Jews, is not leading his holy warriors from inside a secret mountain cave. He lives comfortably with his family in this city adjacent to Pakistan's capital, Islamabad, next to his Koranic girls' school and bookshop, just down the street from a police checkpoint . . . And he is still urging his followers to fight the United States . . . Khalil and his organization's latest incarnation, Jamaat-ul-Ansar or Group of Helpers, openly defy the most recent ban, imposed in November [2003]. One of the platforms for his message is a stridently anti-American monthly magazine, Al-Hilal, which identifies Khalil as its "Chief patron." Khalil uses it to raise funds, notify supporters of meetings and activities and urge volunteers to fight U.S. forces in Afghanistan and Iraq.[132]

Khalil had survived the ban in 1995 on Harkat-ul-Ansar and renamed it Harkat-ul-Mujahideen. Now that Harkat-ul-Mujahideen had also been banned, he ran Jamaat-ul-Ansar. Instead of doing anything about Khalil or his followers after the publication of this report, the ISI threatened the *Los Angeles Times'* Pakistani reporter.[133] Khalil was finally arrested with considerable publicity in August 2004[134] only to be released quietly seven months later.[135]

It is difficult for some members of the law enforcement machinery to look upon Islamists as enemies of the state, after almost two decades of treating them as national heroes. One of the accused in the kidnapping and murder of reporter Daniel Pearl was an employee of the Special Branch of the Karachi police. A member of the paramilitary Rangers has been charged with plotting to murder Musharraf in concert with the group responsible for the car bomb attack at the U.S. Consulate in Karachi.

Junior military officers were involved in a plot to assassinate Musharraf that resulted in a very close shave.

Pakistan's involvement with the jihadi groups and its tolerance of armed extremist religious groups has contributed to generally ineffective law enforcement in the country. Musharraf has himself acknowledged that "Pakistan has become a soft state where law means little, if anything."[136] Sectarian and ethnic murders as well as unexplained bombings have been a common occurrence for the last several years. At least five million small arms are in private hands in Pakistan.[137] The most notable of these is the Kalashnikov assault rifle that served as the weapon of choice during the anti-Soviet Afghan resistance.

Even if General Musharraf decides finally to root out Islamic militancy, it will be years before the terrorist networks are completely eliminated. Resources of the police and intelligence-gathering agencies are overstretched as the military government uses them to stay in power and not just to keep crime and terrorism in check. The terrorists know that and take advantage of the state's weakness.

From the point of view of Pakistan's Islamists and their backers in the ISI, jihad is only on hold but not yet over. Pakistan still has an unfinished agenda in Afghanistan and Kashmir and, given its lack of military and economic strength, subconventional warfare with the help of Islamists remains one of Pakistan's options. Just as the major anti-India jihadi groups retained their infrastructure that could be pressed into service at a future date, Afghanistan's Taliban also continued to find safe haven in Pakistan in the spring of 2005. Afghan and American officials complained periodically of the Taliban still training and organizing in Pakistan's border areas.[138]

Both the Pakistani-Kashmiri militants and the Taliban became relatively quiet after the revival of the India-Pakistan process after a meeting between Vajpayee and Musharraf during the Islamabad Summit conference of SAARC in January 2004. Encouraged by the United States, India and Pakistan resumed the composite dialogue that Vajpayee and Sharif had started in 1999, which had been interrupted by the Kargil crisis. A bus service between the two sides of Kashmir started in April 2005 and was hailed as a major breakthrough. At some stage, however, the two sides would have to discuss the final status of Kashmir.

Musharraf, though far more conciliatory toward India than ever before, clearly stated that Pakistan expects a territorial settlement in Kashmir as essential. India, on the other hand, declared with equal clarity that "there would be no redrawing of borders when it comes to Kashmir."[139] It is too early to tell whether the latest peace process, and the relative inaction of the jihadis, will translate into sustained peace in South Asia.

The Musharraf regime has been careful to take all steps necessary to retain the good will of the United States and its rhetoric of "enlightened moderation" has won it America's support. Pakistan undertook a major military operation in the tribal areas bordering Afghanistan to help flush out Al Qaeda remnants, including possibly Osama bin Laden and his principal deputy, Ayman Al-Zawahiri.[140] After several months of intermittent fighting involving Pakistani tribesmen and "foreign fighters," the operation was called off. Pakistani troops managed to kill some Chechens and Uzbeks in the area but failed to find top Al Qaeda leaders.

President Bush described Musharraf as "a courageous leader" who had risked his life to crack down on the Al Qaeda terrorist network[141] Secretary of State Condoleezza Rice declared during a March 2005 visit to Pakistan that Pakistan "has come an enormously long way. . . . This is not the Pakistan of September 11. It is not even the Pakistan of 2002."[142] American officials regularly expressed the belief that Pakistan had turned the corner and could now be trusted as an American ally. The U.S. ignored the role of Pakistani nuclear scientist Dr. A. Q. Khan in sharing nuclear weapons technology with Libya, Iran, and North Korea and accepted Musharraf's somewhat incredible version that the nuclear sales were transactions of private individuals not known to the Pakistani State.[143] Once again the United States was willing to see Pakistan's glass as half full rather than half empty.

For Pakistan's military, this was good news. With strong relations with the United States, Pakistan could acquire modern military equipment and increased inflows of economic assistance. Confrontation with India would have to be set aside for the time being, as has been done on several occasions in the past. Instead of championing Islamic orthodoxy, Pakistan would seek its place in the sun with the battle cry of moderate Islam. The Pakistani establishment's traditional paradigm for building a state and nation dominated by the military would endure.

8

Conclusion:
From Ideological to Functional State

In an effort to become an ideological state guided by a praetorian military, Pakistan has found itself accentuating its dysfunction, especially during the past two decades. The commitment or lack of commitment of the ordinary Pakistani citizen to Islam has hardly been the major issue in Pakistan's evolution. A large number of otherwise practicing Muslims have demonstrated through the ballot box time and again their desire to embrace pragmatic political and economic ideas. Most Pakistanis would probably be quite content with a state that would cater to their social needs, respect and protect their right to observe religion, and would not invoke Islam as its sole source of legitimacy; but the military's desire to dominate the political system and define Pakistan's national security priorities has been the most significant, although not the only, factor in encouraging an ideological paradigm for Pakistan.

At its birth, Pakistan started life with many disadvantages as the seceding state. Some of its security concerns, such as the need for a credible deterrent against India, are real, but the Pakistani military's desire for institutional supremacy within the country has created psychological and political layers to the Pakistani nation's sense of insecurity. The alliance between mosque and military in Pakistan maintains, and sometimes exaggerates, these psycho-political fears and helps both the Islamists and the generals in their exercise of political power. Support for the Pakistani military by the United States makes it difficult for Pakistan's weak, secular, civil society to assert itself and wean Pakistan from the rhetoric of Islamist ideology toward issues of real concern for Pakistan's citizens.

From the point of view of the United States, Pakistan offers few political choices. Although listed among the U.S. allies in the war on terrorism, Pakistan cannot be easily characterized as either friend or foe. Pakistan has become a major center of radical Islamist ideas and groups, largely because of its past policies of support for Islamist militants fighting Indian rule in the disputed territory of Jammu and Kashmir as well as the Taliban in its pursuit of a client regime in Afghanistan. Since September 11, 2001, however, the selective cooperation of Pakistan's military ruler, General Pervez Musharraf—sharing intelligence with the United States and apprehending Al Qaeda members—has led to the assumption that Pakistan might be ready to give up its long-standing ties with radical Islam. At the same time, the United States cannot ignore the fact that Pakistan's status as an Islamic ideological state is rooted deeply in history and is linked closely with both the praetorian ambitions of Pakistan's military and the worldview of Pakistan's elite.

In the foreseeable future, Islam will remain a significant factor in Pakistan's politics. Musharraf and his likely successors from the ranks of the military, promising reform, will continue to seek U.S. economic and military assistance; yet the power of such promises is tempered by the strong links between Pakistan's military-intelligence apparatus and extremist Islamists.

Pakistan's future direction is crucial to the U.S.-led war against terror, not least because of Pakistan's declared nuclear-weapons capability. The historic alliance between Islamists and Pakistan's military could undermine antiterrorist operations in the short term while contributing to the global radicalization of Islam and fueling India-Pakistan confrontation. Unless Pakistan's all-powerful military can be persuaded to turn over power gradually to secular civilians and allow the secular politics of competing economic and regional interests to prevail over religious sentiment, the country's vulnerability to radical Islamic politics will not wane. With the backing of the U.S. government, Pakistan's military would probably be able to maintain a facade of stability for the next several years; but the military, bolstered by U.S. support, would want to maintain preeminence and is likely to make concessions to Islamists to legitimize its control of the country's polity. The United States is supporting Pakistan's military so that Pakistan backs away from Islamist radicalism, albeit gradually. In the process, however, the military's political ambitions are being encouraged, compromising change and preserving the influence of radical Islamists. Democratic reform that allows secular politicians to compete freely for power is more likely to reduce the influence of radical Islamists.

Since Pakistan's independence in 1947, the disproportionate focus of the state on ideology, military capability, and external alliances has weakened Pakistan internally. The country's institutions—ranging from schools and universities to the judiciary—are in a state of general decline. The economy's stuttering growth depends largely on the level of concessional flows of external resources. Pakistan's gross domestic product (GDP) stands at about $75 billion in absolute terms and $295 billion in purchasing power parity, making Pakistan's economy the smallest of any country that has tested nuclear weapons. Pakistan suffers from massive urban unemployment, rural underemployment, illiteracy, and low per capita income: one-third of the population lives below the poverty line and another 21 percent subsists just above it.

Soon after independence, 16.4 percent of Pakistan's population was literate, compared with 18.3 percent of India's significantly larger population. By 2003, India had managed to attain a literacy rate of 65.3 percent, but Pakistan's stood at only about 35 percent. Today, Pakistan allocates less than 2 percent of its GDP for education and ranks close to the bottom among 87 developing countries in the amount allotted to primary schools. Its low literacy rate and inadequate investment in education have led to a decline in Pakistan's technological base, which in turn hampers the country's economic modernization. With a population growing at an annual rate of 2.7 percent, the state of public health care and other social services in Pakistan is also in decline. Meanwhile, Pakistan spends almost 5 percent of its GDP on defense and is still unable to match the conventional forces of India, which outspends Pakistan 3 to 1 while it allocates less than 2.5 percent of its GDP to military spending.

The dominance of the military in Pakistan's internal affairs is a direct outcome of the circumstances during the early years of statehood. Circumstances have changed considerably over the years, however; and a planned withdrawal of the military from political life is essential for Pakistan to function as a normal state. The partition of British India's assets in 1947 left Pakistan with one-third of the British Indian army and only 17 percent of its revenues. Thus, the military started out as the dominant institution in the new state, and its dominance has endured. Since General Ayub Khan assumed power in 1958, ruling through martial law, the military has directly or indirectly dominated Pakistani politics, set Pakistan's ideological and national security agenda, and repeatedly intervened to direct the course of domestic politics. On four occasions, despite constant rewriting of the country's constitution, ostensibly to pave the way for sustained democracy, generals seized power directly, claiming that civilian politicians were incapable of running the country. Even during periods of civilian government, the generals have exercised political influence through the intelligence apparatus—the ISI—which plays a behind-the-scenes role in exaggerating political divisions to justify military intervention.

Partly because of the role of the military and partly because of their own weakness, Pakistan's political factions have often found it difficult to cooperate with each other or submit to the rule of law. As a result, Pakistan is far from developing a consistent system of government, with persisting political polarization along three major, intersecting fault lines: between civilians and the military, among various ethnic and provincial groups, and between Islamists and secularists.

The first crack in contemporary Pakistan's body politic continues to be this perennial dispute over who should wield political power—the civilians or the military. Musharraf has described Pakistan as "a very difficult country to govern" in view of its myriad internal and external difficulties. Musharraf's view reflects the thinking of the Pakistani military and is possibly self-serving. The military does not allow politics to take its course, periodically accusing elected leaders of compromising national security or of corruption. Repeated military intervention has deprived Pakistan of political leaders experienced in governance, leading to serious lapses under civilian rule. Because the military periodically co-opts or fires civilian politicians, established and accepted rules for political conduct have failed to evolve. Issues such as the role of religion in matters of state, the division of powers among the branches of government, and the authority of the provinces are not settled by constitutional means or through a vote. The military does not let civilians rule, but its own rule lacks legitimacy in the eyes of the general public, creating an air of permanent friction. Thus, instead of governing, Pakistan's rulers, including Musharraf, have been reduced to managing ethnic, religious, and provincial tensions.

The second fault line has its origin in ethnic and provincial differences. Although the majority of Pakistan's ethnically disparate population has traditionally identified with secular politicians, that majority has not always determined the direction of Pakistan's policies, even when expressed in a free and fair election. Highly centralized and unrepresentative governance has created grievances among different ethnic groups, and the state has yet to create any institutional mechanisms for dealing with such discontent. Constitutional provisions relating to provincial autonomy, which could placate each province by allowing self-government, have often been bypassed in practice. Intraprovincial differences—those between the Balochis and the Pashtuns in Balochistan, between the Punjabis and Saraiki speakers in Punjab, between the Pashtuns and Hindko speakers in NWFP, and between the Sindhis and muhajirs (those who have immigrated to Pakistan from India since partition) in Sindh—have also festered without political resolution.

The third fault line is the ideological division over the role of Islam in national life. Starting as a pressure group outside Parliament, Pakistan's religious parties have now become a well-armed and well-financed force that wields considerable influence within different branches of government. Religious groups have benefited from the patronage of the military and the civil bureaucracy, which have seen them as useful tools in perpetuating the military's control over foreign and domestic policy. Because the Islamist worldview is incompatible with the vision of a modern Pakistan, the violent vigilantism of some Islamists has become a serious threat to Pakistani civil society and has also promoted sectarian terrorism. Operating outside the framework of the rule of law, the Islamists have the potential to disrupt the conduct of foreign policy, especially in view of their support for anti-India militants in Kashmir and the Taliban in Afghanistan.

Radical Islamic groups, which portray themselves as the guardians of Pakistan's ideology, have been granted special status by the military-civil bureaucracy that normally governs Pakistan. The Islamists claim that they are the protectors of Pakistan's nuclear deterrent capability as well as champions of the national cause of securing Kashmir for Pakistan. Secular politicians who seek greater autonomy for Pakistan's different regions—or demand that religion be kept out of the business of the state—have come under attack from the Islamists for deviating from Pakistan's ideology.

Establishing Islam as the state ideology was a device aimed at defining a Pakistani identity during the country's formative years. Indeed, Pakistan's leaders started using religious sentiment to strengthen the country's national identity shortly after Pakistan's inception. Emerging from the partition of British India in 1947 after a relatively short independence movement, Pakistan faced several challenges to its survival, beginning with India's perceived reluctance to accept Pakistan's creation. Pakistan's secular elite used Islam as a national rallying cry against perceived and real threats from predominantly Hindu India. They assumed that the country's clerics and Islamists were too weak and too dependent on the state to confront the power structure. Unsure of their fledgling nation's future, the politicians, civil servants, and military officers who led Pakistan in its formative years decided to exacerbate the antagonism between Hindus and Muslims that had led to partition as a means of defining a distinctive identity for Pakistan with "Islamic Pakistan" resisting "Hindu India." Notwithstanding the fitful peace process, hostility between India and Pakistan continues; in Pakistan it serves as an important element of national identification.

Pakistan's political commitment to an ideological state evolved into a strategic commitment to export jihadist ideology for regional influence. During the Bangladesh crisis in 1971, Pakistan's military used Islamist rhetoric and the help of Islamist groups to keep elected secular leaders supported by the majority Bengali-speaking population out of power in East Pakistan before its secession. The Bengalis' rebellion, with India's assistance, and their brutal suppression by the Pakistani military followed an election that would have given power to Bengali politicians in a united Pakistan. After the 1971 war, Pakistan was halved by the birth of an independent Bangladesh, exacerbating Pakistan's insecurity.

Both India and Bangladesh have evolved as secular democracies focused on economic development, but Pakistan continues to be ruled by a civil-military oligarchy that sees itself as defining and also protecting the state's identity—mainly through a mix of religious and militarist nationalism. Hence, in western Pakistan, the effort to create national cohesion among Pakistan's disparate ethnic and linguistic groups through religion took on greater significance, and its manifestations became more militant. Religious groups, both armed and unarmed, gradually grew in power as a result of the alliance between the mosque and the military. Radical and violent manifestations of Islamist ideology, which some-times appear to threaten Pakistan's stability even today, can be inter-preted as a state project gone awry.

Pakistan's rulers have traditionally attempted to manage militant Islamism, trying to calibrate it so that it serves the state's nation-building function without destabilizing internal politics or relations with West-ern countries. Pakistan's emphasis on its Islamic identity continued to increase as the civilian, semiauthoritarian government of Zulfikar Ali Bhutto in the early and mid-1970s channeled Pakistan's Islamic aspira-tions toward foreign policy. Pakistan played a key role in developing the Organization of Islamic Conference and established special relations with Islamic groups and countries.

General Zia ul-Haq's military regime from the late 1970s until the late 1980s took matters a step further when it based Pakistan's legal and edu-cational system on Islamic law, thereby formalizing the preexisting state ideology into an official policy of Islamization. Zia ul-Haq's efforts at Islamization made Pakistan an important ideological and organizational center of the global Islamist movement, including Pakistan's leading role in the anti-Soviet campaign in Afghanistan in the 1980s when it allowed Afghanistan's mujahideen to operate from bases in Pakistan and inflict a heavy toll on the Soviet military.

The success of the jihadist experiment against the Soviets encouraged Pakistan's strategic planners to expand the jihad against India and into post-Soviet Central Asia. Pakistan's sponsorship of the Taliban in Af-ghanistan, together with the presence in Pakistan of Islamist militants from all over the world, derived from Islamabad's desire to emerge as the center of a global Islamic resurgence. Ironically, religious fervor did not motivate all Pakistani leaders who supported this strategy; in most cases, they simply embraced Islam as a politico-military strategic doctrine that would enhance Pakistan's prestige and position in the world. Its focus on building an ideological state, however, has subsequently caused Pakistan to lag in almost all measures that define a functional modern state.

In the past few years, however, the situation has deteriorated further. The Islamists are not content with having a secondary role in national affairs, and they have acquired a momentum of their own. Years of religious rhetoric have influenced a younger generation of military officers; the ISI, in particular, includes a large number of officials who have assimilated the Islamist beliefs they were rhetorically called on to support in the course of jihad in Kashmir and Afghanistan. Because Musharraf and the country's military still believe that secular politicians, not the Islamists, are their rivals for political power, they have continued to use Islamists for political purposes. In 2003, Musharraf's administration sought the backing of Islamists for a set of constitutional amendments that increased the president's power; in return, the administration recognized an Islamist as the leader of the parliamentary opposition. Major figures among the secular opposition have been exiled or jailed on corruption or sedition charges, thereby positioning the Islamists as Pakistan's major opposition group and enabling them to exercise greater influence than would have been possible in an open, democratic political system in light of the Islamists' poor electoral performance in Pakistan's intermittent elections.

Pakistan's civil-military elite's focus on a national ideology has been motivated by its fear that some Pakistani ethnic groups have an insufficient commitment to the idea of Pakistan. This may have been partly true in Pakistan's formative years. Now, however, most of the previously rebellious tribes and ethnicities would be content with their fair share in political and economic power. Regional autonomy and an inclusive democratic political system would be a more effective means of holding Pakistan together than a state ideology. In the absence of an imposed ideology there would be less likelihood of debates over defining that ideology and sectarian conflict would be averted. Most significantly, if a state ideology is no longer central to national discourse, the influence of political as well as militant Islamists would be greatly reduced.

The competition with and fear of India that dominates the Pakistani establishment's thinking over the last fifty-eight years has proven to be equally debilitating to Pakistan's advancement. It is true that the Indians accepted partition only reluctantly and, for some years, spoke of their desire to undo the partition. It was natural for Pakistan's leaders immediately after independence to feel insecure about India's intentions. The manner in which Pakistan dealt with that insecurity, however, made India an obsession of Pakistan's leaders rather than a rationally handled security problem. Pakistan stumbled into wars with India not because India threatened to forcibly occupy Pakistan. On each occasion when Pakistan flexed its military muscle and invited war, Pakistan's psycho-political, as opposed to physical, insecurity was at play. That Pakistan's establishment continues to speak of Pakistan being under threat even after acquiring, and demonstrating, nuclear weapons capability only affirms the psychological nature of Pakistan's avowed security concerns.

Starting out with the desire to secure Kashmir, Pakistan's mishandling of its internal affairs and its confrontation with India led to the country's breakup in 1971. In recent years, Pakistani leaders have argued that they need to be militarily powerful to prevent India from becoming the regional hegemon. India's much larger size and economic and military prowess means that Pakistan is likely to get exhausted while running hard to keep pace with India.

There is no doubt that Pakistanis have strong feelings over Jammu and Kashmir, which might have been included in Pakistan in accordance with the logic of partition. But much of this strong sentiment has been produced by the constant rhetoric of Kashmir's centrality to Pakistan's existence that has been fed to Pakistanis on a regular basis. Fifty-eight years after partition, and in the absence of any incentive or compulsion on the part of India to revise the status quo, it might be prudent for Pakistanis to give priority to normalization and stability in South Asia over settlement of the Kashmir dispute. To make that possible, the Pakistani State must end the rhetoric it has fed to Pakistanis about Kashmir. It appears, so far, that Pakistan's military leadership remains unwilling to change the country's ideological orientation. The Islamists remain important allies of the military in maintaining the country's status as an ideological state as well as to emphasize India's status as an existential threat to Pakistan.

Pakistan's Islamists made their strongest showing in October 2002 in a general election during parliamentary voting when they secured 11.1 percent of the popular vote and 20 percent of the seats in the lower house of Parliament. The decision of the Musharraf regime to bar two former prime ministers, Nawaz Sharif and Benazir Bhutto, and several of their followers from the election helped Islamists achieve these results. The two leading secular parties, Sharif's Pakistan Muslim League and Bhutto's Pakistan Peoples Party, had to contend with corruption proceedings relating to their tenures in office as well as the Musharraf government's intense propaganda in support of these allegations. The candidates of the alliance of Islamic parties—the Mutahhida Majlis Amal (MMA, or United Action Council)—did not face disqualification, and Islamic party leaders campaigned freely. Anti-U.S. sentiment in the areas bordering Afghanistan particularly benefited the MMA, which made electoral gains without dramatically increasing the share of votes traditionally won by Islamic parties. Secular parties suffered because of redistricting as well as the disqualification of some of their candidates. While the leaders of the PML and the PPP were forced into exile, MMA leaders could campaign freely, ensuring a full turnout of Islamist voters at the polls.

The Musharraf government started recognizing the MMA as the main opposition in Parliament even though Bhutto's PPP had the single largest bloc of opposition parliamentarians—eighty-one to the MMA's sixty-three. Musharraf was deliberately projecting the MMA as his primary opposition to create the illusion that radical Islamist groups were gaining power through democratic means, thus minimizing the prospect that the international community—especially the United States while Pakistan offers support in the war against Al Qaeda—would press for democratic reform in Pakistan.

Musharraf has made repeated pronouncements since September 11, 2001, to reassure the world of his intention to alter Pakistan's policy direction radically, moving it away from its Islamist and jihadist past. Musharraf's administration continues to project the war against terrorism as a U.S. war that is being waged with Pakistan's help—even after attempts on his life and the life of his handpicked prime minister, Shaukat Aziz, in 2003 and 2004. Islamabad continues to distinguish between foreign fighters—such as those from Al Qaeda, whom Pakistani forces have been pursuing—and homegrown terrorists who were originally trained to fight Indian troops in Kashmir. Musharraf has reversed Zia ul-Haq's course of Islamization, but only marginally. The government now encourages women's participation in public life, and cultural events involving song and dance are openly allowed and even encouraged. State-owned media have become more culturally liberal, and private radio and television stations with unrestricted entertainment content are now allowed. Controversial Islamic laws, such as those relating to blasphemy and *hudood* (Islamic limits) remain in place, however.

Musharraf and the Pakistani military remain willing to compromise with the Islamists far more than with secular politicians. For example, the MMA has been given greater freedom to organize rallies and manifest its street power than either the PPP or the opposition faction of the PML.

Notwithstanding Musharraf's proclamations of a vision of enlightened moderation for Pakistan, contradictions in his domestic, regional, and international policies are apparent. His greatest commitment is his view that he is indispensable for Pakistan and that Pakistan is safer under the stewardship of the military rather than civilian democratic rule. Musharraf's duality in speaking of enlightened moderation while he keeps alive the perception that he is faced with an Islamist opposition that justifies military intervention and governance reflects the structural problem in Pakistan's politics—the weakness of civilian institutions and the armed forces' dominance of decision making.

Islam has therefore become the central issue in Pakistan's politics because of a conscious and consistent state policy—not just the inadvertent outcome of decisions made after the Soviet intervention in Afghanistan, as has been widely assumed—aimed at excluding from power secular politicians while maintaining a centralized state controlled by the military and the civil bureaucracy. Pakistan's self-characterization as an Islamic, ideological state is thus unlikely to change in the near term. The country's population remains fractured by ethnic and linguistic differences, with Islam used as the common bond in an attempt to unite it.

Several times Pakistan has been seen as a state on the brink of failure, temporarily restored with U.S. military and economic assistance only to return to the brink again. Pakistan, suffering from chronically weak state institutions, continues to face a deep identity crisis and a rising threat from independent, radical Islamists. The government's fears about its viability and security have led Islamabad to seek an alliance with the United States while it simultaneously pursues a nuclear deterrent and subconventional military capability—that is, Islamist terrorism—against India. The U.S. response to September 11 left Pakistan with little choice but to make a harder turn toward the United States. Confronted with an ultimatum to choose between being with the United States or against it, Pakistan's generals chose to revive their alliance with the United States. At every stage since, Pakistan has proved to be a U.S. ally of convenience, not of conviction, as it has sought specific rewards for specific actions.

Pakistan's military historically has been willing to adjust its priorities to fit within the parameters of immediate U.S. global concerns. It has done this to ensure the flow of military and economic aid from the United States, which Pakistan considers necessary for its struggle for survival and its competition with India. Pakistan's relations with the United States have been part of the Pakistani military's policy tripod that emphasizes Islam as a national unifier, rivalry with India as the principal objective of the state's foreign policy, and an alliance with the United States as a means to defray the costs of Pakistan's massive military expenditures. These policy precepts have served to encourage extremist Islamism, which in the past few years has been the source of threats to both U.S. interests and global security. The United States can perhaps deal best with Pakistan in the long term by using its influence to reshape the Pakistani military's view of the national interest.

The United States recognized the troubling potential of Islamist politics in the very first years of the U.S. engagement with Pakistan. In a policy statement issued on July 1, 1951, the U.S. Department of State declared: "Apart from Communism, the other main threat to U.S. interests in Pakistan was from 'reactionary groups of landholders and uneducated religious leaders' who were opposed to the 'present Western-minded government' and 'favor a return to primitive Islamic principles.' "

During the past four decades, however—until September 11, 2001—
the U.S. government did little to discourage Islamabad's embrace of
obscurantist Islam as its state ideology, thereby empowering Pakistan's
religious leaders beyond their support among the populace and tying
the Islamists to Pakistan's military-civil bureaucracy and intelligence
apparatus.

America's alliance with Pakistan, or rather with the Pakistani military, has had three significant consequences for Pakistan. First, because
the U.S. military sees Pakistan in the context of its Middle East strategy,
Pakistan has become more oriented toward the Middle East even though
it is geographically and historically a part of South Asia. Second, the
intermittent flow of U.S. military and economic assistance has encouraged Pakistan's military leaders to overestimate their power potential.
This, in turn, has contributed to their reluctance to accept normal relations
with India even after learning through repeated misadventures that Pakistan can, at best, hold India to a draw in military conflict and cannot defeat it. Third, the ability to secure military and economic aid by fitting into
the current paradigm of American policy has made Pakistan a rentier state,
albeit one that lives off the rents for its strategic location.

The United States might be able to change Pakistan's pretense of being a Middle Eastern state by taking it out of the area of operations of the
American military's Central Command and placing it under Pacific Command, along with India. This would ensure greater interaction between
senior Indian and Pakistani military officers and enable the U.S. military to look at India and Pakistan in a realistic manner. As things have
been since the 1950s, American military planners dealing with the Middle
East and Central Asia feel obliged to include Pakistan in their plans as
the Eastern anchor of their strategy. Pakistani generals offer them operational support significant in their regional context but not necessarily as
important for the big picture of American policy. Pakistan's military has
successfully used its contacts with Central Command officers to promote a more positive view of itself than might have emerged if the same
American officers were also dealing with the rest of South Asia at the
same time.

The other two distortions affecting Pakistan—an exaggerated view of
Pakistani power and the complexities of being a rentier state—are the

direct outcome of American policy relating to foreign aid. U.S. assistance appears to have influenced the internal dynamic of Pakistan negatively, bolstering its military's praetorian ambitions. According to figures provided by the United States Agency for International Development (USAID), between 1954 and 2002 the United States provided a total of $12.6 billion in economic and military aid to Pakistan. Of these $9.19 billion were given during twenty-four years of military rule while only $3.4 billion were provided to civilian regimes covering nineteen years. On average, U.S. aid to Pakistan amounted to $382.9 million for each year of military rule compared with only $178.9 per annum under civilian leadership.

Contrary to the U.S. assumption that aid translates into leverage, Pakistan's military has always managed to take the aid without ever fully giving the United States what it desires. During the 1950s and 1960s, Ayub Khan oversold Pakistan's willingness to help the United States in containing communist expansion. Pakistan provided significant intelligence gathering facilities for a while but never provided the "centrally positioned landing site" the United States sought. Zia ul-Haq's cooperation in bleeding the Soviets in Afghanistan came with Pakistan's plan to install a client regime in Afghanistan after the Soviet withdrawal. The United States never controlled Pakistan's ISI, or for that matter the mujahideen, even though it paid for the operation. Pakistan's role in the jihad against the Soviet Union also inspired Pakistani jihadis to expand jihad into Kashmir. Musharraf's help in the hunt for Al Qaeda also remains selective. Pakistan's unwillingness to fulfill American expectations, rather than American fickleness, has led to the on-off aid relationship between the two countries. The Pakistani military has been unhappy each time the aid pipeline was shut down and turned its people against the United States. While aid flows, however, it is the Pakistani military and not the United States that gains leverage.

United States policy makers need to recognize the limits of aid as leverage with Pakistan. Instead of heaping praise on Pakistan's soldier-politicians, the United States could try deflating their egos. A more modest aid package delivered steadily, aimed at key sectors of the Pakistani economy, would not raise Pakistani expectations and could, over time, create a reliable pocket of influence for the United States among the country's elite. The pattern of large doses of aid, given as strategic rent or quid pro quo for Pakistan's cooperation in a specific sphere, has historically provided the United States with limited leverage. With the dissipation of aid, the United States loses that limited leverage and Pakistan's elite gets embittered.

Washington has never been able to develop a policy that focuses exclusively on dealing with Islamabad and its dysfunction. Instead, Pakistan has generally been placed into broader U.S. policy objectives: containment of communism in the 1950s and 1960s, restriction on Soviet expansion in Afghanistan during the 1980s, nuclear nonproliferation during the 1990s, and the war against terrorism since September 11, 2001. Washington's quid pro quo approach in dealing with Pakistan has often helped confront the issue at hand while it creates another security problem down the road. General Ayub Khan found U.S. eagerness to contain communism during the 1950s useful for extracting a good price for Pakistan's participation in anti-communist treaties. U.S. support during the Cold War enabled Pakistan's military to use force in the Bangladesh crisis of 1971, which led to Pakistan's breakup.

History repeated itself when the Soviet Union's occupation of Afghanistan in 1979 made Pakistan a frontline state in the resistance to communist expansion. Like General Ayub Khan before him, General Zia ul-Haq during the 1980s bargained for additional aid in return for the use of Pakistan as a staging ground for an anti-Soviet insurgency. Zia, circumventing U.S. legislation aimed at nonproliferation, also used the cover of the Afghan jihad to acquire a nuclear-weapons capability for Pakistan. With help from the United States, Zia modernized Pakistan's military and prepared for a broader jihad to expand Pakistan's regional influence, building a cadre of Islamist guerrillas and giving rise to Pakistan's ambitions to create a client regime in Afghanistan that resulted in the Taliban's ascendancy and ability to provide sanctuary for Al Qaeda.

Washington's preoccupation with the success of the anti-Soviet struggle enabled Pakistan to defeat two U.S. objectives—nuclear nonproliferation and security in the Middle East and South Asia—as the Soviet occupation of Afghanistan was beaten back. Meanwhile, the entirely new threat of radical Islamic terrorism was empowered. Islamabad's relationship with Washington has in some ways contributed to the Pakistani crisis because it has allowed Pakistan's leaders to believe they can continue to promote risky domestic, regional, and pan-Islamic policies. The availability of U.S. assistance—offered to secure Pakistani cooperation with the U.S. grand strategy—has exacerbated Pakistan's dysfunction and structural flaws.

Current U.S. hopes in Pakistan are pinned to Musharraf's commitment to U.S. interests. Assassination attempts from which Musharraf has narrowly escaped have raised the question of whether U.S. policy interests would be adequately served beyond the period of Musharraf's indefinite tenure. Although it may be difficult for U.S. and Pakistani policy makers to force an end to Pakistan's status as an Islamic ideological state, changes in the nature of the Pakistani state can gradually wean the country from Islamic extremism. Musharraf cannot. For many years military rule has fomented religious militancy in Pakistan. Under military leadership, Pakistan has defined its national objective as wresting Kashmir from India and, in recent years, establishing a client regime in Afghanistan. Unless Islamabad's objectives are redefined to focus on economic prosperity and popular participation in governance—which the military as an institution remains reluctant to do—the state will continue to turn to Islam as a national unifier.

If Pakistan had proceeded along the path of normal political and economic development, it would not need the exaggerated political and strategic role for Islam that has characterized much of its history. The United States, for its own interests, cannot afford the current rise in Islamic militancy in a large Muslim country that has the capability for nuclear weapons, a large standing army, and a huge intelligence service able to conduct covert operations to destabilize neighboring governments in the Persian Gulf, South Asia, and Central Asia.

The influence of Islamists in Pakistan can perhaps be best contained through democracy. During elections, a majority of Pakistani voters repeatedly demonstrated that they do not share the Islamist vision for the country. Despite the MMA's unprecedented electoral performance in 2002, the alliance garnered only 11 percent of the total votes cast; the Islamist vote as a percentage of total registered voters has been more or less stagnant since the 1970s. The strength of the Islamists lies in their ability to mobilize financial and human resources. Islamists run schools, operate charities, and publish newspapers; moreover, they are able to put their organized cadres on the streets. Thus, in the absence of democratic decision making, Islamists can dominate the political discourse. Pakistan's secular civil society is either apolitical or insufficiently organized, and secular political parties have been dismembered consistently by successive military governments.

Strengthening civil society and building secular political parties as a countervailing force in Pakistan can contain the demands for Islamization made by the religious parties and radical Islamist groups. In recent years the United States has accepted—even endorsed—criticism of corruption and bad governance heaped on Pakistan's popular politicians by Pakistan's military and civilian oligarchy. In the absence of a sustained political process, however, Pakistan is unlikely to produce honest politicians capable of running the country; and the military, which lacks political legitimacy, would continue to influence events with the help of its Islamist allies who extract, as the price for their support, adherence to the notion of the Islamic ideological state. Instead of accepting the military's right to set politics in Pakistan, U.S. policy should insist on a sustained constitutional and political process. Political corruption and fiscal mismanagement need not be ignored, but they should not be allowed to justify the military's continued intervention—intervention that makes it difficult for Pakistan to break away from its ideological tripod.

Moderate and inclusive politics have worked well to contain the Islamists in the past. Whenever an elected political leader has rejected Islamists' demands, fears of a backlash failed to materialize. Between 1972 and 1977, Zulfikar Ali Bhutto successfully expanded the role of women in the public arena despite Islamist opposition, and in 1997 Prime Minister Nawaz Sharif faced only a limited reaction when he reversed the decision to observe Friday as a weekly religious holiday. Conversely, Islamists have won their major policy victories thanks to regimes seeking their support to garner political legitimacy or to achieve strategic objectives. Unlike governments in other Muslim countries like Egypt and Turkey, Pakistan's government—particularly its military—has encouraged political and radical Islam, which otherwise has a relatively narrow base of support. Democratic consensus on limiting or reversing Islamization would gradually roll back the Islamist influence in Pakistani public life. Islamists would maintain their role as a minority pressure group representing a particular point of view, but they would stop wielding their current disproportionate influence over the country's overall direction.

The United States can help contain the Islamists' influence by demanding reform of those aspects of Pakistan's governance that involve the military and security services. Until now, the United States has harshly berated corrupt or ineffective Pakistani politicians but has only mildly criticized the military's meddling. Between 1988 and 1999, when civilians ostensibly governed Pakistan, U.S. officials routinely criticized the civilians' conduct but refrained from commenting on the negative role of the military and the intelligence services despite overwhelming evidence of that role. ISI manipulation of the 1988, 1990, and 1997 elections went unnoticed publicly by the United States while the Pakistani military's recitation of politicians' failings was generally accepted without acknowledging the impact of limits set for the politicians by the military. The United States appears to accept the Pakistani military's falsified narrative of Pakistan's recent history, at least in public. It is often assumed that the military's intervention in politics is motivated by its own concern over national security and the incompetence of politicians. That the military might be a contributor to political incompetence and its desire to control national security policies might be a function of its pursuit of domestic political power are hardly ever taken into account.

Washington should no longer condone the Pakistani military's support for Islamic militants, its use of its intelligence apparatus for controlling domestic politics, and its refusal to cede power to a constitutional democratic government. As an aid donor, Washington has become one of Pakistan's most important benefactors, but a large part of U.S. economic assistance since September 11, 2001, has been used to pay down Pakistan's foreign debt. Because Washington has attached few conditions to U.S. aid, the spending patterns of Pakistan's government have not changed significantly. The country's military spending continues to increase, and spending for social services is well below the level required to improve living conditions for ordinary Pakistanis. The United States must use its aid as a lever to influence Pakistan's domestic policies. Even though Musharraf's selective cooperation in hunting down Al Qaeda terrorists is a positive development, Washington must not ignore Pakistan's state sponsorship of Islamist militants, its pursuit of nuclear weapons and missiles at the expense of education and health care, and its refusal to democratize; each of these issues is directly linked to the future of Islamic radicalism.

The United States clearly has few good short-term policy options in relation to Pakistan. American policy makers should endeavor to recognize the failings of their past policies and avoid repeating their mistakes. The United States has sought short-term gains from its relationship with Pakistan, inadvertently accentuating that country's problems in the process. Pakistan's civil and military elite, on the other hand, must understand how their three-part paradigm for state and nation building has led Pakistan from one disaster to the next. Pakistan was created in a hurry and without giving detailed thought to various aspects of nation and state building. Perhaps it is time to rectify that mistake by taking a long-term view. Both Pakistan's elite and their U.S. benefactors would have to participate in transforming Pakistan into a functional, rather than ideological, state.

Notes

Chapter 1

1. "English Rendering of President General Pervez Musharraf's Address to the Nation (January 12, 2002)," www.pak.gov.pk/President_Addresses/presidential_addresses_index.htm.

2. See, for example, "President's Steps, Views Have Full Support: Gov. Sindh," *Business Recorder*, January 14, 2002. Musharraf's January 12, 2002, address even caused a rally on the Pakistani stock market; see "Pakistani Stocks Rise 2.4% on Musharraf's Speech," *Agence France-Presse*, January 14, 2002.

3. For a discussion of the relatively weak support for Pakistan in the Muslim areas, and the local politics behind it, see Ian Talbot, *Pakistan: A Modern History* (New York: St. Martin's Press, 1998), pp. 66–94.

4. Dennis Kux, *The United States and Pakistan, 1947–2000: Disenchanted Allies* (Washington, D.C.: Woodrow Wilson Center Press, 2001), p. 7; see also Ayesha Jalal, *The Sole Spokesman: Jinnah, the Muslim League and the Demand for Pakistan* (Cambridge: Cambridge University Press, 1985).

5. For an elaboration of this argument, see Ayesha Jalal, "Between Myth and History," *Dawn*, March 23, 2005.

6. Ayesha Jalal, *The State of Martial Rule* (Cambridge: Cambridge University Press, 1990), p. 16.

7. Ibid., pp. 16–18.

8. Ibid., p. 18.

9. British India Library, "Fortnightly Report to the Viceroy by Sir Evan Jenkins, Governor of Punjab, February 1947," *Records of the Political and Secret Department: L/P & J/5/250*, p. 379.

10. Jinnah's conversation of May 1, 1947, with U.S. diplomat Raymond Hare is cited in Kux, *United States and Pakistan, 1947–2000*, p. 13.

11. Jalal, *State of Martial Rule*, p. 18.

12. Human Rights Commission of Pakistan, "Elections in Pakistan: A Brief History," www.hrcpelectoralwatch.org/his_persp.cfm.

13. Khalid bin Sayeed, *Pakistan: The Formative Phase* (London: Oxford University Press, 1968), p. 198.

14. Ibid., pp. 198–99.

15. Dr. Afzal Iqbal, *Islamisation of Pakistan* (Delhi: Idarah-I Adabiyat-I Delli, 1984), p. 38.

16. Khalid bin Sayeed, *Pakistan: The Formative Phase*, p. 203.

17. Ibid., p. 207.

18. Jalal, *State of Martial Rule*, p. 20.

19. Abdus Sattar, "Fifty Years of the Kashmir Dispute: The Diplomatic Aspect," in Suroosh Irfani, ed., *Fifty Years of the Kashmir Dispute* (Muzaffarabad: University of Azad Jammu and Kashmir, 1997), pp. 11–12.

20. Margaret Bourke-White, *Halfway to Freedom* (New York: Simon and Schuster, 1949), p. 99.

21. Jalal, *State of Martial Rule*, p. 36.

22. Ibid. Rupees is abbreviated Rs.

23. For a Pakistani civil servant's view of circumstances at the time of Pakistan's birth and Hindu, as well as British, designs on Pakistan, see Chaudhri Muhammad Ali, *The Emergence of Pakistan* (New York: Columbia University Press, 1967).

24. *Quaid-i-Azam Mohammed Ali Jinnah's Speeches as Governor General of Pakistan, 1947–48* (Karachi: Government of Pakistan, 1964).

25. See, for example, Muhammad Munir, *From Jinnah to Zia* (Lahore: Vanguard Books, 1979).

26. Ardeshir Cowasjee, "In the Name of Religion," *Dawn*, October 5, 2003.

27. M. M. R. Khan, *The United Nations and Kashmir* (Groningen, Netherlands: J. B. Wolters, 1956), p. 62.

28. Bourke-White, *Halfway to Freedom*, p. 103.

29. Jalal, *State of Martial Rule*, p. 49.

30. See, for example, Major General Fazal Muqeem Khan, *Pakistan's Crisis in Leadership* (Islamabad: National Book Foundation, 1973), p. 1.

31. The military in Pakistan's political context generally means the Pakistan army, which is the oldest and strongest of its three armed forces. The Pakistan army's history, structure, motives, and view of self are described in

detail in Stephen P. Cohen, *The Pakistan Army* (Berkeley: University of California Press, 1984); the second edition, with additions and updating, was published in Karachi by Oxford University Press in 1998.

32. Safdar Mahmood, *Constitutional Foundations of Pakistan* (Lahore: Jang Publishers, 1990), p. 52.

33. Ibid., p. 10.

34. M. Rafique Afzal, *Pakistan: History and Politics, 1947–1971* (Karachi: Oxford University Press, 2001), p. 99.

35. Aslam Siddiqi, *Pakistan Seeks Security* (Karachi: Longmans Green, 1960), p. 89.

36. Ibid., pp. 82–83.

37. Ibid., pp. 88–89.

38. Keith Callard, *Pakistan, a Political Study* (London: George Allen and Unwin, 1957), pp. 95–96.

39. The role of provincial special branches (secret services) in Indian provinces under British rule can be gleaned from the documents of the period at the British India Library. Reference to the religious sections in the northwest frontier, for example, can be found in Wali Khan, *Facts Are Facts* (New Delhi: Vikas Publishing House, 1987).

40. Personal interviews with Pakistani intelligence officers of the time helped me confirm that the religious sections continued to operate after Pakistan's independence.

41. For a firsthand account of the anti-Ahmadi riots of 1953 and their influence on Pakistan's future course, see Munir, *From Jinnah to Zia*, pp. 41–73. Munir, then chief justice of Pakistan's Supreme Court, headed a judicial inquiry into the riots.

42. Seyyed Vali Reza Nasr, *The Vanguard of the Islamic Revolution: The Jama'at-i Islami of Pakistan* (Berkeley: University of California Press, 1994), p. 115.

43. For a discussion of Maududi's thought and its impact on the Muslim world, see Seyyed Vali Reza Nasr, *Mawdudi and the Making of Islamic Revivalism* (New York: Oxford University Press, 1996).

44. S. Abul Ala Maududi, *A Short History of the Revivalist Movement in Islam* (Lahore: Islamic Publications, 1963), p. 26.

45. For a history of the Jamaat-e-Islami, see Nasr, *Vanguard of the Islamic Revolution*.

46. Ibid., p. 122.

47. Ibid., p. 116.

48. Musa Khan Jalalzai, *Sectarian and Religio-Political Terrorism in Pakistan* (Lahore: Tarteeb Publishers, 1993), pp. 255–56.

49. Maududi, *Short History of the Revivalist Movement*, p. 38.

50. Ibid., p. 39.

51. For a discussion of this phenomenon, see Brigadier A. R. Siddiqi, *The Military in Pakistan: Image and Reality* (Lahore:Vanguard Books, 1996), pp. 9–12.

52. Jalal, *State of Martial Rule*, p. 42.

53. Homer A. Jack, ed., *The Gandhi Reader* (Bloomington: Indiana University Press, 1956), pp. 454–56.

54. *Time*, August 25, 1947 cited in Kux, *Disenchanted Allies*, p. 4.

55. Khan, *United Nations and Kashmir*, p. 62.

56. For more on the British role in Kashmir, see Alastair Lamb, *Kashmir: A Disputed Legacy* (Hertingfordbury, England: Roxford Books, 1991); and Victoria Schofield, *Kashmir in the Crossfire* (New York: I. B. Tauris, 1996).

57. All Pakistani authors on the subject emphasize the existence of support for the All Jammu and Kashmir Muslim Conference led by Yusuf Shah and Ghulam Abbas. Sumit Ganguly, in *Conflict Unending: India-Pakistan Tensions since 1947* (Washington, D.C.: Woodrow Wilson Center Press, 2001), also refers to Kashmiri leader Shaikh Abdullah while recognizing his limited support in some areas.

58. This argument is advanced in Ian Stephens, *Horned Moon* (London: Chatto and Windus, 1954); and in Chaudhri Muhammad Ali, *The Emergence of Pakistan* (New York: Columbia University Press, 1967). For more on Nehru's one-nation ideal, see Josef Korbel, *Danger in Kashmir* (Princeton: Princeton University Press, 1966).

59. M. M. R. Khan, *United Nations and Kashmir*, p. 52. See also Lamb, *Kashmir: A Disputed Legacy*, and Ali, *Emergence of Pakistan*.

60. See Ali, *Emergence of Pakistan*.

61. See Hari Singh's letter to Mountbatten in Verinder Grover, ed., *The Story of Kashmir: Yesterday and Today*, vol. 3 (New Delhi: Deep and Deep Publishing, 1995), p. 108.

62. See, for instance, M. M. R. Khan, *United Nations and Kashmir*, pp. 45–52; Prem Shanker Jha, *Kashmir, 1947: Rival Versions of History* (New York: Oxford University Press, 1996); and Ali, *Emergence of Pakistan*.

63. For a firsthand account of Pakistan's effort to secure Kashmir in 1947–1948, see Major General Akbar Khan (Ret.), *Raiders in Kashmir* (Islamabad: National Book Foundation, 1975).

64. Siddiqi, *Military in Pakistan*, p. 3.

65. Ibid., p. 70.

66. Kux, *United States and Pakistan, 1947–2000,* p. 13.

67. Bourke-White, *Halfway to Freedom,* p. 92.

68. Ibid., p. 93.

69. Ibid.

70. Ibid., pp. 93–94.

71. Liaquat Ali Khan, *Pakistan, the Heart of Asia* (Cambridge: Harvard University Press, 1950), p. 11.

72. Jalal, *State of Martial Rule,* p. 111.

73. Ibid., pp. 112–13. Jalal cites declassified British and U.S. government documents from the period.

74. Hans Morgenthau, *The Impasse of American Foreign Policy* (Chicago: University of Chicago Press, 1962), p. 14.

75. L. A. Khan, *Pakistan, the Heart of Asia,* p. 28.

76. Kux, *United States and Pakistan, 1947–2000,* p. 38.

77. Shirin Tahir-Kheli, *The United States and Pakistan: The Evolution of an Influence Relationship* (New York: Praeger, 1982), p. 3.

78. Ibid.

79. Ibid.

80. U.S. Department of State policy statement on Pakistan, July 1, 1951, cited in Jalal, *State of Martial Rule,* p. 127.

81. See, for example, Governor General Ghulam Mohammed's conversation with Lieutenant Colonel Stephen J. Meade, former U.S. defense attaché to Pakistan, in Kux, *United States and Pakistan, 1947–2000,* p. 55.

82. Compare with Dennis Kux, *United States and Pakistan, 1947–2000,* p. 57.

83. Tahir-Kheli, *United States and Pakistan,* p. 4.

84. See remarks by Secretary of State John Foster Dulles, cited in Tahir-Kheli, *United States and Pakistan,* p. 5.

85. Ayub Khan, *Friends Not Masters* (London and Karachi: Oxford University Press, 1967), pp. 186–91.

86. Lawrence Ziring, *Pakistan in the Twentieth Century* (Karachi: Oxford University Press, 1997), p. 148.

87. Sir Alexander Symon, letter to Sir Gilbert Laithwaite Lintott, September 27, 1958, in Roedad Khan, ed., *The British Papers: Secret and Confidential India, Pakistan, Bangladesh Documents 1958–69* (Karachi: Oxford University Press, 2002), pp. 13–15. A high commission is the diplomatic mission of one Commonwealth country in another; the high commissioner acts as an ambassador.

88. Sir Alexander Symon, telegram to Commonwealth Relations Office, October 9, 1958, Ibid., pp. 37–39.

89. Sir Alexander Symon, letter to Sir Henry Lintott, August 23, 1958, ibid., p. 11.

90. Sir Alexander Symon, letter to Sir Gilbert Laithwaite Lintott, September 27, 1958, ibid., pp. 13–15.

91. Ibid.

92. Sir Alexander Symon, letter to Sir Gilbert Laithwaite Lintott, September 23, 1958, ibid., p. 12.

93. Sir Alexander Symon, letter to Sir Gilbert Laithwaite Lintott, September 27, 1958, ibid., pp. 13–15.

94. Mohammed Ayub Khan, "Pakistan Perspective," *Foreign Affairs*, vol. 38, no. 4, July 1960, p. 547.

95. Ibid., p. 549.

96. Ibid., pp. 555–556.

97. Huseyn Shaheed Suhrawardy, "Political Stability and Democracy in Pakistan," *Foreign Affairs*, vol. 35, no. 3, April 1957, p. 425.

98. Ibid.

99. S. M. Burke, "Pakistan's Foreign Policy—An Historical Analysis" (London: Oxford University Press, 1973) p. 252.

100. A. H. Nayyar and Ahmad Salim, *The Subtle Subversion: The State of Curricula and Textbooks in Pakistan* (Islamabad: Sustainable Development Policy Institute, 2003), p. 3.

101. Altaf Gauhar, *Ayub Khan: Pakistan's First Military Ruler* (Karachi: Oxford University Press, 1996), p. 93.

102. A. Khan, *Friends Not Masters*, pp. 196–97.

103. Ibid.

104. Ibid.

105. Ibid., p. 172.

106. Ibid.

107. Ibid., p. 183.

108. Herbert Feldman, *From Crisis to Crisis: Pakistan 1962–1969* (Karachi: Oxford University Press, 1972), p. 66.

109. Mahmood Ahmad Madani, editor of Jamaat-e-Islami newspaper, *Jasarat*, interview with author, Islamabad, February 20, 1988.

110. Altaf Gauhar, *Ayub Khan: Pakistan's First Military Ruler*, p. 93.

111. Several Islamic scholars—including Maulana Kausar Niazi, the minister for religious affairs from 1973 to 1977—who argued against a woman's

right to be head of state, confirmed in conversations with the author the IB's role in the 1964 fatwa.

112. Herbert Feldman, *From Crisis to Crisis*, p. 73.
113. Kux, *United States and Pakistan, 1947–2000*, p. 56.
114. Herbert Feldman, *From Crisis to Crisis*, p. 123.
115. Compare with Siddiqi, *Pakistan Seeks Security*, p. 64.
116. Ibid. The author of the study was a senior official in the Bureau of National Reconstruction.
117. Ibid., pp. 65–67.
118. Ayub Khan's address to the nation, September 6, 1965, in Rais Ahmad Jafri, ed., *Ayub: Soldier and Statesman* (Lahore: Mohammad Ali Academy, 1966), pp. 138–39.
119. Siddiqi, *Military in Pakistan*, p. 107.
120. See, for example, Major General Tajammul Hussain Malik, *The Story of My Struggle* (Lahore: Jang Publishers, 1991), p. 45. General Malik saw action in 1965 as a battalion commander, and he was retired from the army for fanaticism in 1976 by the army chief of staff, General Zia ul-Haq.
121. Ambassador Walter McConaughy, telegram to the U.S. Department of State, September 6, 1965, in Roedad Khan, ed., *The American Papers: Secret and Confidential India-Pakistan-Bangladesh Documents, 1965–1973* (Karachi: Oxford University Press, 1999), pp. 19–20.
122. U.S. embassy, telegram to the U.S. Department of State, September 8, 1965, ibid., pp. 43–44.

Chapter 2

1. Herbert Feldman, *The End and the Beginning: Pakistan 1969–1971* (Karachi: Oxford University Press, 1975), p. 13.
2. Ibid., p. 11.
3. "Tweedle Khan Takes Over," *Economist*, March 29, 1969.
4. British high commission in Rawalpindi, letter to South Asia Department of the Foreign and Commonwealth Office, London, May 13, 1969, in R. Khan, ed., *British Papers*, p. 915.
5. U.S. consulate, Karachi, memorandum of conversation with Yusuf Haroon, airgram A-109 to U.S. Department of State, June 5, 1970, in R. Khan, ed., *American Papers*, p. 373.
6. See similar remarks by Sindhi politician Pir Pagara described in memorandum of conversation, August 20, 1969, ibid., pp. 280–82.

7. Roedad Khan, "The Role of the Military-Bureaucratic Oligarchy," *Dawn*, August 25, 2001.

8. Siddiqi, *Military in Pakistan*, pp. 163–64.

9. Ibid., pp. 167–68.

10. Feldman, *End and the Beginning*, pp. 46–47.

11. See Hassan Zaheer, *The Separation of East Pakistan* (Karachi: Oxford University Press, 1994), pp. 123–25. See also Feldman, *End and the Beginning*, p. 81.

12. See, for example, a political assessment from the U.S. embassy in Rawalpindi to the U.S. Department of State, February 13, 1970, in R. Khan, ed., *American Papers*, pp. 327–46.

13. Lieutenant General Kamal Matinuddin (Ret.), *Tragedy of Errors: East Pakistan Crisis 1968–1971* (Lahore: Wajidalis, 1994), p. 151.

14. Zaheer, *Separation of East Pakistan*, p. 125.

15. Matinuddin, *Tragedy of Errors*, p. 150.

16. Ibid.

17. U.S. consul general, Dacca, telegram 113 to U.S. Department of State, June 9, 1969, in R. Khan, ed., *American Papers*, p. 274.

18. U.S. ambassador, airgram A-191 to U.S. Department of State, July 3, 1970, in R. Khan, ed., *American Papers*, p. 382.

19. See, for example, Major General Farman Ali Khan, *How Pakistan Got Divided* (Lahore: Jang Publishers, 1992); Major General F. M. Khan, *Pakistan's Crisis in Leadership;* Lieutenant General A. A. K. Niazi, *The Betrayal of East Pakistan* (Karachi: Oxford University Press, 1998); and Matinuddin, *Tragedy of Errors.* Each laments the 1970 election results that created a political crisis. On page 155, the academic General Matinuddin says, "The result of the election put the military junta in a quandary as neither of the two major parties were national in character," and he accuses the successful parties of being "uncompromising, selfish to the extent of breaking up the country if need be." Although General Matinuddin mentions the pre-polling-day manipulation by military authorities, he does not characterize it as wrong.

20. Matinuddin, *Tragedy of Errors*, pp. 75–76.

21. Sherbaz Khan Mazari, *A Journey to Disillusionment* (Karachi: Oxford University Press, 1999), p. 136.

22. Robert Jackson, *South Asian Crisis: India, Pakistan and Bangladesh* (New York: Praeger, 1975), p. 20.

23. "Current Pakistani Scene—Comment," airgram A-610, November 7, 1969, in R. Khan, ed., *American Papers*, pp. 296–97.

24. A. Khan, *Friends Not Masters*, p. 187.

25. Robert Jackson, *South Asian Crisis*, p. 15.

26. Zaheer, *Separation of East Pakistan*, p. 98.

27. *Report on the General Elections Pakistan 1970–71*, vol. 1 (Karachi: Election Commission of Pakistan, 1972).

28. Talukder Maniruzzaman, *The Bangladesh Revolution and Its Aftermath* (Dacca: Bangladesh Books, 1980), p. 102–3.

29. *Report on the General Elections Pakistan 1970–71*, vol. 1.

30. Roedad Khan, *Pakistan: A Dream Gone Sour* (Karachi: Oxford University Press, 1997), p. 57.

31. "President General Agha Mohammed Yahya Khan's address to the Nation," *Dawn*, March 27, 1969.

32. M. M. Ahmed, quoted in Zaheer, *Separation of East Pakistan*, p. 129.

33. Siddiq Salik, *Witness to Surrender* (Karachi: Oxford University Press, 1978), p. 29. At the time, Salik was the military's public relations officer in East Pakistan. The quote is attributed by others to Major General Muhammad Akbar, head of ISI, but was said to have been specifically aimed at Sheikh Mujibur Rahman. See Matinuddin, *Tragedy of Errors*, p. 156.

34. Quoted in Ziring, *Pakistan in the Twentieth Century*, p. 333.

35. See G. W. Choudhury, *The Last Days of United Pakistan* (Bloomington: Indiana University Press, 1975).

36. See, for example, the accounts of Sherbaz Khan Mazari, an anti-Bhutto politician, in *Journey to Disillusionment*, and accounts of General Matinuddin in *Tragedy of Errors*.

37. See Zaheer, *Separation of East Pakistan*, pp. 136–40, for an account of Bhutto and military leaders' coordinating strategy toward Sheikh Mujibur Rahman and the Awami League.

38. Mazari, *Journey to Disillusionment*, p. 169.

39. Feldman, *From Crisis to Crisis*, p. 317.

40. Feldman, *End and the Beginning*, p. 102.

41. Feldman, *From Crisis to Crisis*, p. 250.

42. Maniruzzaman, *Bangladesh Revolution*, pp. 79–80.

43. F. M. Khan, *Pakistan's Crisis in Leadership*, p. 51.

44. Zaheer, *Separation of East Pakistan*, p. 141.

45. Salik, *Witness to Surrender*, p. 53.

46. Ibid., p. 228, app. 3.

47. Ibid., pp. 74–75.

48. "Admiral Ahsan on Events in East Pakistan," telegram 165 from U.S. embassy, Islamabad, to U.S. Department of State, August 17, 1971, in R. Khan, ed., *American Papers*, p. 643.

49. Robert LaPorte Jr., "Pakistan in 1971: The Disintegration of a Nation," *Asian Survey*, vol. 12, no. 2 (February 1972), p. 102, footnote 24.

50. Matinuddin, *Tragedy of Errors*, p. 260.

51. Muntassir Mamoon, *The Vanquished Generals and the Liberation War of Bangladesh* (Dhaka: Somoy Prokashon, 2000), p. 89.

52. Deputy administrator, U.S. Agency for International Development, memorandum, November 5, 1971, in R. Khan, ed., *American Papers*, p. 705.

53. Siddiqi, *Military in Pakistan*, pp. 208–9.

54. Matinuddin, *Tragedy of Errors*, p. 260.

55. Niazi, *Betrayal of East Pakistan*, pp. 45–46. In his memoir, Major General Farman Ali Khan explained that he had just noted down a phrase from the speech of a left-wing leader reported to him over the telephone; see F. A. Khan, *How Pakistan Got Divided*, pp. 187–88. The Hamoodur Rehman Commission, established to inquire into the circumstances of the separation of East Pakistan, absolved Farman Ali Khan of any wrongdoing and accepted his version of events regarding this phrase.

56. Lieutenant General Gul Hassan Khan, *Memoirs* (Karachi: Oxford University Press, 1993), p. 275–76.

57. Kamal Hosain, conversation with author, Istanbul, April 13, 2004.

58. Salik, *Witness to Surrender*, p. 78.

59. Lieutenant General S. G. M. M. Peerzada, quoted in Zaheer, *Separation of East Pakistan*, p. 158.

60. Zaheer, *Separation of East Pakistan*, p. 174.

61. Ibid., p. 323.

62. Siddiqi, *Military in Pakistan*, pp. 204–6.

63. Maniruzzaman, *Bangladesh Revolution*, p. 101.

64. Two more vacancies were created by deaths of members.

65. For a detailed discussion of the by-election process, see Zaheer, *Separation of East Pakistan*, pp. 337–42 and 500–501, notes 25–28.

66. Zaheer, *Separation of East Pakistan*, p. 342.

67. Report of conversation with Zulfikar Ali Bhutto, telegram 730 from U.S. consulate, Karachi, to U.S. Department of State, July 6, 1971, in R. Khan, ed., *American Papers*, p. 619.

68. Matinuddin, *Tragedy of Errors*, p. 247.

69. Niazi, *Betrayal of East Pakistan*, p. 52.

70. Musa Khan Jalalzai, *Sectarianism and Politico-Religious Terrorism in Pakistan* (Lahore: Tarteeb Publishers, 1993), p. 258.

71. Salik, *Witness to Surrender*, p. 105.

72. Niazi, *Betrayal of East Pakistan*, p. 78.

73. Maniruzzaman, *Bangladesh Revolution*, p. 102.
74. Ibid., p. 106, note 41.
75. Jalalzai, *Sectarianism and Politico-Religious Terrorism in Pakistan*, p. 258.
76. See Ashok Raina, *Inside RAW: The Story of India's Secret Service* (New Delhi: Vikas Publishing House, 1981), which details the role of the Indian intelligence agency in the East Pakistan crisis. Pages 53–54 describe how a RAW operative in Dhaka alerted Calcutta of an imminent military crackdown against the Awami League as early as February. Indian intelligence operatives tried to convince Sheikh Mujibur Rahman to leave Dhaka; he refused and relented to allow only the covert evacuation of his party colleagues at the last minute. Most Awami League leaders made their way to India after the military crackdown.
77. Tahir-Kheli, *United States and Pakistan*, p. 31.
78. Ibid.
79. Cited in Kux, *United States and Pakistan, 1947–2000*, pp. 185–86.
80. Ibid., p. 187.
81. Ibid.
82. Ibid., pp. 187–88.
83. For a critical appraisal of U.S. policy at the time, see Christopher Van Hollen, "Tilt Policy Revisited," *Asian Survey*, vol. 20, no. 4 (April 1980), 339–61.
84. Michael Hornsby, "President Yahya Dashes Hopes of Reconciliation," *Times* (London), July 3, 1971.
85. Ambassador Joseph Farland, airgram A-118, July 2, 1971, in R. Khan, ed., *American Papers*, pp. 614–15.
86. Ibid.
87. Zaheer, *Separation of East Pakistan*, p. 296.
88. See, for example, comments by the army chief of staff, General Hamid Khan, reported in telegram 631 from U.S. embassy, Islamabad, to U.S. Department of State, September 10, 1971, in R. Khan, ed., *American Papers*, p. 663.
89. G. H. Khan, *Memoirs*, p. 328.
90. F. A. Khan, *How Pakistan Got Divided*, p. 161.
91. Zaheer, *Separation of East Pakistan*, p. 297.
92. Van Hollen, "Tilt Policy Revisited," p. 360.

Chapter 3

1. Altaf Gauhar, "Four Wars, One Assumption," *Nation*, September 5, 1999.
2. John H. Gill, *An Atlas of the 1971 India-Pakistan War* (Washington: NESA Center for Strategic Studies, 1999), p. 65.

3. Ibid.
4. Robert LaPorte Jr., "Pakistan in 1972: Picking Up the Pieces," *Asian Survey*, vol. 13, no. 2 (February 1973), 187–88.
5. Siddiqi, *Military in Pakistan*, p. 220.
6. Ibid.
7. Ibid., p. 223.
8. Ibid., p. 224.
9. Ibid., p. 222.
10. G. H. Khan, *Memoirs*, pp. 339–41.
11. Mohammad Asghar Khan, *Generals in Politics: Pakistan, 1958–1982* (New Delhi: Vikas Publishing House, 1983), pp. 45–46.
12. G. H. Khan, *Memoirs*, pp. 341–42.
13. R. Khan, *Pakistan: A Dream Gone Sour*, p. 61.
14. G. H. Khan, *Memoirs*, pp. 343–45.
15. Some accounts, especially Shahid Javed Burki, *Pakistan under Bhutto: 1971–1977* (New York: St. Martin's Press, 1980) give credit for arranging the transfer of power to a group of senior military officers led by Lt. Gen. Gul Hassan Khan and the air force commander in chief, Air Marshal Rahim Khan. Lt. Gen. Gul Hassan Khan's account, cited above and published in 1993, confirms that there was no single leader of the revolt and that he himself was not a principal actor in the transfer of power to Bhutto.
16. The text of the proposed speech appears in Herbert Feldman, *End and the Beginning*, pp. 194–201.
17. See Burki, *Pakistan under Bhutto: 1971–1977*, pp. 69–70.
18. G. H. Khan, *Memoirs*, pp. 346–50.
19. Col. Anwar Ahmad, telephone interview with author, August 16, 2004.
20. See Mubashir Hasan, *The Mirage of Power: An Inquiry into the Bhutto Years 1971–1977* (Karachi: Oxford University Press, 2000), pp. 202–8.
21. Shahid Javed Burki and Craig Baxter, "Socio-Economic Indicators of the Peoples Party Vote in Punjab," in William Howard Wriggins, ed., *Pakistan in Transition* (Islamabad: Islamabad University Press, 1975), pp. 161 and 167.
22. Khurshid Hyder, "Pakistan under Bhutto," *Current History*, vol. 63, no. 375 (November 1972), p. 202.
23. Zulfikar Ali Bhutto, interview, *Spectator* (London); reproduced in Z. A. Bhutto, *New Directions* (London: Namara Publications, 1980), p. 103.
24. Ibid.
25. Anwar H. Syed, "Z. A. Bhutto's Self-Characterizations and Pakistani Political Culture," *Asian Survey*, vol. 18, no. 12 (December 1978), p. 1260.

26. Burki, *Pakistan under Bhutto: 1971–1977*, p. 79.

27. See, for example, Mazari, *Journey to Disillusionment*, pp. 228–29.

28. See Khalid Hasan, *Rearview Mirror* (Lahore: Alhamra Publishing, 2002), pp. 11–118, for a sympathetic account of Bhutto's years in power. Khalid Hasan was Zulfikar Ali Bhutto's press secretary.

29. Saeed Shafqat, *Civil-Military Relations in Pakistan: From Zulfikar Ali Bhutto to Benazir Bhutto* (Boulder: Westview Press, 1997), p. 81.

30. Ibid., p. 89.

31. G. H. Khan, *Memoirs*, pp. 410–11.

32. Shafqat, *Civil-Military Relations in Pakistan*, p. 89.

33. LaPorte, "Pakistan in 1972," pp. 187–98.

34. "Conversation with Pres. Bhutto Wednesday Evening Dec. 22," telegram 891 from U.S. embassy, Islamabad, to U.S. Department of State, December 23, 1971, in R. Khan, ed., *American Papers*, p. 766.

35. "GOP [government of Pakistan] Soundings on US Bases, Defense Pact and Arms for Pakistan," telegram from U.S. embassy, Islamabad, to U.S. Department of State, February 17, 1972, ibid., pp. 795–96.

36. "GOP Willingness to Grant U.S. Base Rights," telegram 505 from U.S. embassy, Islamabad, to U.S. Department of State, ibid., p. 797.

37. "President Bhutto's Proposals for Closer Military Collaboration," memorandum from U.S. secretary of state for the president, March 17, 1972, ibid., p. 811.

38. Simla Agreement, July 2, 1972, available at www.kashmir-information.com/LegalDocs/SimlaAgreement.html.

39. Zulfikar Ali Bhutto, *If I Am Assassinated* (New Delhi: Vikas Publishing House, 1979), p. 130.

40. "Secretary's Conversation with Bhutto," telegram 945 from U.S. secretary of state to U.S. embassy, December 18, 1971, in R. Khan, ed., *American Papers*, p. 774.

41. Ibid.

42. Hasan, *Rearview Mirror*, pp. 97–98. He wrote, "What Bhutto had said was, 'If power is to be transferred to the people before a constitutional settlement, then it is only fair that in East Pakistan, it should go to the Awami League and in the West to the Pakistan People's Party, because while the former is the majority party in that wing, we have been returned by the people of this side . . . '"

43. See LaPorte, "Pakistan in 1971," p. 106, note 40.

44. According to Air Marshal Asghar Khan, a secular opposition leader of the time, "Bhutto was not a democrat . . . by temperament or conviction." See M. A. Khan, *Generals in Politics*, p. 48.

45. Mazari, *Journey to Disillusionment*, p. 292.

46. Ibid., pp. 238–44, 250–52, and 271–327, for a detailed account of the political developments in Balochistan and NWFP during this period.

47. Gen. Khalid Mahmud Arif, *Working with Zia: Pakistan's Power Politics, 1977–1988* (Karachi: Oxford University Press, 1995), p. 300.

48. Ibid., p. 306.

49. "Issues and Talking Points—Bhutto Visit," U.S. Department of State, July 1973, in R. Khan, ed., *American Papers*, p. 960.

50. Lt. General Fazle Haq, conversation with author, Islamabad, September 8, 1988.

51. Zulfikar Ali Bhutto, quoted in "Pres. Bhutto on Pakistan Domestic Political Situation," telegram 663 from U.S. embassy, Islamabad, to U.S. Department of State, June 1973, in R. Khan, ed., *American Papers*, p. 917.

52. Bhutto used the term "Napoleonic order" in an interview with *Le Monde*; cited in Richard S. Wheeler, "Pakistan in 1975: The Hydra of Opposition," *Asian Survey*, vol. 16, no. 2 (February 1975), p. 112.

53. Hasan, *Mirage of Power*, p. 277.

54. Ibid., p. 256.

55. Herbert Feldman, "Pakistan in 1974," *Asian Survey*, vol. 15, no. 2 (February 1975), p. 110.

56. On allegations of Kausar Niazi's ties to the IB, see Hasan, *Mirage of Power*, pp. 271–72. Niazi denied these allegations. In several conversations with the author in 1994–1995, Niazi explained that he represented the Islamic socialist wing of the PPP and had sought from the beginning to dilute the influence of "atheists" from the scientific socialist wing of the party.

57. Khalid Hasan, conversation with author, 2004.

58. Feldman, "Pakistan in 1974," p. 111.

59. Ibid.

60. William L. Richter, "The Political Dynamic of Islamic Resurgence in Pakistan," *Asian Survey*, vol. 19, no. 6 (June 1979), p. 550.

61. Waheed-uz-Zaman, editor's note in *Quest for Identity: Proceedings of the First Congress on the History and Culture of Pakistan, University of Islamabad, April 1973* (Islamabad: University of Islamabad Press, 1974), p. i, cited in Richter, "Political Dynamic of Islamic Resurgence in Pakistan," p. 549.

62. Richter, "Political Dynamic of Islamic Resurgence in Pakistan," p. 550.

63. Ibid., p. 549.
64. Anwar H. Syed, "Pakistan in 1976: Business as Usual," *Asian Survey,* vol. 17, no. 2 (February 1977), p. 190.
65. Hasan, *Mirage of Power,* p. 202.
66. Ibid., p. 280.
67. See, for example, Shahid Javed Burki, "Zia's Eleven Years," in Shahid Javed Burki and Craig Baxter, eds., *Pakistan under the Military: Eleven Years of Zia ul-Haq* (Boulder: Westview Press, 1991), pp. 5–8; and Lt. Gen. Faiz Ali Chishti (Ret.), *Betrayals of Another Kind: Islam, Democracy and the Army in Pakistan* (Cincinnati: Asia Publishing House, 1990), pp. 27–28.
68. Bhutto, *If I Am Assassinated,* p. 59.
69. Burki, "Zia's Eleven Years," in Burki and Baxter, eds., *Pakistan under the Military,* p. 6.
70. Hasan, *Rearview Mirror,* p. 13.
71. Lt. Gen. Jahan Dad Khan, *Pakistan Leadership Challenges* (Karachi: Oxford University Press, 1999), p. 158.
72. Syed, "Pakistan in 1976," pp. 183–84.
73. "General Elections [Top Secret]," ISI document for prime minister, October 5, 1976; document provided to author by officer serving in ISI in 1976.
74. "White Paper on Performance of the Bhutto Regime," vol. 3 (Islamabad: Government of Pakistan, 1977), p. 66.
75. See Bhutto, *If I Am Assassinated.*
76. Kux, *United States and Pakistan, 1947–2000,* p. 218.
77. "General Elections [Top Secret]."
78. Ibid., p. 2.
79. Ibid., p. 7.
80. Ibid., p. 8.
81. Ibid., p. 17.
82. Burki, *Pakistan under Bhutto,* p. 195.
83. Kux, *United States and Pakistan, 1947–2000,* p. 228.
84. Marvin G. Weinbaum, "The March 1977 Elections in Pakistan: Where Everyone Lost," *Asian Survey,* vol. 17, no. 7, July 1977, p. 600.
85. Ibid., p. 602.
86. Ibid.
87. Ibid., pp. 612–614
88. Hasan, *Rearview Mirror,* p. 13.
89. "White Paper on the Conduct of the General Elections in March 1977," (Islamabad: Government of Pakistan, 1978); Mazari, *Journey to Disillusion*

ment, pp. 428–38; and M. A. Khan, *Generals in Politics*, pp. 103–11 for the view that Bhutto himself ordered irregularities in the election.

90. Quoted in Stanley Wolpert, *Zulfi Bhutto of Pakistan* (New York: Oxford University Press, 1993), pp. 278–79.

91. Weinbaum, *The March 1977 Elections in Pakistan*, p. 614.

92. Kausar Niazi, *Last Days of Premier Bhutto* (Lahore: Jang Publishers, 1991), p. 44.

93. M. A. Khan, *Generals in Politics*, p. 107.

94. Talbot, *Pakistan: A Modern History*, p. 241.

95. Arif, *Working with Zia*, p. 72.

96. Chishti, *Betrayals of Another Kind*, p. 31.

97. *Pakistan Times*, April 18, 1977, cited in Richter, "Political Dynamic of Islamic Resurgence in Pakistan," p. 552.

98. See Professor Ghafoor Ahmed, *Phir Martial Law Aa Gaya* [And then came martial law] (Lahore: Jang Publishers, 1986); and Niazi, *Last Days of Premier Bhutto*.

99. "General Zia ul-Haq's Address to the Nation on July 5, 1977," in Hasan-Askari Rizvi, *The Military and Politics in Pakistan 1947–86* (Lahore: Progressive Publishers, 1986), pp. 289–93.

100. See Arif, *Working with Zia*, and Chishti, *Betrayals of Another Kind*, for this view.

101. Brigadier Tafazzul Hussain Siddiqi, conversation with author, Rawalpindi, February 19, 1985.

102. Arif, *Working with Zia*, pp. 73–74.

103. Ibid., p. 74.

104. Nawabzada Nasarullah Khan, conversation with author, Karachi, August 8, 1999. Also see Nasarullah Khan's comments in foreword to Khalid Kashmiri, *General Zia Kay Siasi Tazadaat* [The political contradictions of General Zia] (Lahore: Aks-e-Jahan Publications, 1995), pp. 13–16.

105. See Ghafoor Ahmed, *Phir Martial Law Aa Gaya*, and Arif, *Working with Zia*, p. 85.

106. The chief of Jamaat-e-Islami at the time, Mian Tufail Muhammad, claimed after Zia's death that his first contact with Zia ul-Haq came after Bhutto's overthrow. See interview with Mian Tufail Muhammad in Chaudhry Abdul Hameed, ed., *Shaheed-e-Islam* [Martyr for Islam] (Lahore: Maktaba-e-Karvan, 1989), pp. 53–57.

107. Chishti, *Betrayals of Another Kind*, pp. 53–54.

108. Arif, *Working with Zia*, pp. 76–77.

109. Hasan, *Mirage of Power*, pp. 305–6.
110. Arif, *Working with Zia*, p. 79.
111. M. A. Khan, *Generals in Politics*, p. 113.
112. Maulana Kausar Niazi, interview with author, October 16, 1993.
113. Arif, *Working with Zia*, p. 88.
114. Ibid., p. 86.
115. Ibid., pp. 80–81.
116. J. D. Khan, *Pakistan Leadership Challenges*, p. 163.
117. R. Khan, *Pakistan: A Dream Gone Sour*, p. 72.
118. "General Zia ul-Haq's Address to the Nation on July 5, 1977," in Rizvi, *Military and Politics in Pakistan 1947–86*, pp. 289–93.
119. M. A. Khan, *Generals in Politics*, p. 138.
120. Chishti, *Betrayals of Another Kind*, p. 131.
121. Ibid., p. 132.
122. Ibid.
123. Eric A. Nordlinger, "Soldiers in Politics" (Englewood Cliffs, N.J.: Prentice-Hall, 1977) p. 193.
124 Ibid.

Chapter 4

1. See, for example, Burki, "Zia's Eleven Years," in Burki and Baxter, eds., *Pakistan under the Military*, pp. 4–5; Hameed, ed., *Shaheed-e-Islam*; Mumtaz Liaquat, *Zia ul-Haq: Shakhsiat wa Kirdar* [Zia ul-Haq: personality and character] (Islamabad: Islamic Book Foundation, 1991); and Mahmood Javed, *Zia ul-Haq Shaheed: Aik Tajzia* [The martyr Zia ul-Haq: an analysis] (Karachi: Nizami Kitab Ghar, 1988).
2. Aminul Haq, "Mera Azeem Bhai" [My great brother], in Hameed, ed., *Shaheed-e-Islam*, pp. 31–39. Aminul Haq is General Zia ul-Haq's younger brother.
3. Burki, "Zia's Eleven Years," in Burki and Baxter, eds., *Pakistan under the Military*, p. 5.
4. Ibid.
5. Aminul Haq, "Mera Azeem Bhai," p. 32.
6. General K. M. Arif, *Khaki Shadows: Pakistan 1947–1997* (Karachi: Oxford University Press, 2001), p. 143.
7. Ibid.

8. Ibid.

9. Ibid.

10. Zia ul-Haq, interview by Brian Barron, BBC, in *President of Pakistan, General Muhammad Zia ul-Haq, Interviews to Foreign Media*, vol. 1, March–December 1978 (Islamabad: Government of Pakistan, 1980), pp. 29–30.

11. Ibid.

12. Ibid., p. 32.

13. Khalid Kashmiri, *General Zia Kay Siasi Tazadaat*, pp. 72–74.

14. W. Eric Gustafson, "Pakistan 1978: At the Brink Again?" *Asian Survey*, vol. 19, no. 2 (February 1979), pp. 161–62.

15. President Zia ul-Haq's interview to Ian Stephens, January 6, 1979, in *President of Pakistan General Mohammad Zia ul-Haq–Interviews to Foreign Media*, vol. II (Islamabad: Government of Pakistan, undated), pp. 2–6.

16. Ibid., p. 7.

17. Michael T. Kaufman, "Pakistan's Islamic Revival Affects All Aspects of Life," *New York Times*, October 13, 1980.

18. Seyyed Vali Reza Nasr, "Islamic Opposition to the Islamic State: The Jamaat-e-Islami, 1977–88," *International Journal of Middle East Studies*, vol. 25, no. 2 (May 1993), pp. 261–62.

19. For a discussion of the Pakistani judiciary under Zia ul-Haq, see Paula Newberg, *Judging the State* (Cambridge: Cambridge University Press, 1995), pp. 171–99.

20. Ibid., p. 171.

21. Abdul Qayyum, *Zia ul-Haq and I* (Islamabad: ICCTS Publications, 1997), p. 4.

22. Gustafson, "Pakistan 1978: At the Brink Again?" p. 159.

23. William L. Richter and W. Eric Gustafson, "Pakistan 1979: Back to Square One," *Asian Survey*, vol. 20, no. 2 (February 1980), p. 189.

24. See Victoria Schofield, *Bhutto: Trial and Execution* (London: Cassell, 1979); and T. W. Rajaratnam, *A Judiciary in Crisis: The Trial of Zulfikar Ali Bhutto* (Madras: Kaanthalakam, 1988).

25. Zia ul-Haq, conversation with author, Rawalpindi, September 1984.

26. Nasr, "Islamic Opposition to the Islamic State," p. 264.

27. Ibid., pp. 263–64.

28. Ibid., p. 264.

29. Richter and Gustafson, "Pakistan 1979: Back to Square One," p. 190.

30. Stuart Auerbach, "Pakistan's Official Turn to Islam Collides with Tradition," *Washington Post*, September 8, 1980.

31. Ibid.
32. Muhammad Qasim Zaman, "Sectarianism in Pakistan: The Radicalization of Shi'i and Sunni Identities," *Modern Asian Studies*, vol. 32, no. 3 (July 1998), pp. 689–716.
33. W. Eric Gustafson and William L. Richter, "Pakistan in 1980: Weathering the Storm," *Asian Survey*, vol. 21, no. 2 (February 1981), p. 166.
34. Ibid., p. 167.
35. Stephen Philip Cohen and Marvin G. Weinbaum, "Pakistan in 1981: Staying On," *Asian Survey*, vol. 22, no. 2 (February 1981), p. 139.
36. Ibid.
37. Ibid., pp. 140–141.
38. Ibid., p. 140.
39. Ibid.
40. William Claiborne, "Zia's Islam Metes Strict Tolls; Pakistan Slowly Revamps Its Social, Judicial Standards," *Washington Post*, December 6, 1982.
41. Seyyed Vali Reza Nasr, "Military Rule, Islamism and Democracy in Pakistan," *Middle East Journal*, vol. 58, no. 2 (Spring 2004), p. 196.
42. Steven R. Weisman, "Pakistani Women Take Lead in Drive against Islamization," *New York Times*, June 17, 1988.
43. Ibid.
44. Ibid.
45. Auerbach, "Pakistan's Official Turn to Islam Collides with Tradition."
46. Weisman, "Pakistani Women Take Lead in Drive against Islamization."
47. Claiborne, "Zia's Islam Metes Strict Tolls."
48. Ibid.
49. Steven R. Weisman, "The Islamization of Pakistan: Still Moving Slowly and Still Stirring Debate," *New York Times*, August 10, 1986.
50. Weisman, "Pakistani Women Take Lead in Drive against Islamization."
51. For an anthropologist's view of the limited impact of Islamization in Pakistan's countryside, see Richard Kurin, "Islamization in Pakistan: A View from the Countryside," *Asian Survey*, vol. 25, no. 8 (August 1985), pp. 852–62. Kurin observed a village in Pakistan's Punjab province before and after Zia ul-Haq's Islamization measures and concluded that the villagers did not identify with the government's efforts, and they retained their own sense of being Islamic.
52. Charles H. Kennedy, "Islamization and Legal Reform in Pakistan, 1979–1989," *Pacific Affairs*, vol. 63, no. 1 (Spring 1990), p. 62.
53. Ibid.

54. For a study of the selective implementation of the Hudood Ordinance, see Charles H. Kennedy, "Islamization in Pakistan: Implementation of the Hudood Ordinance," *Asian Survey*, vol. 28, no. 3 (March 1988), pp. 307–16. Kennedy points out that Pakistan's superior courts overturned 50 percent of the convictions under the Hudood Ordinance and that the law was primarily used as "an additional avenue for expressing social and familial conflict."

55. Lawrence Ziring, "From Islamic Republic to Islamic State in Pakistan," *Asian Survey*, vol. 24, no. 9 (September 1984), pp. 931–46.

56. Ibid., pp. 941–42.

57. Lawrence Ziring, "Public Policy Dilemmas and Pakistan's Nationality Problem: The Legacy of Zia ul-Haq," *Asian Survey*, vol. 28, no. 8 (August 1988), p. 799.

58. Ibid., p. 797.

59. Ibid.

60. K. K. Aziz, "The Murder of History in Pakistan" (Lahore: Vanguard Books, 1993), p. 1.

61. Ibid., pp. 188–205.

62. Ibid., p. 227.

63. All above references to textbooks are from Aziz, "The Murder of History in Pakistan."

64. Robert LaPorte Jr., "Urban Groups and the Zia Regime," in Craig Baxter, ed., *Zia's Pakistan: Politics and Stability in a Frontline State* (Boulder and London: Westview Press, 1985), pp. 19–20.

65. Cohen and Weinbaum, "Pakistan in 1981: Staying On."

66. Mary Anne Weaver, "Pakistan's Protests Stir Up Ethnic Divisions," *The Christian Science Monitor*, September 2, 1983.

67. Khalid bin Sayeed, "Pakistan in 1983: Internal Stresses More Serious than External Problems," *Asian Survey*, vol. 24, no. 2 (February 1984), p. 223.

68. Ibid., p. 220.

69. William L. Richter, "Pakistan in 1984: Digging In," *Asian Survey*, vol. 25, no. 2 (February 1985), p. 146.

70. Ibid.

71. Ibid., p. 147.

72. William L. Richter, "Pakistan in 1985: Testing Time for the New Order," *Asian Survey*, vol. 26, no. 2 (February 1986), p. 208.

73. Author's interview with General Zia ul-Haq, Rawalpindi, December 14, 1984.

74. Richter, "Pakistan in 1985: Testing Time For the New Order," p. 209.

75. Author's conversation with Mohammed Khan Junejo, Islamabad, March 16, 1988.
76. Unnamed author, "Zia Decrees Islamic Law to Be Supreme in Pakistan," *Los Angeles Times*, June 16, 1988.
77. Dennis Hevesi, "Mohammad Zia ul-Haq: Unbending Commander of Era of Atom and Islam," *New York Times*, August 18, 1988.

Chapter 5

1. Cited in Barnett R. Rubin, *The Search for Peace in Afghanistan* (New Haven: Yale University Press, 1995), p. 3.
2. Arnold Toynbee, *A Study of History*, vol. 8 (London: Oxford University Press, 1954), p. 20.
3. Diego Cordovez and Selig S. Harrison, *Out of Afghanistan: The Inside Story of the Soviet Withdrawal* (New York: Oxford University Press, 1995), p. 14.
4. Siddiqi, *Pakistan Seeks Security*, p. 24.
5. Lord Birdwood, *India and Pakistan: A Continent Decides* (New York: Praeger, 1954), p. 182.
6. Stephens, *Horned Moon*, p. 108
7. Siddiqi, *Pakistan Seeks Security*, pp. 45–46.
8. Ibid., p. 31.
9. Jeffery J. Roberts, *The Origins of Conflict in Afghanistan* (Westport and London: Praeger, 2004), p. 165.
10. John C. Griffiths, *Afghanistan: Key to a Continent* (Boulder: Westview Press, 1981), p. 142.
11. Ibid.
12. Ibid., p. 150.
13. Siddiqi, *Pakistan Seeks Security*, p. 52.
14. Ibid., p. 53.
15. ISI officer, interview with author, Islamabad, January 4, 2004.
16. Siddiqi, *Pakistan Seeks Security*, p. 45.
17. Griffiths, *Afghanistan: Key to a Continent*, p. 174.
18. Ibid., p. 154.
19. Selig S. Harrison, "How the Soviet Union Stumbled into Afghanistan," in Cordovez and Harrison, *Out of Afghanistan*, p. 14.
20. Rafi Raza, *Zulfikar Ali Bhutto and Pakistan 1967–1977* (Karachi: Oxford University Press, 1997), pp. 268–69.

21. For the Pakistani opposition's view of events in Balochistan, see Mazari, *Journey to Disillusionment*; and M. A. Khan, *Generals in Politics*, pp. 70–72.

22. Raza, *Zulfikar Ali Bhutto and Pakistan 1967–1977*, p. 269.

23. M. A. Khan, *Generals in Politics*, p. 71.

24. Harrison, "How the Soviet Union Stumbled into Afghanistan," in Cordovez and Harrison, *Out of Afghanistan*, p. 15.

25. Peter Marsden, *The Taliban: War, Religion and the New Order in Afghanistan* (London: Zed Books, 1998), p. 23.

26. Ibid.

27. Ibid., p. 30.

28. Ralph Braibanti, "Pakistan's Strategic Significance" (keynote address, Fourth Annual Joint Meeting of Pakistani American Congress and U.S. Senate and House of Representatives Caucus on Pakistan, Washington, D.C., June 5, 1996); published in *Defense Journal* (Pakistan), September–October 1998.

29. See, for example, Kux, *United States and Pakistan, 1947–2000*, p. 220.

30. Raja Anwar, *The Tragedy of Afghanistan* (London: Verso Books, 1988), p. 78.

31. Ibid.

32. Arif, *Working with Zia*, p. 306.

33. Kux, *United States and Pakistan, 1947–2000*, p. 220.

34. Harrison, "How the Soviet Union Stumbled into Afghanistan," in Cordovez and Harrison, *Out of Afghanistan*, p. 21.

35. Ibid., pp. 21–22. See also Arif, *Working with Zia*, pp. 301–3.

36. Harrison, "How the Soviet Union Stumbled into Afghanistan," in Cordovez and Harrison, *Out of Afghanistan*, p. 22.

37. Ibid., p. 25; see also Louis Dupree, *The Accidental Coup* (Hanover, N.H.: American Universities Field Staff Reports, 1979), p. 5, and Anwar, *Tragedy of Afghanistan*, pp. 94–96.

38. Arif, *Working with Zia*, p. 307. All subsequent references to the Zia ul-Haq–Taraki conversation are from this source.

39. Ibid.

40. Ibid.

41. Kux, *United States and Pakistan, 1947–2000*, p. 241.

42. Ibid.

43. Robert M. Gates, *From the Shadows* (New York: Simon and Schuster, 1996), pp. 143–44.

44. Ibid, p. 146.

45. Ibid.

46. Ibid.

47. Ibid.
48. Peter Niesewand, "Guerillas Train in Pakistan to Oust Afghan Government," *Washington Post,* February 2, 1979.
49. Gates, *From the Shadows,* p. 146–47.
50. Kux, *United States and Pakistan, 1947–2000,* pp. 242–44.
51. Ibid., pp. 244–45.
52. Lieutenant General Fazle Haq, interview with author, Islamabad, September 8, 1988.
53. Harrison, "How the Soviet Union Stumbled into Afghanistan," in Cordovez and Harrison, *Out of Afghanistan,* p. 29.
54. Ibid., p. 33.
55. Ibid., pp. 42–49; Harrison argues that the Afghan regime was not in danger of collapse and that the Soviet intervention was aimed primarily at getting rid of Amin and replacing him with the more pliant Karmal.
56. President Carter's secretary of state, Cyrus Vance, was among those who had refused to consider the April 1978 coup d'état that brought the PDPA to power as part of the Soviet agenda for the region; see Cyrus Vance, *Hard Choices: Critical Years in America's Foreign Policy* (New York: Simon and Schuster, 1983), p. 384.
57. Lieutenant General Fazle Haq, interview with author, Islamabad, September 8, 1988. See also Haroonur Rashid, *Faateh: Afghanistan Mein Roosi Shikast kay Memaar General Akhtar Abdul Rahman ki Daastaan-e-Hayat* [The victor: life story of the architect of Russian defeat in Afghanistan General Akhtar Abdul Rahman] (Lahore: Jang Publishers, 1997).
58. Brig. Mohammad Yousaf and Major Mark Adkin, *The Bear Trap: Afghanistan's Untold Story* (Lahore: Jang Publishers, 1992), p. 25.
59. Ibid., p. 26.
60. Zbigniew Brzezinski, *Power and Principle* (New York: Farrar Strauss Giroux, 1983), p. 448.
61. Ibid.
62. Gates, *From the Shadows,* p. 148.
63. Brzezinski, *Power and Principle,* p. 449.
64. Gates, *From the Shadows,* p. 148.
65. Ibid., pp. 148–49.
66. Brzezinski, *Power and Principle,* p. 448.
67. William Borders, "Pakistan Dismisses $400 Million in Aid Offered by U.S. as 'Peanuts'," *New York Times,* January 19, 1980.
68. Kux, *United States and Pakistan, 1947–2000,* p. 256–57.

69. Ibid., p. 257.

70. Ibid.

71. For an analysis of Pakistan's economy under Zia ul-Haq, see John Adams, "Pakistan's Economic Performance in the 1980s: Implications for Political Balance," in Baxter, ed., *Zia's Pakistan*, pp. 47–62.

72. Steve Coll, *Ghost Wars* (New York: Penguin Press, 2004), p. 63.

73. Ziaul Islam Ansari, *General Muhammad Zia ul-Haq: Shakhsiat aur Karnamay* [General Muhammad Zia ul-Haq: the man and his achievements] (Lahore: Jang Publishers, 1990), p. 24.

74. Ibid.

75. Ibid.

76. Gates, *From the Shadows*, p. 427.

77. Yousaf and Adkin, *Bear Trap*, p. 28.

78. Author's conversation with Zaim Noorami, minister of state for foreign affairs, Islamabad, February 7, 1988.

79. Kux, *United States and Pakistan, 1947–2000*, p. 287.

80. The author read the ISI paper outlining the planned referendum while he worked as special assistant to Nawaz Sharif, who was then chief minister of Punjab province.

81. Yousaf and Adkin, *Bear Trap*, p. 8.

82. Ibid., p. 12.

Chapter 6

1. Elaine Sciolino, "Pakistan after Zia: Washington Regrets Death of a Solid Ally but Holds Out Hope for Democratic Change," *New York Times*, August 22, 1988.

2. Rasul B. Rais, "Pakistan in 1988: From Command to Conciliation Politics," *Asian Survey*, vol. 29, no. 2 (February 1989), p. 201.

3. Mirza Aslam Beg, remark to author, Rawalpindi, March 29, 1988. General Beg reiterated that view in subsequent conversations with the author.

4. General Mirza Aslam Beg, "Pakistan's Nuclear Programme: A National Security Perspective," *FRIENDS Quarterly Journal*, vol. II, no. 5 (August 1993), pp. 1–25; see also Mushahid Hussain, "Pakistan Responding to Change," *Jane's Defence Weekly* (October 14, 1989), p. 779.

5. Author's conversation with General Beg, Rawalpindi, April 26, 1999.

6. Christina Lamb, *Waiting for Allah: Pakistan's Struggle for Democracy*, (New Delhi: Viking, 1991), p. 42.

7. R. Khan, "Role of the Military-Bureaucratic Oligarchy."

8. Lamb, *Waiting for Allah*, p. 39.

9. Iqbal Akhund, *Trial and Error: The Advent and Eclipse of Benazir Bhutto*, (Karachi: Oxford University Press, 2000).

10. Author's notes of General Hamid Gul's briefing of four newspaper editors, Islamabad, October 3, 1988, and Brigadier Imtiaz Ahmed's briefing to Punjab Chief Minister Nawaz Sharif, Lahore, October 9, 1988. The quote is from Brigadier Ahmed.

11. Lamb, *Waiting for Allah*, pp. 40, 46–47; see also Hasan-Askari Rizvi, "The Legacy of Military Rule in Pakistan," *Survival*, vol. 31, no. 3 (May–June 1989), pp. 255–68.

12. Akhund, *Trial and Error*, p. 55.

13. Richard M. Weintraub, "Bhutto Takes Power in Pakistan; New Premier Vows to Help the Poor," *Washington Post*, December 3, 1988.

14. Lamb, *Waiting for Allah*, p. 39.

15. Ibid.

16. Ibid.

17. Saeed Shafqat, *Civil-Military Relations in Pakistan* (Boulder, Colo.: Westview Press, 1997), pp. 231–232.

18. Ibid., p. 232.

19. Akhund, *Trial and Error*, p. 64.

20. Ibid., p. 65.

21. Ibid.

22. Lawrence Ziring, "Pakistan in 1989: The Politics of Stalemate," *Asian Survey*, vol. 30, no. 2 (February 1990), p. 127.

23. Ibid., p. 129.

24. Ibid., p. 130.

25. Author's notes, Brigadier Imtiaz Ahmed's briefing to Punjab Chief Minister Nawaz Sharif, Lahore, October 9, 1988.

26. Ibid.

27. Lamb, *Waiting for Allah*, p. 36.

28. Ibid., p. 39.

29. Author's interview with Muhammad Salahuddin, editor of *Takbeer*, Karachi, January 26, 1994.

30. Akhund, *Trial and Error*, p. 58; Lamb, *Waiting for Allah*, p. 39.

31. Author's notes of IJI meeting, Lahore, January 16, 1989.

32. Author's notes of meeting with Aslam Azhar, Managing Director Pakistan Television, Lahore, March 2, 1989. Azhar had several newspaper clippings

quoting ulema and religious party leaders accusing Pakistan television of undermining Islamic morality.

33. Author's conversation with Maulana Kausar Niazi, Islamabad, October 6, 1993.

34. Akhund, *Trial and Error*, pp. 59–60.

35. Richard M. Weintraub, "Mob Storms U.S. Facility in Pakistan; At Least Five Killed as Police Open Fire on Moslem Protesters," *Washington Post*, February 13, 1989.

36. Ibid.

37. Akhund, *Trial and Error*, p. 60.

38. Weintraub, "Mob Storms U.S. Facility in Pakistan."

39. Samina Yasmeen, "Democracy in Pakistan: The Third Dismissal," *Asian Survey*, vol. 34, no. 6 (June 1994), p. 573.

40. Ibid.

41. Ziring, *Pakistan in 1989*, p. 127.

42. Ibid., p. 128.

43. Barbara Crossette, "Gandhi Visit to Pakistan: Hopes for a New Era," *New York Times*, December 29, 1988.

44. Akhund, *Trial and Error*, pp. 90–91.

45. Crossette, "Gandhi Visit to Pakistan."

46. Akhund, *Trial and Error*, pp. 92–94.

47. Author's telephone conversation with Benazir Bhutto, November 23, 2004. Bhutto was in Dubai.

48. Akhund, *Trial and Error*, p. 61.

49. Ibid.

50. Lawrence Ziring, "Pakistan in 1990: The Fall of Benazir Bhutto," *Asian Survey*, vol. 31, no. 2 (February 1991), p. 116.

51. Author's telephone conversation with Benazir Bhutto, November 23, 2004. Bhutto was in Dubai.

52. John Kifner, "Bhutto Ousts Powerful Intelligence Chief," *New York Times*, May 26, 1989.

53. Ibid., see Akhund, *Trial and Error*, pp. 149–199, for an insider's account of deliberations over Afghanistan within the Bhutto government.

54. James Rupert, "Pakistan Seen Favoring Afghan Fundamentalists; Anti-Western Rebel Group in Key Position for Future Power," *Washington Post*, March 6, 1989.

55. Kifner, "Bhutto Ousts Powerful Intelligence Chief."

56. Rupert, "Pakistan Seen Favoring Afghan Fundamentalists."

57. Lamb, *Waiting for Allah*, pp. 234–241.

58. Akhund, *Trial and Error*, p. 137.

59. General Khalid Mahmud Arif, *Working with Zia—Pakistan's Power Politics 1977–1988* (Karachi: Oxford University Press, 1995), pp. 319–320.

60. Dennis Kux, *The United States and Pakistan 1947–2000: Disenchanted Allies*, (Washington, D.C.: Woodrow Wilson Center Press, 2001), p. 299.

61. Ibid.

62. Ibid., p. 257.

63. David B. Ottaway, "U.S. Relieves Pakistan of Pledge against Enriching Uranium," *Washington Post*, June 15, 1989.

64. Stephen Engelberg, "U.S. Sees Pakistan Moving on A-Arms," *New York Times*, June 11, 1989.

65. Ottaway, "U.S. Relieves Pakistan of Pledge against Enriching Uranium."

66. Michael R. Gordon, "Nuclear Course Set by Pakistan Worrying U.S.," *New York Times*, October 12, 1989.

67. Dan Oberdorfer, "Pakistan Has No A-Bomb, Bush Informs Congress," *Washington Post*, October 12, 1989.

68. Author's notes of IJI meeting, Lahore, June 28, 1989.

69. Mushahid Hussain, "Pakistan Responding to Change," *Jane's Defence Weekly* (October 14, 1989), p. 779.

70. Ziring, "Pakistan in 1990: The Fall of Benazir Bhutto," p. 114.

71. Author's conversation with Ghulam Ishaq Khan, Islamabad, July 22, 1993.

72. M. M. Ali, "Former Pakistani Army Chief to Launch Political Party," *The Washington Report on Middle East Affairs*, vol. 14, no. 3 (September 1995), p. 13.

73. Yasmeen, "Democracy in Pakistan: The Third Dismissal," pp. 577–578.

74. Steve Coll, "Rifts Appear in U.S.-Pakistani Alliance," *Washington Post*, October 22, 1990.

75. John Bray, "Pakistan at 50: A State in Decline," *International Affairs*, vol. 73, no. 2 (April 1997), p. 324.

76. "Beg Says He Is Not Answerable to Court," *Dawn*, February 25, 1997.

77. Azhar Sohail, *Agencio ki Hukoomat* [Government by Covert Agencies] (Lahore: Vanguard Books, 1993).

78. Ibid.

79. Author's conversations with Nazeer Naji, Islamabad, March 19, 1991; Mustafa Sadiq, Lahore, August 4, 1994; and Mujibur Rahman Shami, Islamabad, September 21, 2001.

80. Ziring, "Pakistan in 1990: The Fall of Benazir Bhutto," p. 119.

81. Ibid.

82. Ibid.

83. *The October 1990 Elections in Pakistan—Report of the International Delegation* (Washington: National Democratic Institute, 1991), pp. iv–ix.

84. Ibid., p. 38–39.

85. Kux, *Disenchanted Allies*, p. 309.

86. Ibid., p. 312.

87. Barbara Crossette, "Bhutto Defeated in Pakistan Vote; President Sees Orderly Transition," *New York Times*, October 25, 1990.

88. Author's conversation with Major Muhammad Aamir, Islamabad, February 16, 1999; and Sohail, *Agencio ki Hukoomat* [Government by Covert Agencies], pp. 73–75.

89. Steve Coll, "Intrigue Permeates Pakistan; A Political Culture of 'Shadow games,'" *Washington Post*, December 15, 1991.

90. Kux, *Disenchanted Allies*, p. 309.

91. Ibid., p. 313.

92. Author's conversations with General Asif Nawaz, Karachi, January 1, 1992; Rawalpindi, March 18, 1992; and Islamabad, April 3, 1992.

93. Ibid.

94. Molly Moore and John Ward Anderson, "Islamic Law—and Zeal—Rise to Challenge Secular Politics in Pakistan," *Washington Post*, October 21, 1991.

95. Steve Coll, "Afghan Plot Leader Flies to Pakistan; Coup Said to Fizzle," *Washington Post*, March 8, 1990; Steve Coll and James Rupert, "Afghan Rebels Reject Offensive; Pakistan, Backed by U.S., Tried to Press Guerillas into Action," *Washington Post*, March 17, 1990.

96. Edward A. Gargan, "Fiscal and Political Forces Move Pakistan to Seek Afghan Peace," *New York Times*, February 16, 1992.

97. Steve Coll, *Ghost Wars*, (New York: Penguin Press, 2004), p. 234.

98. Ibid.

99. Ibid., pp. 235–236.

100. Ibid., p. 237.

101. Ibid., p. 263.

102. Edward A. Gargan, "President of Pakistan Dismisses Premier and Dissolves Parliament," *New York Times*, April 19, 1993.

103. Tahir Amin, "Pakistan in 1993: Some Dramatic Changes," *Asian Survey*, vol. 34, no. 2 (February 1994) p. 192.

104. Gargan, "President of Pakistan Dismisses Premier and Dissolves Parliament."

105. Amin, "Pakistan in 1993: Some Dramatic Changes," pp. 192–194.

106. Ibid., p. 195.

107. Author's conversation with Benazir Bhutto, Islamabad, November 9, 1996.

108. General Asad Durrani headed MI at the time of Bhutto's first dismissal on August 6, 1990, and became chief of the ISI immediately after the change of government in which he had played a key role. In April 1993, General Javed Ashraf Qazi was Director-General MI before his elevation to the post of DG ISI after the dismissal of the Nawaz Sharif administration.

109. Author's conversation with Lieutenant General Javed Ashraf Qazi, President's House, Islamabad, April 26, 1993.

110. Robert LaPorte Jr., "Pakistan in 1995: The Continuing Crises," *Asian Survey*, vol. 36, no. 2 (February 1996), p. 187.

111. Tahir Amin, "Pakistan in 1994: The Politics of Confrontation," *Asian Survey*, vol. 35, no. 2 (February 1995), p. 144.

112. R. Jeffrey Smith, "Clinton Moves to Ease Pakistan Nuclear Curb; New Bill Would Allow Waiver on Aid Cutoff," *Washington Post*, November 25, 1993.

113. Kux, *Disenchanted Allies*, p. 327.

114. Ibid.

115. David Johnston, "World Trade Center Suspect, One of FBI's Most Wanted, Is Captured in Pakistan," *New York Times*, February 12, 1995.

116. Kux, *Disenchanted Allies*, p. 330.

117. Ibid., p. 333.

118. Dana Priest, "U.S., Pakistan to Renew Talks; Perry Vows to Improve Military Relations despite Congressional Ban," *Washington Post*, January 11, 1995.

119. Author's interviews with ISI officials, Islamabad, October 22, 1994; Rawalpindi, January 9, 2001; and Islamabad, August 5, 2003.

120. Author's conversation with Benazir Bhutto, Islamabad, February 2, 1994.

121. Molly Moore, "The Battle of the Bhuttos Threatens to Split Ruling Party in Pakistan," *Washington Post*, February 1, 1994.

122. Amin, "Pakistan in 1994: The Politics of Confrontation," p. 141.

123. Robert LaPorte Jr., "Pakistan in 1996: Starting Over Again," *Asian Survey*, vol. 37, no. 2 (February 1997), p. 120.

124. Hasan-Askari Rizvi, "Civil-Military Relations in Contemporary Pakistan," *Survival*, vol. 40, no. 2 (Summer 1998), p. 101.

125. Rais Ahmad Khan, "Pakistan in 1992: Waiting for Change," *Asian Survey*, vol. 33, no. 2 (February 1993), p. 131.

126. Amin, "Pakistan in 1994: The Politics of Confrontation," pp. 143–144.

127. LaPorte, "Pakistan in 1995: The Continuing Crises," pp. 182–183.
128. Author's conversation with Benazir Bhutto, Washington, D.C., March 5, 2005.
129. Amin, "Pakistan in 1994: The Politics of Confrontation," p. 144.
130. Aamer Ahmed Khan, "Kashmir Chalo" [Let's Go to Kashmir], *The Herald* (November 1994), p. 30.
131. John Ward Anderson and Kamran Khan, "Pakistan Shelters Islamic Radicals; Militant Groups Train Warriors in Camps Near Afghan Border," *Washington Post*, March 8, 1995.
132. John F. Burns, "Terror Network Traced to Pakistan," *New York Times*, March 20, 1995.
133. Ibid.
134. Staff Correspondent, "India Accused of Tricks to Malign Militants," *Dawn*, August 19, 1995.
135. Author's telephone conversation with Benazir Bhutto, November 23, 2004. Bhutto was in Dubai.
136. Author's interviews with ISI officials, Islamabad, August 5, 2003; Karachi, January 3, 2004.
137. Author's telephone conversation with Benazir Bhutto, November 23, 2004. Bhutto was in Dubai.
138. Amin, "Pakistan in 1994: The Politics of Confrontation," p. 142.
139. Unidentified author, "Karachi's best known social worker flees Pakistan in fear for life," *Deutsche Presse-Agentur* (DPA), December 8, 1994; Staff Reporter, "Edhi Flies to London," *Daily Jang*, December 9, 1994.
140. Zaffar Abbas, "Turban Guerillas," *The Herald* (November 1994), pp. 45–49.
141. Amin, "Pakistan in 1994: The Politics of Confrontation," p. 143.
142. LaPorte, "Pakistan in 1995: The Continuing Crises," p. 184.
143. Ibid.
144. Kamran Khan, "Fundamentalist Coup Plot Reported in Pakistan," *Washington Post*, October 16, 1995.
145. LaPorte Jr., "Pakistan in 1995: The Continuing Crises," p. 184.
146. Coll, *Ghost Wars*, p. 283.
147. Ahmed Rashid, *Taliban*, (New Haven: Yale University Press, 2000), p. 22.
148. Ibid.
149. Ibid., p. 26.
150. Ibid., p. 27.

151. Kamal Matinuddin, *The Taliban Phenomenon: Afghanistan 1994–1997* (Karachi: Oxford University Press, 2001).

152. Imtiaz Gul, *The Unholy Nexus: Pak-Afghan Relations under the Taliban*, (Lahore: Vanguard Books, 2002).

153. Coll, *Ghost Wars*, p. 293.

154. Rashid, *Taliban*, p. 45.

155. John F. Burns, "Pakistan Shifting Stance on Hard-Line Afghans," *New York Times*, March 27, 1996.

156. Ibid.

157. LaPorte, "Pakistan in 1996: Starting Over Again," p. 119.

158. Ibid., p. 120.

159. Kamran Khan, "Bhutto Out as Premier in Pakistan; President Charges Corruption, Dissolves National Assembly," *Washington Post*, November 5, 1996.

160. Author's telephone conversation with Benazir Bhutto, November 23, 2004. Bhutto was in Dubai.

161. LaPorte, "Pakistan in 1996: Starting Over Again," p. 121.

162. Ibid.

163. The 9/11 Commission Report, p. 124.

164. Susan Berfield and Shahid-ur-Rehman, "Who's in Charge Here? Political Chaos Raises Doubts about the Election," *Asiaweek*, January 17, 1997.

165. Ibid.

166. John F. Burns, "Pakistan's Corruption Drive Falters, Creating Political Openings," *New York Times*, December 25, 1996.

167. Ibid.

168. Berfield and Shahid-ur-Rehman, "Who's in Charge Here?"

169. John F. Burns, "Bhutto Foe, a Cricket Idol, Lashes Out at the 'Thievery in Her Heart,'" *New York Times*, November 9, 1996.

170. Author's interviews with ISI officials, Islamabad, August 5, 2003; Karachi, January 3, 2004.

171. Anwar H. Syed, "Pakistan in 1997: Nawaz Sharif's Second Chance to Govern," *Asian Survey*, vol. 38, no. 2 (February 1998), p. 117.

172. Ibid.

173. John F. Burns, "Pakistan Acts to Cut Power of President," *New York Times*, April 2, 1997.

174. Syed, "Pakistan in 1997: Nawaz Sharif's Second Chance to Govern," p. 119.

175. Author's conversation with Farooq Leghari, Islamabad, March 8, 1998.

176. John F. Burns, "Army Takeover Feared as Pakistan Leaders Act to Bolster Power," *New York Times*, November 2, 1997.

177. Reuters, "Pakistan's Premier Is Blamed for Unrest," *New York Times*, November 30, 1997.

178. Syed, "Pakistan in 1997: Nawaz Sharif's Second Chance to Govern," p. 120.

179. Ibid., p. 118.

180. Hasan-Askari Rizvi, "Pakistan in 1998: The Polity under Pressure," *Asian Survey*, vol. 39, no. 1 (January–February 1999), p. 180.

181. Ibid.

182. Syed, "Pakistan in 1997: Nawaz Sharif's Second Chance to Govern," p. 124.

183. John F. Burns, "India Sets 3 Nuclear Blasts, Defying a Worldwide Ban; Tests Bring a Sharp Outcry," *New York Times*, May 12, 1998; "India Carries Out 2 More Atom Tests despite Sanctions," *New York Times*, May 14, 1998.

184. Dan Balz, "U.S. Urges Pakistan to Forgo Tests; Clinton Please Issued as Nation Seems Set on Nuclear Exercise," *Washington Post*, May 18, 1998.

185. John Kifner, "Nuclear Anxiety: In Pakistan; Complex Pressures, Dominated by Islam, Led to Testing," *New York Times*, June 1, 1998.

186. John F. Harris and Thomas W. Lippman, "Clinton Criticizes Tests by Pakistan; U.S. Responds Quickly, Announces Sanctions," *Washington Post*, May 29, 1998.

187. John Ward Anderson and Kamran Khan, "We Are a Nuclear Power; Pakistan Declares Intention to Use Arms in Self-Defense," *Washington Post*, May 30, 1998.

188. Bruce Riedel, "American Diplomacy and the 1999 Kargil Summit at Blair House" (Philadelphia: Center for the Advanced Study of India, 2002), available at www.sas.upenn.edu/casi.

189. Ibid.

190. Sartaj Aziz, "Why Foreign Currency Accounts Were Frozen," *Dawn*, August 5, 1998.

191. Eric Schmitt, "Senate Votes to Lift Most Remaining India-Pakistan Penalties," *New York Times*, July 16, 1998; Thomas W. Lippman, "U.S. Lifts Sanctions on India, Pakistan; Aim Is to Reward, Encourage Nuclear Curbs," *Washington Post*, November 7, 1998.

192. Rizvi, "Pakistan in 1998: The Polity under Pressure," p. 181.

193. Kamran Khan, "PM's Bolt from the Blue Actions Cause Army's NSC Move," *The News* (Lahore), October 7, 1998.

194. Rizvi, "Pakistan in 1998: The Polity under Pressure," p. 183.

195. Author's conversation with Hamid Asghar Kidwai, Karachi, August 9, 2001.

196. Rizvi, "Pakistan in 1998: The Polity under Pressure," p. 183.

197. Ibid.

198. John F. Burns, "India and Pakistan Hold First Meeting Since A-Tests," *New York Times*, July 30, 1998.

199. Unnamed Author, "India, Pakistan Agree on Bus Service," *Washington Post*, November 14, 1998.

200. Kenneth J. Cooper, "India, Pakistan Kindle Hope for Peace; Leaders Meet Near Border after Symbolic Bus Trip, Pledge to Resolve Disputes," *Washington Post*, February 21, 1999.

201. Ibid.

202. Ibid.

203. Barry Bearak, "India Leader Pays Visit to Pakistan," *New York Times*, February 21, 1999.

204. Cooper, "India, Pakistan Kindle Hope for Peace."

205. Author's conversation with MI official, Rawalpindi, September 14, 1999; author's interview with ISI official, Islamabad, August 5, 2003. Urdu daily *Khabrain* reported Qazi Hussain Ahmed's contacts with Military Intelligence at the time and even suggested that MI Chief Major General Ehsan ul-Haq had asked Jamaat-e-Islami to organize the protests against Vajpayee.

206. Riedel, "American Diplomacy and the 1999 Kargil Summit at Blair House."

207. Shaukat Qadir, "An Analysis of the Kargil Crisis 1999," *RUSI Journal* (April 2002), p. 24.

208. Ibid., pp. 25–26.

209. Ibid., p. 26.

210. Ibid.

211. Ibid., p. 27.

212. Riedel, "American Diplomacy and the 1999 Kargil Summit at Blair House."

213. Qadir, "An Analysis of the Kargil Crisis 1999," p. 27.

214. Author's conversation with MI official, Rawalpindi, February 7, 2002; author's interview with ISI official, Islamabad, August 5, 2003.

215. Qadir, "An Analysis of the Kargil Crisis 1999," p. 29.

216. Riedel, "American Diplomacy and the 1999 Kargil Summit at Blair House."

217. Ibid.

218. Qadir, "An Analysis of the Kargil Crisis 1999," p. 29.

219. Ibid.

220. Reuters, "40,000 Reported at Pakistan Opposition Rally," *Washington Post*, September 2, 1999.

221. Pamela Constable, "In Pakistan, Hold on Power Grows Tenuous; Prime Minister Weathers Economic Woes, Army Dissent, Foreign Demands," *Washington Post*, October 10, 1999.

222. Ibid.

223. Author's conversation with Brigadier (later Major General) Rashid Qureshi, Rawalpindi, October 12, 1999.

224. Kamran Khan, "Army Stages Coup in Pakistan; Troops Arrest Prime Minister, Seize Buildings after Firing of General," *Washington Post*, October 13, 1999.

225. Barry Bearak, "Ousted Leader in Pakistan Appears in Public for Trial," *New York Times*, November 20, 1999.

226. Pamela Constable and Kamran Khan, "New Pakistan regime Seen as Moderate; Less Aggressive Policy on India Seems Likely," *Washington Post*, October 17, 1999.

227. "Bush Triggers Row over Pakistan Coup," *BBC News*, November 5, 1999.

228. Ibid.

229. Richard N. Haass, "Pakistan: Democracy Is Not Everything," *IntellectualCapital.com*, November 11, 1999.

230. Tom Clancy and Tony Zinni, *Battle Ready*, (New York: Grosset and Dunlap, 2004), p. 349.

231. Ibid.

232. Tommy Franks, *American Soldier*, (New York: HarperCollins, 2004), p. 214.

233. Ibid., p. 227.

234. Ibid., p. 228.

235. Hasan-Askari Rizvi, "Civil-Military Relations in Contemporary Pakistan," *Survival*, vol. 40, no. 2 (Summer 1998), p. 98.

236. Ian Talbot, "Pakistan in 2002: Democracy, Terrorism and Brinkmanship," *Asian Survey*, vol. 43, no. 1 (January–February 2003), p. 202.

237. Ibid.

238. Ibid., p. 204.

239. Ibid., p. 206.

Chapter 7

1. "Transcript of General Pervez Musharraf's Briefing for Newspaper Editors," *Daily Khabrain*, Islamabad, February 6, 2004.

2. General Jehangir Karamat, ambassador of Pakistan to the United States (speech, Brookings Institution, December 15, 2004). See "Policy of Dialogue 'Irreversible': A Major Strategic Reorientation: Karamat," *Dawn*, December 17, 2004.
3. "President's Address to the Nation, September 19, 2001," Government of Pakistan, available at www.infopak.gov.pk/President_Addresses/presidential_addresses_index.htm.
4. Rizvi, "Civil-Military Relations in Contemporary Pakistan," p. 99.
5. Stephen P. Cohen explains that the Pakistan army's technical and professional competence during the 1950s and 1960s was attained with U.S. help; see Cohen, *Pakistan Army*, p. 103. Despite the inconstancy of U.S.-Pakistan relations, the Pakistan army continues to judge its military effectiveness on the basis of availability of U.S. military equipment.
6. General Zia ul-Haq, interviews with author, Rawalpindi, August 4, 1983, and Islamabad, July 29, 1988. Zia made similar remarks in other interviews with Pakistani and Indian journalists.
7. J. N. Dixit, *India-Pakistan: In War and Peace* (London: Routledge, 2002), p. 241.
8. Ibid., p. 242.
9. Ibid., p. 241.
10. Lieutenant Col. Javed Hassan, *India: A Study in Profile* (Rawalpindi: Services Book Club, 1990), p. 228.
11. General Zia ul-Haq, interview with author, Islamabad, July 29, 1988.
12. Yousaf and Adkin, *Bear Trap*, p. 26.
13. Rashid, *Faateh*, p. 157.
14. Major General M. Amin Khan Burki, foreword to Hassan, *India: A Study in Profile*, p. ii.
15. Hassan, *India: A Study in Profile*, p. 51.
16. Ibid., p. 209.
17. Ibid., p. 111.
18. Ibid., p. 139.
19. Ibid., pp. 125–28.
20. Lieutenant General Hamid Gul, who served as director general of ISI from 1987 to 1989, referred in several conversations with the author to an operational plan to encourage the centrifugal tendencies in India that existed in 1984–1987, when he served as director general of Military Intelligence.
21. Senior ISI official, interview with author, Islamabad, August 5, 2003.
22. Ibid.

23. Dixit, *India-Pakistan: In War and Peace*, p. 245.

24. Rashid, *Faateh*, p. 162.

25. Ibid.

26. "Pakistan Is Not Involved" (interview with Zia ul-Haq), *India Today*, July 15, 1984, p. 68.

27. "Patterns of Global Terrorism 1991" (Washington, D.C.: U.S. Department of State, 1992), South Asia section.

28. Author's interviews with ISI officials, Islamabad, October 22, 1994; Rawalpindi, January 9, 2001; and Islamabad, August 5, 2003. See also Rashid, *Faateh*, pp. 162–63.

29. Spokespersons for Jamaat-e-Islami and JKLF, conversations with author, 1994–1995; also see Mohammad Amir Rana, *Jihad-e-Kashmir wa Afghanistan* [Jihad in Kashmir and Afghanistan] (Lahore: Mashal Books, 2002), pp. 19–20.

30. Schofield, *Kashmir in the Crossfire*, p. 236. For a narrative of the events leading up to the insurgency as well as its consequences, see Sumit Ganguly, *The Crisis in Kashmir: Portents of War, Hopes of Peace* (New York: Cambridge University Press, 1997), chap. 5.

31. Anwar H. Syed, "The Pakistan Peoples Party and the Punjab: National Assembly Elections 1988 and 1990," *Asian Survey*, vol. 31, no. 7 (July 1991), p. 592.

32. Rana, *Jihad-e-Kashmir wa Afghanistan*, p. 18.

33. See Christina Lamb, *Waiting for Allah, Pakistan's Struggle for Democracy* (New Delhi: Viking, 1991), p. 47; and Iqbal Akhund, *Trial and Error, The Advent and Eclipse of Benazir Bhutto* (Karachi: Oxford University Press, 2000), chaps. 4 and 5, for details of the limits on Bhutto's power set by President Ishaq Khan and General Beg.

34. Benazir Bhutto, telephone conversation with author, November 23, 2004. Bhutto was in Dubai.

35. Ibid.

36. Akhund, *Trial and Error*, p. 208.

37. Ibid., pp. 209–10.

38. Ibid., p. 213.

39. Kux, *United States and Pakistan, 1947–2000*, p. 311.

40. Personal diary of author, written during 1990 election campaign when he served as spokesperson for interim prime minister Ghulam Mustafa Jatoi and worked with Nawaz Sharif.

41. See Azhar Sohail, *Agencio ki Hukoomat* [Government by covert agencies] (Lahore: Vanguard Books, 1993), pp. 37–49.

42. For excerpts from the filings by General Beg and General Durrani before Pakistan's Supreme Court, see Ardeshir Cowasjee, "We Never Learn from History," *Dawn*, August 11 and August 18, 2002; see also "Beg Says He Is Not Answerable to Court," *Dawn*, February 25, 1997.

43. Kux, *United States and Pakistan, 1947–2000*, p. 312.

44. Khurshid Ahmed, "New World Order: Daaway aur Haqaiq" [New world order: claims and reality], *Tarjuman-al-Quran*, October 1991.

45. Ibid.

46. The Pressler Amendment, named after Sen. Larry Pressler (R-S.D.), enabled aid to Pakistan provided the president certified that Pakistan did not possess a nuclear explosive device. The Pressler Amendment modified provisions of the Symington and Glenn amendments, which forbade aid to countries pursuing nuclear weapons programs.

47. "Pakistani Quoted as Citing Nuclear Test in 1987 (Reuters)," *New York Times*, July 25, 1993.

48. Kux, *United States and Pakistan, 1947–2000*, p. 310.

49. Ibid.

50. Cited in Khalid bin Sayeed, *Western Dominance and Political Islam: Challenge and Response* (Albany: State University of New York Press, 1995), p. 106.

51. Kux, *United States and Pakistan, 1947–2000*, p. 311.

52. Kuldip Nayar, "'We Have the A-bomb,' Says Pakistan's Dr. Strangelove," *Observer* (London), March 1, 1987.

53. Ibid.

54. Dr. S. M. Rahman, who served as secretary general of General Beg's think tank, described A. Q. Khan's interview with Kuldip Nayar as "a brilliant psychological maneuver" that helped avoid "a fourth round of war [with India] under the smokescreen of Brasstacks."

55. Mushahid Hussain, conversation with author, Islamabad, November 28, 1990.

56. Robert Oakley, former ambassador of the United States to Pakistan, conversation with author, Washington, D.C., August 31, 2004.

57. Two former lieutenant generals, interviews with author, Rawalpindi, March 24, 2002, and August 6, 2003.

58. Ibid.

59. Ibid., p. 308.

60. Ibid., p. 309.

61. Ibid., pp. 308–9 and p. 318.

62. Brigadier General John D. Howard, U.S. defense representative, Islamabad, "Security Assistance Program under Pressler Amendment Suspension," information paper, February 6, 1991 (in author's possession).

63. Kux, *United States and Pakistan, 1947–2000*, p. 313.

64. Ahmed Rashid, *Taliban: Militant Islam, Oil, and Fundamentalism in Central Asia* (New Haven: Yale University Press, 2000), pp. 186–87.

65. Sati Sahni, *Kashmir Underground* (New Delhi: Har-Anand Publications, 1999), p. 37.

66. Ibid.

67. ISI official, interview with author, Islamabad, August 5, 2003.

68. Ibid. Also, ISI officials, interviews with author, Islamabad, October 22, 1994, and Rawalpindi, January 9, 2001.

69. Rana, *Jihad-e-Kashmir wa Afghanistan*, p. 20.

70. Although Muslims constitute a majority in the state of Jammu and Kashmir, Hindus have lived there for centuries and are a majority within the state's Jammu province. The Hindu Pandit community, indigenous to the predominantly Muslim Kashmir valley, has been targeted by insurgents since 1991 in an effort to force them out of the region. Most Pandits have left the valley to become refugees in either Jammu or other parts of India. The communal cleansing has been conducted to create purely Muslim regions within Kashmir in case an international settlement for Jammu and Kashmir requires the state's partition along communal lines. By most accounts, including those by Pakistani, Kashmiri, and Indian authors, the expulsion of Kashmiri Hindus has been conducted by radical Islamist groups backed by the ISI.

71. ISI officials, interview with author, Islamabad, October 22, 1994; Rawalpindi, January 9, 2001; and Islamabad, August 5, 2003. Also, spokespersons for Jamaat-e-Islami and JKLF, conversations with author, 1994–1995.

72. *India: Torture, Rape and Deaths in Custody* (New York: Amnesty International, 1992).

73. Lieutenant General Javed Nasir, complaint no. 107 before the Anti-Terrorist Court, Lahore, October 23, 2002. Lieutenant General Nasir declared his affiliation with the Tableeghi Jamaat in a complaint he filed against the Jang group of newspapers.

74. Ibid.

75. Ibid.

76. Kux, *United States and Pakistan, 1947–2000*, p. 299.

77. Ibid.

78. Author's notes taken at meetings at prime minister's secretariat; author's personal diary entries from September 1, 1991, to May 15, 1992.

79. Ibid.

80. Secretary of State James A. Baker III, letter to Prime Minister Nawaz Sharif, May 10, 1992 (in author's possession).

81. "Ambassador Nicholas Platt's Talking Points for Meeting with Prime Minister Sharif," May 1992 (in author's possession).

82. Author's notes of meeting at the prime minister's house, May 18, 1992.

83. Ibid.

84. James Rupert, "Pakistan Sets Crackdown on Islamic Extremists; U.S. Had Expressed Concern about Terrorism," *Washington Post*, April 2, 1993.

85. Edward A. Gargan, "Radical Arabs Use Pakistan as Base for Holy War," *New York Times*, April 2, 1993.

86. Rupert, "Pakistan Sets Crackdown on Islamic Extremists."

87. Douglas Jehl, "Pakistan Is Facing Terrorist Listing," *New York Times*, April 25, 1993.

88. Kux, "Disenchanted Allies," p. 322.

89. Aamer Ahmed Khan, "Kashmir Chalo" [Let's go to Kashmir], *The Herald* (November 1994), pp. 27–35.

90. Unnamed author, "Charar Sharif kay Hero Must Gul ka Shandaar Kher Maqdam" [Hero of Charar Sharif Must Gul receives grand welcome], *Khabrain* (July 31, 1995).

91. John F. Burns, "Pakistan a Asks for U.S. Help in Crackdown on Militants," *New York Times*, March 22, 1995.

92. Ibid.

93. Staff Reporter, "Bharat kay Khilaf Elan-e-jihad Kiya Jaye –Qazi Hussain" [Qazi Hussain asks for declaration of jihad against India], *Khabrain* (August 5, 1995).

94. Ibid.

95. Zaffar Abbas, "Who's Who of Kashmir Militancy," *The Herald* (August 2000), p. 30.

96. Associated Press of Pakistan (APP), "Peace to Be Maintained During Muharram," *Business Recorder* (April 18, 1998).

97. Kamran Khan and Pamela Constable, "Pakistanis Reportedly Killed in Raids," *Washington Post*, August 22, 1998; Pamela Constable, "U.S. Strike Is Blow to Pakistan's Rulers," *Washington Post*, August 26, 1998.

98. Stephen Cohen, *The Pakistan Army*, (Berkeley: University of California Press, 1984), p. 131.

99. Maulana Masood Azhar, "Guardians of Deen [Faith] and Country," available at www.dalitstan.org/mughalstan/mujahid/azhar005.html.

100. Pamela Constable, "Afghan Hijack Drama Ends Peacefully; Gunmen Free Captives after India Releases Islamic Militants," *Washington Post*, January 1, 2000.

101. Steve Levine, "Killing of Pearl Fit into Web of Radical Islam in Pakistan," *Wall Street Journal*, January 23, 2003.

102. Abbas, "Who's Who of Kashmir Militancy," pp. 29–31.

103. Unnamed Author, "Al-Badr Mujahideen Fighters Reportedly Kill 12 Indian Troops in Ambush," *Daily Ausaf*, January 1, 2001.

104. Author's conversation with Major General Rashid Qureshi, Director General, Inter-Services Public Relations, Rawalpindi, December 31, 2000.

105. "Musharraf: Here's What I'll Do."

106. Office of the White House Press Secretary, "Transcript: Bush, Musharraf Pledge Mutual Support in Anti-Terror Effort," November 10, 2001.

107. Serge Schmemann and Patrick E. Tyler, "Pakistan Leader Seeks Gestures for Backing U.S.," *New York Times*, November 10, 2001.

108. Tommy Franks, *American Soldier*, (New York: Harper Collins, 2004), p. 256.

109. Ibid., p. 273.

110. Celia Dugger, "India Shells Kashmir Area, Imperiling Delicate Balance," *New York Times*, October 16, 2001.

111. Ibid.

112. John F. Burns, "Pakistan Moves against Groups Named by India," *New York Times*, December 29, 2001.

113. Ibid.

114. John F. Burns, "Pakistan Is Reported to Have Arrested Militant Leader," *New York Times*, December 31, 2001.

115. Celia W. Dugger, "Leaders of India and Pakistan Share a Stage, Not a Solution," *New York Times*, January 7, 2002.

116. Somini Sengupta, "Pakistan May Be Unable to Calm Kashmir," *New York Times*, January 2, 2002.

117. Steve Coll, "Excerpts from President General Pervez Musharraf's Interview," *Washington Post*, May 25, 2002.

118. Michael R. Gordon, "New Confidence U.S. Has al Qaeda Leader," *New York Times*, April 1, 2002.

119. Coll, "Excerpts from President General Pervez Musharraf's Interview."

120. Ibid.

121. Celia W. Dugger with Howard French, "To the Drums of War, India Expels Pakistan Ambassador," *New York Times*, May 19, 2002.

122. Howard W. French, "Pakistan Seeks Monitors to Cool the Simmering Crisis in Kashmir," *New York Times*, May 21, 2002.

123. David Rohde, "India Renews Call for U.S. to Declare Pakistan a Terrorist State," *New York Times*, July 17, 2002.

124. Amy Waldman, "U.S. Presses to Keep India-Pakistan Peace," *New York Times*, August 23, 2002.

125. Paul Watson, "A Revolving Door for Pakistan's Militants," *Los Angeles Times*, November 17, 2002.

126. John Lancaster and Kamran Khan, "Extremist Groups Renew Activity in Pakistan," *Washington Post*, February 8, 2003.

127. David Johnston with Douglas Frantz, "Arrests Bring Hope in Hunt for Al-Qaeda," *New York Times*, September 15, 2002.

128. Erik Eckholm, "Pakistanis Arrest Qaeda Figure Seen as Planner of 9/11," *New York Times*, March 2, 2003.

129. James Dao, "Terror Aid from Pakistan Concerns Senators," *New York Times*, February 13, 2003.

130. David Rohde, "Pakistan President Narrowly Escapes Assassin's Bomb," *New York Times*, December 15, 2003; Salman Masood, "Pakistani Leader Escapes Attempt at Assassination," *New York Times*, December 26, 2003.

131. Author's interview with ISI official, Islamabad, January 5, 2004.

132. Paul Watson and Mubashir Zaidi, "Militant Flourishes in Plain Sight; Despite Being Banned by Pakistan, Extremist Leader Fazlur Rehman Khalil, Who Has Ties to Al-Qaeda, Openly Runs His Anti-US Group," *Los Angeles Times*, January 25, 2004.

133. Mubashir Zaidi's e-mail to author, dated January 29, 2004.

134. Staff Reporter, "Militant Group's Chief Arrested," *Dawn*, August 9, 2004.

135. Mohammad Imran, "Maulana Khalil Freed after Seven Months in Jail," *Daily Times* (Pakistan), December 19, 2004.

136. "English Rendering of President General Pervez Musharraf's Address to the Nation."

137. Tara Kartha, "Pakistan and the Taliban: Flux in an Old Relationship?" *Strategic Analysis*, vol. 24, no. 7 (October 2000); International Centre for Peace Initiatives, *The Future of Pakistan* (Mumbai, 2002), p. 63.

138. Carlotta Gall, "Pakistan Lets Taliban Train, Prisoner Says," *New York Times*, August 4, 2004.

139. Somini Sengupta, "Pakistan and India Show New Signs of Reconciliation," *New York Times*, April 17, 2005.
140. Gregg Zoroya, "Pakistanis May Be Near Al-Qaeda No. 2," *USA Today*, March 18, 2004.
141. Sonni Efron, "Bush Lauds the Efforts of Pakistani Ally," *Los Angeles Times*, December 5, 2004.
142. Anne Gearen, "Pakistan Has Come a Long Way," *Associated Press*, March 17, 2005.
143. William C. Rempel and Douglas Frantz, "Global Nuclear Inquiry Stalls; Authorities Fear That the Extent of a Pakistani Scientist's Proliferation Ring Remains Unknown and That It Will Resume Work if Pressures Ease," *Los Angeles Times*, December 5, 2004.

Index

About the Author

Husain Haqqani is a visiting scholar at the Carnegie Endowment for International Peace in Washington, D.C., and an associate professor of International Relations at Boston University.

Born in Karachi, Pakistan, Haqqani acquired traditional Islamic learning as well as a modern education in International Relations. His journalism career started with work as East Asian correspondent for *Arabia—The Islamic World Review* during the turbulent years following the Iranian revolution. During this period he wrote extensively on Muslims in China and East Asia and Islamic political movements around the world. Later, as Pakistan and Afghanistan correspondent for the *Far Eastern Economic Review,* he covered the war in Afghanistan and acquired a deep understanding of militant Islamist Jihadi groups.

Haqqani also has a distinguished career in government. He served as an adviser to Pakistani Prime ministers Ghulam Mustafa Jatoi, Nawaz Sharif, and Benazir Bhutto. From 1992 to 1993, he was Pakistan's ambassador to Sri Lanka.

Haqqani writes a regular column, which is syndicated throughout South Asia and the Middle East, in addition to contributing regularly to international publications. He appears frequently on television news shows in both Pakistan and the United States.

397